Rebellion in Chiapas

Also by John Womack, Jr.

Zapata and the Mexican Revolution

Rebellion in
CHIAPAS

An Historical Reader

J OHN   W OMACK ,   J R.

T HE   N EW   P RESS
N EW   Y ORK

Library of Congress Cataloging-in-Publication Data

Rebellion in Chiapas : an historical reader / [compilation,
   translations, and introductory material by] John Womack, Jr.
      p.   cm.
   Includes bibliographical references and index.
      1. Indians of Mexico—Mexico—Chiapas—Government relations,
   2. Mayas—Mexico—Chiapas—Government relations.   3. Chiapas
   Uprising, 1994–   I. Womack, John, Jr. 1937–   .
      F1219.1.C45R43   1999
   323.1′19707275—dc21   98-30842
                                                                CIP

Published in the United States by The New Press, New York
Distributed by W. W. Norton & Company, Inc., New York

The New Press was established in 1990 as a not-for-profit alternative to the large, commercial publishing
houses currently dominating the book publishing industry. The New Press operates in the public interest
rather than for private gain, and is committed to publishing, in innovative ways, works of educational,
cultural, and community value that are often deemed insufficiently profitable.

www.thenewpress.com

Printed in Canada

9   8   7   6   5   4   3   2   1

Contents

To Richard L. Harwood

"I want there to be democracy, no more inequality—I am looking for a life worth living, liberation, just like God says."

José Pérez, 24, EZLN militiaman, captured at Oxchuc, January 4, 1994

REBELLION IN CHIAPAS

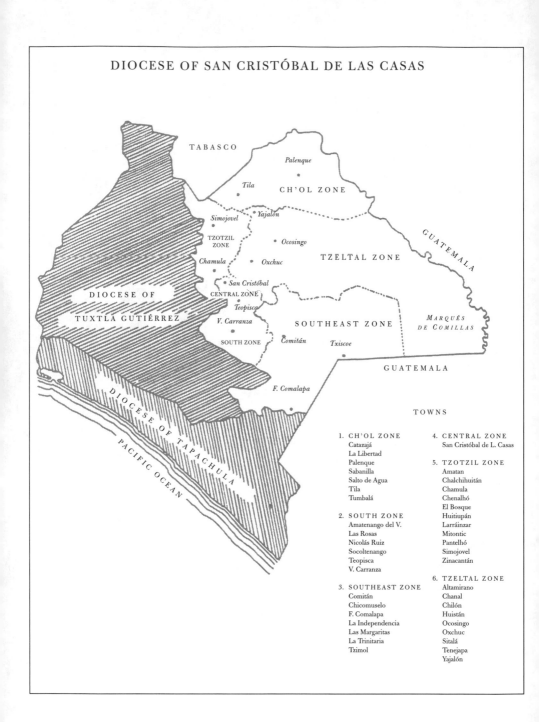

DIOCESE OF SAN CRISTÓBAL DE LAS CASAS

TABASCO

Palenque

Tila

CH'OL ZONE

Simojovel
Yajalón

TZOTZIL
ZONE

Ocosingo

Chamula
Oxchuc

TZELTAL ZONE

GUATEMALA

San Cristóbal
CENTRAL ZONE

DIOCESE OF

TUXTLA GUTIÉRREZ

Teopisca

V. Carranza

SOUTH ZONE

SOUTHEAST ZONE

Comitán
Txiscoe

MARQUÉS
DE COMILLAS

GUATEMALA

DIOCESE OF TAPACHULA

PACIFIC OCEAN

F. Comalapa

TOWNS

1. CH'OL ZONE
Catazajá
La Libertad
Palenque
Sabanilla
Salto de Agua
Tila
Tumbalá

2. SOUTH ZONE
Amatenango del V.
Las Rosas
Nicolás Ruiz
Socoltenango
Teopisca
V. Carranza

3. SOUTHEAST ZONE
Comitán
Chicomuselo
F. Comalapa
La Independencia
Las Margaritas
La Trinitaria
Tzimol

4. CENTRAL ZONE
San Cristóbal de L. Casas

5. TZOTZIL ZONE
Amatan
Chalchihuitán
Chamula
Chenalhó
El Bosque
Huitiupán
Larráinzar
Mitontic
Pantelhó
Simojovel
Zinacantán

6. TZELTAL ZONE
Altamirano
Chanal
Chilón
Huistán
Ocosingo
Oxchuc
Sitalá
Tenejapa
Yajalón

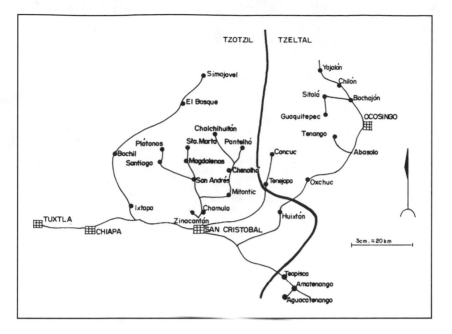

Cities, Towns, and the Villages of Chiapas's Central Highlands, ca. 1960

Source: Jan Rus, "La Comunidad Revolucionaria Institucional: La subversión del gobierno indígena en Los Altos de Chiapas, 1936–1968," in *Chiapas: Los rumbos de otra historia*, eds. Juan Pedro Viqueira and Mario Humberto Ruz (Universidad Nacional Autónoma de México, Centro de Estudios Mexicanos y Centroamericanos, and Universidad de Guadalajara: Mexico City, 1995), p. 254.

Preface

This book is a historian's attempt to explain, especially to Americans, the Zapatista rebellion since 1994 in Mexico's most southern state, Chiapas. From the press, TV, or Internet, most of us have occasionally caught at least some news of the rebellion; from organizations in solidarity with the rebels the most concerned among us have received continual, often detailed reports practically from the front lines. But even at its best the news business can deliver only "the news," not history or historical explanation, and partisan organizations, however honest, can by definition provide only partisan messages, histories, or explanations. What I have tried to do here is go as deep as I could behind the news, as far back as it made sense to go into Chiapas's history, to explain why the rebellion happened. I have wanted especially to open the explanation to include all the important movements and organizations struggling for justice in Chiapas for the last 30 years or more, creating conditions in which one organization, the Zapatista Army, revolted. I also try to show the rebellion's main consequences to date (August 1998).

I put my explanation in two ways. One is in my essay, "Chiapas, the Bishop of San Cristobal, and the Zapatista Revolt" (a part of which appeared earlier in "A Bishop's Conversion," *DoubleTake*, Winter 1998). There I give my historical account of exploitation, oppression, and misery in Chiapas's eastern districts; the struggles to escape, reduce, or (particularly since the 1970s) overthrow these burdens; the rebellion in 1994; and its effects, intended and unintended.

The other way is in the series of thirty-two "readings." There, after a brief background in each case, I offer selections from thirty-seven different "documents" dealing with Chiapas's long history of injustice, conflict, protest, resistance, and rebellion. I chose the documents for any or all of several reasons: originality, the significance of the person, perspective, action, experience, or organization, a revealing or telling quality, variety, authority (scholarly, political, religious, ethnic, professional . . .), and others no doubt unconscious. The first, for example, is a passage from a sixteenth-century Dominican friar's diary about Chiapas's first bishop, Bartolomé de Las Casas, who against local Spaniards' furious opposition started the defense of the diocese's Indian poor. The last is from the Zapatistas' latest official declaration, urging a national referendum on a bill for Indian rights. Neither genre nor political provenance mattered to me. If a document was authentic, pertinent, interesting, and indicative of the long and complicated struggle issuing in Chiapas's tormented present, I considered it for inclusion, and finally chose the ones I thought gave the truest representation of the struggle. Therefore, besides passages from the old diary and all five Zapatista declarations, I have passages from historical articles, anthropological interviews, a novel, a Latin American bishops' conference paper, a new catechism, memoirs, the Mexican press, a Mexican Maoist political pamphlet, a revolutionary organization's statutes, a diocesan missionary plan, a presidential agrarian order, a state criminal code, a bishop's pastoral letter, Zapatista laws, an Indian story about the rebellion, a Congressional-Zapatista agreement on Indian rights, a new Zapatista civil organization's project, the homily at the Mass last Christmas Day for the victims of a massacre, and a couple of recent Zapatista communiqués. All translations are my own unless otherwise credited.

I hope the collection will be useful to readers who want to see for themselves a few of the sources of my explanation, and understand for themselves not only why some of Chiapas's Indian poor revolted in 1994, but also why others equally intent on justice did not, and why the result has been so gripping and so grievous.

John Womack, Jr.
Cambridge, Mass.
August 28, 1998

Acknowledgments

For the encouragement, advice, questions, information, and technical support I needed to make this book, I thank Hugo Araujo, Alejandro Bendaña, Jessica Blatt, César Canavati, José Carreño, John Coatsworth, Robert Coles, George Collier, Robert Darnton, Juan Enríquez, Guillermo Espinosa, Joel Espinoza, Louis Ferleger, Donald Fleming, Vincent Foerstler, Michael Fried, Javier Gil, Guido Goldman, Lilian Handlin, Oscar Handlin, Beatrice Harwood, Richard Harwood, Alicia Hernández, Gonzalo Ituarte, Friedrich Katz, Emilio Kourí, Yvon Le Bot, John Leone, Gary MacEoin, Terrence Malick, Jesús Morales, Mardonio Morales, John McNees, Gaspar Morquecho, Aaron Navarro, Cory Paulsen, Carlos Rojas, Samuel Ruiz, Diane Rus, Jan Rus, Dee Sánchez, Martín Sánchez, André Schiffrin, Jonathan Schrag, Enrique Semo, Dennis Skiotis, Carlos Tello, John Trumpbour, Felipe de Jesús Toussaint, Bernardino Verástique, Juan Pedro Viqueira, Evon Vogt, Alfred Womack, Liza Womack, librarians at the Andover-Harvard Theological Library, the Tozzer Library, and the Widener Library at Harvard University, and others in Mexico to whom I am no less grateful but whom I ought not name. On no account is any of them, named or unnamed, responsible for my sympathies, aversions, judgments, mistakes, or errors of commission or omission.

PART ONE

Chiapas, the Bishop of San Cristóbal, and the Zapatista Revolt

Chiapas, the Bishop of San Cristóbal, and the Zapatista Revolt

Americans tend to think of Mexico as an exotic place, which allows them endless fantasies about it. But Mexico is real. It is a big, complicated, vastly Catholic, still deeply old-fashioned, nevertheless largely modern, and largely poor country. Its territory is over 3½ times that of France, its arable land only 1⅓ times as much. Its population, 95 million, 71 percent urban, is already 1½ times France's (74 percent urban), and growing 5½ times faster.

Contrary to some recent American fantasies, Mexico is not mainly an Indian country. Although the great majority of Mexicans have Indian forebears, and daily reveal, sense, and use Indian cultural remnants, those of all ages who speak an Indian mother tongue number only about 8 percent of the population; 75 percent of them also speak Spanish. Since the 1970s most Indians in Mexico, joining most other Mexicans, have lived in cities, the largest concentration of them in Mexico City, which now includes about 500,000 Indians among its twenty million people.

Despite other fantasies, Mexico has never been a socialist country either. For 100 years the Mexican economy has been predominantly capitalist, which the Mexican Revolution 80 years ago changed mainly to favor Mexican enterprise. Before and since the revolution, except for an interlude of populist reform in the 1930s, the Mexican political system has been an intricate collusion of businessmen and politicians. Through the last ten years it has also been a regime in bitter internal conflict, among and between traditional bosses and various new reformers, some reformers operating inside the system, others outside, with rank antagonism between them.

Mexicans love their country intensely. But for most of them it is a hard place to live, work, or do much good. Of all its hard places, the hardest has long been Chiapas, Mexico's Mississippi. The "Zapatista" revolt there in 1994 exposed it to the world, and excited many old and new fantasies.

The state of Chiapas is on Mexico's border with Guatemala. It covers the northwestern end of the mountain chain that reaches all the way to Panama and connects North and South America. Broken by the mountains and the rivers through them, it has five regions, lying one behind the other, northwest-southeast.

The Pacific coastal plain is fertile, hot, and humid. There coffee, fruit, and sugar have flourished, and cattle too. Inland the Sierra Madre, rising ever higher toward Guatemala, to 13,000 feet on the border, has rich and famous coffee plantations along its northwestern foothills, only poor corn plots on its high southeastern slopes. Below the mountains eastward the state's central valley, through which runs the great Grijalva River from the Guatemala highlands northwest down to the Gulf of Mexico, is 20 to 35 miles wide, over 120 miles long. On the Grijalva now are three of the largest dams in the world. The valley's well-watered, hot lands nourish sugar plantations, hybrid corn farms, and the state's biggest cattle ranches. And there since 1892 is the state capital, Tuxtla Gutiérrez.

Farther east, driven abruptly up from the valley, stand the central highlands, a region as big as the Great Smokies, but manifold in its variety. Los Altos, "the Heights," the mountains, rising to nearly 10,000 feet, fall slowly southeastward in many parallel ridges, between which open steep, long *cañadas*, the canyons that follow their rivers southeast into the mountainous Lacandón jungle and down to the mighty Usumacinta River running from high in Guatemala back down around the mountains northwest to the Gulf. On the cold, foggy Altos, along the chilly ridges, down in the steaming *cañadas*, the soil is poor, and the rains are heavy for seven or eight months a year. Although forests grow robust, the cloud forest, oak, live oak, the rain forest, corn grows but in meager patches. Cleared land cannot take much tilling before it is exhausted. Only in a few valleys and on some confined southerly plains has the soil long borne corn farms or sugar and coffee plantations. This extensive, fractured region is the state's Indian heartland, where from 50 to 90 percent of the people speak a Mayan language, Chol, Tzotzil, Tzeltal, or Tojolabal. To rule them the Spanish in 1528 put their provincial colonial capital of Ciudad Real in Los Altos. For the same reason after Mexican independence, the same city, renamed San Cristóbal, remained the state capital for decades. Its tradition of white rule is still vivid and strong.

Finally, northwestward and northeastward from Los Altos, the land lowers down into the Gulf Coast plain along the state's northern border with Tabasco. The northwest has pastures, cacao and banana plantations, papaya orchards, and natural gas and oil installations, including the Cactus Petrochemical Complex, which recently blew up. In the northeast there are pastures too, few plantations or orchards, no oil, but many tourists to visit the ruins of Palenque.

Migration is Chiapas's oldest story. Three and a half millennia before the Spanish arrived, on primeval trails between central Mexico, Guatemala, and South America, people came to settle Soconusco, the Lancandón jungle, slowly the other regions. As empires emerged at ends of the trails and along them, more migrations followed among the regions, and exchange, conquest, and resistance. The settlements became villages, ancestrally rooted communities. But even these, from farming in extensive, slash-and-burn agriculture, required local migration; villagers continually moved around the community's land to reopen overgrown fallow plots. And many people, probably more than in other parts of village Mexico or Guatemala, continued to move from region to region, freely as pioneers in search of a better life, as resettled captives, or as refugees from tribute, lost wars, or lost rebellions.

The Spanish conquerors did not bring stability. They brought war and epidemic diseases that destroyed most villages. They uprooted many others to concentrate their populations, the better to control them; in these operations they nearly depopulated the Lacandón. And they institutionalized migratory labor in official, periodic conscriptions of Indians for work as farm laborers or two-footed beasts of burden. This was the exploitation against which the first bishop of Chiapas, Bartolomé de Las Casas, raised hell in 1545, in vain. (Reading No. 1.) It still served the conquerors' heirs in the 1620s. (Reading No. 2.) It was the burden Indians hoped to overthrow in a great rebellion in 1712, again in vain. (Reading No. 3.) It remained in force well into the 1800s.

Independence from Spain increased instability. Once in the new Mexican republic the oligarchs of San Cristóbal assumed command of the new state of Chiapas. Like many local oligarchs elsewhere in Mexico then, they were mostly *mestizos*, of both Indian and Spanish descent. But in the Guatemalan fashion they professed themselves *ladinos*, suffered inside a bitter shame over their ancestry, denied it weighed on them, and acted as domineering as Spanish lords and masters, to prove they were white where it mattered. Rich from the rents, trade, and civil and religious taxes of the highlands, champions and protégés of the Church, they were the state's strongest regional power. But they could not prevent the development of other regions and new centers of ladino power, especially in the Grijalva Valley. The conflicts between San Cristóbal and its rivals became frequent wars between orthodox Catholic Conservative clans and Masonic Catholic Liberal clans.

Whatever their loyalties, which varied, Indians fared ever worse. Often they had to pay taxes to both Conservatives and Liberals, and bear arms and military burdens. And their lost villages lost fallow land to ladinos, Conservative and Liberal, who seized it as untitled backwoods. Indians continued to work off and on a month of every year for ladino lords and masters, typically still as migrant laborers and bearers.

By the 1860s Liberals had expropriated the Church, abolished a state head tax and all religious taxes, and made themselves the state's dominant power. During the French Intervention in Mexico, to install Emperor Maximilian, the Conservatives briefly recovered San Cristóbal (1863–64), but the Liberals on recapturing the place set to destroying Conservative control in the highlands. In particular they encouraged Indians not to pay religious dues. Soon villagers around San Cristóbal defied their priests and organized a free Catholic movement. But when the Liberal state government needed revenue in 1869, it suddenly reimposed the head tax. And when the free Catholic villagers evaded the tax and protested in San Cristóbal the arrest of their prophet, for which the local ladinos accused them of threatening race war, state forces including artillery massacred the protesters, killing over 800, driving thousands into flight as refugees. (Reading No. 4.) Migrant labor became state policy in Chiapas in the 1890s (before it did in South Africa). Like the transfer of the state capital to Tuxtla, it was a sign of modern times. A decade before, foreign logging companies had expanded operations up the Usumacinta River to cut the "green gold" of ancient mahogany and cedar; other foreign firms had put coffee plantations in Soconuso. Both regions had attracted migrant laborers, but not enough of them to reduce wages to the level of bare subsistence. This aroused Chiapas's entrepreneurs. The ladino clans of the Grijalva Valley held the state's best land, ready for development to supply Soconusco with food and four-footed beasts of burden. The ladino clans of San Cristóbal controlled the state's largest source of labor, the Indians of Los Altos. Accordingly in 1891 a new governor started the state's first road-building program, and in 1893 managed legislation to compel Indian communities to divide their remaining lands into individually owned private properties, many of which in Los Altos, by hook or crook, ladinos expeditiously acquired. The new roads and the deal between land-rich and labor-rich ladinos ruined many highland villagers. Soon most of them no longer had enough land to support themselves and owed the equivalent of 40 days' labor a year in taxes alone. The men had a choice: revolt with predictable consequences; migrate to try to farm elsewhere, but on any return to their community risk jail or fines for overdue debt or unpaid taxes; or accept contracts that village elders sanctioned advancing loans for a term of work in a logging camp or on the new plantations and farms in Soconusco or the central valley. A few went down to the jungle; fewer returned. Reasonably, most chose the migrant term down on the Pacific, an eight-day walk away. Migrant wages there then fell to nearly the level of subsistence, which made a migrant's net income, after deductions, flimflam, and robbery along the way home, usually very little if anything, so that most migrants had to resubmit to exploitation year after year. Occasionally a critic complained of slavery. Ladinos would fly into righteous denials. They were right. There was no slavery (constitutionally forbidden), only annually recontracted debt peonage.

The Mexican Revolution began naively in 1910 as an "insurrection" to overthrow seven-term President Porfirio Díaz and institute electoral democracy. But scarcely had the Revolutionaries ousted Díaz, when they confronted titanic conflicts among British, American, and German interests in their country, counter-revolutionary movements, feuds among themselves, claims by villagers to lost land, and demands by industrial workers for better hours, wages, and working conditions. The first Revolutionary government, elected in 1911, did nothing for villagers, very little for workers. It fell in a military coup in 1913. A civil war began. Fierce in some regions, negligible in others, it resulted in the defeat of the Mexican army, a U.S. military intervention, a peasant army occupying land in some regions, militant workers striking in others, a different Revolution in every state, then another civil war, this one among Revolutionaries, and another U.S. intervention.

In 1916 one faction of Revolutionaries beat the others. It consisted of a crowd of ambitious northern war lords determined to remake Mexico on their terms. The constitution they prescribed in 1917 was radically nationalist and progressive. In Article 27 it endowed "the nation" with inalienable ownership of the country's land, waters, and subsoil resources; admitted private property not as one of the absolute "rights of man" but as a national policy; recognized villages as corporate bodies entitled to tenure (not property) in agricultural lands; and guaranteed restitution or grants of federal or expropriated private lands as *ejidos* to villages that needed them. Article 123 gave workers the rights to organize unions, bargain collectively with their employers, and strike.

But not many war lords ever agreed on whom "the nation" wanted for president, or which policies it wanted him to pursue most seriously. They formed numerous Revolutionary parties. Attempts to overthrow one president or another, triumphant in 1920, continued through the 1920s. A three-year-long Catholic rebellion aggravated Revolutionary political confusion, conflict, and corruption. Armed violence was rampant in most states, where rival war lords and local bosses fought constantly over office, patronage, business, the distribution of ejidos to villages, and the organization and action of unions to represent workers. A national peasant league and a national federation of labor gained strong positions in the 1920s, not as a result of any benign Revolutionary consensus for them, but at the cost of many bloody struggles and excruciating compromises. The National Revolutionary Party, founded in 1929, was only for war lords and bosses, to institutionalize and civilize their rivalries. It destroyed the peasant league and laid siege to the labor federation.

The Mexican Revolution that was a national movement of working people, by working people, for working people is a myth. The real Mexican Revolution was many improvised, provincial, fluctuating, shifting, and uneven movements, again and again at odds with each other, a few of them actually revolutionary (but eventually defeated, or contained), some of them popular movements for particular lands or unions, most of them movements only of working people, led by ferocious politicians contending for personal power.

Least of all was the Revolution for Indians. It bears emphasis that the constitution of 1917 did not refer to them, either as indígenas (the indigenous, Indians in the American or Canadian sense), or as indios (literally "Indians," but usually meaning poor, brown-skinned country people), and made no special provision for them otherwise. The Plan de Ayala, the principal agrarian declaration of the revolutionary movement that Emiliano Zapata led from 1911 to 1919, which, mythically, all indios then considered theirs, includes neither word. The only specific Revolutionary interest in Indians was local and strategic.

The notion now common in Mexico (and among Mexicanists elsewhere) that "the Mexican Revolution never reached Chiapas," or "came late," is therefore a mistake. The Revolution got to Chiapas about the same time, about the same way, and with about the same limited results as in many other states. When the Porfirian governor resigned in 1911, the ladinos redivided between the Masonic Grijalva Valley and orthodox San Cristóbal, both clans swiftly presenting factions to appropriate the Revolution. When northern Revolutionaries occupied Chiapas in 1914, they hit both factions head on. Their Revolutionary labor law, which abolished debt servitude, set maximum hours, and fixed minimum wages, had a cracking impact. To maintain coffee exports, migrant labor continued in full flow, but under state labor inspectors' supervision. Counter-revolutionaries, some landlords from the Grijalva Valley, others from San Cristóbal, raised rival revolts and ran indestructible guerrillas. Through the local civil wars, famine, and epidemics, many villages dwindled into ghostly retreats, their refugees gone high into the mountains, down into the cañadas, even to other states. By 1920 the counter-revolutionaries had united, negotiated their incorporation into the new Revolutionary army, and swung the election of their first chief as Revolutionary governor. But by then too, based among migrant laborers from the Sierra Madre near the Guatemala border, the Chiapas Socialist Party had formed to represent the state's rural working class. The party began organizing in Soconusco, and by 1922 had established a regional union of peasants and workers, which, coffee planters complained, made its members believe "they did not have to respect any authority." By 1924 the Socialists had become a major political force in Chiapas, and started organizing a Socialist Confederation of Workers across the state. Because of Socialist strength, the governors of Chiapas over the next eight years made substantial grants of ejidos to villages in the southern Sierra Madre and Soconusco, where agrarian reform was at the time among the most radical in Mexico. By the early 1930s Socialists and Communists so threatened the state's landlords that the Revolutionary governor then, a landlord himself, took the preemptive action of opening a state office of "Indian protection," to have village chiefs in Los Altos organize obedient unions of Indian migrant laborers.

Through the Great Depression and political crises in Mexico in the 1930s, the Revolutionary war lords lost power nationally to a second Revolutionary generation that pulled together a popular front to govern the country. Using the constitution for more nationalism and progressivism than any president before him, President Lázaro Cárdenas backed a new nationwide socialist labor movement, distributed more ejidos to villages than all presidents before him, opened a federal department of Indian Affairs, sponsored the organization of a National Peasant Confederation (the CNC), and nationalized the railroads and the oil industry.

These reforms went into effect in Chiapas at once. The new federal Indian Affairs department canceled the previous Indian unions, went around the village chiefs, and organized a new statewide union of Indian workers, most militant in Los Altos. The Cardenista governor taking office in 1936, with the support of Socialist and Communist unions, helped them organize the new state federation of labor, which the new Indian union joined, and assigned more ejidos to more villages than all the governors before. (Reading No. 5.)

So the Mexican Revolution, contradictory, indefinite, contentious, omnivorously and remorselessly political, sometimes radically reformist, happened in Chiapas too. It did not institute democracy of any kind in the state. Nor did it establish liberty, equality, or fraternity. Much less did it turn the world there upside down, socialize the means of production, abolish the labor market or poverty, or stop white or ladino racism. But then it did not work these changes anywhere else in Mexico either. The main change it accomplished in Chiapas was the unionization of Indian migrant laborers, which was more than it did in some other states. But migrant labor continued. It still drew Los Altos' most desperate down east to the lumber camps, where the union meant nothing and bosses worked laborers to death. (Reading No. 6.) And every coffee-picking season it was still the fate of tens of thousands of poor highlander men and boys gone down west for the harvest, entailing every season the fate of heavier toil at home for the tens of thousands of poor women and girls left behind. (Reading No. 7.) Chiapas became Mexico's Mississippi not because the economy had not developed, or because it did not go through the Revolution, but because of the sort of development and the sort of Revolution it suffered.

Since World War II (thanks primarily to the reforms of the 1930s), Mexico has sustained a process of "Institutional Revolution." Compared to the Revolution before, this has been much less violent, much more protective, indeed supportive, of private business, much tougher on struggles for peasants and workers. In this process the country has on several human scores been relatively successful: infant mortality has declined sixfold, the population has nearly quadrupled, the urban population sextupled, society is more and more open and mobile, literacy has increased from 50 to 90 percent, the real national income per capita has tripled, and the government has functioned well enough through its Institutional Revolutionary Party (the PRI), so that no would-be military dictator has even tried to seize power.

As Mexico has grown and modernized, Chiapas has not been an isolated corner. In the country's economic development it has had an integral, important part. It has produced the most coffee and bananas of all the states in the country, accounting for a notable fraction of the national income from exports. Its cacao and beef production each figure second nationally. Its corn farms ordinarily make the third largest contribution to the domestic supply of Mexico's daily staff of life. Its great dams provide half of the country's hydroelectric power. Its gas fields yield a quarter of the country's natural gas (or did, until Cactus Petrochemical exploded). And practically its traditional bosses have regularly delivered huge PRI majorities in national and state elections.

But however safer, more profitable, more productive, and more orderly than the Revolution before, the Institutional Revolution has been nevertheless surprising in the twists and turns it has taken. Mexicans now in their 50s have lived through postwar economic booms cycling into the 1960s, foul Cold War politics culminating in 1968 in the bloody October crisis in Mexico City, government-managed populism in the early 1970s, oil-exporting and foreign-borrowing booms until the financial crisis of 1982, nationalized banks, debt crises, and ripping inflation into the late 1980s, and economic recovery, privatization, free trade, and "social liberalism" in the early 1990s, to find themselves in 1995–96 in new national economic and political crises.

The booms have meant less for the country's morale than the repeated crises. The continual disappointment of so much work undone, so many chances lost, plans wrecked, hopes broken, has created a national dread of failure and betrayal, a national ache for new hope and trust, but an obsessive rejection of public calls for public faith, a bilious cynicism toward the government, an addiction for the old national opium of private anarchism, a national culture of public nihilism. "Crisis" does not appear in William Safire's *Political Dictionary*. But for 30 years it has been one of the conditional nouns, like "weather," most uttered in Mexico. Except in a hospital, "crisis" there almost always means the national condition that has driven the speaker to believe that only God or the stars or a revolution could make things nationally or personally better.

This was President Carlos Salinas's hardest and most amazing feat in the late 1980s and early 90s—that he revived a publicly proud faith that Mexicans could make their work and its worth solid and enduring. In the latest crises it has been the country's sorest loss that this faith feels embarrassing.

Not only has the Institutional Revolution been tortuous and treacherous in the course of time. It has been as uneven as the old Revolution geographically. Through fat years it has favored some sections of the country more than others; through lean or meatless years ruined less in some sections than in others. The northern border states, Jalisco, and Mexico City have prospered most and suffered least. The South Pacific states, Guerrero, Oaxaca, and Chiapas, have prospered least and suffered most. Of all the states, the most agricultural, least electrified, least schooled, least literate, and poorest has been Chiapas. Its population in 1994 was about 3,700,000. Officially half of these people were malnourished. Almost 60 percent of the people working there lived on less than the nationally defined minimum wage, then equivalent to U.S. $1,500 a year. Within each state, regions and districts differ grossly in living standards. Some parts of Chihuahua are as rich as any in West Texas, others as poor as any in Chiapas. Within Chiapas, Soconusco is as rich as some parts of Jalisco; its main town, Tapachula, is "prosperous and cosmopolitan." The Grijalva Valley is rich too; through the 1980s and early '90s Tuxtla was Mexico's third fastest-growing city. What makes Chiapas the poorest state in Mexico is the sorry plight of the central highlands, Los Altos, the cañadas, the Lacandón. There the population in 1994 was around 650,000. Over 40 percent aged 15 and older had no schooling, 56 percent of those 15 and older could not read or write, probably two-thirds of the homes, crowded, dirt-floor shacks, had no electricity, drinking water, or drainage, and almost 70 percent of working people made less than the minimum wage. Excluding the San Cristóbal district, more than 80 percent of working men and women in the region lived on less than U.S. $1,500 a year.

Most galling is that in every district, even in the poorest, different classes of people live in starkly different terms. A villager in Los Altos, who in the oil boom did well enough to buy a truck and thrive in the produce business, rents land (illegally) from 25 dirt-poor men in the village and pays them to farm for him. Other villagers who own trucks do not use them except on high-rate days, since they have gone also into the business. One reputedly has the equivalent of over U.S. $2,500,000 out in loans for interest mostly at annual credit card levels. Some ejidos in the Lacandón hire Guatemalan workers for their harvest at 40 percent of the minimum wage. Meanwhile nine-tenths of the region's country people make from their work only enough for their families to eat, and usually not much, a little corn, salt, beans, and greens.

Salinas knew much about the miseries of Chiapas, and on his policy of social liberalism he acted to relieve them. From 1989 to 1993, through his national antipoverty program, "Solidarity," he pumped some U.S. $500 million into the state, more than went to any other, for jobs and support "for those of us who have the least." In August 1993 he committed another U.S. $50 million for social projects in the cañadas. But it was from the cañadas that the revolt came.

This was not an innocent march into town, like the protest in San Cristóbal in 1869, or a *jacquerie*, an agrarian riot of desperate outrage. On January 1, 1994, some 3,000 booted, uniformed, masked, and well-trained men and women, all armed, many with Sten Mark IIs, AK-47s, M-6s, and Uzis, moved out from numerous clandestine bases, concentrated in several units, and captured San Cristóbal, two towns not far north, six more eastward toward the cañadas, two of them in pitched battles, and many villages elsewhere in the region. As their leadership announced, they were the Ejército Zapatista de Liberación Nacional, the EZLN, the Zapatista Army of National Liberation, at war with the Mexican army and under orders to move on Mexico City and overthrow the Mexican government. On January 2, however, they evacuated San Cristóbal and the towns they had taken, and retreated. The Mexican army shortly thereafter had 14,000 soldiers searching for them to destroy them. On January 12 Salinas declared a unilateral ceasefire and appointed a Commission for Peace and Reconciliation. But by then more than 70 rebels had died fighting, as the cold, bleeding, scared, young survivor of one luckless encounter put it, for "democracy, no more inequality—I am looking for a life worth living, liberation, just like God says."

The poverty in the highlands justifies the revolt there. But it takes more than that to understand why or how the revolt happened. Despite the congestion of poverty in the region, most people there stayed out of the fighting, while others gave all they could for the fight. Why the difference between them? There is much to consider: the organization of local life, Indians, modern medicine, religion, migration, politics national and local. Considering that this is Chiapas, it is, however, a fairly short story, going back only some 50 years.

As late as the 1940s, for all the changes they had endured and absorbed, the Indian villages of Los Altos were still communities where even old people felt that *costumbres* there, local customs, had not basically changed. The Revolution had happened, and unions, and ejidos, and the official National Peasant Confederation, the CNC. But the village still had God, it had its patron saint, its language, and its calendar of holy days, its old families, all related to each other, its continually mending net of god-relations, its witches and its healers, its bone-setter and its midwife, its angels, its beseecher of the mountains, its *principales*, the elders, its occasional assemblies, its seasonal cycle of male migrant labor and compounded female labor. And it had its hierarchy of *cargos*, the public (although not official) communal duties that every year men competed to receive in order to gain rank in the village, which meant prestige and authority among their fellows and a reputation for public responsibility, proven initially in treating the village to a communal, heavily alcoholic binge in gratitude for the honor, then in faithful fulfillment of the duty through the year. The young and the old knew that the village's customs, starting from its reverence for its saint, were only theirs. They knew that in their disputes their elders would find consensus in the village's assembly, and make the consensus work. And they knew that in this profane world the cargos mattered most, to prove who most wanted to serve the village. These were communities of reciprocal constraint and satisfaction, annual dues and annual redemption. Practically small, private, ancestral insurance cooperatives, they ran on trust and mutual obligation. Some fellows in every village usually had more things than others their age there. But from God, nature, their own dreams, and ladinos, they were all always in such peril that they all always needed each other. The traditional duties of rank, low and high, were the guarantee that in a crisis one would be for all, all for one.

But through the 1950s and '60s these villages were transformed from closed, internally bonded communities into broken, bourgeois-ridden, mistrustful bossdoms. The change began with a government decision to do some acculturative good for Indians. In 1951 the Instituto Nacional Indigenista (INI), the federal Indian bureau, established in San Cristóbal its first center of "regional development," to provide the surrounding Tzotzil and Tzeltal villages with public schools, cooperatives, medical services, and legal aid. At first it operated through the old militants still there from the 1930s, who helped the center start training local Indian bilingual teachers as a new generation of local leaders. However, the new center pleased neither state PRI bosses nor San Cristóbal ladinos, who stymied it. By 1954 INI had cut a deal with its opponents, collaborating with the state Indian office, dumping some old militants, coopting others, contracting with ladinos to manage cooperatives, and affirming ladino patronage of coopted militants and new teachers, all so that the center could function. The center then did fine, only as a ladino agency of business, corruption, and control in the villages. The local customs continued, but every year under the sun of this acculturation their old meaning faded. The elders could no longer find consensus in the assembly, lost the authority of age, became mere grandpas, and the cargos turned into alcohol-lubricated rackets. The INI center's ladino-sponsored teachers emerged as the new "principales" and the main cargo-holders. As they developed their careers and businesses, they harped vehemently (which would have been demented for an elder to do) each on his village's "Indian" culture and on his own "Indian" identity. Whatever served their interests, they promoted as "custom" and "tradition, how our ancestors did it." And since despite their new ethnicity they could not find consensus either, they would not even call assemblies, but simply insisted on the village's need for "unity, to be one single soul," the one they had possessed.

Some eventually rose into officially dignified positions. By the 1970s most of the largely Indian townships around San Cristóbal had a PRI bilingual teacher for municipal president (mayor, county commissioner, and sheriff all in one). To describe these fellows, no Mayan word would do. It took a word from the national political culture—*cacique*, or boss. In the name of "custom" and "tradition" they imposed "unity" on their new, broad jurisdiction.

From the center's medical services came more heartwarming successes, but also with unexpected results. The death rate and infant mortality declined. But the birth rate remained high. By the mid-1960s the villages had increased in population altogether by around 50 percent, and of these increased numbers a larger proportion than before was of young people who would themselves soon be having babies. The villages had not meanwhile grown in resources. In 1950, 57 of them had ejidos. This was about all the villages there were, and about all the ejidos there could be (without a radical reform to limit private farms more tightly than even Cárdenas had). By the mid-1960s maybe 60 villages had ejidos, and most, still slashing and burning for their agriculture, could not subsist on them; many of their young men had no plot of their own. It was hard enough then for most villagers with land to earn a rank of honor, some respect and insurance for their family, or to emulate the teachers and make a bundle in the racket. It would be impossible for most youngsters on the way. This was certainly a challenge to the new culture of "traditional unity."

By contrast, most Indians in the highlands' northern and eastern valleys and southern plains in the 1940s lived in new communities where much had lately changed. Chols and Tzotzils to the north, Tzeltals to the east, Tojolabals to the south, they had for many generations been permanently resident peons on local coffee, sugar, and cattle *fincas*, estates in the Guatemalan mold. Around the towns of Ocosingo and Altamirano in the eastern valleys, Las Margaritas on the southern plains, the Dominicans from the seventeenth to the mid-19th century had landless Indian families domiciled on their fincas, and their ladino successors had retained the practice and the people. From finca to finca these families had continued some old costumbres (less faithfully than under the Dominicans), but the relations of most concern to them had been their relations with their landlord. There had been no God or saint but his, if he had one. He had been the father of some of their children, godfather to all, and the only "principal." The most important cargos had been the responsibilities he had assigned. He had decided disputes, obligations, and rank. And there in crises the rule had been simply all for one, him. Among themselves, without an independent base or status, resident peons had ordinarily had no more bond than that of neighbors. It was the agrarian reform of the 1930s that had opened the chance for change: a new right of laborers resident on an estate to petition for official recognition as a community, which would give them the right to petition for an ejido. And it was then on many fincas in these valleys and on the southern plains that neighborly peons discovered a collective courage, gained incorporation as a community, and in many struggles through the 1940s won ejidos. By 1950 there were 53 villages with ejidos in the northern valleys, only 16 around Ocosingo and Altamirano, where fincas still prevailed, but 93 in the plains around Las Margaritas. These new Indian communities had new sorts of "principales," the ejido commissioners; new sorts of cargos, all still celebrated with much alcohol, but for the ejido, the township, the peasant federation; new sorts of rank, to guarantee the various interests in the ejido; and assemblies that ran community and ejido affairs together.

Most unlike the old villages around San Cristóbal, these communities suggested a way of struggle for other landless rural laborers in the region. It would provoke shrewd and vicious resistance by landlords and their agents in the PRI. It would require an absolute commitment from all who joined, steadfast unanimity, and iron determination. But it was the only strategy that worked. Organize a group of landless neighbors resolved to win. Find grantable land, anywhere in the vicinity. Occupy it, secure the perimeter, and declare a community. Fight if necessary. Petition and politick for recognition. Once recognized, petition and politick for an ejido. On receipt of the ejido, guard it as the founders' joint trust. Let others win their own.

But it did not take long before these new communities too turned into bossdoms. No INI or other official program corrupted them. The very process by which they had established themselves, in the nastier pits of Mexican politics, the state and federal agrarian offices, typically brought forth a few forceful leaders who typically soon found that they and their ejido would do best if they managed it in rapport with the local ladinos and the PRI. And soon the ejido became a racket, and one or another leader became a cacique. Short on customs, he would extemporize "traditional Indian unity."

Without a plan the new communities plunged into coffee production. And as they prospered, and by more politicking gained new medical services, the death rate there also declined. The result was the same as in the villages around San Cristóbal. By the mid-1960s the population had so increased in the northern valleys and around Ocosingo, Altamirano, and Las Margaritas, that many of their young men had no land, for corn or coffee.

And by then these communities had reached a limit on their number. This was not for lack of peons wanting land, but for lack of grantable land in the vicinity. Because the agrarian law gave the widest exemption to ranches, many landlords in the 1950s and '60s quit growing sugar and coffee, expelled their peons before they could file for status as a community, and opened their fields to cattle.

Throughout Los Altos then, despite all the appearance of "Indian unity," the pressures inside old villages and new communities were cracking them.

Because of the bossdoms and mounting internal conflicts, some villagers finally accepted a character among them who promised relief here and now and in heaven. This was a Chol, Tzotzil, Tzeltal, or Tojolabal prophet, but in the person of a Presbyterian missionary. Presbyterians had first come to Chiapas from Guatemala around the turn of the century, converted some souls in the Sierra Madre, and eventually had converts in Los Altos working for "Protestantism." For decades they and their successors preached in vain. Even when translations of the Gospel in the Indian languages arrived, the missionaries, the only ones who could read the translation, could not attract an audience for the Good News. But through the 1950s and '60s villagers resentful of the new "principales" and their rackets, especially landless young men, came to them and converted. And their wives, keenly interested in Protestant restrictions on alcohol, came with them, and brought the children. Bred by the material divisions in the village, this religious repudiation of customs and "traditions" was an explicit threat to the village's "unity."

Already in the 1950s, in the mountains, valleys, and plains of Chiapas's central highlands, disgusted young villagers and discarded peons were doing what their ancestors had often done when they could stand no more—migrating to other parts. Very few left the state (which has long had Mexico's lowest rate of emigration). They almost all went east, aggrieved but undaunted pioneers, most of them under 30, maybe on a bus or truck to Ocosingo, Altamirano, or Las Margaritas, perforce on foot down into the then still heavily forested cañadas. This suited the Mexican government perfectly, a private resolution of agrarian conflicts through new settlement of unpopulated federal borderlands. The offices of agrarian reform virtually promised ejidos there, struggle-free, for the asking. But the government did nothing otherwise to help the people who went. The young migrants were moving into uncharted and infamously remote territory, which old timers still called *El Desierto de la Soledad*, the Wilderness of Solitude. The new pioneers called it *La Selva*, the jungle, the forest, the Lacandón. As a Tzotzil accustomed to cold mountains and cloud forests later recalled, it was a dreadful change, "the heat, the gulley washers, the mud, the mites, being afraid of jaguars." Those who found a sweet dell still high in the canyons most often found it occupied, by a ladino ranch, or an earlier migrant settlement in its ejido, or its juniors in their ejido, and had to blaze a trail farther down. Pioneers from an Indian township near San Cristóbal, San Juan Chamula, went southeast toward the Guatemalan border, to the bottoms of the Rio Dolores, the Sorrows River, where there was no one, and settled a little empty place they called in sorrow and hope New San Juan Chamula. Soon they formed a legal community, and had an ejido.

The increasing discord in the central highlands in the 1960s moved some landless young men off to work in construction on the big Malpaso dam in the Grijalva Valley. But many more went for pioneers down into the jungle, in small groups, altogether thousands of people every year. From 1960 to 1970, despite its declining death rate and high birth rate, the population of Los Altos increased only from about 125,000 to about 155,000, 24 percent. Meanwhile the population of the townships of Ocosingo, Altamarino, and Las Margaritas, where the Lacandón was, increased from around 30,000 to around 75,000, 150 percent.

As the young pioneers accumulated in the canyons, typically teenagers and

20-somethings, they made little colonies, which, once incorporated as communities, requested and received their ejidos. These settlements were radically different from villages and communities in the central highlands, and varied bizarrely among themselves. It mattered most that they were practically on their own on a frontier. The government existed in the forest then only in the papers recognizing a community and granting land. There was no PRI. And ladino ranchers remained up near the heads of the canyons. The colonists were therefore free to associate as they wanted and to organize themselves as they judged best. They quickly drew the difference, as they put it, as if in the armed forces or prison, between "the outside" and "the inside." The outside was back where they had come from, towns, rich people, ranchers, medical services, drinking water, electricity, stores, schools—the world the *caxlanes* (Tzeltal for Castilians, Spaniards, ladinos) had made, with no place for them. The inside was where they were now, isolated in the jungle, only "Indians," with no more than they could carry in, trying on their own to make their neck of the woods a fit place to live.

Free inside to choose the company they would keep, they made a medley of choices. Some settlements were of people all from the same village. One was of people all from the same neighborhood, and all Presbyterians. Others were of people who spoke the same language, but came from different villages. Still others were multilingual; there people spoke of themselves no longer as Chol, Tzotzil, Tzeltal, or Tojolabal, but as *choleros, tzotzileros, tzeltaleros, tojolabaleros*, not estranged by language (much less by "culture" or "ethnicity"), but taking their differences as natural and normal. There were even settlements of people from different villages and different faiths. Catholics from Abasolo and Presbyterians from Oxchuc, both Tzeltal villages on the road from San Cristóbal to Ocosingo, settled together in the early 1960s down at the conjunction of the two canyons where the Perlas and the Jataté Rivers join, called their new home San Quintín, and built two churches, one for each creed, right in the middle of the settlement.

The colonists also had a choice in how to use the land to make a living. They could learn to use it as the native Indians there had, to thin the forest's canopy and in miniature clearings like gardens produce tropical vegetables, fruits, fibers, spices, and tobacco, for subsistence and for sale, forever. Or they could follow the example of the earlier migrants, who had opened big clearings for their traditional slash-and-burn agriculture, planted coffee trees they did not tend except at harvests, burned the rest of the trees off their ejidos to open pasture for cattle, and made money off the coffee and the cattle, which so exhausted the land that after 20 years the original ejidos could no longer support the people on them. (Hence the junior ejidos they had passed down along the way.) Because so many of the colonists were young and figured the forest was theirs for the taking, they made the second choice. In freedom and youth then they became frontier farmers and ranchers on their ejidos, ready to wear the land out and move yet another time or two in their life.

Consequently they soon transformed the jungle. By 1970 some 60 percent of the Lacandón was in ejidos. By then in Ocosingo, the state's biggest township, over 4,000 square miles and three-quarters of the Lacandón, vast expanses of the forest had gone up in smoke, at least 30 percent where the fewest ejidos were, as much as 70 percent in the most densely settled canyons. There between 1950 and 1970 the land in grass, to feed cattle, spread as much as 40 percent.

Most remarkable was the new communities' social and political organization. From their native village or finca, the pioneers brought all the interpretive and reassuring customs they could use. If they were Catholic, they almost always carried a patron saint to found their colony, and their communities celebrated holy days, consolidated in kinships by marriage, blood, and God, harbored witches and healers, extolled elders (if there were any), and elaborated a hierarchy of alcoholically festive cargos. But their bonds were necessarily new. Being so far from the outside, so deep inside, so young, and usually of various heritages, the settlers defined themselves not by the old Indian words for village, but simply as "we, the community." They bonded not in moral or material debt, but in a covenant.

Because they could not replicate the old ranks of honor, and (without much of a struggle for their ejido) had no forceful chiefs to command them, these youngsters could not avoid a new kind of politics. Isolated and on their own, they had many concerns in common: mainly the ejido, but also credit, municipal notices from a distant but inquisitive town hall, religious questions, a cooperative, police, housing, the coffee trees, the pasture, a school, stills, local public health, new pioneers joining them. And almost from the beginning they deliberated and decided on them in common, in frequent, regular assemblies that were open meetings ordinarily attended by all local men and women over 16, the age of responsibility there. The language of the assembly was the majority's; whoever knew the languages of the minorities—many did, from working with them in migrant labor—translated for them. Because the community would benefit most if it held together and grew, the assembly would discuss issues through every disagreement, discuss the hard ones to death, sometimes over many meetings, and not until then, when all were satisfied, vote its "accord." In the worst case, if a decision was urgent but held up because of opposition, the opposition would have to leave the community so that the assembly could then vote an accord. An assembly was not a meeting of equals, for the community also had political cargos that distinguished some members more than others. Cargos in the ejido's service, well performed, earned high regard. But duties well done to start a cooperative, coordinate the coffee harvest, or work on other important matters, won respect too. Although ejido commissioners did some of them, they could not do them all.

Many others volunteered, men and women, or the assembly elected them, and they did their part, on one committee or commission, then another, then another, taking turns at the chances for communal appreciation. In time they all learned something about everything they had in common, and learned their value to each other. When the community assembled, of 100 people, maybe 40 would be holding one or another cargo, and most if not all the others would have already served and be expecting to serve again in the future. This made for numerous leaders and guaranteed that no special group could accumulate authority over the assembly.

In the jungle then there were no principales. There the community in its assembly ruled. It elected by consensus not only the necessary committees and commissions, but also a "council of authorities" for terms as long as custom or the law provided. The "authorities" as collegial factotums managed the community's affairs and saw to compliance with its accords. But the "authorities" did not give the orders. It was the community that gave the orders to the "authorities." Having authority there meant working for the community. These were frontier democracies, improvised soviets.

The population of Los Altos increased more than 40 percent in the 1970s. It would have increased much more if tens of thousands of landless youngsters in their turn fed up with poverty and PRI bossdoms had not gone elsewhere. Some went down west to work where the great Angostura dam was under construction. Others went down north for work in the Tabasco oil boom. But most by far continued to migrate down east into the cañadas. The population in the Ocosingo, Altamirano, and Las Margaritas jungle increased from around 60,000 to around 120,000.

There the new pioneers now found more than natural trials and tribulations. National politics had arrived on the scene. In 1972 the officially populist President Luis Echevarría decreed that 2,400 square miles in eastern Chiapas, at least half the Lacandón, belonged to the "Lacandón tribe" as its "communal land . . . since time immemorial." The "Lacandón tribe" consisted then of 66 families, 400 people, used to rain forest garden farming. As this populist generosity developed, it happened that a new federal agency would manage the forest for the Lacandóns on a contract to cut some 10,000 mahoganies and cedars a year, at prices unstated, a splendid racket for PRI politicians involved. It also happened that the new Lacandón Zone included 37 Chol and Tzeltal settlements, 4,000 families, who would have to relocate to two new PRI-prepared camps on the zone's eastern border along the Usumacinta River, one named for Echevarría, the other for Chiapas's governor. Twenty did relocate. The others refused. And when engineers from the Agrarian-Reform ministry arrived directing crews to open breaks through the forest for a survey of the zone, the recalcitrants organized to block them, legally, politically, and physically. In the canyons where they were, this conflict, at times violent, eventually infamous as *El Conflicto por la Brecha*, lasted for 16 years.

By 1978 a new president had complicated business and politics in the jungle. Reducing the Lacandón Zone to the eastern third of the original grant and making the rest into an officially reserved biosphere, he dispossessed one of the earlier relocated concentrations and 26 new settlements, which widened and aggravated the conflict.

Through the decade and into the '80s, despite the oil- and debt-financed boom elsewhere in the country, outside, the inside remained a wilderness, but now ever more occupied and politically harassed. The settlement of so many new colonies in the canyons, their establishment as communities of the new kind, the need of older communities there to enlarge their ejidos, and the official threats of relocation raised in the old and the new communities a new question for their assemblies: security. Some old and new communities joined the PRI. Others turned militant in self-defense. Some of them organized their own armed forces, not just police, but communal soldiers, to protect their work and their hope.

Between 1980 and 1990, through the depths of Mexico's long economic disaster, the population of Los Altos grew by nearly 50 percent. Conflicts over land and religion in the villages there begat feuds, murders, and mass expulsions. As more of its landless young than ever before fled the bossdoms, some to work on the huge new dam building at Chicoasén, most by far as before migrating down to the jungle, the population there swelled from around 120,000 to around 200,000, 67 percent. The newest young pioneers found not only the natural difficulties and the nastiness of official agrarian politics, but also an ugly competition among themselves over ever less land to settle. The jungle had already lost 60 percent of its trees to ejido agriculture and ranching. Rival groups claimed the same little spot for a colony, and fought each other over it. And even when a group settled, made a community, and filed for its ejido, it had to endure other claims, violent reprisals, and ungodly long delays in approval of its grant. By then at best, if a claim was clear and provisionally endorsed at the state level, the process of federal approval took two years of negotiations in the PRI's national agrarian pits. On the average, given the usual disputes, it took five or six enraging years, and usually along the way bloodshed.

In the mid-80s the wars over land and justice not far south, in Nicaragua, El Salvador, and Guatemala, moved the government in Mexico City to take more seriously the conflicts in Chiapas. In league with the Agrarian-Reform ministry, a new governor announced his ominously titled "Program of Agrarian Rehabilitation." On a budget of U.S. $100 million, this was to buy private land in particularly troubled districts and grant it to still landless or but provisionally landed communities there as finally approved ejidos; one of the districts was the jungle.

In all the districts, however, the governor "rehabilitated" many more PRI-dominated communities than others. In Ocosingo 17 communities in the PRI's CNC received federally approved ejidos; only one independent community won a grant. This rankled far and wide. Some in the early 1990s had been working their provisional ejidos, defending themselves, negotiating, and stoking their rage over a decade without official resolution. By then more than 2,000 ejidos statewide occupied something over 50 percent of the farm and ranch land in production. In Ocosingo, officially 206 ejidos held 97.5 percent of the townships' surface. Because there remained considerable private property, and off-limits reserves alone comprised over 30 percent of the township, officials were counting much land in more than one ejido, maybe in three or four. Through the 1980s and into the '90s every community in the cañadas needed more security. More and more assemblies reached an accord to arm men.

From 1989 to 1992, while the national economy recovered through Salinas's reforms, many people in Chiapas suffered a severe depression. The world price of coffee collapsed in 1989, and over the next few years it fell by nearly 60 percent. Small farmers who had invested in the trees lost 65 to 70 percent of their income. Villagers producing coffee in the valleys of Los Altos lost twice: on their own trees and as laborers, because they could no longer compete in migrant labor with the Guatemalan refugees working on the fincas still in operation. Communities in the Margaritas canyons, among them Nuevo San Juan Chamula, had invested heavily in coffee. Old pioneers there, although they were paying their Guatemalan laborers only U.S. $1.60 a day, went broke.

In the thick of this pauperization, in November 1991, news spread across the state of Salinas's plan to reform the constitutional article on agrarian reform. For landless youngsters in the central highlands, still stuck in Los Altos but hoping to migrate, or struggling in the jungle to claim an ejido, the central and outrageous aim was to end the government's obligation to grant lands to any more landless communities. Myriad earnest and honest explanations of the plan—that hardly any land remained to give away, agrarian reform for the last 25 years had increasingly been only on paper, a trick on poor country people, a racket, existing ejidos could stay as they were or receive titles to their grant as their property, the central aim of the new reform was to undermine traditional national bosses and break local bossdoms, an antipoverty program would save the disentitled, and so on—made no difference. In this plan the poorest of the poor Chols, Tzotzils, Tzeltals, and Tojolabals heard the national government's final judgment on them: fend for yourselves. In January 1992 Mexico's Congress passed the reform. In February the new agrarian code went into effect.

That same month two more shocks jolted the cañadas. The Agriculture Ministry stopped the sale of cattle from eastern Chiapas to the regional packing house in Tabasco and put the jungle under quarantine, because of screw worm in Ocosingo. And the state's governor gave an unexpected and particular twist to Salinas's ecological policy, which prohibited commercial logging in the jungle. He canceled all ranching credit to communities there, on the argument that ranching too was harmful to the forest. This was plausible ecologism, except that other ranchers there continued doing business. The governor's actual purpose made sense, however. It was simply to help the state's big ranchers, then losing their share of the national market to smuggled Guatemalan steers and new imports of cheap Argentine beef. As compensation, they could have the communities' share. Because most communities in the canyons ran cattle, the wealthier old pioneer families owning 35 to 45 head, the governor made many enemies. The only people in the state then possibly madder than the small-time coffee farmers and the landless young were small-time frontier ranchers going broke.

Later that year the Mexican debate on NAFTA opened. If the treaty passed, Mexico within 15 years would end all price supports for corn and beans and all duties and quotas on the import of U.S. and Canadian grains and legumes. Mexican corn then sold for U.S. $240 a ton. Iowa corn sold on the U.S.-Mexican border for at most U.S. $110 a ton. Chiapas had nearly 500,000 farmers, nearly all of whom produced some corn, two-thirds of which went to market. Certainly a large majority of those in the Grijalva Valley followed the debate on their future. Certainly not half of the probably 300,000 farmers in the central highlands did, because most of them could not read, had no electricity, and did not understand Spanish well. But it did not take many who did understand the issue to circulate the word in the right language. The future was running out for them in the only farming they knew how to do.

On October 12, 1992, the caxlanes of San Cristóbal celebrated the 500th anniversary of Columbus's discovery of America. That morning over 9,000 Indians from the central highlands marched into the city and demonstrated all day against "500 years of robbery, death, and destruction of the Indian people," a "day of disgrace," and NAFTA. Some of them knocked down a bronze statue of the caxlán conquistador who had founded the city. There were no fights, but not for lack of hard feelings.

So in the midst of national revival a material and moral crisis developed in Chiapas's vast rural areas. It was worst in Los Altos and the cañadas, in the Indian heartland's villages and communities. But despite the Columbus Day protest, it was not basically a crisis for people there as Indians, as Chols, Tzotzils, Tzeltals, or Tojolabals. It was a crisis for them as peasants, villagers, or comrades in a community, as the state's poorest rural poor. Most concretely and sharply it was a crisis on the frontier, which ignited a frontier fury. Through 1993 one of the wealthiest and most respectable ranchers in an old Ocosingo canyon community sold off the last of his steers and the ejido's to buy arms for a rebellion.

But revolt was not inevitable even on the frontier. There inside by then were probably 1,800 colonies and communities. When the time came, some having suffered misery and injustice for years, others newcomers to the ordeal, but all by 1993 full of fury, the great majority of the rural poor who did not belong to the Zapatista Army of National Liberation did not rebel, while the minority who did belong did rebel. The difference between them was not geographic, chronological, economic, social, ethnic, or religious, or in political intelligence or courage. It was principally in the choice made between rival strategies of struggle for "a life worth living." It was in practice a difference of organization—and not between the only locally organized and the Zapatistas, but between other regional organizations of struggle and the EZLN.

Samuel Ruiz is a practical man. Now 74, he has been bishop in San Cristóbal for more than half his life. In his opinion the main change in the diocese is that the Indian poor there have had *toma de conciencia*. This would be a mighty change. *Tomar conciencia* is to take cognizance, to question received faith, wisdom, and conventions, to become conscious in a new frame of mind that people, things, qualities, conditions may not be as they had seemed or been supposed to be, to try to discover, recognize, know them as they truly are, and in this knowledge to accept explicitly the obligations of conscience to do good. It is a powerful mental and moral experience, which especially strengthens the capacity to organize with others to make the wrong right. The poor of Chiapas's central highlands, Indian and otherwise, like the poor elsewhere, like the rich and the rest of us everywhere, make mistakes about wrong and right. But on the evidence the bishop's judgment is accurate. Over the last 30-odd years many Indians in the region have taken a new, critical attitude toward old beliefs and been consciously, conscientiously, and collectively trying to act on a new sense of right and justice. Among countless witnesses, as the bishop remembers, stand 30 commissioners from Indian communities who asked him in 1968, "Does this God of yours know how to save bodies, or is he concerned only with saving souls?" There are the Chols, Tzotzils, Tzeltals, and Tojolabals who have named their communities Bethany, Nazareth, Palestine, Calvary, New Jerusalem, who have for years defied caxlán landlords, defied the PRI, defied the government. There are those who organized, mobilized in secret, and on Columbus Day in 1992 marched in public through San Cristóbal, but did not fight. There are those who, furious as they were, consciously, conscientiously, and collectively did not revolt in 1994. There are the Zapatistas who in the same spirit did revolt.

It has been changing material circumstances that have changed so many minds and allowed so much organization. But what is distinctive is the quality of the change, that the Indian poor have come to feel they are, as Bishop Ruiz says, "the subjects of their lives." More than anyone else he is responsible for their new evaluation and organization of themselves.

This was not the bishop's intention when he first arrived in Chiapas. By all accounts, including his own, he was not then the questioning kind. Born November 3, 1924, in Irapuato, a railroad junction and market town in the central state of Guanajuato, a bastion of Catholicism in Mexico, he had been raised in a devout Catholic family. His father, a small-time grocer, had been a local leader in the Knights of Columbus and Catholic Action, and in the 1930s active in Mexico's major fascist movement, Sinarquismo. Samuel, the first of five children, went to school at the local College of the Sisters of the Sacred Heart and at 13 entered the diocesan seminary in León, the cathedral and small–factory town 50 miles by train north, the Sinarquista capital. He missed his family, soon did not feel at home with them either, and worried that he could not be a priest. On graduation in 1947 he was chosen one of the Mexican seminarians to go to the Pontifical Latin-American College in Rome and study at the pontifical universities. Plus XII made a deep impression on him. So also must have Pius's premier Catholic Actor, the great Jesuit preacher, Father Riccardo Lombardi, whose anti-communist "Crusade of Kindness" conquered Italy ideologically in 1948–49. By 1949 young Ruiz had graduated from the Gregorian University, in Dogmatic Theology, and been ordained. Two years later he had finished the Biblical Institute for a degree in Sacred Scripture. After a two-month Institute tour of the Holy Lands, he had only one more year of study to earn a doctorate. Instead, recalled to León, he returned to teach at the seminary. On November 30, 1951, Father Lombardi preached in León, on "Christ the King," to crowds jamming the town's soccer stadium. Shortly Father Ruiz was named the seminary's prefect of studies, and in 1954, barely 30, promoted to rector. He continued to teach, the Hebrew Bible, the Greek, Introduction to Sacred Scripture, Biblical Exegesis. The bishop appointed him a canon of the cathedral chapter, which in León in the 1950s made him a virtual marquis. The young priest then rose fast in the thoroughly conservative Conference of Mexican Bishops. Sound, industrious, able, from time to time self-doubting, but ferrously dutiful, he was a joy and a relief to the hierarchs. Pope John XXIII's appointment of him to the see in San Cristóbal made him one of them, to his immense joy and relief.

At his consecration in January 1960, the first bishop's consecration ever in the city, grandly staged in fulsome pomp, the 35-year-old Ruiz proudly wore the purple robe with a train 15 feet long. He had become an ecclesiastical duke in a city that bowed even to knights. And duly he paraded his position as the champion of San Cristóbal's conservatism. Against the federal law prohibiting clerical garb in public, he went about the street in his black cassock with red cincture, buttons, and piping.

The diocese then comprised two-thirds of Chiapas, nearly 20,000 square miles, over 700,000 souls, 97.5 percent of them nominally Catholic. Among his new responsibilities the bishop was to make a complete pastoral visitation within five years. There was much to inspect. Besides himself, his capitularies, and a few Marist and Jesuit missionaries, only 13 priests served 32 parishes and hundreds of villages, where, bucking the local pagan culture, maybe 50 meagerly paid catechists tried to keep the faith straight. Dutifully the bishop headed out to the surrounding Tzotzil villages, bearing in mind a modest project of his predecessor's to provide special attention to Indians, to save them from their culture. It was not Guanajuato. He needed a horse or mule to go very far. He had to bring along a translator to communicate. And he found more misery than he had ever seen or could understand. "I was like the fish that sleep with their eyes open," he remembered years later. "I traveled through villages where bosses were scourging debt-slaves . . . and all I saw were old churches and old women praying. 'Such good people,' I said to myself." But soon it got to him, conservatively. The pagan superstitions, the incomprehensible language, so many people barefoot and hungry, a hamlet of only sad men and women—recently the children had all come down with measles and diarrhea, the hamlet had sent three times for a doctor or nurse, none had come, the children had all died, and he was told, "It's the will of God"—it made him angry. Back in San Cristóbal he thought of a new plan for the Indians: "teach them Spanish, put shoes on their feet, and improve their diet." He had no idea how many conservatives, liberals, and Revolutionaries before him had had the same inspiration, to no avail.

His first public campaign was against INI schools in Los Altos, whose teachers he accused of spreading communist propaganda. His first pastoral letter was a barely veiled diatribe against the Cuban Revolution. In the apocalyptic style of Pius XII, he warned of communist infiltration, instructed priests to guard against communist influence on their flocks, and called for the Red Goliath's fall before the Catholic Davidian family praying, thinking Rerum Novarum, acting charitably, and always sure, "Christianity Yes, communism No!"

But on the way to completing his first visitation, Bishop Ruiz matured into a very different person. Through the real difficulties of his diocese, through some long suppressed powers in him that now came out, and through the amazing first session of Vatican II, he lost his sound complaisance toward ecclesiastic, economic, and social hierarchs and began to sense God working on His Own among the Indians.

The immediate trouble in the diocese, as the bishop ably discovered on his more and more distant visits, was neither pagan culture nor communism. Protestants were multiplying in villages and on fincas. And the Church's priests and missionaries were losing contact with ever more young Indians, the landless poor who were migrating east into the jungle, where Protestants were multiplying fastest. In 1962, at the suggestion of the apostolic delegate in Mexico, the bishop opened four schools to recruit and train Indian catechists to spread the Word of God correctly: one in San Cristóbal, which the Marists in charge of the seminary there would run; another in San Cristóbal, where the Sisters of the Divine Pastor, already teaching Indian girls the true faith and the three Rs, began teaching young women to teach others; a third in Bachajón, a village in a northern valley, where the Jesuits already there undertook the new duty; the fourth in Comitán, a town in the southern plains, where newly arrived Marists started training young men. A fifth school would open in 1963, when Dominicans from Oakland's Province of the Holy Name arrived in Ocosingo. The missionaries recruited scores of students, Chol, Tzotzil, Tzeltal, and Tojolabal, from many old villages, pioneer settlements, and new communities.

But from some classes more than half the youngsters left before finishing the three-month term. The others, after being drilled in the rudiments of Spanish, a trade, and Catholic doctrine, went back home to help maintain the faith. Some kept at it. Others quit, some of them to become Protestants. The bishop visited the schools. Students asked him questions that he could not answer to his satisfaction or theirs, about language, customs, values, God and His Word made flesh, the soul and the body, salvation in another world and the fact of wealth and poverty in this world. They were devout, respectful, gravely intent on doing good at home, but angry too, and making friends (and enemies) among themselves. The more the bishop traveled around the diocese, especially through the central highlands, on foot, the more catechists he knew, the more he felt the trouble was the Church itself, its alienation from the Indians. He proposed to Rome a division of the diocese, to allow closer attention to the Indian heartland.

Buried deep under all his education, ambition, and institutional success, his origins began to tell. His parents were both, in his words, "*de cuna sencilla*," of plain and simple stock. His mother, a servant girl orphaned at 15, had left the big house in Durango where a rich family was turning her into a model maid, and gone with a brother to work in migrant labor in Arizona and California. His father had been a migrant laborer then, too. Working in the Mormon-irrigated San Bernardino valley, the two had met in the Catholic Church choir in Colton and married there. They had moved back to Irapuato to rear their children in their language, in the country of their customs and values. And they had been poor for years. They lived behind their store in a neighborhood out on the edge of town, by the municipal water tower and across the road from the produce depot. As a boy, Samuel had known men working there; they were his friends' fathers, teamsters, car loaders, public market sellers. Years later, at school at Rome, he had felt "introverted" and "shy" at "social occasions," and had to push himself to be congenial. He had felt most at home when he found himself with "plain and simple people." Now on his hikes into the villages and new colonies and communities, among the plainest and simplest people he had ever known, he would often speak of "the Indians" and "the poor" as if they were the same, and the strength grew in him to stand up to the rich. "I came to San Cristóbal to convert the poor," he would later say, "but they ended up converting me."

The first ecumenical council of the Catholic Church since the ultra-montane Vatican I of 1869–70 opened in the Vatican in October 1962. It revealed the Church as radically transformed and divided. Of the 2,540 hierarchs attending, most came from outside Europe and the United States—250 from Africa, 256 from Asia, 932, the largest number of all, from Latin America. There were conservatives who wanted nothing new, reformers who wanted almost anything new, and between them a majority of mixed inclinations. Already in *Mater et Magister* the Good Pope John had defined himself: he was for workers and the poor everywhere. The Church, "the loving mother of all," the old man informed the inaugural audience, "must always look to the present, to the new conditions and new forms of life introduced into the modern world . . ." In defense and advancement of The Truth, in "a magisterium which is predominantly pastoral," he declared, the council's duty was to do "that work which our era demands of us" and meet "the modern expectations and needs of the various peoples of the world." Conservatives from the Roman Curia who had controlled most of the preparatory commissions tried from October to the end of the first session in December to win the council's approval of their drafts as its decrees. They failed every time before a preponderance of various reformers, who took control of the revisions to come. But confusion and division emerged in almost every national colloquium.

Among the 932 Latin Americans at Vatican II, one of the most junior in age and tenure was the bishop from San Cristóbal. Given the reality of his diocese and the ever clearer strength of his character, Ruiz quickly knew who he was—a cultural conservative and an economic and social reformer. The debates on every draft interested him: the Church's constitution, revelation, liturgy, the Eastern churches, ecumenical principles, the lay apostolate. This was not a provincial's excitement at princely discourse. Ruiz's interest rose on the reality he was witnessing of the great differences in the Church, and caught on the continual references to the matters of most concern to him at home, God's Word incarnate, "social action," Protestants, catechists, missions. For his feelings on these matters he was learning words and ideas to think about them and argue them. He met French and Italian intellectual priests who introduced him to the social science on "countries in development." The less philosophical, the more historical, Biblical, pastoral, and practical the debates, the more they engaged him.

In the council's sessions in the fall of 1963, 1964, 1965, Ruiz took part in the revisions that issued in the conciliar decrees on the Church's dogmatic constitution, its pastoral constitution in the modern world, ecumenism, and missionary activity. He committed himself in Rome to Pope John's Church, "the Church of all and especially the Church of the poor." He made many friends among other young churchmen there. And he cultivated clerical sociologists and anthropologists of development.

At home between sessions, freed from old constraints on his industry, Ruiz turned out to be a formidable organizer. In San Cristóbal, Bachajón, Comitán, and Ocosingo he expanded his program to train Indian catechists. When his proposal to divide the diocese resulted in the creation of a new see in Tuxtla, he forwent its comforts for the new diocese of old San Cristóbal, the poor half of the state, to concentrate on social action, cooperation with Protestants, and catechetical missions. Back in Mexico from the council's second session, he and the bishops of two other poor dioceses began organizing others in the same situation. Soon they had founded the Mexican Bishop's Mutual Aid Union (UMAE) to distribute conciliar documents among priests and promote social work in the most miserable rural districts. Before the council's next session ended, they had organized 14 dioceses. When the council adjourned in 1965, the year he concluded the first visitation, Ruiz brought back to San Cristóbal a French canon, a sociologist, to direct sociological and anthropological studies of the diocese, to teach the bishop and his priests how better to serve the Indian poor, in the villages and increasingly away in the jungle. By 1967 the diocese had some 600 Indian catechists at work teaching the old doctrine in the new conciliar mode, over 300 of them in the Ocosingo canyons. By then, backed by Father Lombardi's Catholic International, the "Movement for a Better World," 25 bishops belonged to UMAE. Together they had all improved the finances of their dioceses, established new social programs in them, and raised a professional staff for economic and social analyses.

They were also doing ecclesiastical politics. That year, 1967, they moved the conservative Conference of Mexican Bishops to accept Ruiz as head of its Commission on Indians and to establish a national Commission on Pastoral Social Action, with another UMAE cofounder as its head and Ruiz as a member. In 1968 the conservative axis that had dominated the conference since 1942 lost the presidency to a UMAE-supported bishop. Ruiz became head of the conference's new Center for Aid to Indian Missions, where he brought sociologists and anthropologists to study all the Indian dioceses.

Catholic reformers in Mexico then often repeated Pope Paul VI's call in *Populorum Progressio* to overcome the injustice of "underdevelopment" through reforms for "development, . . . the new name for peace." But as Bishop Ruiz organized the new pastoral action for Indians, he sometimes wondered if he really knew what he was doing. He suffered an anguishing exchange at an international meeting held by the Department of Missions of the Conference of Latin American Bishops. After an anthropologist's lecture on Indian cultures, he asked him, half to provoke him, if Catholicism as usually (paganly) practiced in Indian cultures was secondary or fundamental to them. The anthropologist answered that in all the Indian cultures he knew, it was the glue that held them together. The bishop fell silent. "I felt full of despair," he later remembered, "with a load of puzzles in my head . . . What was it to evangelize? Was it to destroy cultures? Should I just sit and contemplate them . . .? Why did God allow so many cultures? Has He let them exist in order that they be destroyed? But He Himself was born in a particular culture and embraced it to the point of speaking the dialect of the Nazarenes of Galilee."

Yet more challenging was the conclusion of a three-month review of his diocese's Indian work that at his request a commission of Indian wisemen had made. Illiterate, speaking no Spanish, they reported not in a statement but in three questions, in Tzeltal. The first was whether the bishop's God could save only souls, or bodies too. The second was, if "the Word of God is like a seed that is to be found everywhere, and . . . already a seed of salvation, . . . can we not assume that these seeds are to be found where we live in the mountains and forests? . . . Why should we have to come to your centers, to your schools, to seek these seeds and harvest them? Why cannot we do it in our own communities?" Third, to the bishop and the missionaries, "You have lived among us and shared our lives. We regard you as our brothers and sisters. Is it your desire to be our brothers and sisters for all time?"

The second general council of the Conference of Latin American Bishops met in Medellín, Colombia, in August–September 1968. There the Latin American Church had its own *toma de conciencia*, a shock of recognition. It was as if the youthful Catholic Action of the 1920s had come alive again all across that part of the world. Catholic Action's essential principles had been in three simple imperatives, "See, Judge, Act." And there many bishops were, decades later, following them in "the new conditions" of "the modern world." Having seen the Church at Vatican II as "especially of the poor," the reformers would now judge and act. Despite conservative resistance, the conference denounced poverty in Latin America as "inhuman," a "sinful situation," a "rejection of the Lord," "institutionalized violence." It gave its "preference to the poorest and most needy sectors and to those segregated for any cause whatsoever." It welcomed the "zeal for full emancipation, liberation from every form of servitude . . ." It recalled that God had sent His Son in the flesh "to liberate all persons from the slavery to which sin has subjugated them: hunger, misery, oppression, and ignorance—in a word, that injustice and hatred which have their origin in human selfishness." And it urged pastoral action to favor "the efforts of the people to create and develop their own grassroots organizations for the redress and consolidation of their rights and the search for true justice."

No less judgmental and agitating were hundreds of priestly and lay staff at the council, privately circulating their views on celibacy, a revolutionary priest in Colombia, "base communities" in Brazil, a new "theology of liberation" in Peru, the Book of Exodus, re-reading which, Ruiz says, made Mexican reformers' "blood run cold."

By papal decision only seven bishops at the council presented papers. One was the bishop of San Cristóbal. His assigned topic was evangelization, spreading the Word of God. What he said not only represented what he had seen and judged, but also indicated where he was going to act: "The poor cannot be evangelized if we own vast estates. The weak and the oppressed withdraw from Christ if we appear as allies of the powerful. The illiterate cannot be evangelized if our religious institutions continue looking for paradise in the big cities, and not on the poor edges of town and out in the disinherited hamlets." (Reading No. 8.) Elected head of the conference's Missions Department, he began learning all he could about missionary organizing elsewhere in Latin America, which now meant the faithful organizing themselves.

Bishop Ruiz then proved himself a formidable manager. Back in San Cristóbal, he delegated authority and headed in his own direction, mentally, morally, and often physically, like thousands of the Indian poor, eastward down into the cañadas. He wanted to know what God had been doing there. A master of Hebrew, Greek, and Latin, able to English, French, German, and Italian, he began learning Tzotzil and Tzeltal to understand villagers and migrants in their own tongue. Jesuits in Bachajón began translating the Bible into Tzeltal. The Dominicans and lay apostles of the Word were walking down to all the settlements they could find in the Ocosingo jungle, talking with the people there, hearing their stories. In real Indian lives the bishop and the missionaries now recognized the story of Exodus, a political story of struggle against oppression and corruption, a divine promise of liberation, a humanly organized escape, the travails of flawed leaders, doubts, and backsliding, and finally, far from perfect, but better than Egypt, the promised land. The bishop decided to reform the entire missionary program, to make evangelization in the canyons, in his word, "incarnate." There would be no "base communities," but many more local catechists. Their work would no longer be individual and instructive, but "communitarian," reflective, evocative, stirring the community, dissolving the Word of God into it. They would have a new catechism, which they would compose themselves, in their own language. They would not only sow the Word in their settlements and communities, but also harvest it, as the faithful put it into their own words and into conscious and conscientious action. The canyon communities would become popular Christian communities.

Reformers did not last long in the offices of Latin American bishops' conferences. In 1971 a new head of the Mexican conference's Social Pastoral Commission gutted it. In 1972 a Colombian conservative took charge of the general Latin American conference, attacked "Marxist infiltration" of the Church, and one by one purged the reformers; in 1974 he rid the Missions Department of the bishop of San Cristóbal.

By then, however, Ruiz had turned his diocese into a model Medellín mission. There were more than 2,000 catechists at work, over 1,000 of them Indians in villages, pioneer settlements, and canyon communities. From regular catechetical meetings, in Chol, Tzotzil, Tzeltal, Tojolabal, many of them knew each other. Since the conflict with the government over the Lacandón Zone had started, the catechists there whom the defiant Chol and Tzeltal communities made authorities had cooperated with each other. In this conflict the Word of God became in their languages the seed of not only spiritual but material and social salvation as well. It resounded in the new catechism the Tzeltal catechists had just finished, which they entitled, "We Are Looking for Freedom": "God wants us to get out to freedom like the ancient Jewish people . . . in the lands of another people, called Egypt, they worked as slaves, suffering many wants. Then God spoke in the heart of one of their principales, . . . 'I have come down to liberate you from your sufferings, and I am going to bring you to another, better land.' . . . [But] they had to get out and fight to gain their freedom. . . . our ancestors too had to unite and struggle to win their lands. . . . We have to gather strength in our hearts, and struggle and suffer much still. We have to struggle against poverty, hunger, and injustice." (Reading No. 9)

Indians in the central highlands then demonstrated their new conscious and conscientious capacity to organize on a regional scale. The occasion was an official event, staged to divert attention from the Lacandón conflict and revalidate the government's pro-Indian credentials by commemorating Bishop Bartolomé de Las Casas's defense of Indians on the fifth centenary of his birth, 1974. Consulted the year before by federal and state officials, Bishop Ruiz had advised that the homage would be empty unless Indians took part. After more consultation, state officials, the bishop, and Indian catechists agreed that Indians would hold an Indian Congress organized by themselves for themselves. As the missionaries lauded Bishop Las Casas and catechists stirred their communities to consider the congress and send delegates, Indians in the highland valleys, plains, and cañadas took their customary time, some months, to deliberate locally, confer through commissioners from community to community, agree on participation, frame questions, articulate statements of their concerns, and organize delegations.

The result was historic, at least in Chiapas. On October 13, 1974, the Indian Congress opened in San Cristóbal. The governor, the one who had bestowed his name on one of the resettlements out of the Lacandón, spoke a few words in caxlán. Then the Indian delegates, 161 choleros, 350 tzotzileros, 587 tzeltaleros, 152 tojolabaleros, 1,250 strong from 327 villages, settlements, and communities, brought their first common assembly ever to order and gave voice to their questions and statements, each speaker in his own language, his words, as at a little UN, translated within each delegation of a different tongue. For two days they recounted the misery and indignity of their lives, denounced particular injustices in vivid detail, analyzed the causes of their poverty, torments, and frustration, and discussed strategies for action, including a union of canyon communities. On the third day, in their customary way, but not quickly, they reached their accords: the need for land to belong to the man who worked it, more land, good land, and honest counselors to teach them their rights under the agrarian code; the need for doctors, effective programs of public health, proper medications, and an end to traffic in government-dispensed medicines; the need for basic services, like running water; the need for more and better schools, and for Indian priests; the need for fair wages and enforcement of the labor law; the need for Indian markets, to avoid "merchants and monolopists [who] are 'A GREAT PLAGUE.' (Reading No. 10.)

This irked the state's PRI. It stunned conservative San Cristóbal. The city's businessmen were the region's *fuerzas vivas*, its live motive power. They were especially the Church's "natural friends." Since Indians on their own could not have staged such a scandal, the diocese's priests must have put them up to it. How could the bishop have allowed it? The PRI and the city's Catholic bourgeoisie took to open criticism of him.

But the bishop had no regrets. He quit wearing his cassock in public, for a plain business suit.

Having managed to evoke new attitudes and induce new organizations among the Indians, he proceeded to consolidate them as a Catholic civil corps. He practically laicized the Indian parishes in the cañadas. It was no longer the missionaries who recruited the catechists there, but the communal assemblies that elected them and a new "authority" the bishop allowed, the predeacon, to move toward an Indian priesthood. Through continual meetings, diocesan priests, missionaries, catechists, predeacons, and canyon community commissioners discussed how to help the communities defend themselves in the Lacandón conflict and begin to satisfy some of their material needs. In November 1975 at the First Diocesan Assembly in San Cristóbal, the bishop proclaimed the diocese's "option for the poor." In December, 18 Ocosingo communities founded a union of ejidos, La Unión Qu'iptik ta Lekubtesel, Tzeltal for "Our Effort [our strength, our push, our driving power] to Do Better." Catechists and predeacons ran it; only Catholics belonged. Several villages in the valleys north of San Cristóbal organized a union of Catholic ejidos there. In 1976, 34 communities promoted their predeacons to deacons, *tuhuneletik* in Tzeltal, "servants" of the community, and the bishop confirmed them. Every year there were more. On funding by foreign NGOs, the bishop brought a private Indian Mission development agency, DESMI, to support the deacons' economic projects and social work.

San Cristóbal's conservatives were fuming that the bishop had gone "Red." The Mexican bishops' conference pretended to ignore him, and angled to isolate him. Pope John Paul II on his visit to Mexico in January 1979 did not go to

Chiapas or mention the church there. The third general council of the Conference of Latin American Bishops meeting then in Puebla, under conservative auspices, did not include Ruiz.

But the pope did affirm the Medellín commitment to a social mission. In Oaxaca he declared before an audience of 40,000 Indians, "You have a right to be respected and not be deprived of the little you have . . . You have a right to throw down the barriers of exploitation." He recommended that they organize "for better coordinated action in greater solidarity . . ." In Puebla, for all their conservatism, the bishops again denounced poverty as "institutionalized violence," condemned social injustice as "social sin," and in a "preferential option for the poor" invited "all, without distinction of class, to accept and take up the cause of the poor, as if they were accepting and taking up their own cause, the very cause of Jesus Christ . . ."

Ruiz could not have hoped for a stronger sanction, except from his diocese's poor themselves. And this too from the faithful poor he soon received. In 1979 the Catholic canyon communities elected a deacon of deacons, their chief moral judge and minister. He was 24 years old.

There remained, however, the "separated brethren" and sisters. Ecumenicist the bishop was, but he could not offer inducement to needy Protestants.

The central highlands, its Indians so poor, so angry, so conscious, conscientious, organized, and militant, were by then powerfully attractive to the Mexican left. Already various factions of the left were at work in the diocese. The two most important were blood enemies. One was the Mexican Communist Party's Farm Workers and Peasants Independent Central, CIOAC, based in the region's northern valleys, trying to organize a farm workers' union. (Reading No. 11.)

The other, which over the next 15 years would matter much more, was a Mao-inspired movement called the Proletarian Line, the LP. Formed in the early '70s among young university teachers and students in Mexico City, it had organized rural communities and poor urban neighborhoods in several northern states to demand land, housing, and social services. Ruiz had met some of the movement's main cadres in 1976, on a trip north to negotiate the release of a priest in jail for working with them. Like most young militants in Mexico then, they had revolution on their minds: "Our central task . . . is to mobilize and organize the great masses to take part in the revolutionary struggle to bring down the bourgeoisie and its government . . . and to extend the revolutionary movement to all of Mexico until the realization of a socialist fatherland." But they had no military configuration, made no appeals for armed action, and operated in public. Their "revolutionary struggle" was actually an "ideological struggle in the bosom of the people," a long process, practically no more than spreading and strengthening their organization among "the people," until maybe decades in the future "the bourgeoisie and its government" could no longer function and finally fell in only transitory violence. Most interesting was the way they organized, which they called *política popular*, "people's politics." This was grassroots organizing from the inside, living and working for years in deliberately selected communities, not as a vanguard, but to elicit critical questions, evoke claims for justice, and induce local leadership, stirring people to solidarity in collective decisions and actions. It would go perfectly in the cañadas, congruent with the diocesan work, but open to Protestants. (Reading No. 12.)

The bishop had invited the head LP cadre to meet his priests and missionaries. In San Cristóbal the head cadre had told the clerics, "You are wizards at pastoral work, but you have no training for strictly political organizing. I come to make you an offer. You take charge of the pastoral work, and we take charge of the political organization." The clerics had accepted the offer. The Jesuits in Bachajón soon backed out, to concentrate on catechetical and social work and discourage outside politics in their districts. But the diocesan priests, the Marists, and the Dominicans had given serious support to their new political partner.

They soon suffered a sharp lesson in "strictly political organizing." Besides the federal government and the Church, the most important organization in the cañadas then was the Ocosingo union of ejidos. The LP cadres had gone straight for it, run into the catechists and deacons who ran it, and found them determined to hold onto it. They had not fought them. As in the north, they had gone to "the masses," lived in the union communities, induced unauthorized communications among them, joined the union's defense of the settlements the government would evict from the Lacandón. Meanwhile, collaborating with them, other young Maoists had been at work in the Las Margaritas canyons. There in 1979 they induced the formation of two more unions of ejidos, including Catholics and Protestants. Statewide the LP cadres organized and won a campaign for federal subsidies of coffee farmers' transport costs, which especially benefited union farmers. And in September 1980 they induced the Ocosingo union of ejidos, the two Las Margaritas unions, and four other organizations, altogether representing 156 communities in 13 municipalities, 10,000 families, to form the Union of Ejido Unions and Associated Peasant Groups of Chiapas, suddenly the entire central highlands' major peasant power. By consensus the Ocosingo union would guide the new organization. Shortly it removed its president, a catechist, and its secretary, the deacon of deacons himself, and new officers following the Proletarian Line took the lead. Unlike other agrarian movements, the Union of Unions did not then launch a struggle for more ejidos or (like the CIOAC) farm workers' unions. It negotiated with the government, and won the authority to administer for its affiliates a big new federal program of rural credits, productivity incentives, and marketing facilities, which would enable them to produce their way out of poverty. And it aggressively defended prospective affiliates, mobilizing, with public support in Mexico City, a Columbus Day sitdown strike in Tuxtla in 1981 to demand federal retraction on evictions from the Lacandón.

San Cristóbal's bourgeoisie led the irate reaction. It published demands for the government to restore order, "or must we take justice into our own hands?" Locally and in Mexico City the press speculated that "since communists had killed Archbishop Romero" in El Salvador, to make a martyr for their cause, they might kill Bishop Ruiz too. One columnist had the bishop in command of 3,000 armed Tzotzils. Another had him running a guerrilla training center at the San Cristóbal seminary, which in hours could bring 300,000 Indians into guerrilla warfare. The death threats began, and police terrorist operations, to create a climate of intimidation.

For two years the bishop and his priests and missionaries worked against the LP to regain the initiative and the influence they had lost. They induced the election of many more catechists and deacons in the cañadas. They founded a secret Indian society, Roots, by which the deacon of deacons and carefully chosen catechists raised Indian opposition to the caxlán Maoists. And they looked for experienced cadres from other movements in the region to help them recapture the Union. The CIOAC, being Communist, would not serve. The new Emiliano Zapata Peasant Organization, the OCEZ, allied with a national left-wing and severely anticlerical public-school teachers' movement, would not do either. (Reading No. 13.) The only other prospects were some new social workers coordinating projects not far north of San Cristóbal, in a very poor Catholic Tzotzil village where Indians a few years before had killed two caxlanes. They were certainly on the left too, but the regional director of DESMI knew them and recommended them. The diocese (except for the Jesuits) soon began collaborating with them in Los Altos, especially through DESMI, Roots, and the deacon of deacons.

This was how the choice opened between rival strategies and organizations of struggle for "a life worth living." Although neither the bishop nor his priests or missionaries knew it, the social workers were cadres of a Che Guevara-inspired clandestine revolutionary movement, the Forces of National Liberation, the FLN. For the last two or three years the DESMI regional director had been a cadre. The deacon of deacons was now one too. The FLN had a proudly secret, violent, and patient past. Formed in the north in 1969 among survivors of earlier guerrilla action, it had suffered bloody losses, betrayals, and purges, reorganized, fought back and come back by the late '70s to run an underground in several states. The movement drew much encouragement from the Sandinista victory in Nicaragua. In 1980, for internal distribution and discipline, it published its statutes. Its highest authority was its commander in chief, who headed a national executive of two other *comandantes*, which directed a political bureau, the commands of combat fronts, and the "clandestine zone directive committees," which among them directed two organizations, the cells of Students and Workers in Struggle and the units of the EZLN. ". . . considering armed struggle as the extension and superior expression of the political struggle of the masses," the new cadres were in Los Altos to open a new front there in the long national struggle "to defeat the bourgeoisie politically and militarily" and "install a socialist system . . ." (Reading No. 14.)

By 1983 the Union of Unions and associated groups had reached a crisis. The CIOAC and the OCEZ were cooperating in campaigns for land in the cañadas to build their organizations there. The Union could no longer maintain the connection between its unions, apprehensive at CIOAC-OCEZ entries into their organizing grounds, and its associated groups, intent on deals to improve credit, production, and marketing. And it split, the Union of Unions sticking together for labor and land, the associated groups founding their own credit union. The main LP cadres withdrew from Chiapas. On support from DESMI, Roots, and the deacon, the FLN cadres went to work far down in the jungle in the Las Margaritas canyons south of Lake Miramar. The FLN national executive then joined them, to reconnoiter bases for the politico-military struggle.

Through the economic disaster then, the new governor's "agrarian rehabilitation" of PRI communities and obstruction of others, the immigration of some 200,000 refugees fleeing reborn-Christian state terrorism in Guatemala, the San Cristóbal diocese did wonders of organization. By 1985 it boasted over 6,000 catechists, more than 3,300 of them Indians, and some 100 Indian deacons. In its clandestine way the FLN too had done well. Its commander in chief had gone to organize other parts, but left behind the two other comandantes, one as chief of staff, to run through DESMI the movement's logistics, the other, the DESMI director's girlfriend, to command operations in the cañadas. Under her orders the cadres had made connections with the Union of Unions, stirred it as the LP cadres had stirred it, helped it regain its standing as the major resistance to ranchers and their gunmen, and in cooperation with the deacon of deacons induced his community, in the middle of the Ocosingo canyons, to form armed guards for self-defense—and "liberation."

In 1986 at a general diocesan assembly the bishop presented a new pastoral plan for evangelization. In the spirit of Catholic Action, Vatican II, and Medellín, he confidently and precisely defined the evangelist's duty "to discover the riches that the Father gave his children even before our humble proclamation of the Good News," and to turn these God-given values, in "indigenous" (i.e., maybe somewhat pagan) Catholics, brothers and sisters of other faiths, atheists too, into practical service of the poor, to make a community of God in anticipation of His Kingdom. The bishop emphasized the egregious inequality and injustice in his diocese, which correctly enough he blamed on U.S. banks, Chiapas ranchers and businessmen, and the Mexican government. He also noted alarmingly "the tendency for armed movements to arise in the state." For his transcendental objective, his program for pastoral action certainly implied some immanentist action: democratize the diocese, incarnate the gospel in the community, learn from the people, inculturate the evangelist, synthesize faith and politics, direct the liturgy and popular religiosity to liberation of the poor, hold workshops for people on "the oppressive system," let women take part in "full equality" with men in making parochial and missionary decisions. (Reading No. 15.)

In this climate the clandestine FLN was thriving. The zone commander established her headquarters just outside the ejido of the deacon of deacons. The secretary of the Union of Unions became a cadre and drew others from the unions into the movement. And the national executive started militarizing the zone. It promoted three of the captains there to *subcomandante*, the senior of them the cadre known as "Marcos," and they began receiving arms and ammunition, raising recruits, and training them as regular insurgents, militia, and active support for the EZLN.

But an old rival of the FLN's soon reappeared in the region. Inside the Mexican government a group of new reformers were emerging under the leadership of the increasingly powerful minister of Budgeting and Programming, Carlos Salinas. Besides enforcing the government's economic policies, Salinas was also developing a social policy and social politics. For some 15 years he had had close contact with the main LP cadres. In 1986 he began discussions with the Union of Unions on the canyon communities' grievances. In March 1987 a national commission and the Union agreed on bases for resolving the problems the Union then regarded as most pressing: regularization of the communities' land holdings, legitimization of their elected authorities, disclosure of expropriable land on large estates, and appreciation of Indian cultures. In March 1988, encouraged by Salinas and stirred by returning LP cadres, the catechists and deacons running the Union registered it as a "rural association of collective concern," an ARIC, to qualify it for credit on a grand scale. In effect the Union was again moving out of the struggle for more land, toward the struggle for more production. That same month the FLN national executive withdrew its zone commander from Chiapas, and made Subcomandante Marcos head of the EZLN's Southeast Combat Front.

Within a year, over politics, the region's clerics and the FLN parted company. National elections occurred in July. Having divided the traditional bosses and beat other inside reformers, Salinas stood as the PRI's presidential candidate. His principal opponent, Cuauhtémoc Cárdenas, the son of the great reformist president of the 1930s, had lately split from the PRI to champion Mexican populism. Many priests and missionaries in the diocese waxed enthusiastic about him and his cause. On their encouragement some FLN cadres in high office in the Union of Unions organized for his new party. Marcos accused them of betraying the revolutionary movement. They quit the FLN. But since Cárdenas barely lost the hotly controversial election, and afterward made clear his intention to rally all the left outside the PRI in a continual campaign for the next election in 1994, they remained active Cardenistas in the Union, persuaded that the new party would be more likely than an FLN uprising to open a way to socialism. Clerics and Roots (despite the deacon of deacons) supported them against the FLN cadres. On the national executive's word Marcos formed his insurgents into seven EZLN regiments under the new command of majors.

By 1989, when coffee prices began falling, eight militant organizations were contending over the poor in the central highlands, and each by then knew more or less what the others were doing. The Church, managed by Bishop Ruiz, continued to expand its social mission, involving ever more catechists and deacons, who in their assemblies, councils, ejido commissions, unions, and the newly reformed Union of Unions–ARIC were (despite Roots) pulling politically in ever more directions. The Proletarian Line, managed by President Salinas, transformed into Solidarity's cadres in the regions, was working hard again in Catholic and Protestant canyon communities. (Reading No. 16.) On January 3, 1989, it won a final presidential resolution in favor of the ejidos in the old Conflicto por la Brecha in the Lacandón, which restored much of its old authority in the Union. (Reading No. 17.) The CIOAC remained strong in the northern valleys, and was organizing in union territory in Margaritas township. The OCEZ, splitting over whether to protest or to negotiate for land, was organizing in union territory in Ocosingo township. The Union of Unions–ARIC itself, reconstituted, redirected, and pulled in several directions, was still the most extensive and powerful peasant organization in the region, still representing over 100 ejidos and running community schools and presidentially subsidized stores. The PRI state machine, having so far failed to repress or capture many communities directly, had a new governor, Patrocinio González, another traditional boss, but Cambridge-(England) trained in economics and law, shrewd and sophisticated, who almost at once reformed the state's penal code to criminalize nearly any public protest and was maneuvering to use Solidarity to impose his brand of PRI across the eastern frontier. (Reading No. 18.) Cárdenas's new party, the Partido de la Revolución Democrática (PRD), barely organized in Chiapas, could not attract support from the CIOAC or the OCEZ, but was finding priests, social workers, and lawyers who in their work promoted it among the poor. And finally there was the FLN, hostile to all other political and social movements, at odds with the bishop, his priests, the Jesuits, and the Dominicans, abandoned by the cadre just elected president of the Union of Unions, but still served by DESMI, still favored by the deacon of deacons, and still dominant in most of the Catholic canyon communities, its loyal cadres preparing the EZLN for war.

As the economy at large recovered, but coffee farmers in Chiapas went under, these struggles all intensified. The arousal of another militant organization in the state, the Mexican army looking for drug traffickers and prospective guerrillas, complicated and endangered every movement but the PRI's. But the movements grew in all directions. The FLN was most successful. The national executive saw that while Solidarity was gaining influence in the Union of Unions and attracting new affiliates there, its operation inside the regime antagonized old affiliates long sick of the system and determined to keep out of its clutches; some of them were quitting the union. In 1991 the FLN outflanked Solidarity by arranging the public constitution of a rival to the Union of Unions, the Emiliano Zapata Independent National Peasant Alliance, the ANCIEZ, nominally with branches in northern, central, and southern Mexico. The Chiapas branch quickly enrolled several ex-Union ejidos and other organizations in the canyons and in CIOAC territory in Los Altos. The FLN then won its most promising political victory—the election of its prize cadre, the deacon of deacons, to president of the Union of Unions. If the deacon could revive the Church's cooperation through Roots and move the Union's ejidos to approve the strategy of armed struggle, the FLN through the Union and the ANCIEZ would dominate the entire region before the EZLN went to war.

On this promise the FLN worked to consolidate its power. In January 1992 the ANCIEZ staged its first demonstration in Chiapas, mobilizing some 4,000 peasants in Ocosingo against the constitutional changes in agrarian reform, the official delays in granting ejidos, army patrols in the cañadas, and the proposed free-trade agreement. The Union of Unions and the ANCIEZ protested the governor's assault on ejido ranching. The ANCIEZ staged another demonstration in Ocosingo in April against the end of entitlement to ejidos, the continued army patrols, and free trade. It took all it could from DESMI and from Solidarity grants to buy more equipment for war. In October it joined the Union, the CIOAC, and the OCEZ to make the anti-Columbus march in San Cristóbal; its members were the ones who knocked down the conquistador's statue.

But the promise proved disappointing. The cadres of Solidarity continued to organize, many for the governor, especially in the towns, but more for the president down in the cañadas, making thousands of committees inside the union for antipoverty projects and resistance to the FLN. And the deacon remained truer to his people and his religious duties than to the revolution. There were in the diocese by then some 8,000 catechists, 400 deacons. He could not rule them, only serve as the people directed him. And they gave him contradictory directions. There were in Ocosingo, Altamirano, and Las Margaritas townships then over 225,000 people in seven or eight towns and maybe 25 villages, 1,350 colonies, and 450 communities, practically all of the colonies and communities down in the cañadas. Of the villages and communities, some 410 held ejidos. About two-thirds of the people in the canyons then, maybe 130,000 people, lived in around 385 communities holding ejidos, some in the PRI's CNC, others in the CIOAC or the OCEZ, most (especially the Protestants) unaffiliated, by far most of the affiliated in the Union of Unions. Altogether through the central highlands the Union then comprised some 120 ejidos, around 90 in the canyons. These communities' assemblies turned again and again through 1992 to the question of an unarmed or the armed way. Most of them, stirred one way by Solidarity cadres, the other way by FLN cadres, could not reach a consensus, could only continue to discuss the question, and the communities remained intact. Most of the others reached a consensus so conditioned that in effect they too postponed the decision, and held their communities together. Only a few decided clearly, about half one way, half the other. Neither from discussions nor from decisions, however, win or lose, did those who oppose the armed way report those who were for it to the army or police. They would not tell on relatives or old friends. And they did not want to start a war among the poor, whatever might happen later.

Counting recruits after the anti-Columbus Day march, in the northern valleys and in the cañadas, in colonies and communities nonunion and union, the EZLN subcomandantes figured their force at 12,000 (a third women), and began holding war councils in the canyons. On January 23, 1993, in the same ejido where 17 years before the Ocosingo communities had founded the first union of ejidos, the FLN met, to decide how soon to go to war. The chief of staff, another comandante, and two other members of the national executive argued for postponement: the movement's forces were still very weak in the northern and central states; the government's army would surround a revolt on the southeast front alone; better wait another 10 years and win in a month. Marcos, with his two junior subcomandantes, argued for action as soon as possible: because of Solidarity and the Church (including that damned deacon), their force was continually losing soldiers and support; the army, which knew where their strongholds were, might attack them if they did not take the offensive; and a war underway in 1994 would gain from the government's disarray in a year of national elections. The commander in chief endorsed Marcos's argument. The chief of staff left the meeting (to leave the movement and eventually the country). The remaining officers formed the FLN Party, the PFLN. By unanimous vote the commander in chief became secretary general and secretary of the interior of its central committee. Marcos became military secretary, and his ex-wife the secretary of the masses, in charge of subsecretariats for peasants, workers, and popular organizations. On Marcos's proposal the central committee created a Clandestine Revolutionary Indian Committee, the CCRI, to ascertain how committed pro-FLN colonies and communities were to a war within the year. In February a CCRI of veteran Chol, Tzotzil, Tzeltal, and Tojolabal cadres worked through as many as 100 localities in the canyons to prepare the voting. On March 25 the colonies and communities voted, about half in favor, enough to satisfy Marcos.

The PFLN soon lost a crucial position and a crucial connection. On May 22 a Mexican army patrol east of Altamirano came under fire in the jungle along the Altamirano-Las Margaritas line from EZLN forces defending a big training camp. Two days later the army occupied the deserted installation. Assuming that the Union of Unions supported the EZLN, it seized a nearly ejido and took away some Union members. The deacon of deacons did his primary duty, publicly denying the Union's engagement in any rebellion, in effect separating the Union from the EZLN.

Once the deacon had defected, Bishop Ruiz could act. He went down into the cañadas with priests and missionaries to advise communities not to support armed struggle. And he composed a pastoral letter for the diocese, which for maximum public effect he delivered to Pope John Paul on the papal visit to Yucatan in August. It was a long summary in plain Spanish of his then 33 years in San Cristóbal, an account of the social mission, the defense of the poor, the incarnation of the Church in Indian cultures, all the Left's standard criticisms of the Mexican regime and Salinas's reforms, but finally a plea for "dialogue," i.e., no military action, negotiations to stop the impending war. (Reading No. 19.)

President Salinas did not want military action either. It would (as Marcos had argued) gravely complicate the presidential succession, always the incumbent's most difficult work, and this time, against traditional PRI bosses' opposition to his reforms, especially hard to manage for another reformer. It would also probably ruin NAFTA's chances for approval in the U.S. Congress. And, since the army's massacre of civilians in Mexico City in 1968 would receive its twenty-fifth commemoration in October 1993, an inevitably bloody offensive among Chiapas's poorest peasants would almost certainly provoke historic civic protests around the country and a national political and military crisis. Instead, the president went on the political offensive. Free from interference by Governor González, whom in January he had promoted to minister of Interior (mainly to check his predecessor, a Mexican J. Edgar Hoover with presidential ambitions), Salinas tried to reclaim Solidarity in Chiapas and accelerate its organizing in the cañadas. In August his minister of Social Development, Luis Donaldo Colosio, in charge of Solidarity, announced in Las Margaritas the government's commitment of $50 million for economic and social programs in the canyon communities, and in Ocosingo conferred at length with the deacon of deacons about the Union, its security, and the EZLN. In September the president and the minister visited a Las Margaritas community and inaugurated a new Solidarity-funded and community-built hospital.

The general command for the EZLN met some days later in an old Ocosingo community. The only item on the agenda, which Marcos proposed, was to replace the pregnant director of the ideological commission with her husband, which the secretary general approved. But the secretary general then questioned Marcos about revolutionary finances, why he kept funds raised in Chiapas for arms procurement only there, why he did not send money to national headquarters for some distribution to other fronts. Marcos answered defiantly. He implied that comrades elsewhere were not doing their jobs. He ridiculed the EZLN's weakness outside Chiapas. The secretary general returned to Mexico City, tail between his legs, with the subcomandante whom Marcos had degraded for the loss of the training camp. In the central highlands Subcomandante Marcos now ruled the EZLN. The word spread quickly through the cañadas, even to the ranchers, that the war would start as soon as he said so.

Chiapas's bourgeoisie at large then rallied, in hopes of finally getting rid of the bishop and using the army to wipe out all its local foes. Their man in the capital, now Interior Minister González, maneuvered with the papal nuncio in Mexico to remove Ruiz from San Cristóbal, which in late October the nuncio leaked that the pope was about to do. Given the sour resentment that many Mexican bishops by then felt toward the nuncio, the support that several of them (as well as the Jesuit provincial and 50 more of the society in Mexico, the secretary general of the Conference of Latin American Bishops, and Rigoberta Menchú), expressed for their brother in San Cristóbal, and a mass demonstration for him there, the maneuver failed. But it seriously distracted the bishop and his clerics from their efforts to prevent war.

The CCRI could not authorize operations to start before the corn harvest was in, late November. On November 17 the U.S. House of Representatives voted for NAFTA, to take effect on January 1, 1994. This would be the date to start the revolution.

Three movements happened in the cañadas in November and December. One was the EZLN's physical movement of supplies and equipment into place for the mobilization. It required much labor. From 12,000 in January, the fighting force had declined, but was still 9,000. Some 130 officers would lead 5,000 troops into battle. Of these, only 200 would carry automatic weapons; 2,000 would have rifles; the remainder, shotguns, pistols, lances. The other 4,000 troops would stay in the canyons as a rearguard. General battle orders were to advance as far as possible. The initial action would consist of four operations. Major Josué and his regiment, to the north, would ambush the government army units on the road from Palenque south toward Ocosingo, and head for the Tabasco oil installations. So protected, Major Mario and his regiment would take Ocosingo. Major Alfredo would lead his regiment through Altamirano, to link up with Major Yolanda and her regiment, Marcos accompanying them, and take the government's army base at San Cristóbal. From the south, Major Moisés would lead his regiment through Las Margaritas to the next town west, Comitán, and proceed under Subcomandante Pedro northwest toward Tuxtla. Then, having sacked the base at San Cristóbal, Marcos would lead a heavily armed and ammunitioned force west, combine with Pedro's force, and attack and capture the state's military headquarters at Tuxtla, after which they would turn north toward Mexico City. Meanwhile, having prepared the northern and central fronts, the secretary general and commander in chief would be coordinating operations in Chihuahua, Michoacán, Puebla, and Veracruz.

Another movement was political. Among the 1,800 colonies and communities in the cañadas, of the 385 communities that had ejidos, 90 of them in the Union, the CCRI asked the ones that had shown most commitment, maybe 30, to take the final accord, to go to war. On this, the ultimate political question, for all their prior stirring and agitation and organization and commitment, the communities came apart. Their assemblies groaned for consensus for the armed way, but it would not come. Maybe 25 voted for it. The most Zapatista community in the canyons could finally do no better than a vote of 67 for war, 21 against. There was no custom to reconcile and unarmed struggles for justice. In the Zapatista canyons the majority ruled.

The last movement was of people. Where communities voted for war, the EZLN tolerated no dissent or pacifism: the minorities had to leave. Not only then did different organizations in the communities separate, but old friends too, fellow catechists, once trusted comrades, members of the same family, fathers and daughters, mothers and sons. The expelled were now displaced persons, migrating again, thousands of them. They could take with them only what they could ride, lead, or carry. They went wherever they thought they might find haven, to Ocosingo, Altamirano, or Las Margaritas, or to another community, Protestant, PRI-connected, or pro-Solidarity, where people also wanted justice, but not war. On December 28 the mobilization of the Zapatistas began, for them to be in place on time to start the war.

In military terms the EZLN offensive was a wonderful success on the first day, a pitiful calamity on the second. Major Josué's regiment, trying to operate across a zone where for the last 15 years the Jesuits had barred any organizing but their own, could not even slow down the government army units wheeling south from Palenque. Major Mario's regiment in Ocosingo on January 2 was therefore surprised, decimated, and driven back into the cañadas. Major Alfredo and his forces joined Major Yolanda and hers in San Cristóbal, and together on January 2 they attacked the base just outside the city, but after a suicidal siege of some 10 hours retreated into the mountains. Major Moisés in Las Margaritas that day lost Subcomandante Pedro, shot and killed in the street by a single unknown gunman, and took his regiment back into the canyons. Over the next 10 days, in firefights, rocket attacks, and strafing runs, the Mexican army and air force regained control of Los Altos and sealed off the canyons. By the ceasefire on January 12 the dead were 13 Mexican army soldiers, 38 state police, the more than 70 Zapatista soldiers, and from 19 to 275 or more civilians. Meanwhile, whatever the FLN commander in chief's efforts, nothing military worth noting happened anywhere else.

But politically the Zapatistas had thrown the country into a tremendous uproar. Their first "Declaration from the Lancandón Jungle" resounded nationwide like the trumpets of Jericho. (Reading No. 20.) And their "Revolutionary Legislation" broadcast a radical egalitarianism deeply dreadful to some, but deeply appealing to many others. (Reading No. 21.) A public hoping through NAFTA to establish itself in "the First World" suddenly had to recognize how deeply a part of "The Third World" it also remained. To their immense credit, within a few days, amid stupefying confusion and bewildering denunciations right, left, and center, most Mexicans outside Chiapas formed two clear, simple opinions: they were for the poor Indians in Chiapas, and they were against war. To his credit, once the Mexican army had resecured its base, Salinas defied the right, dismissed Interior Minister González, ordered the ceasefire, moved Congress to legislate an amnesty, and sent one of his political intimates to negotiate in the cathedral of San Cristóbal, Bishop Ruiz mediating, for "peace and reconciliation" with the Zapatistas. And to his credit, in the course of about two weeks, Marcos carried out a clandestine coup within the failed revolution. He cut loose from his commander in chief, coupled the CCRI and the EZLN's "general command" for a new source of authority, assumed control of Zapatista public communications—and shortly agreed to negotiations. The first EZLN communiqués were in revolutionary bureaucratese. Marcos's communiqués and interviews were playful, sarcastic, poetic, arbitrary, funny, narcissistic, poignant, snide, allusive, Foucaultian, magically realistic, the perfect lingo for contemporary discourse and negotiation, not with a government or rival movements, but through the modern media with a modern public, the message being not war, or peace, or reconciliation, but endless, seductive argumentation. "We did not go to war on January 1 to kill or to have them kill us," the subcomandante in his new mode told the media. "We went to make ourselves heard."

The revolt's repercussions around San Cristóbal continued for months. The EZLN's capture of the city terrified burghers and authorities not only there but in the Indian towns as well. After hiding, then praying harder than for rain in a three-year drought, the Indian bosses still could not tell what to do. They could not even stage a satisfying Mardi Gras on February 15. In this situation their underlings discovered some justice and fun. (Reading No. 22.)

The negotiations in San Cristóbal began on February 21, 1994. On March 1, thanks largely to the bishop, the EZLN delegates and Salinas's envoy reached "tentative agreement" on 34 points. Short of resigning, the government offered about all it could—reform of federal and state laws to meet the CCRI-EZLN's new, undeniable, and robustly attractive demand for "democracy," this before the national elections in August, and their claims, echoing from the Indian Congress of 1974, for Indian rights, land, jobs, housing, health services, education, food for the poor and (apparently on second thought) women's rights, too. (Reading No. 23.) The EZLN delegates reported the offer to the CCRI communities for ratification or rejection.

Three weeks later, while these communities were deliberating, the presidential candidate whom Salinas had prepared to succeed him, Luis Donaldo Colosio, was assassinated. This killed Salinas's project for reform of the regime from within. Since then Mexico has gone through more than four years of turmoil: through 1994 the resurgence of traditional bosses, Salinas's resort (for lack of a better alternative) to the very unprepared Ernesto Zedillo to run for the presidency, the rejection of the March 1 "tentative agreement" by the CCRI communities, Zedillo's election by only a plurality, the assassination of Salinas's most powerful surviving political ally, and President Zedillo's catastrophically mismanaged devaluation of the country's currency; in 1995–96 the worst economic collapse in 60 years, Zedillo's persecution of Salinas, the flagrant miscarriage of the investigations of the assassinations, the abolition of Solidarity, a crime epidemic spread by police, guerrilla action by new revolutionaries, deep indebtedness to the United States, the U.S.-ification of the war on drug trafficking; in 1997 more police-infested crime, more guerrilla activity, high military involvement in drug trafficking, the PRI's (first ever) loss of mid-term elections in the lower house, but the reinvigorated opposition parties' inability to unite on any major question of policy; in 1998 more crime, more U.S. financial and political intervention, more political disarray, and a banking bail-out scandal.

As part of Mexico, Chiapas has been through the same turmoil, compounded by its own continuing strife and subjection to heavy military security. Hardly had the official shooting stopped when 700 delegates from 280 ejidos, unions of ejidos, the Union of Unions-ARIC, and other groups formed the State Council of Indian and Peasant Organizations, the CEOIC, and declared their opposition to armed struggle, but approved the EZLN's demands. By the time negotiations had started, the number of persons displaced by the EZLN and the army had reached some 35,000, over 18,000 of them living in refugee camps. By mid-April 1994 villagers in at least 15 municipalities outside the cañadas had chased away PRI authorities and occupied town hall. And by then, coordinated by the CEOIC, landless peasants outside the canyons had seized nearly 350 fincas covering nearly 250,000 acres. Blaming the bishop, "Commandante Sam," ranchers threatened to use private force unless the state government removed squatters and restored legal order. The new acting governor, sent by Salinas to help negotiate peace, ruled that the state would buy the land seized before mid-April, for resale to the peasants holding it, and evict squatters after mid-April, but refused "under any circumstances" to use the army for evictions. More seizures followed, and police evictions, landlord violence, peasant resistance, and bloodshed. Villagers in Los Altos took to fighting among themselves. It did not help that in the national elections, in August, the deacon of deacons ran for the PRI to represent the Ocosingo district in Congress, and won. The Union of Unions split, between affiliates that backed him (and kept the organization's name) and those that backed the PRD (and became the Independent and Democratic Union of Unions). That state elections in August issued in a PRI gubernatorial victory over an intensely popular PRD candidate sharply aggravated the conflict. In many places PRDistas refused to accept defeat, occupied town halls, or seceded from their municipalities and organized their own local government. By December in the Indian country north of San Cristóbal there were at least 14 such "autonomous municipalities."

San Cristóbal's own bourgeoisie, in the full flush of its traditional ladino presumption and bigotry, contributed a particular malevolence to the strife. Aided by the local PRI, abetted by conservative nationalists throughout the country (including Mexico's Lyndon Larouchers!), the city's self-styled true "San Cristóbalites" publicly and repeatedly vilified the bishop. He was "the Anti-Christ of San Cristóbal, the enemy of the people, Satan's son, the devil's bishop, a communist, the reason for the Zapatistas." Among the graffiti on a downtown wall was "Vote for Peace—Kill Samuel." The fieriest bourgeois stormed the cathedral, shut down the city's churches, called death down on "foreign reporters, hippies, and Indians." A diplomatic and smiling tour guide interpreted their aim to American reporters: "The bishop has created this controversy. There is no injustice here . . . We have lived peacefully with the Indians for over 500 years [sic] and never had a problem. The bishop is all mixed up in politics, and we want our religion to be a comfort, the way it used to be before he came." Some excellent Catholics, he explained, were so discomfited that they would no longer set foot in the cathedral. "It was desecrated by the presence of those filthy Zapatista Indians who lived there like animals during the bishop's so-called dialogues for peace. The cathedral must now be reconsecrated."

In December, in the furor over the new PRI governor taking office, EZLN units without firing a shot snuck through the army's lines to appear in numerous highland towns and villages. The following February, Zedillo sent the army down into the canyons to tighten its lines and try to catch the EZLN's "general command." There was only one casualty (an army officer killed), and when Zedillo ordered a halt the army had effectively surrounded the EZLN and reduced it to the confines of a reservation. But there were another 20,000 displaced persons. If they took refuge where the army ran its new patrols, or fled with the EZLN to its last retreats, they found at least the relief of a truce, a kind of peace. Elsewhere they would have found much worse. Upcountry and across the state rural districts, towns, and cities were suffering all kinds of violence. By April 1995 landless peasants outside the canyons had occupied altogether more than 1,000 farms and ranches, over 370,000 acres. By then in postrevolt agrarian, political, and religious disputes some 700 people had been killed. Between the state police and ranchers' "white guards," especially in the northern municipalities, scarcely a week passed without someone shot for being Indian, poor, uppity, or "communist," maybe as "communist" as the bishop.

After the communities in rebellion rejected the government's first offer, the negotiations restarted and stopped several times, for political reasons on one side or the other. Every time they stopped Bishop Ruiz did his damnedest to restart them. In December 1994, when the antagonism between the new government and the EZLN seemed about to explode in new military action, he went on a fast, for 10 days, until both sides recognized his National Mediation Commission, CONAI, and agreed to resume talks. After Zedillo's military attempt and failure to capture the EZLN leadership in February, the bishop and CONAI were crucial in drawing the government and the CCRI-EZLN back into "dialogue." In March Congress created its own Commission of Concord and Pacification, COCOPA, but in every phase the bishop served as the principal mediator. The government, Solidarity (which still existed then), and other organizations begrudged him the part, well aware that he had his own organization to defend, and in loyalty therefore had to define negotiations to favor his own. But they could not reject him. He was the only authority on the outside whom the communities on the inside trusted. Therefore he did not fade away when in August 1995 the papal nuncio got the pope to assign a reputedly conservative bishop coadjutor to the diocese, in effect to put it in receivership. The bishop's authority in the negotiations was not ecclesiastic, but moral, inevitably partial, but nevertheless moral. His coadjutor soon reinforced it.

Given the radically different positions of the government and the CCRI-EZLN, Ruiz was not able to mediate much. In Mexico as it really was the government could not end poverty or injustice or even the PRI's arrogance and corruption. It could at best announce new policies, pass new laws, establish new programs, fund new projects in Social Development (where the former director of Solidarity was the new minister), and insist in return that for the dignity of the nation the EZLN lay down its arms and take off its mask in trust that nonviolent struggle for reforms would succeed. In the cañadas as they really were, the CCRI communities could not believe in the government; they could only insist that the poor of the nation (or only of Chiapas?) have lives worth living before the EZLN disarmed and showed its face. But precisely therefore the bishop was of vital importance to both sides. By using his moral authority to make the antagonists keep talking, particularly during Zedillo's first year in office, he more than anyone else saved the government from a definitive and catastrophic recourse to arms, and gave the EZLN time to develop the grounds and form for an eventual unarmed struggle.

On different assumptions Marcos evidently began looking for the right time to demilitarize as soon as the government offered to talk. The armed way having failed, if in time elections failed and popular protests brought the regime down, the EZLN could then disarm and triumphantly enter the struggle to reform the country. Already in mid-February 1994, just before the negotiations began, Marcos told the press, "We don't trust anybody but the rifle we carry. But we think if there is another way, it's not political parties; it's civil society." It soon came clear, however, as clear as anything could in Mexico that spring, that outside Chiapas "civil society" would not take the initiative, but only sympathize and worry. In June 1994, in vulnerable isolation after the CCRI communities rejected the "tentative agreement," the CCRI-EZLN high command therefore took the lead. Its "Second Declaration from the Lacandón Jungle" announced in effect a civil strategy for the formation of a nonpartisan popular front against the regime. The tactics were ingenious: under the amnesty, from websites on the Internet, globally, virtually, bring the outside inside, convoke a national concentration of "civil society" in the jungle. (Reading No. 24.) And in August, two weeks before the national elections, near one of the CCRI canyon communities, the Zapatistas staged an internationally publicized rally of some 6,000 representatives of Mexico's old and new leftish social and civic movements, who enthusiastically cheered their hosts and duly founded the National Democratic Convention (CND) to struggle in "civil society" for "democracy and social justice." Concretely, in the hope that the regime would fall apart over the elections, the CND was to create "a provisional or transitional government" that would call a constitutional convention to rewrite the country's basic rules on behalf of the poor. But the regime did not collapse; Zedillo was respectably elected (if only by a plurality).

On January 1, 1995, as the economy crashed deeper and deeper, the CCRI-EZLN high command therefore tried again. In a "Third Declaration from the Lacandón Jungle" it convoked a "national opposition front" to form a Movement for National Liberation (MLN), headed by Cárdenas. (Reading No. 25.) In February, on the anniversary of the Revolutionary Constitution of 1917, in the provincial city where it had been written, the CND and some 4,000 prospective MLNistas convened, and promptly plunged into chaotic and acrimonious accusations among themselves. The CND barely survived. An MLN appeared, but only on paper (and without Cárdenas).

Oddly, Zedillo's military operations a few days later, by not only confining the EZLN to a reservation but also provoking tremendous public protest, may have encouraged Marcos to try yet again to negotiate a Zapatista demilitarization. "Hear civil society's drums," he wrote a comrade, ". . . they say peace, peace, peace." In March the chastened government invited the EZLN to take part in future talks to democratize elections. Marcos refused; the CCRI, he said, would not authorize discussion of democratization with the government or political parties, only with "civil society." But the CCRI-EZLN high command did agree to principles and procedural rules for resolving the issues the government accepted (actually since March 1994) as the reasons for the revolt—"Indian rights, democracy and justice, decent living standards and economic development, women's rights."

As if to justify its new course to its constituents in the canyons, the CCRI-EZLN high command in August 1995 staged a "grand national poll," an electronic referendum on the EZLN's basic demands and way of struggle. Mexico's most respected association of electoral watchdogs, the Alianza Cívica, conducted it, and over a million Mexicans voted (maybe 5 percent of the usual turnout in presidential elections). The results were conclusive: 97.7 percent for the demands, 92.9 percent for the formation of "a broad opposition front," 90 percent to guarantee public offices for women, 57 percent that the EZLN should change from an army into "an independent and new political force." In other words, a majority of the most pro-Zapatista Mexicans in "civil society" wanted the EZLN to drop the disguise, stow its arms, come out from inside, and join the public struggle for reform.

The negotiations suddenly went much better. Despite predictable insults between the two sides, the first substantive talks began in October, on Indian rights, in the little town of San Andrés Larráinzar, north of San Cristóbal. The CCRI-EZLN delegates came with many advisers, including learned scholars, influential intellectuals, experienced and admired Catholic social workers. "We know this is going to be a mountain of words," said Marcos. "We know the government wants to gain time until public attention wears away. But we want to see if we can find a new way to be against the government besides taking up rifles."

One negative condition the Zapatistas put for finding the "new way" was to stay out of official politics. In mid-October Chiapas held its regular state legislative and municipal elections. The PRD reasonably expected to win a strong second place in the legislature and many municipalities, especially in the north. The CCRI-EZLN high command, however, ordered abstention. With a "sad heart," as one said, many Indian PRDistas did not vote. Of 24 seats in the legislature, the PRI won 21, the PRD one. Of the 109 municipalities where all the polls opened (111 minus Ocosingo and Las Margaritas), the PRI won 80, the PRD 18, none in the north. Marcos declared the returns proof that the EZLN was the state's "principal political power." In direct action in December, to check the PRI municipal presidents-elect in the north, PRDistas and pro-Zapatistas occupied town halls or seceded and set up their "autonomous" municipal governments.

Meanwhile, using the August referendum as a mandate, the CCRI-EZLN worked up a positive definition of the "new way" (or an old anarchist way). It turned out to be much like what American social scientists have called "the new institutionalism." On January 1, 1996, in the "Fourth Declaration from the Lacandón Jungle," the Zapatistas high command called for the formation of a new Zapatista Front of National Liberation, the FZLN, a "civil and non-violent organization, independent and democratic, Mexican and national," to struggle for "democracy, liberty, and justice in Mexico." The new front would certainly be out of the ordinary in Mexico, "a political force whose members would not hold or aspire to take power, a force that would not be a political party." (Reading No. 26). This evoked interesting comments on the left, but no surge of offers to form the organization or even join it.

In San Andrés in February 1996 government and the CCRI-EZLN delegates (still in arms, still masked) signed historic accords on Indian rights. (Reading No 27). This agreement, supposed to issue soon in federal legislation, freed both sides to pursue their major, national, political objectives. President Zedillo and his intimates, under mounting pressure for his resignation, hoped in the coming months to negotiate between the PRI and the opposition parties a richly publicized "Democratic Reform of the State" for Congress to pass first thing in the fall, restoring the government's authority and guaranteeing respectable mid-term elections in 1997. The Zapatista high command hoped to use negotiation of the next item on the San Andrés agenda, "Democracy and Justice," to upstage all the political parties and get "civil society" started on an FZLN. Meanwhile, to hold public attention (and hedge against another military surprise), it would draw foreign as well as national celebrities to another grand rally in the canyons.

Zedillo, however, could not muster PRI interest in legislation on Indian rights. Worse, he could not contain the contention inside the PRI over "democratic reform," much less move the party's bosses to accept opposition demands for "free and fair elections," in which the public had lately taken a passionate interest. He could not even keep the talks in San Andrés going, or stop them. Obvious provocations from within the government allowed the CCRI-EZLN again and again to denounce the government's bad faith, suspend the talks, then through CONAI and COCOPA resume them. Neither, however, could the Zapatista high command distract the public from its new hope for "free elections," to support instead "a political force . . . that would not be a political party." Despite all the Zapatista appeals and warnings, "civil society" still would not deliver an FZLN. The sudden appearance of the new revolutionary force in the south shook both the government and the CCRI-EZLN, both of which, in mutual ignorance, had to recalculate how to deal with each other and accomplish their major projects.

Most bedeviling for the government, briefly convenient but in the long run disastrous for the CCRI-EZLN, was the intensified conflict in Los Altos's northern municipalities, or townships. The violence no longer came only from landlords' "white guards" gunning down Indians who looked at their employers' land or them the wrong way. It now came also from within Indian villages and even hamlets, where on a municipal president's orders, or from conviction or fear, or to curry favor, or for land or money, old and new PRIista Indians (some once in Solidarity) were calling their Indian neighbors of other political persuasions (or none) "Zapatistas" and trying to drive them out of the community, if necessary by using machetes and guns. By mid-1996 this feuding was rampant in the northern mountains and valleys. Those in the government who wanted to stop it had no agency for local action except the state and local PRI, the very gang often instigating the expulsions and steadfast in protecting the perpetrators, or the army, under no orders to shelter suspected Zapatistas. The public shame that the violence brought on the government suited the CCRI-EZLN fine for purposes of building public support for its cause. On the other hand, the state PRI's resurgence in the north and the army's reinforcement throughout Los Altos—Bishop Ruiz and CONAI complained continually about the "low-intensity war" the army was waging in the region—were politically fateful Zapatista defeats. The EZLN may have been, as the bishop said then, Mexico's only remaining "convocative power," the only force able to bring out a massive and willing crowd, but its power was no longer political, only moral, a power that would move only the sympathetic.

This was how the Zapatistas' second grand rally succeeded. "The International Encounter for Humanity and against Neo-Liberalism" was a glorious international success in public relations. Régis Debray, Oliver Stone (both of whom, separately, had already gone to the reservation to see Marcos), and many other foreign invitees did not attend. But enough did to create the necessary image. Staged in late July-early August deep in the canyons, the encounter drew to a community really called La Realidad some 3,500 persons, including among other foreign opinion–leaders the French Danielle Mitterand and Alain Touraine, the American Saul Landau, the Russian Pavel Lounguine, and the Uruguayan Eduardo Galeano. The image they took there and sincerely conveyed abroad was of a moral force. Afterward Marcos gave a long, reflective, as usual often playful, but unusually confessional interview, significantly to a most serious French scholar of Latin American violence and popular movements. There the subcomandante again expressed his hopes for "civil society" to create an FZLN, so that Mexico could benefit from "something truly new." (Reading No. 28.)

The shock in late August of coordinated revolutionary guerrilla attacks leaving 15 dead and more than 20 wounded in southern and central Mexico— and guerrilla roadblocks on Chiapas highways—threw the CCRI-EZLN into red alert in all directions. The high command's public reaction to the revolutionaries was hostile, to the government mixed, subtle, and in need of serious interpretation. On August 29 Marcos announced its conditions for a resumption of the talks in San Andrés: absolute fulfillment of the accords on Indian rights, released of jailed Zapatistas, a higher level of government involvement in the talks, a commitment to concrete agreements on "democracy and justice," "dentente and reconciliation" in Chiapas's Indian townships, and an official committee to supervise and verify compliance with subsequent accords.

It was probably the same revolutionary attacks that reminded President Zedillo of the advantages of a law on Indian rights. On September 1, in Mexico's equivalent of the State of the Union message, he indicated his new interest in the question. This reopened the CCRI-EZLN high command's opportunity at least in law to realize its distinctive "Indian" claim and to settle its grievous "Indian debt," which in the circumstances would suffice to justify accepting the parties' electoral reform for "democracy," federal funds for "economic development" as a start on "decent living standards," and making an FZLN to focus the 1997 elections on "justice" and "human rights." The high command cautiously took time to set the proper stage for the deal, to avoid later accusations from outside or inside that it had been coopted. Not until the dying Indian Comandante Ramona, the first EZLN commander to arrive publicly as such in Mexico City, unarmed but still masked, spoke to the multitudes convoked in the national capital's main square on anti-Columbus Day, October 12, did the high command enter secret negotiations with the Interior Ministry and COCOPA. While the government and the CCRI-EZLN delegates at San Andrés in November debated "Democracy and Justice," the government delegates offering representative democracy and economic development, the Zapatista delegates demanding nationwide "direct democracy, substantive democracy, social democracy, civic participation, people's power," the secret negotiations proceeded in Mexico City and San Cristóbal to turn the first San Andrés accords into a draft of a bill for a law on Indian rights. The final draft, carefully corrected by lawyers and approved by the Interior Ministry and Marcos, went to Zedillo for his approval in early December. The sub-comandante and his commanders joked about plastic surgery and retirement.

But the president did not approve. In mid-November the PRI in Congress had defiantly wrecked his last, best try for an electoral reform acceptable to the opposition. Refiguring his own political prospects, Zedillo had already decided by early December to ride with the PRI's bosses into the mid-term elections. It made no sense then for him to propose a bill on Indian rights that Marcos had approved and Congress anyway would not pass. He therefore refused to endorse the draft without gutting the original accords, which he knew the CCRI-EZLN would not accept. As he went to the right, so the last chance for an honorable compromise with the Zapatistas disappeared. The secret negotiations and their failure quickly came out in the media, an embarrassing, depressing episode that the government represented as its constitutional stand for "national unity."

The public took only momentary notice. Nothing could distract it from its increasingly excited speculation over the elections scheduled for July 6, 1997. When the day came and as predicted but nevertheless astoundingly the PRI lost its majority in Congress's Chamber of Deputies and Cárdenas won the mayorship of the Federal District, the public in no less excitement plunged into anticipation of what the new Congress and Cárdenas would do when they took office. In Chiapas, aggravated by the elections, the feuds in the northern villages and hamlets had blown into civil war. PRIista "paramilitaries," with new state and municipal police support, were fighting in bands to impose the PRI's local order, especially where their recalcitrant neighbors had seceded. Their ravaged neighbors, led by local PRDista and pro- (or crypto-) Zapatistas were fighting to defend themselves and refugees in their "autonomous municipalities." But the public's new fixation on national party politics drove even the CCRI-EZLN high command, for all its contempt of parties and elections (lately re-expressed in orders to boycott the polls on July 6), to recognize their new significance and so slight Chiapas's new misery. In August Marcos again denounced PRDistas who would do the government's work against the EZLN, but also declared "civil society" in its electoral "rebellion" had opened a new "space" in which to struggle for "democracy, liberty, and justice," and announced a Zapatista "March to Mexico City" in September (when the new Congress convened) to "witness" the foundation of an FZLN. The march as it happened (of unarmed but in public still masked Zapatistas) was actually a motorized caravan, which the army perfectly protected along its route from San Cristóbal to the national capital's main square. At last, in Mexico City on September 15, the FZLN made its first formal appearance. (Reading No. 29.) Also under army protection the caravan made its way quite safely back to the reservation.

The new Congress did nothing special for Chiapas but approve the federal budget's substantial increase in funds for Social Development there. Against the PRI and the third largest party in the chamber, the Partido de Acción Nacional, the PRD could not even get a vote on the COCOPA-brokered bill for Indian rights. Cárdenas had all he could do in Mexico City while he prepared for another presidential run in 2000; not now but maybe in 2001 he could make an honorable peace with the Zapatistas. The FZLN survived, with occasional positive influence in other states, but none of any kind in Tuxtla Gutiérrez, Los Altos, or the Selva.

Through the fall CONAI and COCOPA continued their efforts to restart talks between the government and the CCRI-EZLN. The government insisted it was ready, although since the elections it evidently preferred to forgo negotiations, strengthen Social Development in the state, and let the FZLN in public and the Zapatistas on the reservation fade into obscurity. The CCRI-EZLN high command insisted it too was ready, as soon as it saw the law for Indian rights, although since the "March to Mexico City" it evidently preferred to wait until Cárdenas became president, when it could deal with a more popular government, get a better compromise, and go "civil" truer to its word and in virtual triumph. But by then the deadlock in negotiations was a concern of secondary importance. The primary source of tension and grief in Chiapas then was the civil war in the northern townships, which neither the government nor the CCRI-EZLN could control and neither CONAI nor COCOPA had any claims or authority to mediate.

Indians being human, there had always been conflict in the northern villages, Chol, Tzotzil, or Tzeltal. Between villages, inside them between neighborhoods, in neighborhoods and hamlets between families, and within families, material or immaterial differences had naturally made for jealousies, trouble, disputes, fights, for which old words existed in all the Indian languages. Normally the conflict did not come too much. Normally, from before the Spanish conquest, in another form under Spanish rule, in yet other forms after Independence, through the nineteenth century into the 1930s, village elders had maintained an impressive local consensus, and the authority to enforce it on the fractious. Under the federal Constitution of 1857 and the Revolutionary (also federal) Constitution of 1917, every state subdivided for local government into municipalities (something like counties in the United States), where municipally elected presidents and councils were (in the first instance) to settle the conflicts in their townships, in the town where the municipal seat was and in the surrounding jurisdiction (e.g., in the municipality's villages and hamlets). But in Los Altos' Indian towns, villages, and hamlets (as in Indian country in other states), generation after generation, it had been the local elders who actually talked local disputes into accords (for which there were also old Indian words), and calmed local fights into peace (in other old Indian words), not every time, but usually, customarily.

The old words for accord and peace had begun to lose their power in the 1930s because the government started its great reforms in the region then. Among them after agrarian reform one of the most important was the imposition of a new rank of municipal authority. State-appointed, young, bilingual Indians, some from the new union of Indian workers, were to organize the Indian villages for the government to support the official struggle for social justice. In practice, on orders or on their own, by fair means or foul, these officers through the 1940s took as much charge as they could of local conflicts, which they often aggravated. From this cohort came INI's collaborators in the 1950s, who in collusion with the region's ladinos built the PRI's first highland Indian bases, provoked the first modern highland emigrations, and raised the first generation of INI-educated Indian school teachers, who in their turn forged the PRI's first willfully "traditional" Indian bossdoms in the 1960s and '70s, forcing many more conflicts in the villages than they resolved.

There were so many conflicts in the northern villages and hamlets then, not only because the new Indian bosses pushed down harder and more selfishly, but also because more of their Indian underlings started pushing up, consciously and conscientiously. It took new Spanish words to tell what the bosses, their followers, and the insubordinates wanted, none of the Indian languages having words for "command" or "favor" or "rights." The first clear sign of the new times had appeared in preparation for the Indian Congress in San Cristóbal in 1974, when the organizers among the Chol, Tzotzil, and Tzeltal found some northern villages and hamlets dangerously hostile, others impatiently welcoming. The Chamulas for the congress showed up only toward the end, to call (in vain) for the congress to overthrow their "traditional" municipal president.

Such conflicts multiplied then as villagers joined contending organizations and formed factions, different organizations and different factions every few years, for the next 20 years. In 1975, to rally its contingents against the Indian Congress's, the government had the CNC organize an official Indian Congress in Chiapas, with "Supreme Indian Councils" for each Indian zone. In 1976, as a hopeful result of the first Indian Congress, some northern villagers founded the Unión de Ejidos del Norte de Chiapas (like the Qu'iptik union in the cañadas). Under official and private (landlord) repression they could not resolve their own differences, and in 1977 the original Indian Congress and the northern union failed. That year some of the dead union's ejidos formed a new union, the CIOAC arrived, the new union and the CIOAC worked together, the army and state police crushed their movement in three townships, some landless villagers accepted a CIOAC-negotiated grant elsewhere, others went back to the landlords for protection and jobs, the union broke with CIOAC and split in two, and CIOAC left. In 1978 the LP arrived, one remnant of the union worked with it, could not resolve its internal differences over the new line, split in two, and the LP left. In 1979 CIOAC returned and started organizing a farm workers' union. In 1980 the Mexican Socialist Workers Party arrived, organized peons to occupy fincas, ran into a massacre (at least 12 killed, 40 wounded), and left. That year other northern villages joined the new Union of Unions. And so the organizing, splitting, reorganizing, and resplitting continued through the decade into the 1990s, complicated after 1988 by national political struggles (for Salinas, for the PRI's traditional bosses, for Cárdenas), Solidarity (federal projects, the state's projects), religion (the diocese, "traditionalists," Protestants), and anything else over which poor, exploited, oppressed, continually disappointed, deeply mistrustful country neighbors could divide and factionalize.

The revolt on January 1, 1994, pulled some highland villagers together across several municipalities. Probably hundreds of Chols, Tzotzils, and Tzeltals in the north, already united in EZLN underground there, joined the rebels from the canyons on New Year's Day. Many more united afterward in sympathy with the Zapatistas or their demands. Many of them and others united politically to vote for Cárdenas that summer; 10 of the northern townships went for the PRD. But many others pulled together only within their villages. As poor as their Zapatista or Cárdenista relatives and neighbors, they seized on the state and municipal PRI's protection of them and united to fight, superficially for the PRI, basically for whatever favors and benefits the government had given them, or might one day give them, i.e., for themselves. Unlike Zapatistas or Cardenistas, therefore, they operated only locally, each band in defense of its local interests or prospects. The "paramilitaries" that formed in 1995–96 did not carry out a broad, state PRI-coordinated campaign against the movement for "autonomous municipalities," but under municipal police protection only fought feuds over particular local secessions. The civil war that racked the northern townships in 1997, for which there was only a Spanish word, *guerra*, was consequently not a coherent, definite contention, but an embroilment of many little continual battles—the "Peace and Justice" band fighting its insubordinate neighbors in one locality, the "San Bartolomé de Los Llanos Alliance" fighting likewise in another, the "Chinchulines" (originally the "Luis Donaldo Colosio Civic Front") in yet another, the "Anti-Zapatista Revolutionary Insurgent Movement," the "Throatcutters," the "Armed Forces of the People," and the "Thomas Munzer" band each fighting in its locality, and others in theirs, among them the "Red Mask" in Chenalhó township. The Interior Ministry, the army, and the state police may have been trying to concentrate "paramilitary" operations to hold strategic passages between the northern highlands and the canyons. But in the villages, neighborhoods, and hamlets where the battles happened, the "paramilitaries" were struggling for local control. This may be why they have fought so brazenly and so mercilessly. It took absolute disregard of high politics or broad strategy for the Chols of "Peace and Justice" in November 1997 to ambush Bishop Ruiz's federally protected motorcade on the road into its stamping grounds. It took absolute disregard of any human concerns but their own for the Tzotzils of the "Red Mask" in December 1997 to massacre 45 unarmed men, women, and children at prayer in the Chenalhó hamlet of Acteal. (Reading No. 30.)

The slaughter at Acteal was so awful that for a while many Mexicans believed some good must come of it, as if by divine justice, some compromise, some reconciliation, some peace. It did result in some mundane legal and political justice—the arrest of scores of Chiapas state police, Chenalhó municipal officials, and local "paramilitaries," the dismissal of the Interior minister, the resignations of Chiapas's interim governor and his advisers, et al. It also obliged Zedillo to reassert his determination to win legislation for Indian rights, even to send a bill to Congress on the question. It brought yet more money for Social Development in Chiapas. And it moved the government to repeated denials that the army would break the official ceasefire in the state, and repeated calls for the CCRI-EZLN to return to San Andrés for negotiations (since August 29, 1996, suspended).

But as usual the innocents died in vain. Since the massacre, regardless of the objections of major international human rights organizations, the PRD's protests (and charges of U.S. military advisers in Chiapas), CONAI's denunciations, and COCOPA's complaints, the government has practically (nothing virtual about its military force) run the state as if it were under siege. Some 40,000 troops, mostly in the highlands and the cañadas, have been doing "social work," but also, with special effort and some 5,000 federal and state police for auxiliaries, flying surveillance, patrolling roads, searching villages, hamlets, and refugee camps, closing churches and chapels, arresting priests, nuns, and PRD, CIOAC, and OCEZ members, dismantling "autonomous municipalities," and detaining for interrogation anyone whose papers (they say) are out of order, all in the name of "the law," in particular the federal law on firearms and explosives. They have not had much success where "paramilitaries" operate. Despite 3,000 soldiers in Chenalhó, so many fellows of the "Red Mask" remain armed and on the loose that eight months after the massacre the Acteal refugees are still afraid to go back. Elsewhere in the highlands armed and unarmed bands, masked or not, have refused to allow Bishop Ruiz and his coadjutor into their villages. On June 7, citing "a constant and growing government aggression" against the diocese, his mediating commission, and himself, "recently executed in signals and words by the president himself," the bishop declared that "clearly one stage of the peace process has ended," and resigned from CONAI, which promptly dissolved. Three days later the government's forces brought "the law" with new zeal to a northern "autonomous municipality" where under the cease-fire EZLN militia had settled. In combined operations, 1,800 soldiers and police charged into one of its hamlets, 1,300 into another, giving such a show of attack in both places that some Zapatistas fired on them, and the soldiers and police unloaded in return, rifles and mortars, helicopters strafing—the first break in the four-year-old ceasefire. Two policemen and eight presumed Zapatistas died. (It deserves note too that Zedillo's bill for Indian rights had already died in Congress.)

Meanwhile the government has sought to reduce international agitation over the new war. To curtail foreign access to its critics in the state (and to harass the San Cristóbal diocese), it has in the last six months there deported more than 76 foreign rights observers, social workers, and diocesan friends, associates, and clergy, including Chenalhó's parish priest, since 1965 serving the township's faithful, but French, and suspected of liberationism. It has lately waxed bolder. When UN Secretary-General Kofi Annan indicated in early July that he might discuss Chiapas with President Zedillo on his visit to Mexico later in the month, the government questioned the notion. The Interior minister declared, "We do not consider it appropriate to internationalize the conflict." Chiapas's substitute interim governor crudely announced he would welcome Annan to his state "as a tourist."

Suddenly in mid-July, after more than four months of most uncharacteristic silence, Marcos reclaimed national attention. In one nine-word communiqué he taunted the army with Speedy González's battle cry against Tom the Cat. In another, 11 words in Nahuatl, he reassured the world that "Zapata lives!" And in a third, as prolix and poetic, analytical and dreamy, scoffing and rousing as ever, quoting Machado, Shakespeare, and Scorza, he lambasted Zedillo (who had "knocked confidence in his [own] government to smithereens"), suggested a new Zapatista respect for COCOPA, and cutely hinted at a Fifth Declaration from the Selva. (Reading No. 31.) On July 21, the day Annan arrived in Mexico, the Fifth Declaration from the Lacandón Jungle hit the press. Beneath some poetry and an explanation of Zapatista "silence, dignity, and resistance," it made an offer to resume negotiations if "mediation, confidence, and credibility [the government's] were restored." This, it specified, would require above all "recognition of the rights of Indian peoples." The EZLN would consequently conduct a "national poll" with the support of "national civil society" in every municipality in the country on the question of "COCOPA's bill" for Indian rights (actually the agreement the CCRI-EZLN delegates and the Interior Ministry had negotiated in November 1996 and Zedillo had then rejected); and if the country endorsed the bill, Congress should pass it. (Reading No. 32.) Evidently, like the government, the CCRI-EZLN high command rejected "internationalization of the conflict." Its plan for a poll and calls for new civic action and legislation took the air out of petitions by scores of Mexican human rights groups for Annan to involve the United Nations in Chiapas.

The declaration raised dutiful hopes among Zapatista sympathizers. But it has not yet moved many others. Zedillo in response went to Ocosingo and urged "direct dialogue" between the government and the EZLN, in other words announcing that the government would continue as before in its application of "the law." The PRD waits, not for the "national poll," but for the CCRI-EZLN's decision on Chiapas's next state legislative and municipal elections, scheduled for October 4, to hear whether (as in 1995) the high command orders abstention, or directs or allows its loyalists to cast their vote (which the PRD would surely win). For the government, the opposition parties, and the CCRI-EZLN, it makes most sense now not to negotiate, to concentrate instead as the public concentrates on the national elections in 2000. By then the government may have imposed "the law" on Chiapas, and Zedillo can leave office with that to his credit (as he would see it). But if the government's imposition on the state aggravates the war among the poor there, the opposition parties will have a bloody case against the PRI, particularly in the presidential election. And if Cárdenas wins the presidency, the EZLN may find as it has hoped for at least a year to find nationwide the "space" to unmask, disarm, and join (or drive) civil campaigns for "democracy, liberty, and justice."

The prospect over the next two years in Chiapas is therefore grim—continued, dangerous, confounding struggles among the poor themselves to develop an effective strategy for their common, crucial struggle, no longer to reach the Promised Land (even without milk and honey), but just to stay in the Wilderness, out of Egypt.

Most significant and problematic is the Mexican public's new faith in national electoral democracy. In the short run it is heavy political insurance, undermining traditional bosses, benefiting reformers still in the system, and fortifying opposition parties right and left. It will be great asset in the presidential election in 2000, the country's next predictable crisis. But it will not cover the public's frustration if electoral democracy yields a new government so representative and as a result so divided—a presidential vote of 40/30/30?, or Cárdenas as president and the PRI again in control of Congress?—that it cannot do anything for the selfish, the generous, or the destitute. The public would then have to become, as for all their differences Salinas, Ruiz, and Marcos have urged, a strong "civil society," to indicate the direction parties and the government should go, to liberate the poor (at least a little) or not. If it does not, it will have to learn to live with its frustrations, which usually leads to denying that politics even matters (a very old Mexican tradition, Catholic and anarchist). This is now how most easily the rich gain and the poor lose. Unless, therefore, national elections deliver a government able and willing to liberate the poor (at least a little) from violence, indignity, and poverty, or "civil society" moves the government firmly in that direction, the poor in Chiapas will have to struggle more grievously than ever to stay out of Egypt.

As hard as concerned Americans have had to strain to understand the Zapatista revolt and its confusing and sorrowful aftermath, we will have to work harder to understand Mexican issues in the future. Our problem is not merely the media, or our notorious inability to learn another language. It is our entire evasive and mendacious culture, which (to the enormous profit of the megacompanies that feed it) makes our selfish decadence entertaining to us, sells us headsets that deafen us to crying injustices in our own country, and changes every real, complicated, painful struggle into a brief sensation of stars, or meteors, gloriously noble or wicked, always somehow erotically intriguing today, dead boring tomorrow. If in this culture we have to hide or fight to comprehend reality right here, we have to leave all that is familiar and comfortable to comprehend reality in Mexico.

John Womack, Jr.
Cambridge, Mass.
August 22, 1998

PART II

Readings

CHAPTER ONE

Las Casas and the Encomenderos of San Cristóbal: Chiapas, 1545

Bishop Bartolomé de Las Casas deserves an extraordinarily respectful introduction. Born in Seville in 1474, the son of a modest merchant of "good old stock," he went out to the new Spanish colony of Santo Domingo in 1502, received like most other Spanish settlers there an *encomienda*, (a royal "trust" or grant of Indians to work for him) and as an *encomendero*, a grant-holder, soon prospered. A catechist, too, he attained the priesthood in 1512 ("the first to sing a new Mass in all these Indies"), served as a military chaplain in the conquest of Cuba, witnessed at least one massacre, and took a "good, big" encomienda of Indians on Cuba's most promising gold mines.

Then his life changed. He began reading *Ecclesiastes*, pondering its "terrible texts." In 1514 he gave his encomienda back to royal authorities and began preaching against the institution, that it was a mortal sin and that by God all encomenderos owed their Indians freedom and restitution. "Bold to the point of temerity, sharp-witted and eloquent, . . . a bundle of energy, of penetrating mind, and phenomenal physical endurance," he sailed for Spain to preach to the king. Condemning encomendero exploitation of the Indians as "the destruction of the Indies," he won royal appointment as "Protector of the Indians" and approval of his plan for the Indians' peaceful conversion and resettlement in beneficently managed villages. Because encomenderos resisted and royal officials did not stop them, the plan failed. He sailed back to Spain, won royal approval for another plan to relieve the Indians, which failed too, then moved the king to approve yet another plan, which also failed, disastrously.

Taking his failures as "divine judgment," Las Casas in 1522 in Santo Domingo entered the Order of Preachers, the Dominicans. For nearly 10 years then, "to all appearances," as he later wrote of himself, "the cleric, now friar, . . . slept." Actually he was studying, steeping himself in civil law, canon law, and theology, thinking, and beginning to write his great *Historia general de las Indias*, never relenting. Named prior of a new convent on the island's rough north coast, he quietly but sternly refused confession to encomenderos until they freed their Indians and made restitution to them.

In 1534, at 60, he returned to public battle. He sailed for Peru, to preach as Protector of the Indians there, got to Panama, in a deadly Pacific calm had to land back in Nicaragua, where he condemned a local Spanish march of conquest, and headed north to take charge of the main Dominican convent in Guatemala. There, seizing the opportunity of a new papal bull that Indians were naturally rational and free human beings, who could understand the Gospel, he mounted a campaign against coercive employment or conversion of them, and in 1537–38 organized a peaceful missionary expedition into Guatemala's last unconquered Indian country, "the Land of War," north toward Chiapas. Recalled by Guatemala's bishop to prepare a trip to Spain to raise more recruits and royal support for the mission, he went first to Mexico City, for his first time, and there, delayed for a meeting on missionary questions, fought two battles, one in the first book he finished, *The Only Method of Attracting All People to the True Faith*, which was by peaceful conversion, the other in denouncing the Franciscan practice of baptizing uncatechized adult Indians *en masse*. Back in Spain in 1540–41, he raised the necessary recruits and support, and continued his battle against wholesale baptisms. And he entered the biggest public battle of his life and the most significant in the history of the Spanish empire.

It happened that Emperor Charles V, once Erasmus's tutee, was for many reasons then reviewing imperial policy on encomiendas and Indians. In 1542 Las Casas won a hearing at court, read there his hair-raising *Very Brief Account of the Destruction of the Indies*, advised the emperor to revoke all encomiendas, abolish Indian slavery, dismiss venal officials (several of whom he named), and so on. After testimony from other, moderate souls, the emperor in his wisdom signed the so-called New Laws on November 20, 1542. These forbade future enslavement of Indians, ordered all officials to give up their encomiendas, prohibited the grant to officials or private subjects of any new encomiendas, and barred the transfer of current grants, including by inheritance. The emperor also nominated Las Casas to the bishopric of remote and barely conquered Chiapas. As soon as the New Laws were known in the New World, encomenderos fiercely resisted them, some in outright rebellion; and they all blamed Las Casas for them.

In this atmosphere, after a harrowing trip back to Mexico, Las Casas arrived in Chiapas in March 1545. For months he fought continual battles for the New Laws and the Indians there, with encomenderos, clerics, and Guatemalan authorities. In 1546 he learned that the emperor had withdrawn the ban on inheriting encomiendas, and left Chiapas for Mexico City and Spain to reenter the battles at court.

In 1550 in Spain he resigned his bishopric and became the Protector of the Indians *ex-officio* wherever the court shifted around the kingdom. Wilier, tougher, and bolder as he aged, he won some mighty battles. He died in 1566, at 92, begging his Dominican brothers to continue to protect the Indians. He stands still as the greatest moral figure in Spanish history.

The following is an early-eighteenth-century Dominican historian's transcription of a diary/memoir by one of the young Dominicans who accompanied Las Casas to Chiapas in 1545–46, Brother Tomás de la Torre. It shows how intensely the encomenderos in San Cristóbal resented Las Casas, how thoroughly they defied him, and how resolutely, then aged 71, he fought them in defense of the Indians.

HISTORIA DE LA PROVINCIA DE SAN VICENTE DE CHIAPA Y GUATEMALA DE LA ORDEN DE PREDICADORES*

. . . Chapter XLIII. Of the Beginning and Motives That There Were for the Great Quarrels and Persecutions That Were Raised Against the Bishop and the Dominicans

There would be . . . in this Province five Clerics in all of it, a Dean, a Canon, and the others plain Clerics; the Bishop [Las Casas] brought a Maestreescuela [a cathedral dignitary to teach divinity] who was the only Cleric who arrived here with him; the Dean was a jurist and canonist and a great Lawyer, the Canon a Theologian very withdrawn and quiet and a true Priest of the Lord . . . The Maestreescuela was also a Learned canonist, the others [already there] were idiots and boys and of those who were making a living in the Villages baptizing Indians, one even a Tribute-Collector or little less, another planting sugar cane and running a sugar mill for part of the sugar; infamous things in these lands.

Seeing this the Bishop collected them all in the City and promised them to make use of them in the Church's work when he could and to help them at the cost of that miserable income of his and that they would eat with him, although his table was not pleasant to all, because since he did not eat meat there was no abundance of it at his table, nor of anything else, because he did not change anything from his old and Dominican way of life; his clothes were of

---

*Francisco Ximénez [1710–1720], Books I and II, Serie "Biblioteca Goathemala," vol. 27 (Guatemala: Academia de Geografía e Historia de Guatemala , 1977), I, pp. 370–373. (Translation by John Womack, Jr., with help from Kathryn Burns and Mary Gaylord.)

coarse cloth, his common mode of travel was on foot and in sandles, his food eggs and no more of what the members of the Order are accustomed to eat, his exercise was to study and preach most fervently against the tyrannies of the land, showing his flock the true path of salvation, and at night to say prolix and fervent Prayers, giving testimony to this the great sighs and sobs that those were listening at the door of his room heard him give.

Seeing, then, the tyrannies that were happening, and wanting to oppose the wolves and not carry about the bishop's staff for pure ceremony, he tested all the confessors that there were, Clerics as well as Brothers of Our Lady of Mercy, to see if they knew anything, and approved for confessors only the Dean and the Canon, giving them a memorial of cases that he did not want to absolve or that they should absolve, noting they should reserve them for him, who being very prodigal of his authority would advise those confessors to come to him with these things, so that he might be able to guide the confessor and the penitent in the truth, because this land was then corrupt in this, and without fear I say that the ecclesiastics were blind and more so than the laymen, because to these sacrileges and iniquities that we abominate they paid no attention at all, such as having Indians for slaves, it being manifest to the world how they were made slaves, to take Gold from the mines with free Indians, and other unheard of tyrannies in which this world of the Indies abounded without the King being able to remedy it with holy and just laws that he has always sent, because of the insatiable greed of his Governors and Officials.

Of this Holy and good Doctrine of the Bishop, the Canon drank abundantly and has suffered for it more than any of the rest of us. Not so the Dean, although at first he made a show of obeying the Prelate. The Maestreescuela he [Las Casas] did not approve for confessor because he [the Maestreescuela] did not know the customs of the land, for which reason we [the Dominicans who had come with the bishop] did not want ourselves to be approved either. In these times there was no justice at all in this land, the Municipal Magistrates ruled, conquistadors like their neighbors, and since the High Royal Court that had been put in these parts at the petition of the Bishop did not have anyone to guide it, there were born so many evils that I do not know how to tell them to you.

The poor old man tormented with this did not know what was to be done except speaking out in the pulpit and in his house against them. What was to be done when the Indian woman came privately and put herself at his feet saying, look, Lord, he has taken me a Christian to be sold and I am not a slave and I have no brand on my face? So these and other things the poor Pastor saw his lambs of his flocks suffering. Since he abominated these things and kept shut the doors of the confessors, people began to rage so much against him, that there is no language that can explain it: some because it seemed to them that this was a way to take their slaves and profits from them, others from shame before the Indians because all around there the Indians understood that those who oppressed them were bad, others also because to most other people they were Christians and the word went around that they would not be given the Sacraments by the custom of the land unless they restored what they had stolen and quit stealing. They made a thousand attempts and tricks to corrupt the old man, they threw a thousand supplicants on him, they got a thousand interdictions on him with bulls from the Pope, they threatened to accuse him because he did not obey the bulls, they got injunctions on him from Magistrates and Notaries swearing they would complain about him to the King and his high councils, to the archbishop and the Pope, that he was denying them the sacraments and excluding them from what Christians enjoy; and with all this they could not get from him any other reply but this: blind cowards, whom Satan holds deceived, come all of you, for I will hear your confessions, only put down what you have stolen or at least stop stealing.

They answered, let the King determine that and then prostrate on the ground they would do so; he showed them the King's new laws [on enslavement and encomiendas], in which the King commanded to do everything that the bishop was asking them to do, they answered that those laws they had already appealed and they were not worth anything; they told him that lawyers absolved such things in the Indies and that to him they were not obliged to give credence, that he was an enemy of the Christians and that he was trying to throw them out of the land.

Meanwhile, the talk of the People was: that the Bishop knew nothing and that he had graduated from school in Gerez [Jerez, famous for sherry, but not for schools, meaning he drank to excess and had no education], and that he did not know how to study except in Juan Bocasio [Giovanni Bocaccio, meaning he was a glutton too], and although he was a known confessor in Seville and the most learned Canon Lawyer and in Theology who I believe has passed through this land, they called him a Lutheran, who did not give the sacraments, and they said in the city square, do not call him Bishop, he is worse than the Anti-Christ, and others things of this kind, threatening to kill him, and for that they shot off a harquebus, hard by the window where he slept, and they took away all the household service that the Indians did for him and commanded them not to sell him bread, and to the landlord of the house where he lodged, who was away in his villages, they sent word to come to the City to throw the Bishop out of that house where he lodged so that he would have nowhere to go. They said that he was not Bishop because not all the town councilmen were present when he was received in the City, and other absurdities that it would take a long time to tell; they sent word to him that he not preach because if they saw him revive the dead, they would say that he did it by sorcery. Many whom he sent the notary or Constable to call would not come, and they said that he was not Bishop, that not all the Councilmen were there when he came, and so they said: Brother Bartolomé who says he is the Bishop.

Although he was in his Church, gave communion, and excommunicated and ordained and blessed the oil and confirmed, no one accompanied him and many called him Your Reverence and even Father, and the women especially would not rise in Church when he passed, although he wore the vestments for a high Pontifical Mass. The greeting that those who wrote to their Pastor from elsewhere gave to him was: you Devil who has come to us. Others said, I do not know what sin this City has done that God gave it such a Bishop. A man swore that he had to be killed, and as he [Las Casas] was days without appearing, so we were greatly afraid that he had been killed; then that man himself almost came to death from some knife-wounds he was given, and the Bishop visited him and consoled him, and after that the man remained very much his Servant and reformed.

To see the perseverance that the Holy Bishop had, made us admire him. We counseled him many times that he leave his Bishopric and he answered that if the persecution were against him he would leave; but since it was against his flock he would not dare to and that he was prepared to die for them and that from his work he had hopes that some benefit would come to his flock. He would tell us that God gave him so much consolation in his work, that he did not even feel the work, nor did any of the persecution matter anything to him, because those cries against him were old to him, and where could he go and be well received considering what was involved? This the Holy and very worthy Bishop told us and never stopped preaching, bringing to us and to his subjects that passage from the prophet Ezequiel . . . [sic, a break in the original, in Brother Tomás's diary, maybe because he could not recall or find the passage to cite].

If all the things of this man were to be written, more space and more paper would be necessary. Let us come to the conclusion of the strife of that Holy Week [of Easter 1545]. The Dean, when one of those Conquistadors was going to confess, sent him to the Bishop with a little Slip of paper saying: "the bearer has slaves or mines, Your Honor may see what is to be done, although what Your Honor excludes I do not find excluded in law, or bulls," not understanding or pretending not to understand what the Prelate ordered. The Bishop tried to correct and enlighten him, saying that those were mortal sins and that those men were persisting in their impenitence oppressing the poor. The Dean, seeing that this was already moving forward, seems to have absolved everything, because it was seen one day during Easter Week that some of those who were known for being in those sins were taking communion; and the Bishop wanting to correct him paternally invited all the Clerics to eat, and the Dean dissembled and did not go; afterward the Bishop had him called and they found him playing cards and he answered that he was sick and then he went to bed: the truth known, the Bishop again had him called, since their lodgings were right across from each other; the Dean answered that he could not go, the Bishop called him a third time and he answered the same, he had him called the fourth time with a Note signed in his name, and he still would not go; he called him the fifth time on pain of excommunication to come, and he would not go either; and then he [Las Casas] sent a constable to arrest him and the Clerics who were there, and the Dean grabbed a sword to defend himself and they did not dare go after him; and the Canon being there talking to him about the matter and what evil he was doing, seeing him [the canon] safe, they attacked the Dean, and the Constable was wounded in the instep of the foot from which he suffered very badly and remained crippled. Then the Dean gave cry to the City, saying, "help me, Señores, for I will confess you all." Then all the City came running and the Magistrate gave cry, here from the King ["Stop in the name of the law"], and they all came out with swords drawn and lances and took away the Dean whom the Clerics had been holding; and fearing that the Dominican Brothers were going to come out to favor the Bishop, because the lodgings were just opposite from each other, they put themselves at the door of our lodging with lances and swords. We did not go out or go to the doors or windows, but we were quiet, entrusting to God the Holy old man. At this, the Alcalde came giving cry, "here from the King," and they entered with a great rush into the lodging of the Bishop, giving cry saying that they were not heretics, and that he was destroying the land.

Brother Domingo de Medinilla was there and a Gentleman from Salamanca called Villafuerte who by chance was in the City, and barely by pleading could they contain the people in the hall while the Bishop went into a Chamber. Afterward the Bishop was about to go out to tell them, what were they looking for, believing that they would be ashamed before him; but Villafuerte feared that they would kill him, and by violent shoves presto put him back in the Chamber, and there they threw themselves after him, with swords and bucklers against the tame lamb, but he did not answer anything to their incivilities, and so they left confused. It was feared that if they took him into the hall where many people could reach him, that someone would cunningly put a dagger in him and kill him, because in all the Indies then there would be no better animal's head to cut off and show for bounty than that of the Bishop. The Bishop declared the Dean publicly excommunicated, and stopped him from confessing, so that no one could confess to him, and the Dean fled that night, and after he had left, the Magistrate came with a coat of mail, saying that if His Lordship ordered the Dean arrested, he was ready to do him the favor.

This Dean afterwards absolved many in Chiapas, and later the Bishop on his way to the Synod in Mexico City asked the Bishop in Oaxaca to arrest him, and he would not because the required testimony was not available there. Later in Mexico the Dean threw himself at the feet of the Bishop, and not long ago, going to Spain, he died.

This was the first strife of the Bishop with his flock; another Cleric also tried to knife the Vicar-General and so fled, and it has been said that they hanged him in the Province of Nicaragua, and another also left here, saying that the Bishop could not detain him in his presence, and gone from here in a short time he died; and so there remained with the Bishop only the Canon and another Cleric whom they call Galiano. . . .

CHAPTER TWO

Presumptuous and Arrogant Gentlemen, Poisonous Gentlewomen: San Cristóbal, 1626

Thomas Gage was the first Englishman to live in the Spanish empire in America—and then write and publish a book about it. This could have happened only because he was an egregiously perfidious man who lived in especially "interesting times." Born in England probably in 1603, scion of a proud old Catholic and pro-Spanish noble family (an uncle executed for treason against Queen Elizabeth, his own father and mother once sentenced to death for sheltering a Jesuit, and barely saved), he had two brothers in the priesthood and two others who became Jesuits. His father meant him too for a Jesuit. But after Jesuit schooling in Flanders and Rome, young Thomas went to Spain, acrimoniously left the Jesuits, and joined the Dominicans. In 1625 he and another young Dominican volunteered for missionary service in the Philippines. On the way there, in Mexico, they heard dismal stories about their destination, and fled south. They spent some months among the Dominicans in Chiapas. Gage's friend stayed there. (A missionary among the Tzeltal, he was elected first prior in Ocosingo in 1639, and died there in 1646.) Gage himself went on to Guatemala, where after a few pleasant years teaching in the Dominican seminary he grudgingly ran a series of missions out in Indian districts. In 1637 he abandoned his mission without notice, made his way to Panama, sailed for Spain, and returned to England, claiming among Catholics that he was back to help reestablish Catholicism. But after a quarrel with the Dominicans there and frustration in Rome, he decided in 1640 to join the Church of England. Having carefully negotiated the switch, he publicly recanted his Catholicism in August 1642, joined the Anglicans in London, and, to prove his new loyalty in the turmoil of the civil war just breaking out, got himself married and gave fatal testimony against a schoolmate and old friend, a Catholic priest accused of saying Mass in England, for which the priest was convicted of treason, hanged, drawn, and quartered. In 1643 Gage testified against a Catholic cousin's chaplain, clinched his conviction and execution, and received appointment as rector of a parish. Through the next five ever more Puritan years, he conveniently slipped his Anglicanism, displayed Presbyterian leanings, won a better parish, and wrote and published *The English-American His Travail by Sea and Land* . . . , by which the author intended to encourage a grand English liberation of Guatemala and the Spanish Main. In 1651 a Jesuit in whose arms Gage's eldest brother had died on a civil war battlefield came to trial for treason. Gage's testimony brought his conviction and execution. The next year, evidently on information from Gage, another of his brothers was arrested for being a priest; he died in prison. The more hateful Gage was, the more influential he became. In 1654 he won an invitation to submit to Lord Protector Cromwell his notions on the prospects for English expansion against the Spanish in the Caribbean. Cromwell chose his recommendation of Santo Domingo as the strategic key to capture. In 1655 Admiral William Penn's expedition sailed into the Caribbean, 38 ships, 8,000 men, with Gage as General Robert Venables's chaplain. It suffered heavy losses at Santo Domingo, but recovered to capture Jamaica, where Gage remained as chaplain to the English conquerors. There the next year he died, before he could use his sharp mind and twisted heart to gain from the island's coming boom in sugar and African slavery.

From his months in San Cristóbal in 1626, the following is Gage's foul impression of a foul colonial elite.

THOMAS GAGE'S TRAVELS
IN THE NEW WORLD*

. . . The city of Chiapa Real [San Cristóbal] is one of the meanest cities in all America, consisting of not above four hundred Spanish householders, and about an hundred houses of Indians joining to the city, and called *el barrio de los Indios* [the Indian quarter], who have a chapel by themselves. In this city there is no parish church, but only the cathedral, which is mother to all the inhabitants. Besides, there are two cloisters one of Dominicans and the other of Franciscans, and a poor cloister of nuns, which are burdensome enough to that city. The fact that the Jesuits have got no footing there (who commonly

*J. Eric S. Thompson, ed., *The English-American* . . ., [London, 1648] (Norman: University of Oklahoma Press, 1958), pp. 140–145.

live in the richest and wealthiest places and cities) is a sufficient argument of either the poverty of that city, or of want of gallant parts and prodigality in the gentry, from whose free and generous spirits they [Jesuits] like horseleeches are still sucking extraordinary and great alms for the colleges where they live. But here the merchants are close-handed, and the gentlemen hard and sparing, wanting of wit and courtiers' parts and bravery, and so poor Chiapa is held no fit place for Jesuits. The merchants' chief trading there is in cacao, cotton from the adjacent parts of the country, in pedlar's small wares, in some sugar from about Chiapa of the Indians [the town now called Chiapa de Corzo, down the mountains west of San Cristóbal], and in a little cochineal. But commonly the Governor (whose chief gain consisteth in this) will not suffer them to be too free in this commodity, lest they hinder his greedy traffic. These have their shops all together in a little market-place before the cathedral church, built with walks and porches, under which the poor Indian wives meet at five o'clock at evening to sell what slap [slop] and drugs they can prepare most cheap for the empty Creole stomachs.

The richer sort of these merchants go and send yet further to Tabasco for wares from Spain, such as wines, linen cloth, figs, raisins, olives, and iron, though in these commodities they dare not venture too much, by reason the Spaniards in that country are not very many, and those that are there are such as are loath to open their purses to more than what may suffice nature. So that Spanish commodities are chiefly brought for the friars who are the best and joviallest blades of that country.

The gentlemen of Chiapa are a by-word all about that country, signifying great dons (dones, gifts or abilities I should say), great birth, fantastic pride, joined with simplicity, ignorance, misery, and penury. These gentlemen will say they descend from some duke's house in Spain, and immediately from the first Conquerors; yet in carriage they are but clowns, in wit, abilities, parts, and discourse as shallow-brained as a low brook, whose waters are scarce able to leap over a pebble stone, any small reason soon tries and tires their weak brain, which is easily at a stand when sense is propounded, and slides on speedily when nonsense carrieth the stream. The gentlemen Creoles or natives of Chiapa are as presumptuous and arrogant as if the noblest blood in the Court of Madrid ran through their veins. It is a common thing amongst them to make a dinner only with a dish of frijoles [beans] in black broth, boiled with pepper and garlic, saying it is the most nourishing meat in all the Indies; and after this so stately a dinner they will be sure to come out to the street-door of their houses to see and to be seen, and there for half an hour will they stand shaking off the crumbs of bread from their clothes, bands (but especially from their ruffs when they used them), and from their mustachios. And with their tooth-pickers they will stand picking their teeth, as if some small partridge bone stuck in them. Nay, if a friend pass by at that time, they will be sure to find out some crumb or other in the mustachio (as if on purpose the crumbs of the table had been shaken upon their beards, that the loss of them might be a gaining of credit for great house-keeping) and they will be sure to vent out some non-truth, as to say: *"A Señor que linda perdiz he comido hoy,"* "O Sir, what a dainty partridge have I eat to-day," whereas they pick out nothing from their teeth but a black husk of a dry *frijol* or Turkey bean.

Though they say they are great in blood and in birth, yet in their employments they are but rich graziers, for most of their wealth consisteth in farms of cattle and mules. Some indeed have towns of Indians subject unto them, whereof they are called *encomenderos,* and receive yearly from every Indian a certain poll tribute of fowls and money. They have most cowardly spirits for war, and though they will say they would fain see Spain, yet they dare not venture their lives at sea, for they judge sleeping in a whole skin the best maxim for their Creole spirits. One hundred fighting soldiers would easily lay low those Chiapa dons, and gain the whole city, which lieth so open to the fields that the mules and asses come in and graze, the streets being very commodious to entertain asses from within, and from without. Yet in this city liveth commonly a governor, or *Alcalde Mayor,* and a bishop.

The Governor's place is of no small esteem and interest, for his power reacheth far, and he tradeth much in cacao and cochineal, and domineers over both Spaniards and Indians at his will and pleasure. But ill-gotten goods never thrive, as was seen in Don Gabriel de Orellana, governor of this city and country in my time, who, having sent the worth of eight thousand crowns in cochineal, cacao, sugar, and hides by the river of Tabasco [the Grijalva] towards Havana, lost it all into the hands of the Hollanders, who doubtless knew how to make better use of it than would have done that tyrannizing Governor. The Bishop's place of that city is worth at least eight thousand ducats a year, which truly he had need of that comes so far from Spain to live in such a city where are such able dons and where asses are so freely fed and bred. Most of this Bishop's revenues consisteth in great offerings which he yearly receiveth from the great Indian towns, going out to them once a year to confirm their children. Confirmation is such a means to confirm and strengthen the Bishop's revenues, that none must be confirmed by him who offer not a fair white wax-candle, with a ribbon and at least four reals. I have seen the richer sort offer him a candle of at least six-pound weight with two yards of twelve-penny broad ribbon, and the candle stuck from the top to the bottom with single reals round about. Nay, the poor Indians make it the chief masterpiece of their vanity to offer proudly in such occasions.

Don Bernardino de Salazar was the Bishop of the city in my time, who desired my company to ride with him his circuit but one month about the towns near to Chiapa, and in this time I was appointed by him to hold the basin wherein the Spaniards and Indians (whilst he confirmed their children) did cast their offerings, which I and another chaplain did always tell and cast up by good account before we carried the money up into his chamber. I found that at our return at the month's end he had received one thousand and six hundred ducats of offerings alone, besides the fees due to him for visiting the several companies, or sodalities and confraternities, belonging to the saints or souls in their purgatory, which are extraordinary rich there, whereof he and all other bishops in their district take account yearly. This Bishop, as all the rest are there, was somewhat covetous, but otherwise a man of a temperate life and conversation, very zealous to reform whatsoever abuses committed in the church, which cost him his life before I departed from Chiapa to Guatemala.

The women of that city, it seems, pretend much weakness and squeamishness of stomach, which they say is so great that they are not able to continue in the church while a Mass is briefly huddled over, much less while a solemn high Mass (as they call it) is sung and a sermon preached, unless they drink a cup of hot chocolate, and eat a bit of sweetmeats to strengthen their stomachs. For this purpose it was much used by them to make their maids bring to them to church in the middle of Mass or sermon a cup of chocolate, which could not be done to all, or most of them, without a great confusion and interrupting both Mass and sermon. The Bishop perceived this abuse and gave fair warning for the omitting of it, but all without amendment. Consequently he thought fit to fix in writing upon the church's doors an excommunication against all such as should presume at the time of service to eat or drink within the church. This excommunication was taken much to heart by all, but especially by the gentlewomen, who protested if they might not eat or drink in the church they could not continue in it to hear what otherwise they were bound unto.

The chief of them, knowing what great friendship there was between the Bishop and the Prior and myself, came to the Prior and me desiring us to use all means we could with the Bishop to persuade him to revoke his excommunication so heavily laid upon them, and his threatening their souls with damning judgment for the violation of it. The good Prior and myself labored all we could, alleging the custom of the country, the weakness of the sex whom it most concerned, and also the weakness of their stomachs, the contempt that might from them ensue unto his person, and many inconveniences which might follow to the breeding of an uproar in the church and in the city, whereof we had some probable conjecture from what already we had heard from some. But none of these reasons would move the Bishop. He answered that he preferred the honor of God, and of his house before his own life.

The women seeing him so hard to be entreated, began to stomach [be angry with] him the more and to slight him with scornful and reproachful words. Others slighted his excommunication, drinking in iniquity in the church, as the fish doth water. This caused one day such an uproar in the Cathedral that many swords were drawn against the priests and prebends, who attempted to take away from the maids the cups of chocolate which they brought unto their mistresses. These ladies seeing at last that neither fair nor foul means would prevail with the Bishop, resolved to forsake the Cathedral, where the Bishop's own and his prebends' eyes must needs be watching over them. So from that time most of the city betook themselves to the cloister churches, where by the nuns and friars they were not troubled nor resisted, though fairly counselled to obey the command of the Bishop. Nevertheless, his name they could not now brook, and to his prebends they denied now all such relief and stipend for Masses which formerly they had used to bestow upon them, conferring them all upon the friars who grew rich by the poor impoverished Cathedral.

This lasted not long, but the Bishop began to stomach the friars, and to set up another excommunication, binding all the city to resort unto their own cathedral church. This the women would not obey, but kept their houses for a whole month. In that time the Bishop fell dangerously sick, and desired to retire himself to the cloister of the Dominicans, for the great confidence he had in the Prior that he would take care of him in his sickness. Physicians were sent for far and near, who all with a joint opinion agreed that the Bishop was poisoned, and he himself doubted not of it at his death, praying unto God to forgive those that had been the cause of it, and to accept that sacrifice of his life, which he was willing to offer for the zeal of God's house and honor. He lay not above a week in the cloister, and as soon as he was dead, all his body, his head and face, did so swell that the least touch upon any part of him caused the skin to break and cast out white matter, which had corrupted and overflown all his body.

A gentlewoman with whom I was well acquainted in that city, who was noted to be somewhat too familiar with one of the Bishop's pages, was commonly censured. She was said to have prescribed such a cup of chocolate to be ministered by the page which poisoned him who so rigorously had forbidden chocolate to be drunk in the church. I myself heard this gentlewoman say of the deceased Bishop that she thought few grieved for his death, and that the women had no reason to grieve for him, and that she judged, he being such an enemy to chocolate in the church, that which he had drunk at home in his house had not agreed with his body. And it became afterwards a proverb in that country, Beware of the chocolate of Chiapa; which made me so cautious that I would not drink afterwards of it in a house where I had not very great satisfaction of the whole family . . .

CHAPTER THREE

Rebellion in the Highlands: The Revolt of Cancuc, 1712

This was not the first, but it was the major Indian uprising in Chiapas under Spanish rule. Nothing comparable would happen again until January 1, 1994—and then among very different kinds of Indians in a very different part of the state.

No one anywhere in 1994 understood better than Mario Humberto Ruz and Juan Pedro Viqueira how Chiapas's past weighed on its present. Ruz, a native Yucatecan, had come to Chiapas decades before to do his national service as a medical doctor in Comitán. His official service done, he became an anthropologist, concentrating on the Tzeltals and the Tojolabals, then a magisterial historian of colonial Tabasco and Chiapas. From his position in the Centro de Estudios Mayas in the Instituto de Investigaciones Filológicas at the National University, he had an extensive comparative perspective as well as his own deep learning, analytical sophistication, and finely balanced judgment to bring to bear on the history of Chiapas's many conflicts.

Viqueira, nephew of a great Mexican anthropologist, Ángel Palerm, held an undergraduate degree in rural sociology and a master's in history from El Colegio de Michoacán (Mexico's premier center for the study of "microhistory"), had lived in San Cristóbal and worked at the Centro de Investigaciones y Estudios Superiores en Antropología Social since 1987, had published extensively on the causes, course, and consequences of the revolt of Cancuc, enjoyed a justly deserved reputation as the world's paramount authority on eighteenth-century Chiapas, and was finishing his dissertation on colonial Chiapas for the École des Hautes Études en Sciences Sociales in Paris (from which he now holds his doctorate).

"After January 1, 1994," Ruz has written, "Chiapas stopped being conceptualized as the Mexican frontier with the past, and turned into a referent of the national future: it went from the last trench in the rear up to the vanguard." But in Chiapas and elsewhere in Mexico (never mind other countries) there were questions and answers immediately flying about the rebellion—It was a resurgence of Mexico's 1968, maybe even an alien intrusion from Central American revolutions! No, it was a direct continuation of Chiapas's age-old conflicts! It was a manipulation of the Indians! No, it was an Indian movement! It was anachronistic! No, it was quintessentially contemporary! It was a political maneuver! No, it was a struggle for land! Liberation theologians were behind it! No, liberation theologians were not behind it! It was unique to Chiapas! No, it was a movement that could erupt anywhere in Mexico! All this frantic controversy revealed pervasive and profound ignorance of the people there past and present. "In the face of such disinformative confusion," Ruz, Viqueira, and other scholars, who among them had accumulated some 250 years of intimate professional study of the region, put together in six months a book that explained as best they could the enormous historical complexities behind the state's latest and most important rebellion. It is a book that does honor to them, their discipline, the people of whom they wrote, and their country, a book that should make historians anywhere proud of their craft. But it took exhausting efforts and three university presses to bring the book into print, and then to produce only 1,000 copies. Happily, it is now in a second edition that may reach a broader public.

LAS CAUSAS DE UNA REBELIÓN INDIA: CHIAPAS, 1712*

. . . Years of Prosperity (1670–1707)

After several decades of economic depression, the Kingdom of Guatemala after the years 1660–70 experienced an important increase in commercial exchange and productive activity. During the period when the Guatemala Royal High Court Chief Justice Gabriel Sánchez de Berrospe ruled (1696–1701), a quantity of silver was sent to Spain greater than that sent during the previous 20 years.

A yet more significant proof of this economic bonanza is the fact that in the years from 1694 to 1697 successful campaigns were launched to conquer the Lacandón and the Petén [jungles], which implied great expenses; in the previous 100 years no serious effort for conquest had been made there. These conquests, moreover, were justified with the argument that it was necessary to open a direct road between Campeche [on the Gulf of Mexico] and Guate-

---

*Juan Pedro Viqueira, in *Chiapas: Los rumbos de otra historia*, eds. Juan Pedro Viqueira and Mario Humberto Ruz (Universidad Nacional Autónoma de México, Centro de Estudios Mexicanos y Centroamericanos, and Universidad de Guadalajara: Mexico City, 1995), pp. 109–126.

mala, which constitutes one more index of an intensification of economic activity that required breaking the isolation of the different regions in order to broaden markets and multipy commercial exchange.

DEMOGRAPHIC RECUPERATION

In Chiapas after the 1670s there occurred a slow but continuous recovery of the population, on the order of 0.5 percent annually. This recuperation was stronger yet in the province of Los Llanos [south of San Cristóbal]. Los Zendales, for its part [northeast of San Cristóbal], continued the demographic growth initiated there at the beginning of the century, although now at a slower rate, especially in the northern area, which made foreseeable in this province the appearance of grave problems in the not distant future.

In a district like that of Chiapas, which lacked such natural resources as mines of precious metals, which could generate great wealth without need for an abundant labor force, this demographic growth turned logically into an important incentive for Spanish enterprises. Nevertheless, the economic revival, clearly visible in various macroeconomic indicators, would not translate into an improvement of the situation of the Indians, but on the contrary would take place at their expense.

NEW BURDENS

To begin with, the increase in population caused the authorities in Guatemala and Chiapas to update the tribute rolls much more often. This meant not only brusque increases in the payments that Indians had to make to the Crown or their *encomenderos*, but also that the officials responsible for making up the new rolls used their offices to extract from the Indians unduly important quantities of money and food, on the pretext of various salaries and fees.

Between 1670 and 1690 there was established in Chiapas a new and original mechanism for collecting tribute that allowed the authorities responsible for extracting it—the lieutenants of royal revenue officers until 1692 and the district magistrates afterward—to obtain juicy and illegal profits and at the same time impress a greater dynamism on the district's economy. This mechanism had its point of departure in the difference between the prices that these officials reported to the Crown that the taxed goods had and the price that these goods actually sold for in the market, which, depending on the harvest, could be two, three, four, or even six times higher. All they had to do then was collect from the Indians in money, at market prices, the part of the tribute the Indians owed in corn, beans, and chile, and pocket the difference. It is clear that to be able to manage a fraud of these dimensions required the interested complicity of the private powers in Chiapas. To achieve this complicity, the district magistrates distributed at the "official price" the tributes of the villages near Ciudad Real [San Cristóbal] payable in kind, among the bishop, the convents of the religious orders and nuns, and notable residents, who thus supplied their houses and haciendas with corn at fixed and ridiculously low prices.

This bundle of interests resulted by the turn of the eighteenth century in a peculiar tributary geography: the villages of the Priorship of Chiapa [westward] and Los Llanos . . . close to Ciudad Real . . . and Simojovel [north] were paying tribute in kind, thus supplying Ciudad Real and the haciendas of the Guardianía of Huitiupán [north] their necessary corn. Beyond, there extended an intermediate area that in years of good harvests, when no one there needed corn from elsewhere, paid in money, while in times of scarcity it paid in kind. Finally, the villages most distant from the capital [San Cristóbal] always paid their tribute in money.

To obtain the cash necessary to discharge this burden, the Indians of the most distant area had to work for some three months a year in the Tabasco cacao and vanilla plantations, or on the Dominican haciendas in Ocosingo, Chiapa, and Comitán, or on the Spanish haciendas in Jiquipilas, Los Llanos, and Soconusco.

Their efforts yielded triple for the Spaniards: first, they enriched the lieutenants of the royal revenue officers, and later the district magistrate and his protegés; second, they provided cheap labor to the haciendas and plantations of Chiapas, Tabasco, and Soconusco; and third, in a period when money was scarce in the Kingdom of Guatemala, they furnished Chiapas cash from Tabasco.

With these sums paid by the Indians as tribute, the economy of the district of Chiapas gained greater dynamism. In fact this income permitted the district magistrate to trade with Tehuantepec [in Oaxaca], to buy cotton there that he resold to the natives in Chiapas for them to make the cloth they owed in tribute; to invest in various wares that he sold to Spaniards and "distributed" in more or less forced sales among Indians; to acquire rough cloth in Puebla that he then sent to Guatemala as if it were what had been collected for part of the local tribute, while the locally collected cloth, of better quality, he sent off for sale in the Honduras mining camps; and finally to finance the production of cochineal in some [northwestern] Zoque villages, to smuggle it to Spain, via Tabasco and Veracruz.

Thanks to this tributary system, Ciudad Real, well supplied with agricultural products and cash, began to flourish. Around 1675 the Jesuits arrived in Chiapas, perhaps attracted by the new economic possibilities of the region. They founded a seminary and built the Church of San Agustín. Between 1676 and 1698 a new bishop's residence was built, and complete renovations were done on the cathedral's chapter, sacristy, and façade. During these years the tower went up on the convent today called El Carmen. The Franciscans undertook works on their monastery and church at the end of the 1670s and the beginning of the next decade. Bishop Brother Juan Bautista Álvarez de Toledo founded, in 1709 and 1712, respectively, the Hospital of Santa María de la

Caridad and a poor house for women. In 1713 various works were underway on the church of the Dominican monastery. . . .

Given the enormous profits that came to Ciudad Real from the so-called "fraud in tribute sales," few Spaniards were interested in denouncing the fraud to the Crown. On the other hand, the hate that Indians felt over tributes so difficult for them to pay, the hate they felt for a city that demanded these tributes with implacable cruelty, was growing inexorably . . .

CONFLICTS AMONG SPANIARDS

Between 1670 and 1707 the district of Chiapas experienced serious conflicts among various groups of Spaniards who repeatedly upset public order. . . . in 1674 the Spanish crown designated Marcos Bravo de la Serna bishop of Chiapas and Soconusco. His loyalty to the interests of the Crown and his eager modernizing efforts quickly brought him big problems with all sectors of the population. The prelate saw everywhere only corruption, abuses, negligence, superstitions, and idolatry. He therefore quarreled with the district magistrate of Chiapas and various judges of the Royal High Court in Guatemala City, whom he accused of using their office to enrich themselves illegally. The campaigns that he launched against "idolatry" showed the relative failure of the evangelization of the Indians, which had been mainly the responsibility of the Dominican Order, which controlled 80 percent of the parishes in the district of Chiapas. To limit the Order's exorbitant power, Bravo de la Serna proposed to the Royal Council of the Indies [the king's colonial ministry] to take the seven parishes of Los Zendales away from the Dominicans and put them under parish priests, which earned him the Dominicans' wrath. Despite his intrepid efforts, the fruits of his ecclesiastical government were few. Death surprised him before resolutions from the Council of the Indies favorable to his designs arrived, so that these resolutions did not go into effect, except in a few cases, and then almost a century later.

The next bishop, Brother Francisco Núñez de la Vega, a Dominican, born in the colonies, . . . put into practice a radically different policy. Alleging the absence of parish priests capable of running the parishes the Dominicans held, he managed to bury this project of his predecessor's. On the other hand, he continued with greater energy the persecution of "idolatrous Indians" and "teachers of witchcraft" that his predecessor had begun. Thanks to this campaign he restored, under his own command, the unity of the Church in Chiapas. But instead of serving the interests of the Crown, as Bravo de la Serna had done, he turned into a great champion of the rights of the Church, which it is fair to say he often identified with his own. His long tenure as bishop allowed him to consolidate exorbitant power that he often used, with the weapon of excommunication, to oppose district magistrates and Royal High Court judges. In 1689–90 he had a violent dispute with Judge Scals of the Royal

High Court; in 1695 he opposed the campaigns against the Lacandón Indians that the High Court's chief justice . . . was directing; and in 1701 he excommunicated the court's armed forces when they came to arrest the royal inspector . . ., to mention only the most famous cases.

The struggle over the administration and collection of tribute, from which . . . it was possible to obtain juicy profits through the . . . "fraud in tribute sales," was at the origin of some judgments that several district magistrates of Chiapas then won against the lieutenants of the royal revenue officers in Ciudad Real. While in the rest of the Kingdom of Guatemala and in New Spain generally, control over tribute was exercised by the district magistrates, in Chiapas it was a lieutenant of the royal revenue officers, strongly tied to local interests, who managed everything related to the royal treasury, including the tribute the Indians paid. At least twice district magistrates received judgments favorable to their claims, but the royal revenue officers . . . managed to recover management of the tribute just a few year later. In 1689 District Magistrate Manuel de Maisterra brought the problem before the Royal High Court again. On this occasion the royal revenue officers and their lieutenant, who was a brother of one of them, defended their interests with special ill will and persistence, resorting to dilatory maneuvers of little elegance when there arrived from Spain the decision of the Council of the Indies favoring the district magistrate's claims. Consequently the district magistrates, given this important source of income that allowed them to finance forced sales of very diverse kinds, took control of the economic life of Chiapas, generally displacing their competitors, the local merchants . . .

The Crisis of 1707–1712

THE AGRICULTURAL CRISIS

In 1707 there began a period of bad harvests—a cyclical phenomenon typical in traditional societies—that brought hunger and illness to many villages in the district of Chiapas. The consequences of this agricultural crisis were especially devastating in villages that habitually paid their tribute in money or that did so only in times of scarcity. On the one hand, the oppressive system of tribute collection that had been functioning for several decades had exhausted those villages' monetary and food reserves. On the other hand, in years of agricultural crisis their inhabitants not only could not raise crops sufficient to assure their own subsistence, but in addition the amount of tribute converted to money rose in direct proportion to the rise in the prices that corn, beans, and chile fetched in the markets, and which, according to how serious the scarcity was, could double or even triple.

To top it all off, the new bishop, Juan Bautista Álvarez de Toledo, started his tour of inspection in 1709. This ambitious prelate was very fond of doing works of charity, about which he punctually informed the king. Besides distributing once a week corn among the needy of Ciudad Real, he put all his effort into founding a hospital and an asylum for wayward girls. But these pious works required important sums of money, which necessarily had to come out of the Indians' pocket. So on his visits of inspection the prelate imposed new duties and demanded the payment of a tithe on the Indian confraternities' savings, which funds usually served in part to attenuate the consequences of bad harvests . . .

MUTINIES AND MIRACLES

Together with these economic and political troubles, there were strange religious events and movements of protest in the Indian villages. Between 1709 and 1711 the province of Los Zendales was the scene of three important commotions. The first took place in the village of Bachajón, where the Indians mutinied against their priest. . . . The next year the natives of Yajalón locked up in jail for several days the Dominican Brother Pedro Villena, who, obeying an order from the bishop, had tried to remove some relics from the village church to take them to Bachajón. A little later, in the neighboring village of Chilón, there were "new discords and inquietudes among its natives as well as among the Spanish citizenry" against the same friar.

About this time the so-called hermit of Zinacantán appeared. A mysterious character . . . not Indian . . . sitting up in a hollow tree, he was having himself worshipped by the natives of this village. He was arrested once, but the bishop, judging him to be crazy, let him go free. A little later he returned to his old haunts. He put an image of the Virgin of La Soledad in the Zinacantán town council and paid the priest for Masses. Later he convoked the Indians of Totolapa, San Lucas, and Chamula to a great fiesta at which he distributed tablets of chocolate and a lot of bread. His fame was beginning to spread when he was again arrested and exiled to New Spain [Mexico, a different jurisdiction].

In 1711 an Indian passed through Simojovel, preaching that he was the cousin of the Virgin of La Soledad and that she would not be long in coming back to this world. At the same time another Indian who said he was Saint Paul went around the region announcing the end of time.

In 1712 word spread over a broad zone of the miracle of the Virgin's appearance in Santa Marta Xolotepec. Its diffusion was the work not only of the people of this village, which had no more than 60 tributaries; in the construction of a chapel for the Virgin the neighboring villages of Las Coronas also collaborated—Chalchihuitán, Santiago Huixtán, and Magdalena Tenezacatlán. The fame of the Virgin quickly spread and attracted Indians from Totolapa, San Lucas, and Jototol, from the Guardianía de Huitiupán, and even from places as distant as San Bartolomé de Los Llanos, the Valley of Jiquipilas, and Los Zoques.

On the other hand, the Indians of San Pedro Chenalhó, although neighbors of Santa Marta Xolotepec, did not come to worship the Virgin, because they were very busy with their own miracle: a few days before, the image of their patron saint had sweated.

The bishop and the district magistrate, facing this religious exaltation, which foretold nothing good, had to resort to tricks to confiscate the image of the Virgin of Santa Marta Xolotepec and to arrest the miracle's promoters. For his part, a Dominican, Brother José Monroy, sought to check the veneration that the statue of Saint Peter was exciting in Chenalhó.

The Outbreak of the Rebellion

DEVELOPMENT OF THE REBELLION

In mid-June 1712, in the village of Cancuc, in the province of Los Zendales, an Indian girl of 13 or 14 years, María López, daughter of the village sacristan, told the justices and the people that at a place near her father's house, the Virgin had appeared to her in the form of a very pretty and very white lady, and had asked that a chapel be built for her so that she could live among the Indians. The news was taken at first with a certain scepticism on the part of the villagers; but little by little the firmness and conviction that the Indian girl showed and the support that some principales and elders offered her, elders from her village and from others, all of great prestige in the region, convinced many of the truth of her words. The priest in charge of the parish, Brother Simón de Lara, the only non-Indian inhabitant of the village, tried to put a stop to this dangerous "deceit" and had María and her father, Agustín López, whipped. But the only thing the Dominican accomplished was that practically the whole village took the Indian girl's side and that she reaffirmed that the Virgin appeared to her and talked to her. The chapel was then built in a few days. The Spanish authorities, civil and ecclesiastic, fearful of the commotions that word of a miracle of this kind could cause in a region where the Spanish and mestizo population was very small, ordered the destruction of the chapel, to which every day more and more Indians from the neighboring villages were coming. Their orders were not only not obeyed, but at the end of July Brother Simón de Lara had to flee Cancuc, threatened with death by his parishioners. On August 8, before a crowd of Indians from some ten villages from . . . Los Zendales, the Indian girl, who now was having herself called María de la Candelaria, gave the sign to start the rebellion against Spanish rule. Months later, Juan Pérez, the young Indian organist in Cancuc, would narrate these events to his Spanish judges:

After the prayer, the people being in the chapel and around it, lying prostrate on the ground, María López came in, accompanied by an Indian woman called Magdalena Díaz (now dead), with a bundle covered by her skirts . . . and they put the bundle behind the petate [a sleeping mat they used for an altar screen], and said that there they had placed Our Lady who had appeared to her. And then the whole village was coming into the chapel, and they were adoring the petate, touching the rosary, and crossing themselves, and kept doing it. And the miracle having been told in the other villages of the province, there were coming to this village the sons of those others, some bringing pine needles, others candles, and others alms, which one and then the other were giving to the Indian girl María López, who, when all the villages were here, said to them, "Believe me and follow me, because there is no more tribute, or king, or bishop, or district magistrate, and do no more than follow and believe this Virgin whom I have behind the petate."

To all the villages of the region then came dispatches written by the rebels, communicating to the Indians the good news that "the end has come and the prophecy was fulfilled of throwing off the yoke and restoring their lands and liberty," because it was "God's will that [the Virgin of Cancuc] had come for her sons the Indians to liberate them from the captivity of the Spaniards and the ministers of the Church and that the angels would come to plant and take care of their corn patches, and that by signs that they had had in the sun and the moon the king of Spain had already died and it was necessary to name another" and that "the king who was to govern them would be of their election and they would be free of the work they suffered and free from paying tributes." In these dispatches the rebels ordered the Indians to come to Cancuc to see the Virgin, bringing cases for crosses, other church ornaments, staffs of justice, and jail irons. The revolt of the 32 villages of Los Zendales, Las Coronas and Chinampas, and the Guardianía of Huitiupán, as the Spaniards called the rebellion, referring to the tributary provinces that took part in it, had begun.

On August 12 and 14, respectively, the rebels attacked and took Chilón and Ocosingo, towns in which the few Spaniards in the district's northeastern part had concentrated. With these actions the rebels gained control of all the villages in . . . Los Zendales and . . . Huitiupán, the sole exceptions being Simojovel and Los Plátanos. The Spaniards of Ciudad Real tried to counterattack, but on August 25 they were besieged in Huixtán. Only the arrival of reinforcements, composed mainly of Indians from the village of Chiapa who had remained loyal to the Crown, saved them from imminent defeat.

After this battle, the Spaniards judged it more prudent to entrench themselves in Ciudad Real and ask for help from Guatemala and Tabasco. Thus for almost three months the rebels had time to outline a new social order in the broad region under their control, . . . Los Zendales and . . . Huitiupán, joined then by . . . Las Coronas and Chinampas, so including Tzeltal, Tzotzil, and Chol villages.

The restructuring of this region had as its base a new miracle: a few days after the battle at Huixtán, an Indian from Chenalhó, Sebastián Gómez, arrived in Cancuc saying that he had ascended to Heaven, where, after conversing with the Most Holy Trinity, the Virgin Mary, and Saint Peter, he had received from Peter the authority to appoint new bishops and vicars. For this purpose there was a quick convocation of all the Indians who could read and write, generally sacristans and choirmasters. Sebastián Gómez de la Gloria, aided by María de la Candelaria, annointed them as vicars and ordered them to return to their villages to preach the Gospel, celebrate Mass, and administer the divine sacraments to their villagers. At the same time Sebastián Gómez de la Gloria imposed a certain order and hierarchy among the captains who had led the fighting; he appointed three of them captain-general, so giving them preeminence over the others.

However, this Indian republic did not resist the sudden attacks by the numerous and well-munitioned troops who arrived from Guatemala under the command of the chief justice of the High Court. . . . Defeated first at Oxchuc, the rebels tried to resist at Cancuc, using their position on the heights of a wooded hill surrounded by deep ravines, but on November 21 they were conquered by the stone mortars and rifles of their attackers. The closest villages then surrendered, while the inhabitants of the district's northern region continued to offer some resistance, taking refuge in the woods. Although the Spaniards did not have to fight more battles, the task of driving the Indians out of the woods and back to their villages took several months of hard work.

The consequences of the rebellion were disastrous for the Indians. Deprived of metal tools by the conquering troops on the pretext that they could be used as weapons, their planted fields having been destroyed, the Indians throughout the region were overwhelmed by famine followed by deadly epidemics that decimated them . . .

CHAPTER FOUR

Ladino Massacre of Highland Indians: The Caste War of 1869

In the wake of the French military withdrawal from Mexico in 1866, after the Mexican Republican Army defeated the remaining Mexican Imperial Army, executed Emperor Maximilian, and restored Liberal command in 1867, Liberals encouraged Indians in old Conservative regions to give up their old Conservative loyalties and take part in Mexico's new freedom. In Chiapas, accordingly, in the Tzotzil country north of San Cristóbal, Indians in 1867–68 adopted a new religious cult and stopped worshiping and trading in ladino towns. Their unexpected independence alarmed ladino priests, merchants, and politicians, who in 1869 launched a ferocious war on them. For more than a century the standard story of this war was the ladino story, that the Indians had revolted against the ladinos in a "caste" or race war to destroy them, which the ladinos had successfully resisted in a fight to the death for civilization.

Not until the 1970s did any scholar seriously search the primary sources, and discover that the offensive had come from the ladinos. The scholar who finally got the story right was a young American anthropologist, Jan Rus, who had first gone to Los Altos on the Harvard Chiapas Project between his junior and senior years of college in 1968, then returned again and again, in repeated devotions, to understand Tzotzils historically and anthropologically, to work with them, to use archives to write true histories of their forebears, and to help them tell their own stories of their own lives. The terms in which he set right the history of the "Caste War" of 1869 did not yet fit in the canon of anthropology of the 1970s, but it made excellent historical sense then and now. Engaged for the last 30 years in Tzotzil studies, from outside and from inside, author of some 30 publications on Los Altos, Rus from 1985 to 1998 served as director of the Native Language Project at the Instituto de Asesoría Antropológica para la Región Maya, A.C., or INAREMAC, a private institute in San Cristóbal for anthropological, historical, agricultural, health, and educational research, consulting, and publishing on Mayan districts. He is also coordinating editor of the American scholarly periodical *Latin American Perspectives*, published at the University of California at Riverside.

WHOSE CASTE WAR?
INDIANS, LADINOS, AND THE CHIAPAS "CASTE WAR" OF 1869*

. . . The Separatist Movement, 1867–1869

. . . [Despite Liberal anticlerical reforms in 1856–57] religious income from the vicariate of Chamula [the Tzotzil town north of San Cristóbal] actually rose after 1865, for a while even rivalling that of the pre-reform period. In part, this was due to the piety—and uncertainty—of the Indians themselves: given doubts about who would finally emerge in control of the highlands [the Liberals or the Conservatives], they seem, at least for the time being, to have been willing to accept a return to the status quo ante. Equally important, however, was the rigor of their new vicar after mid–1865, Miguel Martínez. In a period when the rest of the highland clergy seems to have been in retreat, Martínez was almost uniquely zealous in his efforts to restore the Indian parishes to their former profitability. According to later allegations, he extracted funds improperly from the native *cofradías* [confraternities], withheld religious services from those too poor to pay for them, and even flogged native officials who failed to meet their tax quotas . . .

The first sign of unrest came in late 1867 with news that people from a large area of the townships of Chamula, Mitontic, and Chenalhó had begun gathering to venerate a set of magical "talking stones" discovered near the hamlet of Tzajalhemel by a Chamula woman, Agustina Gómez Checheb. So important had this phenomenon become by the end of the year that Pedro Díaz Cuzcat, a fiscal [practically a deacon] from Chamula, journeyed to Tzajalhemel to investigate. After a brief inspection, he announced that he too, like Checheb, could "talk" to the stones, and almost as quickly declared that they represented the saints and had asked that a shrine be built for them on the place of their appearances. By the end of January 1868, the crowds at Tzajalhemel had become larger than ever, attracted now not only by the stones but by the regular sermons of their priest, Cuzcat.

---

*Jan Rus, in *Spaniards and Indians in Southeastern Mesoamerica: Essays on the History of Ethnic Relations*, eds. Murdo J. MacLeod and Robert Wasserstrom (Lincoln: University of Nebraska Press, 1983), pp. 144–156.

It is significant that Cuzcat was a fiscal. According to an 1855 document describing Chamula's religious structure for future priests, the fiscales were the principal brokers between the church and the local community: in addition to acting as translators for the priests, they also kept all parish records, taught catechism to the young, and even led religious services themselves in the priests' absence. For this they were paid a small stipend, and often served for a decade or more at a time. They were, in fact, the closest thing to a native clergy. Not only, then, did Cuzcat undoubtedly know of the government's decrees with respect to Indians and the church when he set out for Tzajalhemel, but he also had the religious authority necessary to attract others to the new cult he intended to found.

So quickly did worship at the shrine grow after Cuzcat's arrival that, by mid-February 1868, Father Martínez himself was forced to visit Tzajalhemel to try to put a stop to it. What he found there was a small native house, a box-altar with candles and incense burning on it, and a small clay "saint" that worshippers tried at first to hide from him. Perhaps mindful of the government's decrees, his reaction on this first occasion was relatively mild: after lecturing those present about the perils of idolatry, he ordered them to disperse and, apparently convinced they would, returned forthwith to Chamula.

In fact, however, the next two months proved to be one of the new religion's periods of fastest growth. Having been mistreated by ladinos of all parties, especially during the preceding civil wars, many Indians seemed to find in the isolated shrine a kind of sanctuary, a place where they could not only pray in peace but could meet and trade with their neighbors without fear of ladino interference. By March, Indians from throughout the vicariate of Chamula and from such nearby Tzeltal communities as Tenejapa had begun to attend regularly, making Tzajalhemel not only an important religious center but one of the highlands' busiest marketing centers as well.

All of this, of course, had profound effects on the ladinos. As attendance at Tzajalhemel increased, religious income and commerce in the surrounding ladino towns necessarily decreased. To the lowlanders [the Liberals of the Central Valley], this was a great triumph. Because their reason for attacking the church in the first place had been to strike at the power of the highland conservatives [the traditional San Cristóbal elite], these economic side-effects were an unexpected bonus. To the highlanders, on the other hand, the new developments appeared in a much more ominous light. If it continued, the growing Indian boycott could only mean one thing: utter ruin. Their anxiety became particularly acute in the weeks following Easter (April 12), 1868, when for the first time in memory Indians were almost completely absent from the ceremonies—and businesses—of San Cristóbal. Crying that the long-feared "caste war" was finally upon them, the city's ladinos organized themselves into self-defense companies and sent out urgent pleas for aid to the rest of the highlands.

Finally, on May 3—the Día de Santa Cruz, another important Indian celebration that San Cristóbal passed without native commerce—the new conservative jefe político of the highlands struck. Accompanied by a force of twenty–five men, he raided Tzajalhemel, seized Checheb and the "saints," and ordered the Indians to go home. Much to the highlanders' consternation, however, the liberal state government—seeing in this raid proof that its anticonservative policies were working—promptly ordered Checheb released and the Indians' freedom of worship respected. In attacking the separatists directly, the conservatives had inadvertently strengthened them.

Their hands thus tied politically, the highlanders tried a new tack. On May 27 they sent a commission of three priests to reason with the Indians, to try to talk them back into paying religion. Finding the masses gathered at Tzajalhemel "sincere" in their beliefs—that is, still Catholic—but nevertheless "deluded," the members of this commission blessed a cross for them to worship and warned them in the direst terms of the dangers of praying before unconsecrated (that is, "unfranchised") images. Convinced that their superior theology had won the day, they returned triumphant to San Cristóbal that same afternoon.

Whether due to this commission's persuasiveness or something else, activity at the shrine did in fact decline during the next two months, a normal crowd attending the fiesta of Chamula's patron saint, San Juan, on June 24. In August, however, before the feast of Santa Rosa, Tzajalhemel became busier than ever. Emboldened by the continued, tacit support of the state government, the Indians enlarged their temple, purchased a bell and trumpets, chose sacristans and acolytes to care for the building and altar, and named a *mayor-domo* [steward] of Santa Rosa to organize the festivities. Indeed, they showed every intention of making ceremonies in Tzajalhemel as full of pomp and satisfaction as those in the traditional pueblos themselves.

After Santa Rosa, life in Tzajalhemel settled into a routine closely modeled on that of the older pueblos in other ways as well. By this time, Cuzcat had begun to assume more and more of the duties of the parish priests with whom he had formerly had such close contact. On Sundays, he donned a robe and preached at dawn and vespers—services announced by the sacristans with a touch of the bell. On other days, there were petitions to hear, sacraments to dispense, and always the cult of the saints to tend. In addition, there were small daily markets to supervise, and larger, regional gatherings on Sundays and feast days. Although imitation may be the sincerest form of flattery, highland ladinos were far from pleased. Aside from the few alcohol sellers and itinerant peddlers who had begun to frequent the new pueblo, Tzajalhemel remained for most anathema.

Finally, on December 2, 1868, they could stand it no longer: concerned more with their own economic survival than with legal niceties, San Cristóbal's leaders dispatched a force of fifty men to put an end to the separatist movement once and for all. Although the Indians tried briefly to resist this invasion and defend their shrine, the ladinos fired into their midst and easily set them to flight. Checheb and several others were arrested, the images and implements were impounded, and the shrine itself was stripped of its decorations. Although Cuzcat escaped, he too was captured as he passed through Ixtapa on his way to beg the state government for relief. He was sent on to Chiapa in irons, and it was to be almost two months before he could prove his innocence of any wrongdoing—at which point the governor, instead of releasing him unconditionally, merely returned him to San Cristóbal, where he was promptly re-arrested by the conservatives on February 8, 1869.

The "Caste War," 1869–70

. . . in early 1869, [Liberal Governor Pantaleón Domínguez] . . . announced his intention to begin enforcing the state tax code, particularly the head tax, counting on it not only to provide the funds for needed public services but also to win the support of local officials throughout the state who were to be granted eight percent of what they collected in commissions. The new taxes were to be paid quarterly, the first installment coming due May 30—and, to make them more compelling, the collectors were authorized to jail indefinitely the *ayuntamiento* [town council] of any township that failed to cooperate.

Unfortunately, Domínguez, his attention fixed on ladino society, does not seem to have given much thought to the effect his decrees might have on the Indians. From December 1868 through mid-April 1869 there had been no activity in Tzajalhemel, and apparently he assumed that the Chamulas and their neighbors would continue to accept meekly whatever new conditions were imposed on them. The assumption, however, was wrong—tragically so. When the new secretaries and schoolteachers began detaining people in their pueblos in April and early May to charge them the first quarter's head tax, the Indians, led this time by dissident members of their own ayuntamientos, simply returned to their refuge in the forest. Again commerce with non-Indians fell off, again church attendance declined, again ladinos throughout the vicariate of Chamula complained to the regional authorities in San Cristóbal.

Events moved rapidly toward a showdown. By mid-May, feeling in San Cristóbal was running strongly in favor of another raid—one that promised to be even more violent, more of a "lesson," than that of the preceding December. Before such an attack could take place, however, Ignacio Fernández de Galindo, a liberal teacher from Central Mexico who had lived in San Cristóbal since early 1868, and who on several occasions had defended the Indians' rights in public debates, slipped out of the city on May 26 with his wife and a student, Benigno Trejo, to warn the Indians of their danger.

What happened next is largely a matter of conjecture. Those who would see the separation of 1869 as a simple continuation of that of 1868—and both as the result of a conspiracy between Galindo and Cuzcat—claim that Galindo convinced the Indians he was a divinely ordained successor to Cuzcat and then organized them into an army to make war on his own race. According to his own later testimony, on the other hand, he merely informed the Indians of their rights and offered to help them turn aside raids on their villages—and that only with the intention of preventing bloodshed.

Whichever of these explanations is the more correct, the one that was believed in San Cristóbal in 1869 was the former. Under its influence, the Indians' withdrawal was by early June being seen not as just another annoying boycott but as the concentration of forces for an all-out attack on whites. Finally, in what appears to have been a last attempt to talk the Indians into submission (and perhaps simultaneously to survey their forces), Father Martínez and the secretaries of Chamula, Mitontic, and Chenalhó arranged to meet in Tzajalhemel the morning of June 13. As it happened, Martínez and his escort from Chamula—the secretary-teacher, the secretary's brother, and Martínez's own Indian servant—arrived early for this appointment. Finding only a few Indians at the shrine, they nevertheless went ahead and tried to persuade them to abandon their "rebellion" and go home. The Indians, for their part, are reported to have received these representations respectfully, even asking the priest's blessing before he left. Unfortunately, they were so respectful that they turned over the shrine's new religious objects when he asked for them. With that the die was cast: before Martínez and his companions could return to Chamula, they were overtaken by a body of Indians who, learning what had happened in Tzajalhemel, had pursued them, determined to retrieve their possessions. In the ensuing struggle, Martínez and the ladinos with him were killed. The "Caste War" was on.

Ladino blood having been spilt, panic swept the highlands. In the city, the self-defense companies, certain an Indian attack was imminent, prepared for the siege. In the outlying villages and hamlets, those who had no immediate escape route gathered at a few of the larger hamlets and prepared to fight. Perhaps the Indians saw in these gatherings potential acts of aggression; perhaps, one set of killings having been committed, some among them felt they no longer had anything to lose. In any case, on June 15 and 16, in what were arguably the only Indian-initiated actions of the entire "war," men from the southern end of the vicariate of Chamula attacked and killed the ladinos sheltered in "Natividad," near San Andrés, and "La Merced," near Santa Marta. At about the same time, the people of Chalchiguitán assassinated their schoolteacher and his family and their priest as they fled toward Simojovel, and the Chamulas dispatched five ladino peddlers on the road to San Cristóbal. Even at its height, however, the violence does not appear to have been indiscriminate: eleven cattle buyers from Chicoasén seized near Tzajalhemel on June 13 were released unharmed a day later, and ten ladinos and their children resident in Chenalhó during the entire "Caste War" emerged unscathed in mid-July. Apparently most of the Indians' rage was directly at those with whom they had old scores to settle or who had in some way threatened them.

Finally, on June 17, Galindo, in what was evidently an attempt to redirect the Indians' energy, led several thousand of them to San Cristóbal to secure the release of Cuzcat. Despite the terror this "siege" seems to have caused San Cristóbal's already edgy citizens, the Indians' behavior was not what might have been expected of an attacking army: not only did they come under a white flag, but they came at dusk, when fighting would be difficult. What Galindo offered in their behalf was a trade: Cuzcat, Checheb, and the others in exchange for himself, his wife, and Trejo as good-faith hostages.

. . . [A]fter the exchange had been consummated, he not only showed no fear of his fellow ladinos but actually "headed for his house as though nothing had happened"! San Cristóbal's leaders, however, were not so complaisant: no sooner had the Indians withdrawn than they invalidated the agreement, claiming it had been made under duress, and arrested Galindo, his wife, and the student.

From June 17 to 21, the Indians celebrated Cuzcat's release in Tzajalhemel. Expecting reprisals at any moment, however, they left some six hundred of their number camped above the roads leading from San Cristóbal as sentries—sentries whose digging sticks and machetes would be of but little use if a ladino attack did come. Nevertheless, this continued Indian presence played right into the hands of [the San Cristóbal weekly newspaper's] editors, who now wrote that there could "no longer be any doubt that the Indians were sworn enemies of the whites," that their most fervent desire was to "ravish and kill San Cristóbal's tender wives and sisters, to mutilate the corpses of its children." The only solution, they wrote, was a "war to the death between barbarism and civilization," a war in which—and here was the key—Chiapas's ladinos would for the first time in decades recognize their essential unity.

In spite of the passion of this appeal, however, San Cristóbal's situation at first aroused little sympathy in the lowlands. Indeed, as late as June 18 news of Father Martínez's death was carried in the official newspaper under the restrained heading "Scandals." On the morning of June 20, however—more than a month after the crisis had begun, and a week after the first killings—Domínguez suddenly activated the lowland militia and set off to relieve San Cristóbal. What had happened? First, news of the continuing "siege" of San Cristóbal after June 18 does seem to have aroused many in the lowlands, who now feared that the Indians were escaping any ladino control. Second, and perhaps even more important, there had been elections for local office throughout the lowlands on June 11. When the results were announced the evening of June 19, Domínguez's party had been resoundingly defeated, and, since the elections had been widely regarded as a vote of confidence, a pronouncement [military revolt] against the governor was expected momentarily. By mobilizing the forces that would have carried out such a coup, Domínguez neatly sidestepped his own ouster.

From the moment Domínguez and his 300 heavily armed troops marched into San Cristóbal in the mid-afternoon of June 21, the Indians' fate was sealed. Within minutes they had attacked those camped north and west of the city—people who in almost a week had taken no hostile action—leaving more than three hundred of them dead by nightfall. Forty-three ladinos also died in this "glorious battle," most of them apparently local men who turned out to watch the sport and got in the way of their own artillery.

After this first engagement, Domínguez and his new conservative allies looked to their own affairs in San Cristóbal. Fear of the Indians now lifted, San Cristóbal tried Galindo and company on the twenty-third, the "defense" attorneys being the very ex imperialists [local supporters of Emperor Maximilian, 1864–67] who had fanned the flames of the "Caste War" during May and early June. Naturally Galindo could not win, and he and Trejo were executed June 26. Domínguez, meanwhile, his government penniless, his expulsion from office delayed only by the "Caste War," occupied himself with composing urgent appeals to local authorities around the state for volunteers and contributions to the cause of "civilization versus barbarism." Within a week, these requests brought him more than two thousand pesos and seven hundred men, more than enough to preserve his government and provide for the coming military campaign.

Finally, on June 30, their ranks swelled to over a thousand men, the ladino forces set out for the definitive attack on Chamula. [Here is an account of their action, in which they may have killed 300 more Indians, by] one of the lowland soldiers present, Pedro José Montesinos:

> When we first spied the Chamulas, hundreds of them were scattered in disordered groups on the hillsides, and before we were within rifle distance all, women and children as well as men, knelt on their bare knees to beg forgiveness. In spite of the humble position they took to show submission, however, the government forces continued to advance, and they, undoubtedly hoping they would be granted the mercy they begged with tears of sorrow, remained on their knees. At a little less than 200 meters, the soldiers opened fire on their compact masses—and despite the carnage done to them by the bullets, despite their cries for mercy, continued firing for some time.
>
> When the government forces finally reached the Chamulas, their thirst for the blood of that poor, abject race still not slaked, there were suddenly such strident yells that even knowing nothing of what they said one knew their meaning: with those shouts they [the Indians] threw themselves against the government forces with an almost inhuman valor. These poor men, unable to secure the clemency they implored with tears and prostration, charged with a barbaric bravery.

Following this triumph of "civilization over barbarism," Domínguez repeated a call he had first made several days earlier for the "rebellious" communities to present themselves and surrender. Almost immediately, what was left of the ayuntamientos of Chamula and Mitontic sent word through the teacher of Zinacantán that they wished to make peace. Their suit was accepted on July 4. Meanwhile, on July 3 a squadron of soldiers had been sent to reconnoiter Tzajalhemel. Although they found the site deserted, they also found a note, written on official paper, nailed to the door of the shrine. It was a plea from Cuzcat to Governor Domínguez that he be forgiven, that he was innocent of any part in a plan to attack ladinos. Considering that he had been in jail for the half-year before June 17, this claim is not hard to believe. The soldiers burned the temple and returned to San Cristóbal.

. . . Meanwhile, survivors of the attacks of June 21 and 30 had by this time fled back into the forests north and east of their communities. On July 7, the militia remaining in San Cristóbal had word that one of the "mobs" of these refugees was camped in the hamlet of Yolonchén, near San Andrés. Immediately a force of 360 men was dispatched to deal with it, engaging the Indians—men, women and children—in a fight that left 200 of them dead as against four ladinos. Following this raid, on July 16 an army of 610 infantry, 30 cavalry, and one crew of artillery left San Cristóbal to begin the tour of the Indian townships prescribed by Domínguez. Through July 26, when they returned to the city, they tramped through all the communities as far north as Chalchiguitán—650 ladinos foraging on Indian lands, routing from their homes hundreds of terrified natives who, thus deprived of their livelihoods, were forced to join the refugees from the south in pilfering the stores and butchering the cattle of the abandoned ladino farms that lay in their path. Perversely, the soldiers' descriptions of these ruined farms were then published [in the San Cristóbal newspaper] as further evidence of the destruction being wreaked on the state by the "Indian hordes."

Perhaps most sadly, Indians themselves participated in all these persecutions. Irregular militiamen from Mitontic and Chenalhó took part in the July 16 expedition, and when a second one left San Cristóbal on August 7, it took with it several hundred men from Chamula itself. In their eagerness to prove themselves, these "loyal" Indians were even more ruthless than their ladino masters at hunting down and killing their fellows. Indeed, after mid-September primary responsibility for restoring order was left in their hands, the only direct ladino participants being a squadron of sixty infantry and fourteen cavalry stationed in San Andrés.

Through the fall, there continued to be occasional "contacts" with the "rebels"—from their descriptions, cases in which individual refugees, or at most small family groups, were run down by the soldiers and their native allies and killed. Then, on November 13, the government forces finally caught up with one last camp of exhausted fugitives north of San Andrés. Rather than waste munitions on them, the ladinos sent in 250 Indian lance bearers, an action that produced the following glowing report from Cresencio Rosas, the expedition's commander: "After an impetuous attack that yielded sixty rebel dead, we retrieved lances, axes, machetes and knives from the field, and took many families prisoner. I send my congratulations to the government and the entire white race for this great triumph of the defenders of humanity against barbarism."

Following this battle, pacification of the central highlands itself was finally judged complete. Some resistance did continue just to the north among bands of highland Indians who had taken advantage of the confusion to flee the haciendas where they had been held as laborers. However, on April 18, 1870, and again on July 27, volunteers from Simojovel attacked the camps of these people, killing 32 on the first occasion and 36 on the second. With that, the great "Caste War" was finished . . .

CHAPTER FIVE

The Mexican Revolution in Tzotzil: "When We Stopped Being Crushed," 1914–1940

Everywhere in Mexico, anywhere in Mexico, sooner or later someone will break into a talk on the Revolution, the great complication of civil war, banditry, and social and political reform in the 1910s, social and political organization in the 1920s, and new reforms in the 1930s, the institutions and values of which remain powerful even 60 years later. The talk turns different ways in different places. In public it usually sounds like what children hear *en la escuela*, in the schoolhouse, as the Mexican federal school system teaches the Revolution in its nationally standardized textbooks, official, national, patriotic talk. At home, at work, out in the countryside *en la milpa*, in the corn patch, it is usually the private recitation of privately inherited memories of the Revolution, personal, familial, parochial, sometimes rebellious talk. Especially in villages that survive as villages, it is literally folklore, the local people's private collective teaching of the deliberately remembered lessons that the village privately accepts as the Revolution's local meaning. Particularly in rural Chiapas it is old men and women telling what they remember to their juniors as moral and civic lessons, to fortify their community's own sense of its history and consensual identity. These are *pláticas*. The word *plática* in Spanish comes from Low Latin *practica*, for "confidential friendship," or "familiarity," which came to mean "conversation." In time it also took on the meaning of "talk," or "a talk," much less than a speech or a lecture or a sermon, open for listeners to join or contest, but always with the purpose of explanation or reassurance or encouragement of consensus. In the Chiapas highlands old people used to give such talks for all three purposes at once.

The "talk" that Andrés Aubry analyzes below came from Tzotzil elders in Zinacantán who gave it to informants for John Burstein's Tzotzil Workshop at INAREMAC (see Reading No. 4) in 1978–79. The Tzotzil draft was then polished by the Chamula Mariano Méndez and the Zinacanteco Anselmo Pérez (one of Robert M. Laughlin's two local "collaborators" on *The Great Tzotzil Dictionary of San Lorenzo Zinacantán*, Smithsonian Contributions to Anthropology, No. 19 [Washington: Smithsonian Institution, 1975], and published in Tzotzil and Spanish with Aubry's commentary as *Cuando dejamos de ser aplastados* ["When We Stopped Being Crushed"], 2 vols. (México: Secretaría de Educación Pública-Instituto Nacional Indigenista, 1982).

Aubry, a French anthropologist who had worked previously for the Conference of Latin American Bishops and UNESCO, settled in San Cristóbal in 1973. "A privileged witness" to the preparation and meeting of the Indian Congress in San Cristóbal in 1974 (see Reading No. 10), he then served as INAREMAC's director until its legal extinction in February 1998. In this capacity he coordinated regional projects by the National Polytechnic Institute's medical school and the Comitán regional hospital in public health, by French agricultural schools and local producers' organizations in agriculture, by the Tzotzil Workshop in linguistics and language (including the publication of 30 books in Tzotzil), and by various historical researchers (including himself) in collecting and classifying historical documents and publishing the *Boletín del Archivo Histórico Diocesano de San Cristóbal*. He writes therefore from much intimate experience in the region and with much authority.

EN LA ESCUELA Y EN LA MILPA,
LA PLÁTICA NO ES LA MISMA:
HISTORIA TZOTZIL DE LA REVOLUCIÓN MEXICANA
EN CHIAPAS*

Since the Conquest, the history of Chiapas has been controversial: one chronicle of the province would be barely published, when another witness representing other interests would hurry to get out a "new" or "true" version, of course different, of the same facts.

The history of the Revolution in Chiapas does not escape this rule. It does not turn out the same if the view is from Mexico City, from Tuxtla Gutiérrez, or from San Cristóbal de Las Casas. From the national capital, the sources, scarce or still hidden as military secrets, present this history as a desperate effort of Carrancismo [the so-called Constitutionalist Revolutionary forces of

---

*Andrés Aubry (Instituto de Asesoría Antropológica para la Región Maya, A.C., Doc. 026-IX-84), pp. 1–12. (Translation by John Womack, Jr., with help from Andrés Aubry.)

Venustiano Carranza, who eventually served as president of Mexico from 1917 to 1920]. But from the state capital the Revolutionaries are Mapachistas [local anti-Carranza and landlord-led forces based in the central valley], and from the capital of Los Altos, they are Pinedistas [local anti-Carranza and landlord-led forces based around San Cristóbal]. The failure of the Constitutionalist attempt and the anti-Carrancista character . . . of the other two ordinarily lead to the thesis that the Mexican Revolution never reached Chiapas.

All these sources (1) are urban, (2) spring from politico-military personalities or chiefs, (3) are written, shaped into books, archives, or newspapers, (4) are polemical in that they all cite and question each other, (5) are partial, not only for their partisan positions, but also because they view only one region of Chiapas or one phase of the revolutionary contest in the state.

But if we leave the books and go out into the field, suddenly there appear different sources, which do not belong to any of the above factions. These are not written; they come out only in the talk of illiterates headed for the corn patch, or in meetings of the elders, as well as on moonlit nights. They are not the property (intellectual or ideological) of any national or Chiapan personality, because they reflect the collective position of a village, a people. A last characteristic, important for the historian: they embrace the Revolution in all the geographic stages of the state, and in all the phases of the movement, from start to finish. In sum, the illiterates are the only ones who show concern to keep a complete story of the globality of the revolutionary movement, in space and in time.

The peasant sources with which we are familiar are Tzotzil. Some have already been transcribed, but others were born oral. They are little known, because access to them requires a "peasant passport" or implies a linguistic initiation.

Yes, this is the case: the Tzotzil dictionary does not have the word "Revolution." Any question with this vocabulary falls therefore into a void or silence. But most *ejidatarios* [members of an agrarian community holding an inalienable federal land grant] or *comuneros* [Indians who constitute a local community and hold their land in common] turn lively if there is allusion to the period of "when we stopped being crushed" (*k'alal ich'ay mosoal*) [or, "when we stopped being mozos," indentured servants]. By this stereotyped formula the Tzotzils evoke the times when they decided not to be either *baldíos* [squatters reduced to debt peonage] or servants and day laborers. This linguistic code, hermetic to the Mexican from outside their world, opens the doors of the history of the Revolution in Chiapas, and revolutionizes it . . .

We have two kinds of stories: (1) the "Talk of the Elders of Zinacantán," and (2) other Tzotzil commentaries, memories, or narratives.

In the case of Zinacantán, the elders' talk does not pretend to be a reconstruction of revolutionary events, but a historical reflection in the form of a story, that is, a message to Zinacantecans today, grounded throughout in historical memories ordered by the elders' analysis, which follows a chronological frame. Linguistically, one would say that the elders do not offer us a story *of* the facts (not historical information) but tell a story *to* the community (an analysis of the history).

The other stories usually confirm the talk of Zinacantán, although they flow from different and independent sources. Underlying the exposition there also runs an interpretation, not always explicit, of the Chiapan revolutionary process . . .

1. The Facts: Scenario and Stages of the Mexican Revolution in Chiapas

A. IN CHIAPAS, THE REVOLUTION CAME FROM THE COUNTRYSIDE, BUT THE COUNTER-REVOLUTION SPRANG FROM THE CITY.

. . . the Tzotzils realize that history is not told the same way in the city and the countryside. In the schoolhouse and out in the corn patch, the talk is not the same.

In San Cristóbal, the revolutionary period is marked by the eruption of new family names: Madero, Carranza, Obregón, Tiburcio Fernández Ruiz, etc. But in the hamlets of Zinacantán municipality, they speak of groups: "Pajaritos," Mapaches, Pinedistas, etc., which mobilized the people against them.

On the urban side: personalities, money, power, and failure. In the countryside: collective movements, poverty, suffering, and popular success.

From the beginning the Elders of Zinacantán choose their side.

B. THE TZOTZILS CHANGE THE OFFICIAL DATING OF THE REVOLUTION.

The Revolution (Tzotzil version) begins in 1911 and triumphs almost 30 years later in Cárdenas's government. It starts with a political fight for power, continues with a cultural victory against the "saint burners" (peasant tag for the "red shirts" . . . [a militant anticlerical movement, based in neighboring Tabasco in the 1920s and '30s]), and is resolved economically by the conquest of land, called "liberation of the laborer" (*ich'ay mosoal* or *spojobail mosoetik*). From the struggle is born a new society (*ach' rason*) that postulates a new man.

The "dispute" began with the faction of Jacinto Pérez Pajarito in 1911. He recruited his counter-revolutionary forces among the Indians of various villages, with counsel, blessing, and Guadalupan medals from the bishop of San Cristóbal, Francisco Orozco y Jiménez. Recalling this period, the Zinacantecans take elaborate care with the Tzotzil vocabulary of their analysis: in order not to divide the Indians, they never allude to the ethnic character of the rebels, and underline that the people of Chamula [the adjacent and often rival Tzotzil municipality] also rejected them . . .

C. THE PEASANT REVOLUTIONARY ALLIANCE OF INDIANS AND LADINOS DEMYSTIFIED THE FALSE COUNTER-REVOLUTIONARY ALLIANCE OF LIBERALS AND CONSERVATIVES.

In 1914 the landlords . . . try to achieve what Pajarito's forces did not. Despite the Act of Canquí . . . [supposedly uniting the state to drive out Carranza's forces], they reach only a twisted fusion of two contentious factions: one based in the state's Central Valley . . . , led by El Mapache (Tiburcio Fernández Ruiz), with the Liberals from Tuxtla; the other based in Los Altos, captained by [Alberto] Pineda, with the Conservatives from San Cristóbal.

But the Zinacantecans had the wisdom not to divide among themselves. To fight against the landlords, they made an alliance with ladino peasants. Here they contribute historical details that are new and of great significance: on the Zinacantecan mobilization, on the military strategies of the Constitutionalists and the Canquí group, on the dark role of the Guatemalan president in the conflict, and on the ideological indecision of Pineda's forces.

D. THE INDIAN REVOLUTION IN CHIAPAS WAS ALSO A CULTURAL REVOLUTION.

With the official triumph of the Revolution in 1920, the Tzotzils win nothing. Our stories are completely quiet on the counter-revolutionary offensive . . . that scourged Chiapas in 1923. But they turn lively again after 1934, when the Tuxtla bourgeoisie, excited by big bribes and pressured by a friend of ex-President Calles, Governor Victórico Grajales, invade the countryside with their saint burners, apparently to avoid a revival in Chiapas of the Cristero movement [the national Catholic rebellion of 1926–29, which surfaced in some other states in the early 1930s].

This episode of Tzotzil cultural resistance, springing from their churches and ceremonial centers, offers Tzotzils the strategic opportunity to learn the benefits of clandestine activity, evoked in a moving and vibrant way in our stories. In the woods popular unity strengthened.

E. WITH THE REVOLUTIONARY EJIDATARIO IS BORN A NEW MAN.

Cárdenas was the only president to remember Chiapas after he took office. In a tour of the state . . . by car, boat, train, down mule trails, on long hikes, he comes to distribute land. . . .

Erasto Urbina [see Reading No. 7] will put the seal on the process. Using the organization learned in previous clandestine activity, he advised the Indians to take possession of the fields they had won by constructing churches or installing in their new plots [the parts of the federal land grant assigned to individual ejidatarios] the images that the saint burners had violated.

In summary, the Tzotzils won the political battle with arms in hand; the cultural struggle was achieved by the organization of clandestine action; and the economic dimension of the Revolution, which its Tzotzil name gives it, was resolved with the conquest of the land. The ejido plot transformed the Porfirian laborer into a peasant, founding a new social order (ach' rason).

2. Analysis: The Political Cathedra of the Tzotziles

. . . the Zinacantecans are not motivated to reconstitute the historical facts of the Revolution in Chiapas, because any Indian raised in the tradition of the Elders already has the information. Their aim is different: . . . to deliver a message to the Tzotzil people.

In the following lines we will therefore try to synthesize the Zinacantecans' authoritative political teaching. In passing, we will be able to measure the ideological level and the historico-political consciousness of the Indian peasants of Chiapas.

1. Although the word "revolution" does not exist in Tzotzil, the Zinacantecans elaborated the concept with a long semantic sequence that reveals the depth of their revolutionary sense. The "organization of their thought" (specialists would say, the Tzotzil conceptual apparatus) is structured in the following manner:

Some word of information (k'op) comes up that before long is a problem or conflict (k'oplal), until "the thought for seeking" is whirling round and round, which opens the possibility for political problematicization. Precisely, sa k'op is "the word that revolves or turns around or mixes up or scrambles," or provokes, that is, the Revolution in its political sense.

Once the resources of "the word" (k'op) are exhausted, inevitably violence (tzak' bail) breaks out, or the "physical revolution" . . . of machetes and stranglings, which began happening in 1911, to give a warning to the Pajaritos. But revolutionary violence, later, in 1914, had to grow into an armed movement to throw out the landlords. Ak' k'ok' is "to take up the rifle," because the "anger of the people" (kap jol) had no other outlet.

The result was immediate: in 1914 there appears the "Law of Liberation of Laborers" and in 1917 the Constitution that reestablished "what is correct and right" (smelol), so cementing the bases of a new social relation (ach' rason). These two juridical documents have a narrow relationship, because the man who inspired the first and the man who was the [Constitutional Convention's] reporting secretary of Article 123 of the second [i.e., the Constitutional article on labor rights] are one and the same Chiapan: Luis Espinosa. The Chiapan law of 1914 is like a draft of the Constitutional Article 123, and makes clear that pressure from Chiapas's laborers benefited the entire republic.

All this is expressed by a linguistic formula that clearly defines the process, *k'alal ich'ay mosoal*, which we could translate into cultivated Spanish as "the historic liberation of the oppressed." In the "*castilla*" [Spanish] of Chiapas, it is the transformation of the peon, of the baldío, or of the servant or laborer, into a peasant, with all the dignity of the term: owner of his land. This happened in 1940, with Erasto Urbina, promoted by Cárdenas.

Let us synthesize the synthesis: this semantic sequence is ordered in the story according to chronological stages, structuring the Tzotzil dating of the Revolution. But it also classifies the qualitative dimensions of the Revolution, announcing its successive achievements: its political, ideological, and economic watersheds. In their conceptualization, carefully analyzed and measured, the Zinacantecans reconcile history (the dates, periodization) and society (the process), that is, they reach a formulation of the Tzotzil historico-social consciousness.

2. With this conceptual clarity, it is not at all strange that the Zinacantecans knew immediately how to lay bare the maneuvers that impeded the process thus semantically defined, that is, the attempts at counter-revolution.

First, their humorous story of the Pajarito uprising teaches that it is necessary to distinguish between revolt and revolution.

Second, by demystifying the "generals of the Revolution" (Pineda and El Mapache) as the sordid landlord captains they were, they explain how not to confuse disorder and Revolution.

Third, with the moving story of cultural resistance to the religious persecution by the saint burners, they show clearly that the Revolution would cease to be a revolution if the Tzotzils had to stop being peasants and Indians.

3. With pride, the Tzotzils teach in their "Talk" that Zinacantán had a good nose for how society would develop; it never got the path of history wrong.

Even when revolutionary surnames divided . . . San Cristóbal, Zinacantán had opted for them, despite their status as unknown outsiders. Zinacantán, before any other place in the state, always recognized the historic revolutionaries . . . Zinacantán has always chosen the paths of history . . .

4. The Revolution also interests the Zinacantecans because it achieved in passing a local success: it fortified the unity of their people.

The Pajaritos, despite their ethnic identity [as Indians], did not manage to create a Zinacantecan faction (this being perhaps a discrete allusion to the same failure by the [Protestant] "evangelicals" today, who, infesting all their neighbors, are not able to "stick" in their territory). When by Pineda's cunning a fellow of his faction emerged as municipal president of Zinacantán, the entire village turned upside down against him and installed the first revolutionary municipal council with firm popular support. When the invincible

Mapache ("look, not even bullets hurt him, only gave him a scrape") tried to recruit Zinacantecans, he had to abandon the territory. When the "Villista" forces (actually only Mapachistas) or Pinedistas were marauding around Zinacantán, "we had to go in groups because of the danger," and the resistance of the whole people solidified. The cultural victory over the saint burners sealed this unity.

Zinacantán's unity is at once a fruit and a lesson of the Revolution . . .

Chapter Six

Migrant Labor in the Lumber Camps: The Jungle, Mud, Oxen, and Doomsday, c. 1925

The mystery man who wrote Mexican novels in German under the pseudonym B. Traven may never have known the name his mother gave him, or much else about his origins. (For the most authoritative study now of the man and his work, see Karl S. Guthke, *B. Traven: The Life Behind the Legends*, tr. Robert C. Sprung [New York: Lawrence Hill Books, 1991.]) But he knew Mexico, where he lived from 1924 until his death in 1969, as well as any foreigner of his time. And of all the country's regions, he knew Chiapas best, particularly the Lacandón Jungle, which he first explored as an official "Norwegian" photographer on a Mexican anthropological-archaeological expedition in 1926 and where he spent the better part of the next five years traveling with Indian guides, taking hundreds of photographs and detailed notes on the people, especially the workers in the mahogany lumber camps. The series of novels that he then published, the so-called Mahogany series appearing from 1931 to 1940, eventually translated into English as *The Carreta, Government, March to the Montería, Trozas, The Rebellion of the Hanged,* and *General from the Jungle,* were not fiction, Traven himself insisted, but "documents, that is all; documents which . . . [I put] in the form of novels to make them more readable." And although he set the fictional time of the stories before the Revolution in 1910, he had heard them as contemporaneous accounts. His main personal source on the camps, his "key informant," as anthropologists used to say, had worked in them from 1918 to 1925. ". . . [A]ll the circumstances reported," wrote Traven of his first two Mahogany novels, ". . . are still the same today, in 1931 . . . ." If asked, he would have written likewise of the last four, only more vehemently. To make his "documents . . . more readable," he did dramatically describe the managerial, political, and penal horrors of the jungle's most infamous camp as if they were typical of all camps. But his accounts of lumbering operations and work then were accurate, as Jan de Vos, the historian of the Lacandón lumber industry, attests in his excellent book, *Oro verde: La conquista de la Selva Lacandona por los madereros tabasqueños, 1822–1949* (Mexico City: Fondo de Cultura Económica, 1988), 198–201, 253–57.

Through the decades that followed, Traven stayed in touch with old friends in Chiapas. That was where he wanted to go when he died. In April 1969, the last wake for him took place in the poorest Tzeltal hut on the outskirts of Ocosingo. It was a Tzeltal ceremony. The next day, as Traven had requested in his will, a bush pilot took his ashes up into the air over the Lacandón, and scattered them down over the jungle and the canyons and the Jataté River.

The reading below, from the fourth of the Mahogany novels, the one most focused on the lumbering as a business and as work, shows most clearly the kind of work that highland migrant laborers who went east had to do.

TROZAS [*TREE TRUNKS*]*

. . . The last trozas were dragged out of the ditch, and then they began hauling the trozas stacked on the edge of the ditch to the tumbo [the landing, from which the trunks would float away at high water].

"Now, keep your eyes wide open, Nene," said Andrés to Vicente. "Now you're really going to learn something. Up to now you haven't really been working, just going for a walk with the oxen. El Gusano ["The Worm," an assistant foreman] knows very well why he's cleared off just now. Now it's real fun. Now we get the trail on which you can slip into the mud up to your ears; and if no one sees you at the right moment you just stick there, and the ten or twelve spans of oxen tread you so deep in the morass that even God won't be able to find you on Doomsday. Don't go too near the oxen. When they begin to pull they kick out right and left and tread anything that gets in their way under their feet."

The next five hundred meters were a real pleasure: they went downhill. The boyeros [drovers] made the most of it. They coupled three or four trozas together and sent them to the steepest part of the falling terrain with a single team. That didn't last long, and then all the trozas were lined up again.

The way from there to the ditch for floating was a very wide hollow in the

---

*B. Traven, tr. Hugh Young (Ivan R. Dee: Chicago, 1994), pp. 222–232.

ground. Trees and plants had decayed there for thousands of years, and that created a soft soil. Because of the dense crowns of the great jungle giants, hardly any rays of sunshine came down which sometimes could have dried out the soft earth of this hollow. From both sides, and from the hill as well, all the moisture ran into this hollow, whether it was rain or the heavy dew that dripped from trees and bushes in the early hours of the morning. As a result, a morass was built up in the hollow that could very well have been described as a swamp. But in a swamp there is generally more water. This morass was in many ways more dangerous than a swamp, when it came to wading or riding through it or dragging through heavy tree trunks. It was easier to haul trozas through a swamp than through such morasses, which are so remarkably frequent that one gets the impression that the whole jungle consists of them. With long enough chains and a good number of spans of oxen it could be a pleasure to shift trozas, compared with hauling them through those morasses. In a swamp, if it was not too overgrown, a troza could sometimes float. But the soft earth of the morass was so sticky, so adhesive, so heavily loamy, that a troza hauled through it was grasped by the sticky, loamy, chalky mass as if by a huge monster that, once it has caught its prey, is unwilling to let it go. A troza that reached the tumbo and had passed through that morass on its last stretch was three times its natural thickness, because the sticky mud clung to the troza and was hauled along with it.

This mud was so sticky that often it could not be peeled off the troza just by hand; they had to use machetes, axes, and thick branches to help scale off the hard, sticky mud.

A couple of weeks earlier, when Don Severo [president of the logging company] and El Pícaro [the district foreman] , with the aid of some muchachos, had reconnoitered the new area to be opened up, in order to establish the regions to be exploited and to locate and record the ditches to be used for floating, they had no doubt seen this hollow in the terrain over which all the trozas that were felled in the campo would have to be hauled. They spent a whole day trying to find another, better way to this tumbo. But it was clear that over a breadth of five kilometers every trail that led to the main ditch went through similar hollows in the ground. And since all those hollows were morasses of the same sort, it was decided simply to choose the shortest route, and that was the one before which the boyeros had now lined up the trunks . . .

There were twelve spans of oxen hauling the troza. Three boyeros were wading on each side, shoving the troza here and there with their hooks and dragging it out of the morass. The lads were up to their hips in the mud and had little control over the troza, which was always liable to disappear in the morass and then could only be found and fished out by following the chain attached to it.

The boys and the other boyeros waded next to the oxen, driving the animals with sharp sticks, with shouts and oaths. The oxen too were wading up to their loins in the sticky morass, and maybe they had even more trouble than the lads in moving ahead. They never raised their legs completely out of the deep slimy mud but dragged their legs and bodies through it.

Every five paces the whole column stopped. Boys and oxen panted and gasped for breath. And what was visible of men and animals above the morass was dripping with sweat. The dense swarms of biting flies above the column bit into the lads' or the oxen's flesh at one place, tore a piece out leaving a shining stream of flowing blood behind them, flew off, bit their way in at another point, tore out another little scrap, and flew off to come down again at yet another place.

While the spans were standing still the lads were hard at it with all their strength, digging out and bringing up the troza, which was completely submerged and had become trapped in roots and lianas. When it was fully freed, the long line of spans was driven on. It advanced maybe twenty paces, then the troza was sunk in the mud again and disappeared from sight. The oxen, still pulling their hardest, hauled the troza a few paces farther before they stopped, and by then the troza was so firmly rammed into the morass that even twice the number of spans could not have pulled it farther. The whole column stopped again with curses and groans. The troza had to be dug out once more. And when it was finally brought to the surface, the lads succeeded in hauling it another twenty paces before it was submerged again and had to be dug out again.

The muchachos who were walking beside the oxen, driving them on and pulling up and dragging out the towing chains all the time so that they did not get caught under roots and sunken bushes, were standing in the morass rather than beside it. With one careless step they could fall under the oxen's feet. The animals, pulling forward with all their strength, tortured by thousands of insects, half blinded with the infernal damp heat and by the strain of the work, maddened by the yelling of the boys driving them and the continual pricking of the goads, trod mercilessly into the morass any lads who carelessly fell under their feet. Every fifty meters a lad disappeared under the feet of the oxen. The column could not be halted at that very second, for if the muchachos tried to stop even the two spans nearest to them, the spans in front pulled them on and those following pushed from behind. Only their great skill in maneuvering their bodies and the suppleness of all their limbs saved the lads that fell under the oxen's feet. That was why the first advice a new boyero got from the experienced ones was always: "Boy, take care that you don't get under the feet of the oxen! But if you are down, don't wait for the column to stop but wriggle out quicker and smarter than a hunted iguana." The reason for that advice was that new boyeros didn't go near enough to the spans when the column was on the move, and therefore those novices slowed down the day's work considerably.

Every span had to have a boy of its own to keep the column moving and to watch the towing chains so that they didn't get caught. But that made it necessary for them to go so close to the working oxen that most of the time the boy was half under the body of one of the two oxen, and needed only to let one foot slip into a hole from which an ox had just pulled its foreleg, and then he was already lying full length under both animals. Every muchacho had to look out for himself, for his own life. No one could help him; for every one of them had three times as much work to do as is normally expected of a man . . .

With each new troza that was brought to the tumbo the morass grew deeper. If it might still have had a certain density and firmness when the passages began, with the dragging of the heavy trozas, the stamping of the feet of twelve or fourteen pairs of heavy oxen, and the movement of the lads' legs, the morass grew pasty and muddy, like dough. The more it took on the consistency of dough, the deeper the trozas sank in the mud, the harder and more tiresome it became for the animals to drag their feet out of it, and the more strength which should have been devoted to the work of hauling had to be wasted just to keep moving through that deep and sticky mud. Not only that. The softer the dough, and the deeper it became softened and broken up, the more the heavy cakes and lumps of it clung to the troza and to the legs of the animals and the lads. The legs of the oxen began to look like elephants' legs while the troza tripled in weight. As soon as the troza was pulled to the surface the lads naturally scratched off the excessive burden of mud. But the passage hardly went five meters farther and already the troza had grown to twice its size and weight.

But what good was it to weep! If the troza was to earn money it had to be sold, and if it was to be sold it must be taken to market. How it gets to the harbor is not the purchaser's affair but the vendor's. The vendor would prefer to bring the caoba [mahogany] out of the jungle with tractors that run on steel caterpillar tracks. But where the tractors could carry it there is no caoba growing. The high price of gold is due to the rarity of that metal and the difficulty of obtaining it. The high price of mahogany, in contrast, is due to the difficulty of transport. It takes less trouble, less time, and less money to bring pine wood from the interior of Finland to a port in Central America than to deliver caoba from the Central American jungle to the same port. That is why lumber that comes from the woods of Russia, Sweden, and Finland is many times cheaper in the seaports of America than wood from the primeval forests of those American republics . . .

When the sixth troza of the day stuck on the way to the tumbo, deep in the morass, the oxen felt it their duty, for their own self-preservation, to quit work for the day.

While the lads were doing all they could to dig out the sunken troza, one span after another began to lie down. When the troza was at last free, every span was resting, lying in the mud. The boyeros knew that neither pricking the oxen with the goads nor whipping them would get them to go on working.

They had already worked two hours longer than they usually did. But since they formed part of such a big team, their herd instinct and their social consciousness had made them forget for a time that they were overworked. Now, however, that same herd instinct persuaded them all to lie down and refuse to work anymore.

A panting Vicente, lungs gasping and covered in sweat, went up to Andrés: "At last we've finished work today. I can't go on."

"None of us can go on, Nene. But it's only the oxen that will have a rest, until one o'clock tonight. Not us. We're going to the campo now, to eat. But then we have to work half the afternoon before we can rest."

"We can't shift any trozas without the oxen," said Vicente.

"Quite right, my child." Andrés chuckled. He too was panting like all the other lads. And his body too was streaming with heavy sweat; in many places it was pink where it ran down on him, because it was mixed with the thin streams of blood that flowed where he had been stung. Yet, despite his exhaustion, he could still laugh with Vicente, and he repeated: "Of course not, Nene. Without oxen we can't shift any trozas. I see you know how to use your head."

"But I'm saying, Andrés, if we don't have any oxen then we can't haul any trozas and don't need to go on working."

"It may have been like that on your finca, my son. Not here. Here you work as long as you can still stand. And when you can't stand any longer, then you work crawling on your arse. But you just have to work. El Gusano told me yesterday that we're clearing the trails on the other side of the ditch, where they've already been felling, and have to cut away the thicket to get the trail open. The caoba is ten times richer on the other side. But the trail is even more marshy."

"Even more marshy and muddy than here?" asked Vicente in astonishment. "How is that possible?"

"Everything is possible here. And on the other side, because of the slope of the land, the marsh is so soft that the trozas can sink ten meters deep in the ground when they're hauled, so we shall have to build calzadas [timber roadways]. And that's what we shall be doing this afternoon until we all fall down and just sleep where we drop."

"Calzadas, what's that then?"

"You'll learn this afternoon, and when you're building the calzadas you'll also be learning that every job here is the same in its terrible difficulty and strain. There's never any easy work here, and no rest at all . . ."

Migrant Labor on the Coffee Plantations: Debt, Lies, Drink, Hard Work, and the Union, 1920s–1930s

The work that migrant laborers from Los Altos in the 1920s and '30s did on the coffee plantations down west toward the Pacific coast was particularly coercive because of the debts that drove it, and particularly bitter because of the violence, the low wages, and the hours the landlord dictated as he willed. Migrant laborers in northern Mexico in the 1920s, especially if they went to work in the United States, could make enough to support their families during their absence, and on their return (like Bishop Ruiz's father) start a little business. Migrant laborers in Chiapas then and later could do neither. At best they could eventually repay their debts. Even then the seasonal cost to their families at home, in the extra work the families did to support themselves, in physically coping without husbands, fathers, sons, and brothers, and in emotional stress and strain, was heavy, sometimes crippling. The work, the conditions, the wages, the hours, and the consequences are not much better now, although the victims are not Mexican but Guatemalan Indians.

The history of any kind of work may be clearest (if not full or most powerful) in short stories about it. The following stories below are from a remarkable collection of oral histories about migrant labor in Chiapas mostly from the late 1920s to the early '40s. Old Tzotzils recall their times in debt, on the road, and on the finca. (The stories about more recent times are "What Maruch Did . . .," about the 1950s, and "Words of a Woman . . .," about the 1970s.) All the stories originally appeared in print as they were told, in

Tzotzil, in a collection published in San Cristóbal in 1986. Tzotzils themselves then urged a bilingual edition, in Tzotzil and Spanish, so that other Indians and others not Indian could learn how migrant labor on the coffee plantations used to be. This is the edition from which the following selections come.

The editors and translators know their work, too. For an introduction to Jan Rus, see Reading No. 4. Diane Rus, like her husband, first went to Tzotzil country on the Harvard Chiapas Project between her junior and senior years of college in 1968. Later a graduate of the Harvard School of Education, in Los Altos for years at a time in the 1970s and 1980s, she has now accumulated her three decades of work with Tzotzils and of devotion to Tzotzil studies, from the outside and the inside, to understand the people of the highlands anthropologically, historically, sociologically, and biographically, to be with them in the telling of their stories, to make their stories lore and literature. She has collected, edited, and translated numerous Tzotzil stories for IN-AREMAC (see Reading No. 4). Her latest publication is a book, *Mujeres de tierra fría: Conversaciones con las coletas* (Tuxtla Gutiérrez: Universidad de Ciencias y Artes del Estado de Chiapas, 1997), on women in San Cristóbal.

José Hernández is a Tzotzil writer in the Tzotzil Workshop of INAREM-AC's Native Language Project.

Readers who appreciate the following stories may be happy to know that the editors and translators expect to publish soon an English version of the entire collection, in a scholarly series of works of "native literature."

ABTEL TA PINKA, TRABAJO EN LAS FINCAS*

. . . Talking About Labor Contractors.

In those times there were labor contractors in San Cristóbal—we call them "money-givers." People who needed a loan, even some 20 or 30 pesos, went to look for them. "OK, come such and such a day, such and such a time," they'd say. OK. He grabs the money and goes home. When the time comes, the contractor says, "So you're going to pay your debt, off you go." If you had a debt and didn't come, they were looking for you. Even here in Chamula they knew how to look for you in those days. The ladinos pursued us even out to the little hamlets on the paths where we lived. But once a ladino came, and people got together and they cut off his head and threw it in the river. End of problem. You didn't know in those days if the municipal president ran things here, or the owners of the fincas.

---

*(San Cristóbal: INAREMAC, 1990), pp. 5–37. Jan Rus, Diane Rus, José Hernández, eds. and trans. (Translation by John Womack, Jr., with help from Jan Rus.)

. . . Talking About the Contract

Well, before, the contractor didn't always tell the whole truth about the loan. "You, I already gave you so much," he'd say, though it wasn't true. Uh, poor Indian, what could he do, even though it wasn't so? Since there wasn't any union, he didn't have anywhere to complain.

Other contractors, liars, they'd say that the worker had taken advance money when it wasn't true. But in those days nobody said anything. Not a thing. The contractors would even hit us. That's how it was, that ugly. But poor Indians, nobody knew how to read or write, and we didn't know how to speak Spanish either. We just stood there looking at the ladinos.

. . . Story of the Labor Gang

When the gang got ready to leave, many men would get together and get drunk at the contractor's house. There they had to wait for their *compañeros*. [Literally "companions," but really "fellows" in the old sense, or "mates," as English workers used to say, nearly but not quite "comrades."] Sometimes they didn't come. Sometimes everybody came. There you had to wait for everybody before you left for the finca. Some left without any money. They knew their families had no money, that they were going to have to send a money order through the contractor. But the pay was very little then. You couldn't leave but five or ten pesos.

So many, many people were collected together. They'd be together in a cabin that was the finca's property in those days. There a lot of people would be sleeping. One night, two nights they'd sleep there. They'd get drunk, fight, people from many different municipalities. There were people from Tenejapa, Chenalhó, San Miguel, and other places. There was a gang boss, a kind of warden, let's say. He'd watch when people were getting drunk. He'd keep people from going out into the streets in San Cristóbal, and he kept close count of the workers, just like lambs, counted out. On the road to the finca, every night, every morning, he'd go through the list, if everybody was there or if somebody'd run off. If somebody escaped, well, he knew who it was. It wasn't possible to look for them on the way, because you didn't know where they'd gone to hide, since we were walking loose, on our own. Some got to the finca, and others stayed on the way. That's how it was in those days.

. . . About Pay

Well, on the finca they had to pay us every week. They'd ask us if we wanted to collect every week, or if we wanted to save. So we collected by the week three or four pesos, no more, because the pay was very poor. "OK, take this bit, and I'll keep this bit for you," the chief'd say. OK, if we kept the contract, he'd give us the rest of our money. But he discounted a lot. They discounted our expenses as each landlord pleased. They charged us for our meals every day, every day. So very little was left, maybe 20 or 30 pesos, at most 50 pesos a month. That's how it was when I was a boy.

. . . A Woman Tells of When Her Husband Went to the Finca

Before, I was very poor. I know well when my first husband had to go the finca. He was going from San Cristóbal, and I was going with him to see him off. We had to sleep there several nights, two or three at least, and people there got drunk a lot because the boss gave them money. They were going to the San Cristóbal and Hamburgo fincas. Lots, lots of people were going, who knows to how many fincas. But lots of people. So, when he got drunk in San Cristóbal, my first husband, he beat me up a lot! I almost died from getting hit so much. It was very ugly. When he went off to the finca, he got very mad. I went home, but with my face all swollen. (She cries.) All beaten up. Things were very bad. I went back all beaten up, but I still had to tend my sheep, sweep out the house, go cut firewood, work in the corn patch, harvest it—lots of things. If I got all this done, I spun, carded, weaved. So I was working a lot.

So he'd gone to the finca again. "I'm going to the finca," he used to say. "Go, then," I'd say. I was very happy when he'd leave, because there weren't any more beatings. He wouldn't give me food, he wouldn't give me corn, or beans, or meat. Just beatings. It was a very sad life I had with my husband who went to the finca.

. . . What Maruch Did When Her Husband Went to the Finca

After we got married, he went off to the finca four times. But I didn't know what finca. I was still a girl. "I'm going to the finca," he said. "Go," I said. "Here, I'll leave you a little money," he said. It was like 10 pesos. "OK," I said. "Think seriously about what you're going to buy," he said. "OK," I said.

So I went to the market and bought two bags of brown sugar. Two, no more. I went home. From there I went into the woods, and I put the sugar in a pot to make sugar beer. The next day I went back, boiled it, and that afternoon I already had *aguardiente* [rum]. OK, with the aguardiente I went to a farm manager's house here in Santa Ana, and I delivered the liquor to him. He paid me, and now I had 20 pesos. The next day I went on foot to San Cristóbal and bought four bags of brown sugar. I put it in the pot and cooked it. Then I had 40 pesos. I looked for firewood, I made sugar beer, and I cooked it. Just that. When my husband came back after like five weeks on the finca, he brought barely some 200 pesos. When he got here, he said, "Are you here?" "I'm here," I said. "Did you bring any money?" I said. "I brought some," he said. "Aaah, you brought some," I said. "How many pesos did you bring?" I said. "Not much," he said. "Some 200 pesos," he said. "But now I've got quite a bit of money," I said. "How much have you got?" he said. "I made aguardiente, and sold it to the farm manager," I said. "Aaah," he said. "So you've got a lot of money," he said. "I don't have that much money, it's a shame," he said. "It's not worth the trouble going to the finca," he said. And he didn't go again.

. . . How I Went to the Finca When I Was a Boy

When I was little, like eight years old, I went for the first time to the finca. We went to cut fodder with other boys, but even real little boys. We had machetes, but mine had no edge, and since the grass was very tough, I didn't cut anything. So I went back to the galley [the migrant dormitory]. There I stayed just playing around. When my papa came back from the coffee groves, he gave me a whipping, he punished me hard, and I had to stand it. Well, I went on growing up, growing up, spending five or six months at a time on the finca. We'd go, we'd come back, until I'd grown up; then my spirit was strong. I now knew how to work: to pick coffee, box it, plant the little trees—everything you do on a finca. My father didn't hit me anymore, because I'd learned how to work. And so that stopped.

So, then, I'd go, and come back. I almost grew up on the Santa Anita finca, down from Hamburgo. I went some 10 years there. We'd make the season, staying half a year, or eight or even nine months there. We stayed a long time every time. And so I got to be a man. Already I was working in the patio [where the coffee beans are spread out to dry]. I was grown then and had the strength to lift the coffee bags. There I made my first money . . .

. . . About Work on the Fincas

Well, there were various kinds of work, each one different. Some people worked by the task. If they were strong and worked well, it was possible to finish even two tasks in a day. But many didn't finish even one task. In those days they paid $1.50 [pesos] a task for chopping out the weeds and grass, a task being 20 square *brasadas* [*brazadas*, c. 120 sq. ft.]. But it was very hard to finish a task, and often you couldn't do it. If you got an easy task, let's say just big-leafed weeds, you could do one or two. But others, they'd get nothing but rock and grass, and it was hard to walk, much less finish the task.

The work was far from the galley too, sometimes a walk of an hour or two. Other times it was close. But we always went out early, when the sun was just rising. That way you could finish the task.

. . . On the Galleys

The galley was our house on the finca. It had a plain board door. Inside, there were just beds, like shelves, sometimes two or three one on top of the other.

Lots of people slept there, somebody for each bed. So there was really lots of noise at night Sometimes till eight or nine at night there was noise from so many people talking. They'd tell jokes, laugh. They were happy to be together.

. . . About the Cooks

Work on the finca was hard, and worse than that was the work of making the tortillas, corn gruel, coffee. There were always three or four cooks, all men. There was a corn grinder, a tortilla maker, somebody in charge of beans, and somebody in charge of coffee. They had to get up at midnight, and the beans they had to get started before they went to bed. Well, when breakfast was ready, they'd sound a horn to wake people up. When the horn blew, everybody brought his little pot for coffee and his plate for beans, and he'd put his tortillas in his little food sack. So we'd take the food to the galley like at four in the morning. Others would put their meal just in their food sacks to take it to the coffee groves. We'd eat there later, like at eight or nine in the morning . . .

. . . Talk About the Gang Boss

The gang boss supervised when the people were out in the coffee grove. He gave the orders, and would check if the work was done right or not. "It's badly done here, it's no good, do it right," he'd say. But there were people who didn't learn, or who didn't do what the boss wanted, and then the bosses would even hit them. But there were no authorities on the finca, and there was nowhere to complain about bad treatment. So sometimes there were men who wouldn't stand for getting hit, and then the fight would start. They'd look for compañeros from their same village, and sometimes they'd leave the boss almost dead from the beating. The gang boss couldn't complain either, because as I said there was no authority or law on the finca. He couldn't complain to the owner, because the owner came just to see the coffee grove from the road. He left authority in the hands of his gang bosses and the manager . . .

. . . Story of Robbers on the Road

When we returned from the fincas, there were always robberies on the road. The thing is, the thieves knew that as we'd been a long time on the finca, we'd be carrying money. Nothing ever happened to me, but my deceased papa said that once when he was returning from the finca, four ladinos with machetes tried to rob him and his compañeros. As it was an eight-day walk, it was easy to rob people between villages. "Put down your bundles so we can see what you're carrying," the thieves said. OK, but my papa didn't come by himself. He had three friends with him. They put their things down, but also took out their machetes. As some of them were carrying wild tobacco in a little pot, but ground up, dust, they took it out and blew it in the thieves' eyes. These guys started shaking and were all covered in snot. Then, "boom," said a rifle, and they left three thieves dead there on the mountain. One managed to escape. Three stayed, thrown off to the side of the road. So they didn't get robbed; they didn't lose a thing. At least that's how my deceased papa used to tell it.

That's how it always goes with the ladinos. They always want to go against the Indians. Sometimes they put us in jail. Sometimes they don't pay us what they owe us, or don't pay it all. Always enmity. They never want to treat us with justice, they always get mad, always hit us. But they make a lot of money with us. Who knows how much money they make? But they live well. But they live well.

. . . When the Union Came

When there was no union, there was nowhere to complain. The labor contractors used to give orders according to their own whims. Just on their own they'd decide how much they were going to give us, how they were going to make up their gangs. But when the union came, the law came. Then even the landlords began to respect us a little more. Then we began to feel a little more human. The food on the finca got better, the work got better. That's because the deceased Erasto [Erasto Urbina, organizer around San Cristóbal for the Indian Workers Union, 1936; first director of the State Department of Rural Education and Indian Incorporation, 1937; later state legislator and municipal president of San Cristóbal] was giving the orders. Don Erasto went out to see the fincas, and left word to improve the food, not to leave us hungry, that the task be more fair. He said how many hours we could work; it couldn't be "that's just how it is," as the landlord pleased. "Eight hours of labor," Don Erasto said. When there was no union, we used to work a lot more. The landlords before would give us what they wanted: more work, every task much bigger. Also, before, the labor contractors would hit us, and even the owners of the fincas would hit us—even give us a kicking. But after the union, everything on the finca got better. I worked two years in the union, watching that the contractors paid the advances fair and square. The landlords had to come with the contracted workers to the union.

. . . Words of a Woman Who Worked on a Finca

I went to the finca a time ago, when my son was very little. Now he's 15. I was living alone—my husband went away with another woman and abandoned me. I suffered a lot living alone. I had no corn. So I went to the Catarina finca for eight weeks. I asked for the job in San Cristóbal, from a labor contractor named Manuel. And I went. There on the finca I got up very early to prepare my breakfast, because I had to take care of myself on my own. It wasn't dawn yet when I'd go out to pick coffee. I'd take my basket well tied up. When I went to the finca, I had to walk a long way after the bus let me off. But I hurried right along. The road wasn't any good either—nothing but pedregal [sharp, broken rock], bad.

By main force I had to finish a task a day, because I wanted to work like a man. I had a wooden hook to pull down the coffee. We had to work like men because the work was measured by tasks. There wasn't any truck; we used a tumpline to carry the sacks. Sometimes it took me till four or five in the afternoon to fill my sack. I suffered a lot. When my son cried, I had the basket all tied up, and still I'd give my baby the breast, first one side and then the other. The men'd finish their tasks earlier because they didn't have distractions.

Every week they gave us our meat, and we bought the tortillas. Sometimes we ate palm root instead of corn—we'd look for it when we got back from picking. "If you feed yourselves," the boss said, "I'm going to pay you more." So I decided it was better to support myself. Well, we had to buy corn and beans. So when I got back from picking late, I still had to prepare my meal and make tortillas.

The boss gave me a room apart; the men had rooms in another place. So I felt very lonely on the finca. I had no company, and I was very sad. Almost all the others were from other villages, besides the fact that they were men. It made me ashamed to be the only woman.

When I finished the contract, I had the same problem as when I got there. I had to walk a long way, and my feet hurt a lot. I had to run to catch the bus in Arriaga. In two days I got back here again.

So I got to San Cristóbal about five in the morning, after traveling all night. I got off near Don Manuel's house. He'd ordered my money in a money order, so they didn't pay me on the finca. I had to go to Don Manuel's house to get my money.

"Did you do the work well?" he asked me when I got there. "Well, yes," I said. "Aaah, good," he said. "Did it go all right with your son?" he said. "Well, it seems so," I said. That's how it was. I got to San Cristóbal at five, and afterward he gave me a coffee. "Want some more coffee?" he said. "Well, yes, give me a little more," I told him. So I drank the coffee that Don Manuel gave me. The pay I collected bought me some carding combs and a blouse sewed by machine. I was making 50 pesos a week [four dollars at the time]; the wage was very little. Now they have to pay more.

The Church's New Mission in a De-Christianized Continent: Bishop Ruiz in Medellín, 1968

The first General Conference of Latin American Bishops had met in the Vatican in 1899, for Pope Leo XIII to remind the bishops what he had said in *Rerum Novarum* (1891). Since these bishops had so far done next to nothing in response to his encyclical, and the United States had just taken Catholic Spain's islands in the Caribbean (and looked as if it would not stop there), he clarified their new social duties to them. Most of them went home and went to work, eventually developing substantial movements of Catholic Action (which in time, in some countries, turned into Christian Democracy).

Two generations later and in a very different world, the Latin American bishops rallied enthusiastically in Medellín, Colombia. Inspired, most of them, by their experiences of Vatican II, they designed scores of social and religious programs for the Church to regain at least its moral authority in potentially and often actually revolutionary circumstances. Speaking on "evangelization," Bishop Ruiz modestly disclaimed any originality, but went on to deliver a particularly concrete, perceptive, and powerful call for new kinds of missionary organization and action on the geographic and social margins of modern Latin American society. The following is a selection from his address to the conference.

EVANGELIZATION IN LATIN AMERICA*

. . . Without fear of exaggeration it can be stated that the primary task of the Latin American Church is to evangelize . . .

---

*Samuel Ruiz García, in *The Church in the Present-Day Transformation of Latin America in the Light of the Council, Second General Conference of Latin American Bishops*, 2 vols. (Bogotá: General Secretariat of CELAM, 1970), I, pp. 155–177.

Undoubtedly, the sixteenth century had an evangelizing force which left a long-lasting mark on our continent. Our religious ways have their roots in the method of preaching, the style of catechesis, and content of the message then presented.

Despite all its defects, that first evangelization of our continent *did have a kerygma* [emphasis in original, here and below] which led to conversion and to union with Christ. It held that idols were evil, that Christ—Lord of heaven and earth—suffered and died on the cross to save us, that sacred scriptures were the word of God and gave us life, that Christ—God and man through whom we are saved—wanted to incorporate us into His Kingdom without end.

Furthermore, although evangelization because of its historic conditioning opted to break with everything pagan, occasional examples are *to be found of concern for the Indian culture and religion*.

However, this interest was not widespread, and though the Indian language was used to communicate the religious message, this was frequently the work of Indian translators who were forced to learn the new religious ideas without relating them to their own religious concepts. By the seventeenth century the evangelizing crusade could be said to be over. The baptized dedicated themselves to moralistic instruction by rote. To this we add the fact that these baptized people perhaps realized the obvious advantages of incorporation into civil society by reason of social and economic privileges accorded Indians and mestizos; that catechesis was merely a method of instruction that offered isolated doctrinal points which at best were memorized, etc. No one can accuse us of exaggerating when we conclude that generally speaking, *evangelization in Latin America was incomplete* . . .

Our pastoral on the Word of God in Latin America presupposes that we are in a continent where the majority are baptized. We assume that adequate catechetical instruction will automatically help the baptized attain a mature faith . . . with the exception of places which are juridically considered mission territory and those which enjoy a keen awareness of the Church as not yet completely established . . . the Church does not evangelize, but rather catechises, and this catechesis is far from ideal. It is a catechesis without kerygma which runs the risk of being little more than mere religious instruction and which does not truly penetrate the heart of the faithful . . .

For this reason a large number of baptized persons do not attain a conscious and matured faith, and though they receive the sacraments, it is debatable whether they consider them signs of faith or mere rites. Because of this infantile catechesis, many Catholics (and I include, perhaps to the astonishment of many here today, religious [members of orders, e.g., Dominicans] and priests) go through life without being truly converted to the Gospel, without a personal encounter and commitment with Jesus the Savior. A weak faith is incapable of enlightening new problems confronting the adult man. This leads to a schizophrenic life where the religious and the everyday life of a person not only do not coincide, but often collide . . .

The lack of evangelization . . . engenders . . . a "substitute religion" on the one hand that is converted into an atheism increasingly characteristic of the Latin American leader, and on the other, a Christianity of the masses, which is ritualistic and associated with natural religion. In this type of Christianity we find a providential God, a God who acts alongside natural forces; or else contact with God is exclusively through rites based on objects, not attitudes. Thus there is no contact with internal feelings either before or after the particular rite.

. . . *Several questions about evangelization suggest themselves*. Should we dedicate ourselves to actively evangelize the illiterate syncretist, lover of rites and processions? Or should we concentrate on the increasing number of unbelievers and work out a way of presenting the Word of God in secularized form for a secularized man? Do we need two types of evangelists? If popular religion is transitory, is it without value and should we let it perish without compassion or tears?

. . . What is happening in Latin America? Do we need a heart transplant for a continent in need of evangelical charity? Or should we prepare ourselves to Christianize a new culture whose imminent birth manifests itself in crisis, tensions, in the pain of violence which our continent experiencies?

. . . *The rise of a predominantly urban-industrial society* . . . produces a more radical change on those who migrate from the countryside to the large cities. On the regional level it produces an imbalance between urban and rural development, and modifies the social and economic structures; on the urban level the haphazard growth of certain areas, the long distances to work and social contacts produce anonymity, depersonalization, standardization of the individual, the reorganization of his life under new values and a new environment. All of these produce a clash of conflicts among emigrants to the cities.

. . . *From this comes a pluralism* where unanimity no longer reigns. Ways of thinking are diversified, moral criteria are no longer Christian; political ideologies—that at times replace religion in Latin America—exert an absorbing influence. In any case, Christianity becomes merely one way of living and thinking. Therefore those who claim to be Christians only by cultural motivation, or social pressure or habit are in a state of crisis. They cannot resist these multiple influences, and fall into practical atheism . . .

. . . *A culture of the masses* is emerging which implies new social relationships, new types of personalities, new measures for value judgments, etc. One particular element in this culture is mass media of communication, for it strongly influences the formation of the popular mind.

. . . There is also a *crisis in religion* (desacralization). The man of this industrialized society is urbanized, technologized; he is a man who trusts increasingly in himself, in organization, in technology . . . Society is "desacralized," that is, it is independent of religious expressions. Desacralization carries with it (except in nontechnologized and nonurbanized areas) the decline of religion, of the Christian ritual practices, and even the extinction of the faith.

. . . Development, that is, the temporal conditions that free and promote growth of the human person, can materialize and dehumanize as well as liberate and increase awareness. To see that development not only effects well-being and culture, but also that it humanizes, frees, and perfects, is the task to which Christians should feel committed, for this prepares them for a better understanding of the Gospel, which itself is liberating and humanizing. It is a great challenge for Christians who need to live a religion that frees and perfects, and not an alienating, obscurantist religiosity that disappears as soon as development occurs . . .

. . . The *imperialism of the nonterritorial milieu* is one of the most important consequences of these changes and should be carefully taken into account in present-day evangelization. The "milieu," that group of values, ideas, and models which influences well-defined areas—work, professional life, amusements, mass media, intellectual and cultural media—unconsciously forms mentalities, imposing criteria and ways of action more or less blind according to the maturity of the persons involved. In past societies, a person was exposed almost exclusively to the influences of his particular area; his town was his place of work, where his family, his parish, and his amusements were found. To influence this territory was tantamount to influencing the whole person. Today, the home in the urban society is a secondary place, and public opinion, the office, the club, the means of communication all carry much greater weight than the family or parish. Therefore, the task of evangelization should not be directed only at the individual person, but at the milieu . . .

. . . As a result of changes in Latin America, we are realizing the urgency of a new type of pastoral action relevant to each situation, and of studying just what the focus of evangelization should be.

. . . We can point out the following missionary situations:

1st area): Where there are no indications of Christian life, because *the Church is not present* or really established (non-Christian religions, syncretism, de-Christianization, marginal indigenous communities, black syncretist groups practicing Voodoo, Candomblé, or Umbanda, marginal urban masses and intellectual minorities led by non-Christian ideologies which are rapidly gaining in influence and importance).

2nd area): Where there is Christian initiation and some religious practice, but a weak presentation of the Gospel. In other words, where there is an ambiguous Christianity resulting *from poorly established Churches.* (In this area we find many indigenous comunities, rural or mining zones, and some Mestizo towns.)

3rd area): Finally, ecclesiastical communities with some local apostles and fervent practicing Christian cells, but where because *Christians are in the minority and the pastoral structure is weak*, they are considered as mission territory.

. . . Special consideration should be given to the Indians on the Latin American continent. There are 30 million of them, a considerable number by any standard, and they are still socially, politically, economically, and most important of all, *pastorally marginal*, with the exception of a few who are cared for by a truly missionary action. In the majority of cases, religious attention is focused on white and mixed groups.

Symptoms of the problem. The right of an Indian to receive the message in his own tongue is not always recognized, much less the right to receive it in his own mentality and thought patterns. Oral communication involves only language, mental and cultural communication is quite another thing.

The evangelical message is generally transmitted through translations of pre-conciliar [pre-Vatican II] texts. There are as yet no plans on the diocesan or national level resulting from a serious study of the indigenous cultures.

These are rather improvised, "Latin American style." There does not exist a responsible organization, enjoying collective and effective solidarity, which would seek in each country the solution to the problem of the total integration of the Indian. It is generally unknown of what that integration should consist, and it is commonly assumed to mean the death of their cultures.

It is believed that the mere increase in personnel and educational institutions will solve the problem. Or we go to the other extreme and promote a charitable and welfare-type assistance which does not take into consideration marginality and underdevelopment, and which does not see the necessity of basing this help on Indian values, cultures, and ways of thinking.

The prevailing opinion in Episcopal [Catholic bishops'] Conferences seems to be the following: The Indian problem is not the most urgent one, and therefore not the most important. We would like to strongly state that in our pastoral action we must distinguish between *what is urgent and what is transcendental* although less urgent. If not, time will continue to accumulate on this shameful problem, which could well be characterized as the methodological failure of the evangelizing action of the Church in Latin America.

. . . The great danger for the Latin American Church is not Communism or secularization. The problem lies in continuing to be bound to outdated ways of life and action. . . . All these structures, although created by the Church, must now be transformed by her so that they can function as a light among the nations and evangelical leaven of the masses . . .

As an almost inevitable result of . . . de-Christianizing changes—

evangelization which was formerly incomplete and now is inexistent, new mission areas of great scope—we realize the urgency for Latin America to be declared missionary territory with a program for in-depth evangelizing work. Missionary activities of the Church are not limited to legally recognized "mission countries." The Church's missionary activity flows from her nature based on the designs of God, on the redeeming work of the Son, and the enlightening action of the Holy Spirit. This missionary action should take on different nuances according to the degree of implantation, that is to say, of adherence to Christ. We need a far-reaching Church in open dialogue with the world.

. . . Especially in Latin America it is basic for us to distinguish between the ministry of evangelization and that of catechesis in the prophetic mission of the Church. Faith, in fact, has two aspects: *an effective one* of conversion, humble union with God and his plan of salvation, of change of heart, thinking, and acting. The second aspect is of *knowledge*, enlightenment of the spirit. *It is the function of evangelization* or kerygma to proclaim the essence of the message, the main points of the history of salvation, in order to convert. *The function of catechesis* is to reveal the meaning of these incidents, to study them. In catechetics, faith in Christ is the starting point; in evangelization, faith is the goal. These two aspects of the ministry of the word exist and are necessarily present in the living faith, but they are distinct. If faith saves, it is due to its aspects of conversion. Faith cannot be static. Because of its personal dynamism it must constantly be relating to the saving action of God. On the other hand, the process of conversion never ends for a Christian. Kerygma is not like a doorway which leads to the nave of catechetics; rather, it is the crypt that supports the nave and must continually be reinforced.

. . . If the task of the primitive Church was to *baptize the converted*, our task today is to convert the baptized. For a long time now, perhaps, we have given the impression of having forgotten that Baptism in the case of an infant gives the *habit of faith* (in simplistic language, the potential and motion to make an act of faith); but it does not give the act of faith itself, which is something that the individual person must make with the help of grace. *The faith of the convert* is not reduced to following the dogmatic truths revealed and proposed by the Church, a kind of endorsement of the creed; it is a change of life, of mentality, an event which embraces all of his being, a personal encounter with Christ. But the faith of the convert—"encounter of persons"—is not distinct from another faith which could be described as "to hold as true"; it is the same faith which from the beginning of conversion is led by God Himself in a further stage to the deepening of the various aspects of its mystery, to a life of faith. Thus, we can see that pastoral implementation of the prophetic ministry ought to be the same for converted adults and for baptized children, when they reach psychological maturity.

. . . It is necessary not to take for granted, but to make certain of a conversion after the preaching of the kerygma, as an indispensable prerequisite for catechesis. It is impossible to catechise before converting, just as it is impossible to grow without first having been born.

The stages which normally mark the passage to adult faith are: *pre-evangelization*, which takes man where he is and awakens in him a sense of God; *evangelization*, or kerygma, the dynamic proclamation of the essence of the Christian message; and *catechesis* proper, which systematically develops the message, building on the conversion achieved by the former stages . . .

The Church nowadays faces an unbelieving world, where the means normally employed are ineffective. Everything is demanding that the Church adopt a method of evangelization, of pure kerygma, of prophetic ministry, exercised as it was in apostolic times; that it be a word directed in such a way so as to elicit a complete and personal response. But before man can respond, he must be aware that he has been spoken to. And here exactly is where the problem lies: the *apostles* preached the good news to the Jews and not to religious pagans of the time; *we* have to face a world which is becoming more irreligious every day, materialistic, pagan, secularized . . . In the present world, God barely has a place. Authority does not come from Him; rights are not based upon religious principles; the Church is considered a "sub-cultural" society which defends its privileged position in places where underdevelopment still endures it.

. . . Before proclaiming the Gospel, it is necessary to prepare souls to receive, to desire it . . . That preparation whereby the kerygma acquires meaning in this milieu . . . is called pre-evangelization.

Pre-evangelization is not conducted *a priori*; it presupposes an objective study of the non-believer, his psychology, his milieu, his culture, his religious ideas . . .

It goes without saying that the attitude of the pre-evangelizer should be supported by the living testimony of the Christian community. If the principal "sign" which accompanies pre-evangelization and kerygma continues to be the Resurrection of Jesus Christ, the promise of Christ, our own current situation, so similar to that of the primitive Church, leads us to hope that in this kerygmatic springtime we will find other "signs" such as those which were a part of the apostolic teaching.

As pastors, we must not continue to belong to a kind of "Church of Silence" faced with today's ocurrences. "Speak, preach, write, take stands," said the Roman Pontiff, on the dramas of contemporary civilization be they great and beautiful, or sad and dangerous. Our word should be evangelical, sincere, joyful, sure, merciful, adaptable.

The Christian community and apostolic groups in formation should speak the language of the two "signs" which the Lord left by which His Church would be known and recognized: *Charity* and *unity*, and all they imply in the present Latin American reality.

We should excuse, on the other hand, the numerous "counter-signs" which are insurmountable obstacles to evangelization. We cannot evangelize the poor if we are a power elite. The weak and oppressed will alienate themselves from Christ if we appear to be allied with the powerful; we cannot evangelize the ignorant if our religious institutions continue seeking the comforts of large cities, and ignore the small towns and suburbs. [My translation of this passage—in my introductory essay—is a little different, in some places more literal, in others more interpretive.] The gospel will not shine in its splendor if those responsible for local Churches appear to be reticent to adopt new attitudes demanded by Vatican II.

We must find new forms of presence, new means of evangelization, and make better use of existing resources. We must evaluate popular religiosity, purify it, and convert it into a "sign" and evangelizing instrument; we must make evangelization the goal of Catholic school education; we must give an evangelizing dimension to those shrines which attract pilgrims; we must enlist the help of the omnipresent mass media; we must elaborate the theology and meaning of poverty in developing nations.

. . . We must change our view of the Church as being either out of the world or against it. The Church is the people of God committed through history. The Church is in the world, not next to it, or competing against it, but within it in an attitude of service. The mission of the Church is a new type of divine presence in human history.

. . . The existence of vast indigenous areas in Latin America is an anti-sign as well as a task and a hope.

It is an *"anti-sign"* because though centuries of Christianity have elapsed in our continent, the Indian problem—at times exploited under the guise of folklore—has yet to be solved. Either their cultures are destroyed or their communities disintegrated; they either lose their cultural values or keep true values which are not imbued with the Christian spirit. It is an anti-sign because before our unaware or helpless eyes, religiosity coexists alongside underdevelopment and marginality on all levels. It is an anti-sign because their religious syncretism indicates a lack of incarnation and accentuates the image many people have of a Church which favors underdevelopment and is disinterested in human advancement. It is an anti-sign finally because this image is opposed to the testimony of charity of a community which does not know how to mobilize its resouces and members in relation to its needs.

The existence of these Indian communities is a ray of hope because they provide the occasion for the formation of a kerygma in ecumenical cooperation with our separated brethren who have concentrated their missionary work in these marginal areas. It is a hope for a joint Latin American pastoral plan, which is more easily attainable here because the areas are not as large as the entire continent and because they have a common denominator despite the tremendous variations (there is more of a psychological closeness among

Indians in Mexico, Ecuador, or Peru than there is between us and any one aboriginal group); it is a hope for the discovery of the true road evangelization shoud take in other rural areas in Latin America. Finally it is a hope which shines in the horizon with the possibility of enriching both culture and religion, and which could be viewed as an example of the contribution Latin America is destined to make to the rest of the world in this field . . .

CHAPTER NINE

Exodus in Chiapas:
The Tzeltal Catechism of
Liberation, Ocosingo, 1972

In the Roman Catholic Church catechists are the faithful who teach the
Church's doctrine to the baptised in need of it for salvation. If they can read,
they usually teach it from a catechism, a manual of its rudiments; if not, they
teach it from memory, by heart. *Ex officio* they have been missionaries, diocesan religious, that is, bishops, priests, and associates under vows, and faithful
parents and godparents; *voluntate*, parochially, they have been pious laity. The
Church in Chiapas has never had enough of them. In 1905, in his encyclical
Acerbo nimis against "the present religious crisis," Pope Pius X prescribed
throughout the Catholic world an extensive, rigorous, detailed program of
catechesis, including in every parish canonically mandated Confraternities of
Christian Doctrine, to give religious instruction to "adults no less than the
young." Forty-five years later not a single regular missionary served in Chiapas. For some 900,000 souls in 40 parishes there, the bishop had only 30 priests,
46 sisters, and maybe 60 Confraternity venues. Of the priests, all of them in the
diocese's few cities and towns, the most dutiful would sometimes visit outlying villages, fincas, hamlets, even distant migrant camps, but only to perform
baptisms and marriages. The sisters and trusty Confraternitarians taught catechism in the cities and towns on Sundays and feast days. Their manual, in
Spanish, dating from 1591, was for teaching the Credo, the Our Father, Ave
Maria, and Salve Regina, the Ten Commandments, the seven Sacraments, the
fourteen works of mercy, the seven mortal sins, the three theological virtues,
and so on. Out in the country not one parent or godparent in 500 knew enough
to teach the children, and the Confraternities were *nullae*. By Vatican standards Chiapas was still in the Dark Ages.

In 1952 Pope Pius XII, the first pope to speak of "Catholic social doctrine,"
launched a major new offensive against communism. Decrying "the total cri-

sis that agitates the world, . . . a general condition that We do not hesitate to call explosive," he urged the faithful everywhere to hear the Apostolic alarm: "The hour has now come for us to rise from sleep" (Rom. 13:11). He warned, "It is an entire world that must be remade from its foundations, that must be transformed from savage to human, from human to divine. . . ." He stood himself as "the herald of a better world, willed by God," and charged the faithful everywhere "to start a powerful revival of thought and action, a revival in which you are all commited, without evasion of any kind, the clergy and the people, the authorities, families, groups, every single soul, on the front line of the total renovation of Christian life, in defense of moral values, in the realization of social justice, in the reconstruction of the Christian order. . . ."

So began the Movement for a Better World, postwar Catholicism's most attractive and important international social movement before Vatican II. Its organizer was a phenomenal Italian Jesuit, Riccardo Lombardi. Editor of Italy's main Catholic political journal, author of ten books on atheism, Marxism, and Catholic "mobilization," he was Pius's favorite public intellectual. While priestly scholars who questioned the Church's social theory and practice, (e.g., Hans Küng, the Dominican Yves Congar, the Jesuits Henri de Lubac and Karl Rahner), languished nearly in disgrace, Lombardi had brilliantly justified, elaborated, and popularized the then orthodox social gospel. And he was probably the best Catholic preacher of his time. Leading his "Crusade of Kindness" in Italy, speaking for hours to crowds in the hundreds of thousands, he had gained a reputation as "God's microphone." Carrying the crusade through the rest of Western Europe, Latin America (including León, Guanajuato, in 1951), the United States, and Canada, exciting Catholic masses everywhere, he became "the Catholic Billy Graham." Under his direction, with the pope's personal endorsement, the Movement for a Better World was soon training Catholic "officers" and "cadres," clergy and laity, to organize the excited masses and mobilize them in militant Catholic social action for its declared goal, "World Conquest for Jesus." Through the 1950s two cardinals, more than 250 archbishops and bishops, 1,200 religious superiors, 10,000 priests, 5,000 sisters, 15,000 of the laity emerged from the movement's retreats of prayer and study, on every continent, to lead, in all the dimensions and relations of their lives, in "mutual charity and unity," the formation of a Catholic "united front" to fight "the Crusade of the Twentieth Century . . . for a new world . . . the common good . . . the triumph of love . . . a Christian society . . . the new Jerusalem . . . the era of Jesus. . . . "

From one source or another funds eventually flowed to Mexico sufficient to establish the movement there in 1956. Soon, on such stimulation and support, Mexican bishops were contending more vigorously with communists and their then presumptive allies (equivalents?), Masons, Protestants, and Jews, in part by disbursements to parishes to pay laymen to promote the faith in previously ill-served localities. There formed then the movement's humblest practical result, "the institution of the catechists." In some parishes, for a pittance, selected "men of good will" in outlying villages began teaching the catechism (the same old manual) to their neighbors and the children, leading the community in singings of the missal hymns and sayings of the rosary, and admonishing the lapsed to revive their faith. Even in Chiapas this happened.

There too, in Chiapas in 1958, after 44 years of exile, the Jesuits returned institutionally. The bishop put their mission northeast of San Cristóbal, in the township of Chilón, in the Tzeltal village of Bachajón. On an trajectory different from Lombardi's, the brothers, all four of them, settled among the villagers not for a revival but to learn the language and make a permanent base.

For some 1,200,000 souls in Chiapas in 1960, still in only 40 parishes, this was the catechetical corps that Bishop Ruiz found—in his diocese's cities and towns 33 priests, 67 sisters, and maybe 150 pious laity in the Confraternities, out in the country (almost all in Los Altos) the four Jesuits, some 50 hired catechists, and no more than one in 500 parents and godparents, all still teaching by text or by heart the old story of subjection and supplication in this world, salvation in the next.

It was in the spirit of Catholic Action and the Movement for a Better World that the bishop started the schools for catechists in 1962. The courses that the Marist brothers, the Divine Pastor sisters, the Jesuits, and after 1963 the Dominicans devotedly taught their young Indian students, in the Bible, the catechism, and vocations, were in Spanish, doctrinaire, authoritarian, and on the local premises of Indian inferiority. And they achieved their purposes, explicit and unconscious. Successful graduates taught the same Word of God from the same texts back in their communities, in their own languages, but in the same authoritarian mode, denounced *costumbres malas* (boozing, feuding, witching), opened shops, bought cattle, farmed and ranched better, and by judging who of their neighbors had learned the catechism came to determine whose children could be baptised, who could be married, who could stand as godparents; that is, as militant catechists, they gained a locally new and divisive power. The courses were not for students who continued to think in their own languages, in which "teaching" and "learning" were the same word, "to say" was the same as "to do," and there was no word for "commandment," there being no word for "command." They were not for students who wondered if God could speak only castilla, or why Jesus was both ladino and Indian, or what happened in the Church to the special souls, the visions, tigers, miracles, owls, monsters, companions, that God gave principales so that they could right wrongs, or how from suffering not healed in this world could come peace and harmony in the next. Such students were therefore not successful, and sooner or later went home in confusion, anger, disgust. As it developed in Los Altos from 1962 to 1965, this first catechetical movement strengthened the orthodox, paternalistic, racist, triumphally Western faith in the highlands and the canyons, but caused new conflicts in the catechised communities.

The Movement for a Better World, its derivatives, and its imitations, however enthusiastic, however powerful, began to sink in the tremendous upheaval of Vatican II. Already during and between the council's sessions many bishops, priests, brothers, and sisters in various parts of the world started a different kind of Catholic action, catholic, heterodox, empathetic, egalitarian, and liberating movements for the poor. In Chiapas, even while the first catechetical movement proceeded, the bishop and his religious, worried over its results, began to question its prejudices and in light of the council's debates to reform its methods and mission. Among the changes was a new concern for language, no longer merely a means of practical communication, but a liturgical, evangelical, and catechetical necessity. (See Reading No. 8) For "incarnation" and "inculturation" of God's Word, the experts in Rome were insisting, it was crucial to learn and teach in the language of the people. In 1964 the Jesuits in Bachajón organized a team of Tzeltal catechists (fluent in Spanish) to begin the first Catholic translation of the Bible into Tzeltal. As soon as the council published the new liturgy in 1965, in Latin, the Jesuits translated it into Tzeltal, before it appeared in Spanish.

The council's constitutions, decrees, and declarations gave direction and form then to Bishop Ruiz's massive expansion of his diocese's catechical program, practically a new catechical movement. The Latin American Bishops Conference meeting in Medellín in 1968 gave the movement marching orders against poverty and for liberation. But the diocese's religious and its hundreds of new catechists were still using the old catechism, implicitly teaching despite themselves that this world, especially for the poor, would never be more than "this valley of tears."

In 1970, in line with the council's Declaration on Christian Education, the bishop decided to require "baptismal catechesis" of his flock. Lay catechists out in the country then came under religious obligation to teach intending unbaptized adults and baptized but lapsed parents and godparents of unbaptized babies in their communities, which in effect gave them religious authority to determine whom the priest on his rounds there could baptize. As they duly used their new authority, they provoked serious protests in their communities, even threats of violence. On the council's warrant the bishop and his religious considered authorizing "the community" to conduct the catechesis and decide admissions to the sacrament. But the communities would not take the responsibility. They could not, they made clear, because they had no part in the catechism. And many catechists could not understand why they should lose their authority. Like most other conflicts in Chiapas, the disputes over eligibility for salvation were worst in the canyons.

The Dominican missionary parish of Ocosingo, the catechetical center for the canyons, had by then developed a remarkable team of talented organizers, teachers, and social workers. Under the American Dominican Vincent Foerstler, it included the Mexican Marist Javier Vargas (newly arrived from ten years work at the Marist mission in San Cristóbal), an American Maryknoll sister, an American sister of the Presentation, and two lay Colombians recruited at Medellín. In 1971 they ran special courses in Ocosingo in which missionaries and catechists together discussed how to organize a new "communitarian catechesis, not only with the community physically present, but also with it having its say." Whether or not the catechists understood "inculturation," they promptly grasped their new role, not (like little Lombardis) to transmit God's Word from the catechism to their neighbors, but to gather the Word from the communities and spread It there. So began a third and very different catechetical movement—to engage the communities in the discovery of God in them and for them.

In 1972 the Ocosingo team went down to work with the Tzeltal catechists in the Selva. It was there, suffering hopefully the hardships the highland refugees suffered in their remote, struggling, but still hopeful canyon communities, colonies, and pioneer camps, thinking on the new Jesuit translation of the Bible's second book into Tzeltal, that Vargas called their struggle Exodus. In retrospect this may seem an easy insight, but at the time it was a brilliant stroke, for it canceled the old catechism and gave the new movement its own organizing vision, spirit, and theme. In periodic meetings with the missionaries the canyon catechists would discuss which Biblical chapters of oppression and liberation they should bring into the settlements to evoke God's Word. In the settlements' classes on the Word the faithful would reflect on the Biblical stories, tell their own stories of their struggles together, and find the Word in them. The catechists would take these stories back to their meetings, discuss them, fit them into "Exodus," and bring a more engaging and suggestive story back into the settlements to evoke more of God's Word. (Oddly, because the missionaries could not entirely purge themselves of Lombardi's language, or because the catechists and their faithful drew the words from their own experience, or both, the stories often prescribed attitudes and action for "a better life, a better community, a better world.") Before long the catechists were gathering and spreading not only the Word of God but also the word of God's people. This was how they stopped being teachers and became (in Tzeltal) *jtijwanejetik*, drivers, conductors, instrumentalists, movers, stirrers of the communities, colonies, and camps, which was how they served in organizing the great Indian Congress in San Cristóbal in 1974.

Their new work was also the origin of the Tzeltal catechism. At the first periodic meetings the missionaries would tape the catechists' discussion and write a synthesis for them, for their reflection and use in the settlements. Soon the catechists began writing their own syntheses, which they had printed in Tzeltal as "lessons." These they collected for their classes, and eventually recognized as a new catechism. In their new mode they would not teach it, they said, only use it to "talk" (which they did not consider teaching) of "what the communities had taught themselves in the light of the faith. . . . the faith of the people, who, in reflecting on their faith, turned more into the community of the Lord." For example, they would talk of "what we learned" about "cultural oppression" (one of the following excerpts). Even so they tried to compose the catechism's last section in the old terms of Faith, Hope, and Charity. They did Faith, (excerpted here) and they did Hope. But they decided not to do Charity. Of Faith and Hope, they said, you could talk, but Charity you did not talk, you had to live. They would write the last chapter in their lives, they said, and it would end in the Kingdom come, where Faith and Hope are fulfilled and Charity abides.

The text by 1974 the missionaries translated into Spanish under the title "We Are Looking for Freedom: The Tzeltals of the Selva Announce the Good News." It was not for catechizing elsewhere, they explained, because "life is unique and unrepeatable," but only to show other communities how to search for freedom. Evidently it received such use. Much of its language, substance, and spirit reappeared generally in the Indian grievances and demands in the Indian Congress later that year—and in the Qu'iptik union ("our effort to do better") in 1975.

The reference to "guerrillas and soldiers" on the text's penultimate page may be to the first force the FLN had in the Selva, in 1972–74, and the army units that destroyed it. There is no hint of foreboding that 20 years later some veteran catechists would be officers in the FLN's reincarnation.

ESTAMOS BUSCANDO LA LIBERTAD:
LOS TZELTALES DE LA SELVA ANUNCIAN
LA BUENA NUEVA*

. . . Part II. How We Live in Oppression

. . . CHAPTER IV. CULTURAL OPPRESSION

Third Lesson

Prayer: Lord, here we are united in Your name.
We give You thanks for all that we are and have.
Lord, help us to grow every day more.
Help us to form truly a community in which we realize how valuable we are.

---

*Misión de Ocosingo-Altamirano (Ocosingo, 1972–74), pp. 43–52, 60–62, 76–81, 86–92, 117–118. (Translation by John Womack, Jr., with help from Jan Rus.)

Song: I discovered one day
        That I am unique in the world,
        But that I need the others.
        Being on my own is of no use.
        Being on my own kills me.
        My true life
        Is to live with my brothers,
        They give me life
        And I do the same for them.
        Community is life.
        Community is life.
        It takes me to freedom.

Reading: Is It True That We Are No Longer Indians?

1. Brothers, what I am going to tell you here is what I said with brother Manuel, who no longer wants to be our Indian brother.

2. Last Sunday I was walking along, carrying my bag, headed for the colony to go to church with my community.

3. On the road I met Manuel, who lives on the farm on the other side of the river.

4. He was coming riding his horse, wearing his pants and his new shirt, his good hat and his fine shoes.

5. I said to him, Good morning, brother Manuel, how is your heart?

6. Hello, *indito* [little Indian], he answered me in castilla.

7. I said to him, Are you not Indian too? Maybe you are not Manuel, son of my Uncle Tomás, who is of our Indian race?

8. Yes, I am Manuel, and I am the owner of that farm on the other side of the river.

9. I am the owner of those cattle you see in the pasture. I am the owner of that land where the boys from the colonies go to make some money.

10. But I am not Indian like you, he told me. I do not know how to speak your language. My language is castilla.

11. Boy, do not say that my papa is your uncle. My family does not deal with Indians.

12. I answered him, yes, your father is my uncle. Your father did the same work in the corn patch and planting beans as all the men of my race do.

13. I told him, Some years ago your father also wore white cotton country clothes and sandals. Together my father and he took candles to the festival of San Tomás.

14. Then he laughed and said to me,

15. You stupid Indian, you are Catholic. That is why you are poor, you are

wasting your time. It is from going off to pray that you have no cattle, no farm, or animals, or money.

16. It is from going around praying that you do not know castilla and you speak your language that no one understands.

17. Better stop praying, get out of your colony that is so poor, and come to my farm to make some money. Become ladino and you will see how you make money.

18. Stop believing in God, because money is what is useful. Your God is of no use. God is money.

19. When I heard all this that Manuel was telling me, I felt angry and sad.

20. I told him that I did not want to work on his farm, I have a special duty in my colony, and I told him goodbye.

21. Along the road here I kept thinking about many things and I asked myself many questions like these:

22. Is it true that we Indians, to be able to live comfortably, have to scorn our race?

23. Is it true that to be able to grow we have to forget our language and crush our brothers?

24. In the colony we do work for the community: school, pastures, paths. But we do not do it with pleasure. We do it out of fear and obligation. I believe that it is because we do not like our race.

25. We think the will of God is that we be always poor.

26. That is not so.

27. God wants us all to get out of poverty together.

28. Brothers, I believe in God and I believe that it is possible that with the work of all of us united we may come to be a great people, a respected Indian people, where we may live as brothers.

29. We must keep the wealth God gave us from rotting in the hands of the rich or from being lost in the hands of those who are not capable of using it for the good of all.

Prayer: Lord, we ask You for the strength to forgive those who have offended us.
Give us Your strength, Lord.
Lord, we ask You for the strength to work with pleasure so that the life of our colony is better.
Give us Your strength, Lord.
Lord, we ask You for the strength to deal with everyone like a true brother.
Give us Your strength, Lord.
Lord, we ask You for the strength to live always as Your sons.
Give us Your strength, Lord.

Fourth Lesson

Prayer: God, our strength, we ask You to be with us now and forever.
Help us understand that it is not necessary to change what we are to
make our lives better. What is necessary is to make what we are grow.
We are Your children, Lord, worthy of living better.

Song: Community, Community,
How much joy I find in you.
My heart finds love
And in my brothers charity.
So I want
To commit myself to the creation
Of a great community,
Full of faith, full of love,
To reach happiness.
We come looking
For a new path to live better.
Now we have found it, it is the only path:
To create community, create community.

Reading: We Crush Ourselves and They Crush Us

1. Brothers, we are going to think today about something that for a long
time has made me sad.

2. Many times I have asked my friends in the colonies what it means to be
of the Indian race.

3. And they have answered me like this:

4. The Indians are us, the poor.

5. We Indians do not speak castilla.

6. We only speak the language of our ancestors. That is why we do not
know how to think.

7. We Indians do not know how to work. That is why we are poor and
have no money or cattle.

8. We have not studied, we do not know how to read or write.

9. Just because that is how it is, we are poor and we do not know how to
think.

10. Brothers, this is how we talk and I cannot believe these things we say.

11. I do not believe that we Indians have to be poor forever.

12. I do not believe that from speaking the language of our ancestors we do
not know how to think.

13. In our language is how we can think best.

14. I believe that it is good to learn Spanish, but it is very bad to forget the language of our race.

15. I believe it is good that our sons get out and learn other work like teachers, engineers, and doctors.

16. But it is bad that those who get out do not return to help us. They abandon the land of their fathers and scorn their Indian brothers.

17. There is a thing that I do believe, and it is that we are crushed and we accept being a crushed people.

18. We Indians believe that our race, our language, and our customs are of no use. This means that we are crushing ourselves.

19. As no man has a right to crush another man, neither does he have a right to crush himself.

20. The Second Commandment of God's Law says this: Love your brother as you love yourself.

21. God commands that we love ourselves, that we love our race, our people, our family.

22. We Indians are made by God and therefore we are of value and have a force of growth in our heart.

23. Brothers, let us not crush ourselves.

24. Let us recognize the force that there is in our Indian heart and let us make it grow.

25. Let us not scorn or forget our race.

26. He who scorns his race, it is as if he scorned his mother. It is as if he scorned God's work.

Prayer: Lord, help us come out of oppression because we are Your children.
Hear us, Lord.
Lord, help us not to oppress others, because we are all Your children.
Hear us, Lord.
Lord, help us love ourselves, because this is Your law.
Hear us, Lord.

Fifth Lesson

Prayer: Our Father who loves us forever, help us in this moment when we are united here in Your name.
Help us understand that You put in our heart the power to grow, the power to make our lives better,
the power to struggle to live happily.
Help us discover the way we can use Your power in us.

Song: The community
       is the encounter of persons,
       where all can speak and work
       for the common good.
       In community
       many persons and one heart (three times).

Reading: Thought Is Our Greatest Strength

1. Brothers, let us think today about all we can do for our race to grow.

2. The ejido commissioner works so that we can have our land.

3. The municipal agent here wants us to fix the roads, the bridges, and the houses in the colonies.

4. The committee wants us to have a school for our children.

5. Others of us want there to be cooperatives and clinics.

6. Others think that if we sell our produce better, corn, beans, pigs, we can grow better.

7. And to be able to do all this they ask us for cooperative contributions, meetings, and communal work.

8. We pay taxes and still we do not all have land.

9. The teachers are not to be found in the schools, and they leave.

10. They trick us in the coffee business, the pig business, and everything else.

11. We find no medicine to cure the sick.

12. All the time we are suffering and going through times of need, disease, poverty. We do not have land. There are no teachers or clinics.

13. Some brothers think the ejido commissioner, the municipal agent, and the committee are of no use.

14. They think the meetings and communal work are a waste of time.

15. Others think the cooperative contributions are a waste of money, because nothing is resolved.

16. Many of us brothers think this way, but none of us says it to the others.

17. If we want to grow and get what we want, we have to say what we are thinking.

18. If we think the authorities are of no use, we have to say so and change them.

19. When we believe the cooperative contribution is unfair, let us say so without fear.

20. When they call us to meetings, we have to go and help with our thought.

21. When we are going to sell our produce, let us not sell by ourselves one by one.

22. Let us not sell at the price the buyer asks [sic].

23. We all have to make ourselves strong and sell at the price that seems fair to us.

24. We have to help our community. We have to say the good things and the bad things we see.

25. Brothers, if I do not help the ejido commissioner with my thought, I have no right to say the commissioner is of no use.

26. If we do not go into the market with one idea in mind and one thing to say in common, the buyers will rob us.

27. He who stays quiet is not helping.

28. He who stays quiet steals strength from the community, and lets us be crushed.

29. If we do not give our thought, we are paying taxes in vain, we are giving our communal labor in vain.

30. When we give our communal labor, we are giving the strength of our body.

31. Man is different from animals, because man has strength in thought.

32. To grow as a community of men, we have to give the strength of our thought.

Prayer: Lord, help us to understand that by being men, by that alone, we can think.
This we ask You, Lord.
Lord, help us to understand that by being men, our word has value.
This we ask You, Lord.
Lord, help us to understand that by being Your children, we have to concern ourselves with the
good of the others.
This we ask You, Lord.

Sixth Lesson

Prayer: God, our Creator, You made men to live in communities, like brothers.
Open our hearts so that we understand what it is to live in communities.

Song: Community, Community . . .

Reading: We Look Again at What We Learned

1. Brothers, we have already met here many times in the chapel.
2. We have met to speak of our land, our food, our customs.
3. Some brothers can think this is not God's Word.

4. Let us remember, brothers, that what God wants is our growth, our freedom.

5. God wants us as a community to get out of poverty and being crushed.

6. He wants us to get out to freedom, like the ancient Jewish people.

7. In the lands of another people, called Egypt, the Jewish people lived.

8. The land was not theirs, they worked as slaves, suffering many wants.

9. Then God spoke in the heart of one of their principales, and He said to him:

10. I have seen the suffering of My people, I have heard the weeping that the foremen wring from them.

11. I have come down to liberate you from your sufferings, and I am going to bring you to another, better land.

12. And God said to Moses:

13. I command you to take My people out of Egypt. I will be your God, and I will be with you forever, helping you (Ex. 3:7–12).

14. Brothers, this is what God said in ancient time, and His Word is for all men.

15. God wants us to stop everything that crushes us.

16. The Word of God tells us that as a community we must get out to look for freedom.

17. God says that if we are looking to make our lives better and for freedom, He will be accompanying us.

18. We have already said that we are crushed because there is no accord among us, because we are divided.

19. Then let us look for our union, and God will help us.

20. We said that we are crushed because we do not have land.

21. Let us help one another, for God is accompanying us.

22. We see that we are crushing ourselves, because we scorn our race and our customs.

23. Let us look to grow and to unite, and God will help us.

24. We are crushed because we do not say what we think.

25. If we speak without fear and with love, God will help us.

26. The buyers and the authorities crush us.

27. Then let us defend ourselves together, let us help one another, and God will help us.

28. God helps us if we work together as a community.

29. God helps us if we want to get out of being crushed.

30. God helps us in the struggle to get our freedom.

Prayer: Lord, help us to understand that an assembly is for our good, when we all give support with our thought.
Hear us, Lord.

Lord, help us to help our authorities, telling them our word.
Hear us, Lord.
Lord, help us to accept the responsibility that we have for the growth of our community.
Hear us, Lord.

. . . PART III.

FAITH, HOPE, AND CHARITY

. . . Chapter VII. The Path of Faith

First Lesson

Prayer: Lord, increase our faith to believe in You. Your heart willed us, together with Christ, to struggle
and work for the good of all, because only in this way will we save ourselves.

Song: One Lord, one faith, one baptism, one God and Father.
Called to keep the unity of the Spirit by the bond of peace, we sing and proclaim.
Called to form one body in one same Spirit, we sing and proclaim.
Called to share one same hope in Christ, we sing and proclaim:

Reading: To Better Ourselves Is to Gain Salvation

1. The Spirit of God is present as a force of betterment in the midst of our community.
2. Brothers, I have thought of all the work we do in common.
3. This force that moves us to work in common to better ourselves is the sign of God's presence in us.
4. And the sign the community has to show its faith in God is working for a better life.
5. To help the growth of the community is to show our faith in God's Plan.
6. He who struggles to put an end to injustices, this is a man of faith.
7. Our community will have true faith when we decide to work with the force of the Spirit.
8. This force of the Spirit is what takes us to freedom.
9. Liberty is obtained with the work of each day.
10. Since before Creation, God chose us to be His children.

11. He chose us to be free (Ephesians 1:3-5).

12. But God did not chose only a few. God chose us all, and that is why God is in the whole community.

13. The first thing God did to save us was to create the world.

14. And with the Creation began the path of our salvation.

15. Now we have to help to make the world ever better.

16. To help to make better everything that God made is to work on God's Plan.

17. That is why we say to better ourselves is to gain salvation.

18. The faith of the community is shown in its struggle for freedom.

19. We cannot say that we have faith if we do not struggle to put an end to evil.

20. The community that does not struggle for the freedom of all is scorning the presence of the Spirit.

21. The community that in union looks for its freedom is a community that has faith and receives the Spirit.

Prayer: Lord, we believe in You because since before creating things, You already willed our freedom.
We believe in You, Lord.
Lord, we believe in You because with Your Word and Your example, You show us how to gain salvation.
We believe in You, Lord.
Lord, we believe in You because Your Spirit, which lives in the community, moves us to work for
our salvation.
We believe in You, Lord.

Second Lesson

Prayer: Christ, our Brother, we believe in You. You want the salvation of all. We ask You to give us Your strength to reach salvation, because we know that the path to gain it is very difficult.

Song: (As in the previous lesson)

Reading: What Our Faith Does

1. Brothers, our union with God the Creator and Savior is shown by our faith.

2. Our Faith goes in search of salvation, the freedom of all.

3. The man who looks for salvation has to struggle against hunger, disease, and pain.

4. The man who looks for salvation cannot stay quiet when there are injustices.

5. The man who loves God also loves what God did.

6. To love God is to work for us to come to be a people where no one crushes anyone else.

7. The sufferings and wants that we go through are not going to end by themselves.

8. Let us not believe, brothers, that salvation will arrive when this life of suffering is over.

9. Salvation will arrrive when we decide to put an end to the evils and sufferings we go through.

10. If we have faith in God, let us struggle for there to be no more suffering.

11. When the Israelites lived as slaves, they had to get out and fight to gain their freedom.

12. When our ancestors lived as *mozos*, peons, they too had to unite and struggle to win their lands.

13. These were men of much Faith and they showed it by their work.

14. By their Faith and their struggle we have land today and live free in colonies and farms.

15. But true freedom has not yet arrived.

16. We have to gather strength in our hearts, and struggle and suffer much still.

17. We have to struggle against poverty, hunger, and injustice.

18. We have to struggle against those who crush our race.

19. We have to prevent ourselves from crushing one another.

20. Freedom is not for cowards.

21. Salvation is for those who have a strong heart and much love.

22. Salvation will not happen after our death.

23. Salvation is happening every time we change bad for good.

24. Salvation began when God made the world. But we have to do our work to gain it completely.

25. Salvation is for everyone and is gained in this life every day.

Prayer: Lord, we want to live our faith.
      Help us, O Lord.
      Lord, You are with us to banish all our ills.
      Help us, O Lord.
      Lord, we recognize that we need to have a strong heart, without fear, to look for our salvation.
      Help us, O Lord.

Third Lesson

Prayer: Lord, we know that You want the good of all. Help us say what we think and carry out together the accords we take in the community. In this way we are showing our faith in You, Lord.

Song: The community is people coming together, where all can speak and work for the common good.
In community, many persons and one heart, many persons and one heart.

Reading: Let Us Take an Accord

   1. After a meeting with the ejido commissioner, some brothers stayed and talked.

   2. They were sad because in the meeting they had not taken any accord.

   3. One brother said:

   4. Always in the chapel [where they met] we are saying pretty things, but we do not carry them out.

   5. We say we want to better our lives.

   6. We say we want to work in common.

   7. We say we show our faith by the work we do together to better our lives.

   8. I do not understand why there are brothers who do not say their thoughts in the meetings.

   9. There are other brothers who are at the meeting, but without any interest in it, just playing.

   10. There are others who speak so much they do not let the others have a chance to speak.

   11. They think they know everything and do not respect the thoughts of others.

   12. But the accord has to be for the good of all, because we are all in need.

   13. The accord cannot be for the good of a few. That is to crush us.

   14. What is pretty is that we each be capable of suffering a little so that the community betters its life.

   15. Then another brother spoke and said:

   16. The commissioner is the one who has to think.

   17. He is the one who has to give the orders and say what we are going to do, and we others are going to obey him.

   18. Then the others answered:

   19. No, brother, the responsibility is not only the commissioner's.

   20. Freedom is for all, and we have to gain it together.

21. The commissioner only has his thought, but if we join together the thoughts of us all, this way will be better.

22. If we have faith in God, we have to show it by having faith in our brothers.

23. And we can show our faith in God, working on His Plan, only with our brothers.

24. Because salvation is gained by the work of all, not by that of a few.

25. That is why I am not happy with the meetings we have.

26. We still do not know how to take accords.

27. We have to make an effort, brothers, for if we do not take accords, then we are divided.

28. And if we are divided, we have no strength to better ourselves...

Chapter VIII. Faith in Authority . . .

Second Lesson

Prayer: Our God and Lord, You commanded us to dominate the earth.
Christ taught us that we must do so with love.
In Your Spirit we unite to fulfill your commandment.

Song: Every man carries written
within his heart
the mandate of the Lord
that brings us toward good.
United we work to make the world better.
We are the brothers of Jesus the Savior.
He gave us the example of serving others.
He is the voice of the heart.

Reading: Authority

1. Brothers, persons are the greatest wealth the community has.

2. A person is wealth because he can think and work.

3. But we are richer and accomplish more with our work when we are united.

4. God commands us: "Dominate the earth."

5. Therefore when we work united to make the world better, we are obeying the authority of God.

6. When God showed us His Plan, His authority also gave us the power to be able to fulfill it.

7. Our community, by means of His authority, must organize all its strength and wealth for work.

8. In this way then authority is the meeting of all the community's thoughts in search of bettering the community's life.

9. That is why the community cannot allow its wealth to be wasted.

10. That is why it needs to organize its people, their thoughts, their work, and all their other wealth.

11. Authority is not a man who imposes himself and dominates the community.

12. Authority is in the heart of the community.

13. God said: "I shall write My Law in their hearts and I shall be their God and they will be My people" (Jeremiah 31:33).

14. Therefore the community has the authority to name capable and responsible persons to organize its work.

15. And those persons who hold authority do not hold it just because of who they are.

16. They hold it because the community gave it to them.

17. And authority is in the community because God gave it to us.

18. In this way then the authorities—municipal agents, presidents, catechists, and others—are nothing but servants of the community.

19. To be a servant is to dedicate yourself with all your heart to the betterment of the community.

20. And to serve the betterment of men is to obey the Plan of God.

Prayer: Lord, help us to understand that we are obeying Your commandment when we
work united to make the world better.
Hear us, Lord.
Lord, help us to understand that authority comes from You and is manifest in the union and accord
of the whole community.
Hear us, Lord.
Lord, help us to understand that Your Law is written in our hearts.
Hear us, Lord . . .

A Letter to Brothers

Dear Brothers,

For almost two years, every Sunday, the new lessons from God's Word keep coming. With these lessons there are many who have found a new strength in their hearts, and they say: This Word is good, because it speaks of our life, of our community, of the Bible, but everything in one, because it is God who is with us.

But there are other brothers who say: These lessons are not God's Word, because they are not the letter of the Bible. They also say: It is not God's Word because it speaks of the ejido, of the commissioner, the agent, the school, of food.

Brothers: How can we truly know what is God's Word? Is it that God's Word is only kept in books? Is it that only those who know how to read can understand God's Word?

No, brothers. God's Word is Christ, and Christ lives in us. God's Word is a living Word. God's Word speaks to us and asks us to answer.

Now life is not like before. Life keeps changing. Now highways are already coming out to our colonies. And what are we going to do?

Already more buyers and sellers of things are coming out. Produce leaves, products arrive. And maybe our life is going to stay the same? What are we going to do?

Already many in the colonies have radios, and we hear voices in Spanish and in Tzeltal. What good does it do us?

Already the government is more interested in doing agricultural programs and highways and many things with the Indians. What for? Is it that the government is looking out for our good?

Already we have seen guerrillas and soldiers arriving in our colonies. All armed. We have known how they shoot at each other and even kill each other. Why?

Now we now that there is still much oppression. Why?

By means of all these things in life God speaks to us and asks us to answer Him.

How are we going to answer God's Word well? Saint Paul tells us: Brothers, the Word of God is written in our hearts, and all can read it and recognize it. In truth each of us is a letter that Christ has written through our lives. We are a letter that has not been written on paper and with a pencil, but with the Spirit of God who lives in our hearts. So we must not be followers of the book, because the book does not give life, but believers in the Spirit who lives in our hearts and gives us understanding and strength (2 Cor. 3:1-4).

So it is, brothers: Christ is in us. The Spirit of Christ gives us life. Therefore it is our responsibility to look for the growth of life, to answer God's Word.

Let us give the community our thoughts and our work, as seeds that must bear fruit. If we do not cast the seed, the new fruit will not be born. If we do not give our thoughts and our work, the new life for which we hope will not be born.

Saint Paul encourages us and says: Brothers, keep on till the end, showing enthusiasm in your work; do not turn lazy (Heb. 6:11-12).

Let us ask God to light our minds so that we know what is the hope that is in our hearts. Let us ask God to give us strength to say our word and to work to gain what our hearts hope (Ephesians 1:18).

CHAPTER TEN

Las Casas Recalled, Indians Informed, Organized, United, and Defiant: The Congress of San Cristóbal, 1974

The Las Casas Indian Congress that convened in San Cristóbal in October 1974 was an event in a process, the movement that began in August 1973, when Bishop Ruiz assigned the missionaries he thought best at "the pastoral practice of incarnation" to organize the state-sponsored commemoration of Las Casas explicitly so that Indians would "have their own say."

The initial organizers—their official title was "promoter"—were only six: a young philosopher-theologian in Sabanilla for the Chol zone; a priest in Chamula and a priest in Chenalhó for the Tzotzils; a Jesuit in Bachajón and a young ex-Marist schoolteacher in Ocosingo for the Tzeltal zone; and a young Marist sociologist for the Tojolabals. The bishop would raise the funds (eventually from the Inter-American Foundation) to cover some expenses. The promoting would depend on donated labor for the rest. Using a UN-funded state agency for "socioeconomic development" to convene local Indian authorities in the various zones, they proposed the congress to them and explained that Las Casas was only a pretext, that the purpose was to build separate from Church and State an organization of Indian villages and communities to defend Indian interests. That they offered no government grants or projects disappointed some authorities, who walked out on them. But many others endorsed the plan, and in October 1973 the promoters commenced moving village and community assemblies to consider participation in the congress.

Some assemblies were hostile, others so angry and demanding that the promoters fled from them. But most responded in customary style, deliberately, and then strongly in favor. As these came to number in the hundreds and began framing their denunciations and demands, the promoters recruited a team of translators for preconvention training, and induced participant villages and communities to elect "coordinators" to organize and manage "sub-congresses" for cooperation within each zone and across the zones. Most significantly the sub-congresses agreed to "have their say" at the convention under four common rubrics: land, commerce, education, and health; neither in the local assemblies nor in the sub-congresses did partisan politics come up. Over the entrance to the San Cristóbal municipal auditorium when the congress proudly convened on October 13, 1974, was a big banner that read, "Equality in Justice."

The grievances and denunciations that the delegates presented there on land, commerce, education, and health surprised no one who knew Chiapas. But it was striking that Chols, Tzotzils, Tzeltals, and Tojolabals had for the first time come together in one place in protest, and were expressing their indignation no longer along ethnic lines but in solidarity with each other. And as the promoters and coordinators prepared the successive accords, in effect demands, the delegates carefully discussed them, and expeditiously voted for them. The proceedings took only one odd turn, when the Chamula Tzotzils presented an outright political question, a request for a demonstration in their town against state-police evictions the day before. The congress denounced the evictions, but did not leave the hall. It would soon suffer worse political challenges.

After the convention, its promoters, coordinators, and counselor for translation induced the formation of a congress executive council to bring the movement into social action. The council president was the Marist sociologist who had first organized the Tojolabal zone; the secretary general, a Tenejapa Tzeltal from a Lacandón pioneer community; the other councilors, the former zone coordinators. They ran immediately into political battles they had not chosen: 40 Chamulans jailed in a corral, the PRI's concoction of a CNC National Indian Congress, which went right after the San Cristóbal congress's best cadres. The new council tried to distinguish its movement from the CNC's, naming it the Brother Bartolomé de Las Casas Indian Congress. On the bases of the San Cristóbal accords, it then mounted social campaigns on the issues of land, commerce, education, and health, made substantial gains in organization in most of its zones, but also discovered the politics of the established resistance to reform—and much worse, the politics of its own inherent regional, ideological, and class differences.

By late 1976 the Las Casas Indian Congress was in crisis. The council president and another of the founding promoters resigned and left the state. In January 1977 the council elected as its new president the founding promoter in the Chol zone, and decided to reform the congress. The movement's new objectives in the short run were "a) to awaken proletarian consciousness in ourselves and in our communities, b) to constitute ourselves as a true independent organization, c) to develop programs for economic, ideological, and political struggles, with the budgets that these require" (nothing "ethnic"). Its objective in the long run was transcendent: "The Indian Congress pursues the change of the present socio-economic system for a society in which there will be no private property in the means of production." This led to deeper divisions.

In a meeting of the council in San Cristóbal on March 17, 1977, the president declared the congress dissolved. "Let each region," he concluded, "follow the course that in its judgment it considers appropriate."

In this disarray, a few months later, there arrived the organizers of the Línea Proletaria.

The following are excerpts from documentary appendices to an historical account of the congress by one of its founders and its last president, the philosopher-theologian in Sabanilla, Chol zone.

EL CONGRESO INDÍGENA DE CHIAPAS: UN TESTIMONIO*

. . . Speech on Brother Bartolomé de Las Casas . . .

Life of Brother Bartolomé de Las Casas: he was born in Seville, on the other side of the ocean, in 1474. He was bishop of this city of San Cristóbal.

First a gentleman called Christopher Columbus came to these lands, the one who crossed the ocean the first time. He saw lots of Indian people, admired our customs, the land so good of our old people. He went to let his compañeros who lived on the other side of the ocean know, and told them that here there was good land and a lot of unknown people.

At that time our old people had good organizations. They had doctors, engineers, lawyers, builders. They had authorities like we'd like to have.

Columbus came with his compañeros to know the people here and to bother them. With them came Brother Bartolomé de Las Casas. They began to bother the old people, to take away their land, and to make them work without pay, working hard the whole day. They took away all our organization that we had. Then all the ladinos treated us like animals.

Brother Bartolomé de Las Casas saw that it was very bad what his other compañeros were doing. So he began to defend the Indians, because we're just as much the same Christians being Indians as caxlanes are. As the ladinos

---

*Jesús Morales Bermúdez, in *Anuario del Instituto Chiapaneco de Cultura*, 1991, pp. 292–352.

were quite a few, they even wanted to kill Brother Bartolomé, for defending us.

He fought hard and asked the authorities on the other side of the ocean to make the caxlanes stop bothering us, that there be a law for us all to be equal. This bishop went traveling several times, . . . 14 times [to Spain] to get the law that we're all equal.

Right here in San Cristóbal Brother Bartolomé de Las Casas was defending the Indian. I believe we all know that church that's to one side of the Church of Santo Domingo, up from the union hall. That was where Brother Bartolomé de Las Casas used to celebrate Mass.

We Indians, it's time now that we begin to think and see if really we have the liberty that Brother Bartolomé de Las Casas left us, because we all, Tzotzils, Tzeltals, Chols, and Tojolabals, we live in the mountains, while all the ladinos live in the city and have good farms and fincas.

But if we demand our rights or want to ask for our land, we can't. They've already taken away from us our old organization. That's why now they impose even our own authorities on us, and even federal authorities. So in Chamula we've suffered going to jail for defending our rights to elect our municipal president. The authorities send soldiers so we'll be afraid.

That's why the landlords run all over us, like in Altamirano, where soldiers burned down people's houses just for asking for land.

That's why they trample on our customs. This is not an authority like we want.

So where is the liberty Brother Bartolomé left?

We have been suffering injustice for 500 years, and we're still in the same situation. Injustices continue against us. They always want to manage us like children, because we're Indians. They think we have no rights.

Well, comrades, now Brother Bartolomé de Las Casas is no longer alive. It's only in his name that we're holding this congress. He's dead now, and we don't expect another one like him.

Who's going to defend us against injustices and so that we have our liberty?

The ladinos, I believe they're not going to defend us.

The government, maybe yes, maybe no.

So, who's going to defend us?

I think that organizing ourselves we can all have liberty and work better. We all have to be Bartolomé. So we are going to defend ourselves through the organization of all of us, because union makes strength.

. . . Chol Position on Land

Before, all the territory that we occupy was the community's. We are in the municiplities of Tila, Tumbalá, Salto de Agua, Sabanilla, Palenque, and some communities that have gone to the Nationals [public lands] in Chilón and

Ocosingo. We would not know how to explain how and why we have been despoiled of our old communal lands . . .

The situation of poverty and misery in which Chol laborers resident on the fincas live is extreme. This is due to the labor system imposed on them, starvation wages, company stores, the lack of medicine, alcoholism, and commerce.

We work from sunup to sundown for wages that don't come to seven pesos a day. From the age of ten children have to start working for wages of a peso or two a day. These wages aren't paid in cash, but in scrip or merchandise or drink. This situation the labor authorities aren't aware of, due to the isolation in which we live. Only very recently roads are beginning to be built. We have to work for free on Sundays on the system they call "the page." At coffee harvest time the women and children have to work just like the men. On the finca there is no medical service for the laborer.

The corn fields have little by little been converted into pastures. The owner of the finca generously offers his laborers a big tract, magnificent land for corn. The only condition he puts on them is that with the corn they also plant grass. So the next year this magnificent field is turned into pasture. The next year he gives them another tract. The Indian clears it, prepares the land, plants his corn, together with the grass. So after four or five years the finca has turned into a cattle ranch. And the landless laborers resident on the place, what are they going to eat? So emigration to the Nationals has been massive. They go fleeing the hunger and misery of the fincas. The land of their fathers, which saw them born, is left forever behind.

Despite working from sunup to sundown, they never have money for anything and ask for loans. Generally they ask for them when corn is scarce, in July or August. If they ask for 100 pesos, by the next February at the latest they have to pay 200. Alcoholism in these circumstances is their escape from reality . . .

Tzotzil Position on Land

The Tzotzil community is the one that has suffered most the colonizing and invading action of the ladinos from colonial times to our day, as is clear in concrete denunciations we now present . . .

The Lázaro Cárdenas ejido in the municipality of Huitiupán has been struggling for its land for 42 years. There was a presidential resolution [of the case] on August 19, 1964, published in the *Diario Oficial* [the federal gazette] on January 20, 1965. But the authorities have not turned over 454 hectares [1,132 acres] to the ejido, because the resolution affects properties abandoned by an owner, which are now public land, but held by Mariano Ruiz Ruiz. The Lázaro Cárdenas ejidatarios denounce the engineer Manuel Gutiérrez Meneses of the State Agrarian Department in Tuxtla, who conceded legal protection to the false owner Mariano Ruiz Ruiz against the presidential resolution. According to a statement from the Federal Agrarian Department in Mexico City . . . the properties in question are under a provisional certificate of exemption from agrarian reform, which no one has ever seen and which contravenes Articles 203 and 204 of the New Law of Agrarian Reform. Over these 42 years the Lázaro Cárdenas ejidatarios have spent 420,840 pesos, in the last three years alone (14 fruitless trips to Mexico City) 30,060 pesos. There are 85 men eligible for grants who have lost hope that the law will be applied . . .

Tojolabal Position on Land

. . . We don't find at the agrarian authority an effective answer to the petitions we make. For example, in one of the colonies, we have been asking since 1948 for expansion of its grant, and to date nothing has been resolved.

We see that our word carries no weight with the authorities. When we go to their offices they pay no attention to us, they scold us, they send us back and forth. But they give us no orientation on how to resolve our problems. Specifically we note that the Joint Agrarian Commission seems to be functioning for interests definitely not Indian. So we simply waste our time and our money on trips, and the problems aren't resolved. It's worth noting that every trip is costing the community over 300 pesos.

Another source of problems are the abuses and injustices on the part of the finqueros [the finca owners]. The mestizos have the best lands, for crops and for pasture for animals. When Tojolabals need pasture for their animals, they have to pay the mestizo 20 or 30 pesos a month for every head.

Or if we want the right for our animals to go into their pasture, we have to go work for them free or at starvation wages, seven pesos for a laborer from sunup to sundown.

If a mestizo's cattle get into an Indian's field, the mestizo pays no damages, and the Indian has no chance of a favorable ruling on his complaint to the judicial authorities. There have been cases when the landlords close their pastures and block the roads, forcing the Indian to make long detours.

One of the principal problems is that the little land we have is of bad quality. Corn doesn't grow well, nor is there pasture for our animals, which die in the summertime. And we ask ourselves, why is it that we have the worst lands, yet we have lived in this country since time immemorial, and the mestizo is a recent arrival? It's a question that deserves an answer.

We want to denounce with all clarity the abuses and tricks on the part of the authorities. There are many cases where the agrarian authorities have tricked us, especially the engineers, who ask for money to do their work. Examples: in the colony Jerusalém, the engineer asked for 10,000 pesos. Or like the colony Guadalupe Victoria, in the municipality of Altamirano, where they gave 2,000 pesos to the engineer and 2,000 pesos to the lawyer, got no official documentation, and so lost the money and got nothing settled. There are cases . . . when the engineer making the survey leaves great stretches unsurveyed and later sells them. The lands he separates off like this are the best. This happened in the colony Guadalupe Victoria and in the colony 20 de Noviembre [November 20, the date in 1910 when "the Mexican Revolution" started.]

We feel that internal problems divide us and the community finds no support or orientation. In a Tojolabal community with land in the communal form [as Indian communities may hold land, not in the form of an ejido], they thought they would change to the ejidal form and named their representatives to go through the administrative process, but the representatives tricked their compañeros and sold the community's timber, . . . and this has caused a great conflict . . .

Tzeltal Position on Land

We feel disorganized. We don't have our ejido plots duly demarcated, which is the origin of internal disputes. Since 1935 we've been trying to legalize our lands and until now have not been able to get the documentation up to date. We judge that this is the fault of the responsible officials at the Agrarian Department.

The engineers they send us never turn over the complete report, either because they don't finish their surveys or because they get mad at the comuneros or ejidatarios. They ask for much money for each of their trips to us. Every ejidatario or comunero has to contribute 20 or 30 pesos. If, for example, in San Sebastián Bachajón, there are 3,000 ejidatarios, you see how much the gift comes to. It's worse in that our internal authorities—generally youngsters who know some castilla—learn how to extort money from their brothers and take part in the booty. If there is no such cooperation, the engineer gets mad and doesn't do the work, so the administrative papers we need go on sleeping in the office.

The zone chief at the Agrarian Department, for every administrative step in which he has to intervene, whether for the whole community or to solve a particular conflict, also demands money aside from his travel expenses and food. Almost always he leaves the problem half solved, to have the opportunity for more money. Of course they never give receipts for all this money. They call them voluntary contributions. So it's impossible to make a judicial claim against them.

The ejido commissioners [elected managers of the ejido], given the bad example of the agrarian officers, also lay a charge on their brothers and get rich at their expense. Other times, although they're working properly, they have to be asking for cooperation from the others in the ejido for the administrative business in Tuxtla and Mexico City. With the bureaucratic slowness, the vested interests, and the immorality of the engineers and zone chiefs, the administration of the case doesn't advance. This provokes the ejidatarios and the comuneros to lose confidence in their internal authorities, and so they look for some crime they may have done.

Judges and police detectives take up cases that don't pertain to them in order to get money out of them. Often they intervene in purely agrarian cases. So both the defendant and the plaintiff pay a fine, of course without either of them getting a receipt. This custom of asking for money from both sides is generalized, whether there is guilt or not, in all court proceedings . . .

The forestry office is another chapter in exploitation. It's true that often we don't know how to take care of our forests; we aren't familiar with the value they have. No one is concerned to orient us. There are no campaigns by the forestry authorities to show the Indian what he has, or to teach him the importance of the forest. What is very effective is repression. Year after year we have to ask for permits to plant our corn, and we pay heavy for them. If we ask for permits to cut high timber, we can't get them. And they fine us if we use dead wood.

This chaotic situation has as a result, besides the systematic impoverishment of the communities, . . . many internal conflicts that have cut short many lives and caused resentment and hatreds among *us*. It leads to persons outside the community and with strong economic interests *invading lands* by the system of simple invasion, or through trickery in commerce, alcoholism, or lending money [emphases in original]. Because of everything previously indicated, it is impossible to arrive at a legal and expeditious solution.

Another chapter that complicates the matter is ignorance of prevailing legislation. We don't know our duties or our rights, which makes it possible for engineers as well as zone chiefs and judicial authorities to take advantage of this ignorance. So we fall into the hands of lawyers without conscience who instead of orienting us exploit us more.

We want to make a clear denunciation of how they treat us in the Joint Agrarian Commission. Above all the engineer Enoch Cruz, besides insulting us and delaying our cases, takes money from those who have invaded our lands, and resolves internal conflicts on the basis of whoever gives him more money . . .

The groups who have fled to the Nationals . . . suffer the same difficulties. . . . Given the numbers of people who have fled there, the new ejidos (colonies) are getting saturated with people, and we foresee that serious problems will soon arise in these groups. We foresee that the policy of dragging out the administrative process and public officials getting fat results will continue . . .

Because of this saturation and the lack of solutions to the problems that arise, there is the phenomenon of Indian ejidatarios who are on a continuous pilgrimage in search of a place to settle. It worries them that those to whom responsibilities are given in the community, like agents and commissioners, turn into exploiters. They think that this is due to them quickly learning the path of extortion that the officers of the Agrarian Department show them. In many of these colonies the people don't receive an adequate agrarian education, and consequently think the highest internal authority is the commissioner and not the assembly, so that local bossism worsens.

They are also sensitive to . . . the social disorganization in which they live, for the colonies are formed of Indians who come from various groups and traditions, even various languages. This makes people feel distant from each other and causes sharp problems difficult to solve. It is one of the many problems that these people have to confront when they abandon the place that saw them born.

Cantinas are introduced, and sell a lot of beer. Although many colonies have reacted positively against this exploitation, they do not feel they have the support of the authorities and the schoolteachers. There are even some fincas, strategically located in the jungle, that are a force of exploitation, like, for example, the finca El Diamante, located along the line between the municipalities of Ocosingo and Chilón, surrounded by little colonies which it exploits in trade, in the sale of aguardiente, and in continual attempts to invade their land . . .

SUMMARY OF GRIEVANCES: COMMERCE

. . . The peasant, the Indian, works hard, and is always exploited, selling his products cheap and buying things high. So we leave our money and our work with the merchant.

. . . For us, merchants and monopolists are "A GREAT PLAGUE."

. . . Exploitation in commerce goes from little things to big and expensive things. We are always at a disadvantage.

. . . "Intermediaries" snatch our products, in markets and on the road, and pay what they want.

. . . The pig dealers trick us, for example, stuffing their pigs with grain [like "watering the stock," to put false weight on them] . . .

. . . And when we buy products or sell them, often they trick us with weights and measures.

. . . We know there are very powerful gentlemen who take advantage and are getting very rich from stealing or paying very low prices for products of high price.

. . . Here we want to DENOUNCE . . . the coffee dealers, the timber dealers in Los Altos (and in the jungle), the cattle dealers. For example, with timber, they trick us, and because the community does not know how to defend itself or know its rights, they exploit it. They bribe the ejido commissioners. Before, for a mahogany tree that costs $10,000 [pesos] or more, they paid us $25 or $50. Now they do not pay us anything anymore, and they haul timber out day and night in big trucks.

. . . The buyers and sellers set prices at their whim. So, for example, the corn we sell at 50 centavos, we buy at three pesos.

. . . The sale of liquor and beer is a great source of exploitation.

. . . Besides, the liquor is often moonshine. (For example, Tocoy in Huixtán is a place that produces and smuggles liquor.)

. . . There are high taxes that are private businesses.

. . . The taxes in the markets are arbitrary. For example, for a sack of apples they charge us three or four pesos in taxes. For example, when we get out of the trucks at the San Cristóbal market, they right off charge us a tax, without knowing if we have brought any merchandise.

. . . And we want to know where our taxes go, because we see no improvements in our communities.

We see that often the big merchants do not pay taxes as we do.

. . . Another big business in commerce is loans. When we are needing to sell, they will trade us a bag of corn for a bag of our coffee.

Also they pay us 100 pesos for a bag of coffee that is worth 600 pesos.

The lenders give us liquor, trick us, and when they see us drunk they put us in jail, and we have to pay a fine. So the lender wins, the judge wins, and the jailers too.

The loans in money are at high interest. For example, loans at 100 percent interest in seven months.

Summary of Grievances: Education

. . . It is a very bad system of education. Even the teaching is bad.

. . . what they teach is of no use for the improvement of the community.

. . . they only teach how to read and write, which the children soon forget, but they learn nothing about how to make a living.

. . . it is an education that prepares the children for exploitation.

. . . those who finish the sixth year know nothing, they become exploiters following the example of their teachers.

. . . the school is against our customs, and makes people leave.

. . . it does not teach anything about improvement of the land, agriculture, care of animals, agrarian law, medicine.

. . . there is a lack of schools.

. . . schooling is incomplete. For example, there is a school that has been going for 38 years, and no one has finished the primary grades.

. . . we see that schooling only really serves the ladinos.

. . . Most of the teachers and INI agents give a bad example.

. . . They do not respect the local authorities, they turn into local bosses themselves.

. . . They do not respect the older girls in school. There are many cases of rape.

. . . They do not keep the schedule.

. . . They turn into enemies of the community.

. . . They are merchants and exploit their students.

. . . They run cantinas.

. . . They do not teach well.

. . . They get drunk.

. . . They are ashamed of being Indians. They do not respect the custom of their communities.

. . . The INI agents in Tila and Tumbalá are working VERY WELL, AND THE COMMUNITY LIKES THEM. The same goes for the INI agents in the Tojolabal zone.

Ladino teachers . . . think they are superior.

. . . They ask for a lot of cooperation [money] for their airfare [to take a bush flight down to the jungle communities].

. . . They do not teach well because they do not know the Indian language, and the children do not know Spanish.

. . . They ask for money for grades, enrollments, free textbooks, food.

. . . They join the local bosses and bother the community.

. . . They do not respect anything.

. . . There is a group of Tzeltal teachers who work on their own private initiative. The government does not support them. They are good, but they need training. They have asked for positions in INI, but are not given them . . .

Summary of Grievances: Health

. . . We suffer many diseases and epidemics.

. . . There are many zones where there is a lot of tuberculosis.

. . . Intestinal diseases, hemorrhages, rheumatism.

. . . The reasons why we suffer this are: malnutrition and poverty; lack of land; lack of knowledge about domestic hygiene, water, food; lack of shelter; rain.

. . . our living conditions are conditions of disease.

. . . The vaccination campaigns do not get to us. Or when they do, instead of giving us the prescribed triple vaccination, they give us only one shot.

. . . The lack of roads means that many vaccinations or medicines never get here.

. . . Only in some places are there big clinics. In most places there are none.

. . . For example, there is not a single hospital in the entire Chol zone, or in Tila, Sabanilla, Tumbalá. Because of the isolation in which we live, only those who have money can get out to be cured; the others have to die from their disease.

. . . Where there are health centers, neither the doctors nor the nurses know how to go into the country. We want there to be more doctors, but for them to see people in their homes.

. . . They often treat us badly. They give us something to calm us down, but not real medicine.

. . . In the health centers we suffer discrimination; it is that they do not know how to speak our language.

Over the radio they tell us about hygiene and health, but our conditions do not improve just because of what the radio says.

. . . In Sabanilla there is a foreign clinic that attends to [Seventh–Day] Adventists.

. . . In the Salto de Agua health center, our people contributed money and work, and now they charge us a lot for services. In Sabanilla the municipal president asks for a lot of cooperation [money] for the health center.

. . . Medicine is a very expensive business for peasants.

. . . Trickery and commercial exploitation in the pharmacies. Very expensive medicines.

. . . They trick us, selling us medicine that has passed its expiration date.

. . . They sell us medical samples or federal hospital medicine [that should be free].

. . . Traveling salesmen sell medicine at high prices, and it has passed its expiration date.

. . . Merchants practice medicine without knowing what they are doing, and charge a lot.

. . . They charge high for vaccinations.

. . . Indians have more trust in Indian medicine than in ladino medicine.

. . . Impoverishment and loss of knowledge of traditional medicine.

. . . There is a lot of trickery and enmity that the traditional healers cause.

. . . Indian medicine is good, but people use it to do harm.

. . . We are lacking instruction on how not to mix Indian medicine and ladino medicine.

. . . We are lacking instruction on how to use Indian medicine right and to use it to cure people . . .

Accords: Land
The Land Belongs to He Who Works It

1. We all want to solve the problems of land, but we are divided, each for himself, and so we feel we have no strength. We are looking to organize each group so that it will have strength, because union makes strength . . .

2. We demand that the communal lands taken away from our fathers be returned to us.

3. That the employees of the Agrarian Department effectively resolve pending administrative questions. We demand an end to extortion by engineers and zone chiefs and forestry officers.

4. That there be an Agrarian Department branch office in San Cristóbal for the administrative business of our agrarian affairs. And above all that it have complete authority to resolve our agrarian problems.

5. That the problem of the Tuliljá dam be justly resolved, and that they take us into account.

6. That the minimum wage be paid to Indians who work on fincas and in cities, and that they receive all the benefits that the law provides.

7. That taxes not be imposed on sterile land. That taxes be fair.

8. We demand that to settle our problems the government not send in the army. That problems be settled with the community, not with the army.

Accords: Commerce
Equality and Justice in Prices

1. We want an Indian market, that is, that we ourselves be the ones who buy and sell, that this be organized in each municipality, starting with hamlets, colonies, and settlements, concentrating produce in our warehouses, so that among ourselves, Tzeltals, Tzotzils, Tojolabals, and Chols, we can sell each other our various products . . .

2. We want to organize ourselves into cooperatives for selling and producing, to defend ourselves from monopolizers and so that profits do not leave the community.

3. We demand that Inmecafe [the federal coffee-purchasing agency] not sell itself out to monopolizers, that it buy [from us] at guaranteed prices through the representative elected by the community.

4. We want to study well and in groups the matter of alcoholic drinks, knowing that liquor is bad when it becomes a means of exploitation. Because of liquor they have despoiled us and ruined our health. . . .

Accords: Education
To Renew the Education of Our Children

1. We want Indian teachers to be trained who will teach in our language and our custom, and that they also teach Spanish. We do not want teachers who do not know our language and customs.

2. We want teachers who will respect the communities and their customs. We want them to teach us our rights as citizens. We want the community to be taught its rights.

We do not want them to be merchants.

We do not want them to get drunk.

We do not want them to set bad examples.

We do not want them to ask for a fine when a girl over 15 who is in school gets married.

We do not want them to be lazy.

We want them to commit themselves to the service of the community.

3. We want our communities to organize themselves better, that there be a committee independent of the teachers, elected by the community, to watch over the teacher's work.

4. Education and teaching are very necessary, but they should help to improve our human conditions and respond to the needs of the community, in land and animals, social integration, cultivation, tailoring, bricklaying.

5. That there be an Indian newspaper in our four languages [Chol, Tzotzil, Tzetzal, Tojolabal]. That the paper be the Indians' and that it serve for our own communication.

Accords: Health
Health Is Life

1. We need to organize our community so that we can take care of our health.

2. We want the old medicine not to be lost. It is necessary to know the medicinal plants in order to use them for the good of us all.

3. We ask that there be clinics in the big Indian villages and that they serve the smaller communities with Indian nurses who know both medicines, that of pills and that of plants. This way medicine will get to us all.

4. That the sale of medicine by merchants be prohibited, because they trick people a lot on prices and medicine past its expiration date.

5. In many of our zones there is tuberculosis. We ask for an effective campaign against tuberculosis.

6. That there be education on health to prevent diseases, and for hygiene, so that the two medicines are not mixed up . . .

CHAPTER ELEVEN

Tzotzil and Chol Struggles in the North: Land, Labor, and the CIOAC, the Farm Workers and Peasants Independent Central, 1977, 1978, 1984

By 1970 the most dangerous part of the state was the north. Through the mountains and valleys down from San Cristóbal toward Tabasco and the Gulf, in the coffee and ranching municipalities of Huitiupán, Sabanilla, Simojovel, Tila, Tumbalá, and Salto de Agua, where 60 to 80 percent of the people were Tzotzil or Chol, governments since the 1930s had expropriated many estates and distributed the land in ejidos. But many other estates remained, holding the region's best land. And despite much emigration south and east to the Lacandón jungle, there remained many landless laborers, some on the ejidos, waiting for land, working for a pittance now and then on the estates, others actually resident on the estates, praying for the landlord's continued patronage, working his land and crops and cattle for him in return for the use of a patch where they exploited themselves. Of these estate laborers, miserable as they all were, some had more for themselves than others. The baldíos actually rented idle patches from the landlord, and paid him in shares or money, but also, always, in labor when needed, as sharecroppers, tenant farmers, and the master's servants. The *peones acasillados* (literally, "housed peons"), stuck permanently on the estates, even to the third generation, used their patches to survive only to labor for the landlord, as his perpetual servants, in effect his serfs. By 1970 the region featured some 10,000 such landless and practically bonded laborers. Other laborers often called them slaves.

Immediately after the Indian Congress in 1974 30-odd communities in the region united to try to take lands already long granted to them but not yet ceded to them. (One case in Huitiupán—see, in Reading No. 10, the part on "Tzotzil Position on Land"—was that of the ejido Lázaro Cárdenas, granted land in 1964, but ten years later still administratively prevented from taking it.) They also raised a movement to improve wages and working conditions for landless laborers. They failed at both efforts. When they fought again, harder, they triggered massive state-police repression throughout the region. They got no help from the PRI's then worse than useless CNC. It took two years for the communities to reunite. In 1977 they turned to the CIOAC, the new Farm Workers and Peasants Independent Central, the only (putatively) national agrarian organization in Mexico then offering to defend the rights of rural laborers under the federal labor law as well as press claims for land due to peasants under the federal agrarian law.

The CIOAC's origins were in the Mexican Communist Party's struggles in the 1950s to rebuild its popular support in the countryside. In 1963, in the excitement over the Cuban Revolution, one of the party's principal agrarian leaders, Ramón Danzós, had helped to organize (against the CNC) a broad leftist agrarian association, the Peasants Independent Central, the CCI. The new organization split the very next year. Two CCIs, one increasingly in cahoots with the PRI, the other communist, had then contested the field until 1975, when the latter reorganized for action on farm labor as well as land disputes, and renamed itself the CIOAC. Two years later coffee workers in Huitiupán, Sabanilla, and Simojovel, following the CIOAC's lead, formed the Independent Union of Peasants of Northern Chiapas, a CIOAC affiliate.

After the repression of July 11, 1977, described in the first selection that follows, the still protesting communities broke with the CIOAC, and in 1978 turned to the Línea Proletaria. This involved them in broader strategies and struggles, the fiery result of one of which appears in the second selection that follows. The initially united communities fell apart. Some joined the CNC, praying for its patronage. Others stayed with the Línea Proletaria, which brought considerable benefits for three or four years, then (in the national economic crisis of 1982) sinking losses.

But others returned to the CIOAC when it returned in 1979, on a unionizing campaign for the long haul. Concentrating on Simojovel, CIOAC organizers in 1980 led peones acasillados on 36 estates there to form a statewide farm and ranch workers' union. The state labor board would not register it. In 1981 the new union, with more locals and legally better prepared, again met the board's refusal to register it. In 1982 it went yet again to the board, yet again in vain. In 1983 it organized a "Peasant March from Chiapas to Mexico City" to publicize its members' grievances. Meanwhile the CIOAC national office and the union, despite its juridical invisibility, were continuing to organize in Simojovel and other northern municipalities, to press landlords to negotiate contracts, to fight for fair prices in the state's sale of land to northern communities, to protest exorbitant indemnities to landlords for land taken for a new dam in the region, to demand full indemnities and agreeable relocation of the communities that would lose their land to the dam, in short to infuriate landlords and their stewards in the state and federal governments. One violent reaction in 1984 appears in the third selection. But the CIOAC continued its struggle. Ten years later, although old and new rivals had gained substantial support in the north, the CIOAC remained the deepest and strongest organization in the region.

Proceso, from which the following reading is excerpted, is a Mexico City weekly news magazine. Founded in 1976 by journalists purged from Mexico City's daily *El Excélsior* for their independent political reporting, it has since then been the world's best source of information on economic, social, and political injustice in Mexico.

AUGUST 1, 1977[*]

In a combined operation on July 11 the army with helicopters and land forces besieged some ten villages in Chiapas in the region of Simojovel, Huitiupán, and Sabanilla. More than 250 persons were captured, . . . mostly women and children, then freed after four days of detention in the federal school at Simojovel. Three children drowned in the river when peasants were driven out of San Isidro, and several more died [from lack of medical attention] . . . in an epidemic of whooping cough in the region.

Peasants from San Isidro, Pauchil, Naquém, San Antonio, La Lámina—their houses burned, all their work tools and belongings stolen, from clothes, food, and domestic animals to radios and village loudspeakers—were the main victims of the aggression. Others managed to flee before the army arrived . . .

This was the culmination of a series of aggressions against peasant groups that have claimed land in the region. In many cases these are Indians who for three generations have been living as landless laborers on the fincas, and now refuse to remain in this situation of virtual slavery.

Dr. Mercedes Olivera, who is coordinating a study in the region for the Institute of Anthropological Research of the National University, writes in a statement to Governor Jorge de la Vega Domínguez, dated last April 18, that in this region there are at least 10,000 such laborers.

---

[*] Pp. 20–21. (Translation by John Womack, Jr., with help from Jan Rus and Emilio Kourí.)

When peasants begin to fight for the land where they have lived for decades, the landlords "free" them because they no longer need their labor, but do need the land they occupy. As a result, "freed" or expelled laborers have formed colonies and are asking for the creation of ejidos: Limas, Chañival, Mercedes Isidoro, Ramos, Naquém, and others, such as those recently evicted by the army.

For their part, landowners have pressed the government, the police, and the army to evict the laborers, whom they call "invaders"—in some cases after official grants of land to them—, and it is now clear that the landowners have received state support.

The situation in the zone has turned explosive. . . . On June 9 authorities in Tuxtla Gutiérrez called peasants from Simojovel, Huitiupán, and Sabanilla to the state capital with the promise that their agrarian problems would be resolved. But the governor refused to receive them, and sent them to the state agrarian officer, Leandro Molinar Meraz, and to the deputy attorney general, Fernando Reyes Cortés, who threatened to jail them and send the army to their villages. The meeting to "solve" problems ended in the detention of five peasant leaders, who were freed hours later only by the pressure of some 1,000 petitions for land.

The next day the army went into Nuevo San Antonio, "headed by Blas Morales, owner of the San Antonio Las Montañas finca," according to a report by the Independent Union of Peasants of Northern Chiapas, an organization of the region's landless farm workers. Houses were burned, women raped, peasants taken prisoner, their personal effects stolen, as would happen a month later in ten other villages.

After the army's latest violent entry into the villages—other peasants, at the service of the region's landowners, accompanied the army and identified the independent leaders in each community—, the victims in an assembly of 27 localities and 800 peasants agreed to ask for an indemnization for the death of the children, Domingo Pérez García, Herminda García, and Mariano García, who all drowned crossing the river under army orders, another child who died in Chichimeca, and the theft of their personal effects.

"The governor denies that there were thefts, and says the state won't pay a cent. Besides, he repeats that as 'often as necessary we will again use the forces of public security to guarantee private property,'" according to Dr. Olivera and José Rodríguez Mendoza, of the CIOAC, the Farm Workers and Peasants Independent Central.

In a single-spaced, six-page declaration the peasants recount the abuses and harm done to them. They tell how in Naquém the owner of the estate there, Capt. Jorge Mazón Penagos [paternally and maternally a grandly landed officer], came with the army and insulted and struck peasants.

In Simojovel, where the Marcos E. Becerra School was used as a jail, several peasants from San Isidro, where 14 houses had been burned, and from

Naquém, were thrown out of helicopters from heights of 15 or 20 feet. There the landlords themselves, local ranchers and coffee planters, pushed peasants around and threatened them with death for being "land grabbers."

Under detention, the peasants were interrogated as to the names and location of their leaders. Most were not given anything to eat. Some were given crackers and coffee once a day.

The peasants of Pauchil, 42 families, who have fought for land for many years, were moved to Socoltenango, near the Pujiltic [sugar] mill, where they were promised they would be given land.

But they demand that the owner of the finca Covadonga, Humberto Hidalgo, who claims to own Pauchil, pay them for their harvest and the work they lost because of being evicted from the property. This amounts to half a million pesos. He wants to pay them only 100,000 pesos.

In the army's operation two persons were wounded by gunfire. According to peasants in the region, landlords in Simojovel and Huitiupán had been meeting for several weeks to plan the eviction. "They raised money to pay armed men," the peasants said, and mentioned Arnulfo Zenteno, another landlord whose last name is Cancino, also Capt. Jordan Mazón Penagos, and Manuel and Antonio Hidalgo Niño, Humberto Hidalgo's sons, who run the regional cattlemen's association. "The soldiers' quarters are the office of the cattlemen's association, and it costs the landlords thousands of pesos to maintain the soldiers and feed them."

. . . Dr. Olivera states that the peasants have demanded that authorities survey the estates in question "in accord with the titles of property that are presented," because many landlords simply take over land and then say that it is theirs. The peasants also demand that all procedures be expedited for grants and amplifications of ejidos that have been under petition for many years in this region.

APRIL 17, 1978*

On Sunday April 3 a group of Indians was playing basketball on the ejido court in Taniperla [in northern Ocosingo municipality], Chiapas. At three in the afternoon 41 armed soldiers and several cattlemen from the region arrived. A lieutenant announced that "for good or bad" the Indians had to leave the village and their fields. The Indians refused.

The next day at seven in the morning the rattle of machineguns firing in the direction of the village emphasized that the lieutenant would enforce his order. Half an hour later the soldiers threatened to burn the Indians' huts if

_____

* Pp. 20–22.

they did not leave them. At noon, protected by the army, 54 landlords burned the village, two schools, and a Mexican flag.

Taniperla is between the Lacandón jungle and the zone of Los Altos, an area inhabited by some 500,000 Tzeltal, Tzotzil, Chol, Tojolabal, and Lacandón Indians, who survive in misery, suffering agrarian problems that date from colonial times and cause permanent social tension . . .

Taniperla is also some 90 kilometers from Comitán, where the Defense Ministry is building the biggest military base in the country, according to General Juan F. Tapia García, commander of the 24th Motorized Cavalry Regiment there.

Comitán, some few kilometers from the Guatemala border and very near the biggest hydroelectric dams and the most important oil fields of the country, is regarded as the door to the jungle and Los Altos.

The federal government is also building a system of roads, with parallel airstrips, which, starting from Comitán, will surround the oil fields, the dams, the jungle, and Los Altos. In the center of this system will remain the half a million Indians with their social problems . . .

On last March 26, 3,000 soldiers from the military zones of Chiapas, Oaxaca, and Guerrero paraded through the streets of San Cristóbal de Las Casas—the metropolis of the Indian zones—to commemorate the 450th anniversary of the city's foundation by the conquistador Diego de Mazariegos . . .

In Chiapas the army is under the command of General José Hernández Toledo, who achieved public notoriety in 1968 when he led the so-called "Olympic Battalion," which took part in the events of October 2 of that year [the violent repression of a massive civic demonstration in Mexico City, resulting in at least 250 civilian dead].

Governor de la Vega Domínguez said in his first annual report on the state's affairs, "Here our soldiers, officers, and commanders have worked in a tireless manner and with a great sense of responsibility. At their head we have the prestigious Divisional General José Hernández Toledo."

Nevertheless the Indians have reasons for distrust. . . . The leaders of 27 ejidos in Chiapas have protested the assaults committed against peasants who work on the Naquém finca. They demand that the hired gunmen who have fired on the peasants there to frighten them away be withdrawn from the finca. On July 11 last year the peasants were driven out by the army and their personal effects stolen. The army then withdrew, but shortly the gunmen arrived.

Attached is a statement signed by 15 Tzotzil and Chol ejidatarios from Huitiupán, Simojovel, and Sabanilla in which they protest the arbitrary acts being committed with the support of soldiers against these Indian groups to take away their land. In the letter the Indians denounce Chiapas Deputy Attorney General Fernando Reyes Cortés, who has distinguished himself by personally leading the repression throughout the state . . .

APRIL 24, 1984*

Simojovel de Allende, Chiapas. In the mountains of this . . . part of Los Altos . . . , with 16 Indian municipalities, people don't sleep. Day and night messengers run the roads from community to community to warn of the arrival of the public security forces. This is how the Tzotzils have organized to repel the police and landlords who threaten to drive them again from their lands . . .

"The situation now is very difficult," declared Ernesto López, Indian leader of the zone. "We're not standing for any more threats, beatings, or bullets from the police and the landowners."

Peasants from the CIOAC, the OCEZ, and even from the CNC in Simojovel have been punished and repressed for the sole crime of recovering their lands. The list is long: Vergel, Paredón, La Ilusión, Zacatón, Tres Casas, Pechuag, Jotolchén, La Pimienta, Galeana, San Antonio Los Altos, Arrayán, El Amparo, Concepción, Cacaos, Buena Vista, Santa Anita, and others.

This is the story: The peasants of Jotolchén, members of the CNC, were informed on the morning of April 11 that 40 state security police and eight armed landowners were headed for the community "to evict the invaders." The news terrified the villagers, who had already learned of other aggressions in several regions. Immediately a messenger from the community went to ask for help from the peasants of La Pimienta, also members of the CNC. But when the Pimienta peasants arrived at Jotolchén, its inhabitants had already fled into the mountains.

At 2 p.m. that day the police arrived, accompanying the landowners. The peasants of La Pimienta, who had arrived just minutes before in Jotolchén, decided to talk with the police; many of them put down their machetes to avoid any provocation. But . . . the police began to throw tear gas at them and then fired on them.

Juan López Hernández died immediately when one of the landowners shot him. The death of Fernando Sánchez was more cruel: while two police held him by the arms, the lieutenant of the detachment shot him from a distance of two meters.

There were also wounded, 28 in all. Four of them—Román Pérez Rojas, Rafael Hernández Pérez, Miguel Pérez Díaz, and Andrés González Ruiz—

---

* Pp. 27–30.

were taken in serious condition to a hospital under the custody of the state judicial police.

The state government . . . , in its eagerness to justify the police intervention and avoid responsibility for the murder of the two peasants, issued a press bulletin . . . saying, "Peasants from the ejidos of Jotolchén and La Pimienta, incited by leaders of the CNPA [Coordinadora Nacional del Plan de Ayala, another radical peasant association demanding more redistribution of land to landless laborers] and the PSUM [Mexican United Socialist Party, successor to the Mexican Communist Party, which had dissolved in 1981], Sebastián Pérez Núñez, Enrique López Ruiz, and Luis López Vázquez, confronted another group of Indians from Las Palmas in this municipality, whom they tried to evict from their lands in a premeditated invasion."

The bulletin adds, ". . . the CNPA and PSUM peasants, from Jotolchén and La Pimienta, had known about the action . . . 24 hours ahead of time, due to the fact that by loudspeaker they had been called by the leaders of both organizations to carry out the invasion."

But the bulletin contains serious contradictions. First, Jotolchén and La Pimienta are ejidos that belong to the CNC, which was confirmed, a day after the aggression, by the leader of that organization in Chiapas, Oscar Ochoa Zepeda. Also, the communiqué reflects a complete ignorance of the zone's problems, or, what is worse, a premeditated distortion of the facts to justify the arrest of the leaders mentioned, who belong to the Farm Workers and Peasants Independent Central.

Two days before these events, on April 9, peasants and Indians from La Pimienta, Jotolchén, Galeana, Virginia, and Berlín, all in the CNC, had taken part in a march that was to go to the state capital, where the marchers were going to demand that the governor withdraw the police from Simojovel municipality and turn over the lands claimed by the peasants. The march was broken up by the police. . . . Only representatives of the communities managed to reach the capital.

On the next day, April 10 [the date of Emiliano Zapata's assassination in 1919, which every year agrarian organizations all across the country commemorate], contingents from the CNPA, the CIOAC, and the CNC marched to the municipal seat, Simojovel, with the same demands and in support of the mobilization that was taking place that same day at the national level . . .

On April 11 came the government's response: the murders of the Jotolchén peasants.

In the face of this violence, the Indians decided to carry out a series of actions repudiating the state government's policy. During Holy Week they did not allow landowners to hear Mass in Simojovel, where prayers were being said for the murdered peasants. And they announced a sit-in of 50 communities to ask the governor to indemnify the families of the murdered peasants.

The miserable conditions in which the Indian population of this region lives sharpen day to day because of the systematic repression comparable to a state of siege in certain villages. Peasants who normally spend their time at work in their corn patch now pass most of the day expecting the police to appear.

Besides, the confinement of laborers to the farm where they work, the requirement that they use the company store, and the employer's right to give his laborers a kicking are matters of daily life on the fincas of the great landlords here, Trejo, Hidalgo, Anzures, Flores, Mazón, Zúñiga, Penagos, Del Carpio, and Vallinas, who have held economic and political power for decades in the region and the state.

The key problem of the region—super-exploitation of landless laborers living on estates, monopolization of land, inadequate ejido grants, and the climate of violence—has paradoxically worsened with the project for the Itzantún hydroelectric installation and the discovery of great oil fields. The Itzantún dam will flood 11,000 hectares of the zone's best land.

Anthropologist Ana Bella Pérez Castro . . . emphasizes three transcendental facts about the region: [1] In 1934 Cárdenas recognized landless laborers resident on estates as subjects with agrarian rights. [This change in the agrarian law actually dates from before Cárdenas, 1933, but Cárdenas did use it broadly and effectively.] From that date to 1940 eight ejidos were formed in the region. From 1940 to 1958, as agrarian policy folded back into defense of private property, invasions of land broke out in Simojovel and Huitiupán.

[2] Years later, in April 1975, the struggle began again, when lands were taken for the Lázaro Cárdenas ejido, a movement that was brutally repressed by the army on June 10, 1977.

History repeated itself with each governor in turn. Manuel Velasco Suárez, Jorge de la Vega Domínguez, Salomón González Blanco, Juan Sabines Gutiérrez, and now Absalón Castellanos Domínguez have only responded with violence to the historic claim of the Indians of the region . . .

[3] On October 26, 1980, the farm workers union backed by the CIOAC was born in Los Altos. Enrique López Ruiz, a member of the CIOAC state committee, recalls that seven months later—in May 1981—laborers on 30 fincas went on strike. Their demands were elementary: an eight-hour day, the minimum wage, social security, and benefits as the labor law provides.

Luis López Vázquez, the CIOAC general secretary in Chiapas, declares that in Los Altos there are 10,000 farm workers subjected to servile labor relations on the cattle ranches and coffee plantations. "In this zone," he says, "the landlords extract their profit not so much from the investment of capital, but from the super-exploitation of workers by their confinement to the estate."

"Today," he adds, "they produce cattle . . . , coffee, and basic agricultural products under the same forms of exploitation as were practiced in the nineteenth century."

On a trip to various fincas it was possible to collect testimony from several landless estate laborers that reflected the exploitation they suffer.

Andrés Díaz López, from the finca El Vergel, recounted, "I got to last until when the boss was paying us five pesos a day, but the oldest, they used to pay them for all their work only 25 centavos a day, later 50 centavos, then a peso, till they got up to five. I worked 16 years, loading lumber, running the coffee-processing machines, in the corn field, picking coffee, stringing wire fence, carrying rock out of the field. Doing that work, the oldest men died, and the landowner wouldn't even give them medicine. When we got sick, they'd give us an aspirin for medicine. And if we asked for money to buy something that might cure us, the boss would tell us that the aspirin had run up our bill and we owed too much for any more advance."

Sebastián Pérez Gutiérrez, from the finca El Porvenir, recalled, "I started to work when I was ten, making 20 centavos a day and working from six in the morning to six at night. When I got bigger, I began to make 25 centavos, and the bigger boys 50 centavos. When I got to be a man, the landowner paid me a peso for 12 hours of work. I cleared pasture, chopped weeds out of the coffee, picked corn, carried rock. After so much work, I saw nothing from it. The more I worked, the poorer I was, and the owner was getting richer. I was seeing so much suffering in my family, that's why I began to think of organizing and the struggle that we are making right now."

Meanwhile, because landless estate laborers have organized and filed a demand before the state labor board that any estate be seized if the landowner does not pay debt contracted with his laborers, . . . the landlords have decided to abandon the land and to accuse the laborers of being invaders and communists, denying that they have hired them and justifying in this way the repression against organized laborers.

During the term of the previous governor, Juan Sabines Gutiérrez, the state twice refused to register the Farm Workers Union of the region. Now Governor Absalón Castellanos Domínguez not only is refusing registration, but also, say the independent peasant organizations, "increasing his use of the police . . . against communities that claim their land and labor rights."

CHAPTER TWELVE

The Proletarian Line: From Torreón to the Canyons, 1976–1977

Bishop Ruiz first invited irreligious leftists to work in his diocese in 1973 to help prepare the Indian Congress in 1974. The reason was not ideological but practical, and the leftists chosen not deliberately but as luck would have it. The "promoters" in charge of organizing the congress needed to develop a corps of translators for its sessions. They contracted with a young historian-linguist from the National Institute of Anthropology and History, already teaching at the diocesan seminary, to recruit and train the translators. As they then went with the Indian "coordinators" of the congress to meetings with delegations in the four Indian zones, they saw that the coordinators would need "advisers" to frame multitudinous denunciations and protests into coherent demands—and organize post-congress excitement into a coherent Indian movement. It happened that their man for translations had friends at the National School of Agriculture, in Chapingo, just outside Mexico City, running a project to organize Indians in Oaxaca. Liberationist clergy in Oaxaca thought well of their work. At the promoters' request the head of the project, a professor of economics at Chapingo, sent a few students to the diocese. They proved to be excellent advisers. The promoters wanted more of them, indefinitely. The professor agreed, but explained that so engaged his students would do "broader sociological work, different from [the Church's], based on Marxism." There was hardly any other kind of rural social work taking place in Mexico then. The promoters showed "much interest." On the bishop's invitation the professor supplied a full complement of advisers, cadres of his clandestine organization, the Unión del Pueblo, revolutionary Maoists.

Sprung from the student movement and its bloody repression in 1968, secretly formed at Chapingo in 1969 to mount armed protection for "the people" against the government, but one of several such groups in the country then, the People's Union had split in two in 1971. Che Guevarists wanted immediate guerrilla action. Maoists wanted to establish bases of support, mass organizations, a party, a front, before launching "protracted and uninterrupted popular war in stages." The Guevarists had made armed units and started bombing public offices and banks. The Maoists, under academic cover in "social projects," had begun organizing in Mexico City and in various rural districts, mainly in Oaxaca. Some of their best cadres went to Chiapas in 1973–74, above all Jaime Soto.

Working closely with the missionaries, predeacons, and catechists in the canyons, the People's Union advisers were vital to the success of the Indian Congress. Together Javier Vargas (see Reading No. 9) and Jaime Soto gave the special courses for the predeacons, catechists, and ejido officers who would found Chiapas's first Union of Ejidos in December 1975. It was Soto, from his base on one of the ejidos preparing La Qu'iptik, who organized La Organización, the cryptic committee that wrote the union's statutes and regulations and later served practically as its board of trustees. He and another outstanding Chapingo cadre, René Gómez, played essential parts in organizing La Qu'iptik's expansion in 1976 against the federal government's move to evict communities from the Lacandón zone.

Why then, in October 1976, did Bishop Ruiz invite a second faction of the irreligious left to work in his diocese? It is most improbable that he acted simply out of enthusiasm or hospitality, without reflection. It is also unlikely that he worried about depending only on the first faction and wanted a second for balance, because his new deacons held firm control of the union. It seems most likely that he was already figuring the first faction had shown him all it could do, and he needed more. The reason he needed more was the very reason the union had expanded, El Conflicto por la Brecha, the government's action on the Lacandón, which posed a mortal threat to the entire diocesan program in the canyons. Soto and Gómez, for all their admirable qualities, had no better response to the threat than to denounce La Brecha and organize as before but harder. To contend with the government and the powerful new interests in the Lacandón, the bishop needed a bigger, better, and savvier advisory service. When in October, on other business in the northern city of Torreón, he unexpectedly met leading Proletarian Line cadres and heard about their multiple operations, it made perfect sense to invite them to San Cristóbal. The first Maoists had done much good. These Maoists might do much better.

They certainly had much more theory and practical experience. Started in November 1968 among young professors and students in the National University's Faculty of Economics, organized as the "Coalición de Brigadas Emiliano Zapata," their public movement had quickly produced a strategically sophisticated, brilliantly argued, actually useful call for "decentralized" struggle through "people's politics" for "an organization of a new type" and "people's democracy." Remarkably (anywhere), it had then proceeded to practice what it preached. Its two outstanding intellects had published a masterly analysis of "the national reality," and the movement had gone publicly to work in a Mexicanized and nonviolent Maoism of "protracted and uninterrupted popular struggle [N.B., not war] in stages." In but a few years, in every case against officially protected interests and often violent reactions, it had organized Mexico's first union of ejidos (producing tobacco, on the Pacific Coast just north of Puerto Vallarta), negotiated finance and marketing for a big "coalition" of collective ejidos (farther up the coast, in Sonora), won control of several locals in the National Mine and Metal Workers Union (in three different states), the National Telephone Workers Union (in Mexico City), and the National Educational Workers Union, and put down deep roots around Monterrey and Torreón. And it had continually fought tendencies to become a party. Self-defined as the Línea de Masas, it was a movement ever more broadly informed, articulated, and theorized, but deliberately changing for the people among whom its cadres lived and worked to decide themselves on the struggles they would fight. When eventually some cadres around Monterrey "fetishized the organization," the others nationally broke with them, made new engagements in the area, and renamed the movement the Línea Proletaria. This was when the bishop discovered it in Torreón, expanding, turning crises to advantage, inventive, always looking (like a collective Schumpeterian entrepreneur) for the dynamic initiative.

The one constant in the movement had been the preeminence of its primary intellect and "ideological director," arguably the most remarkable organizer of his generation, Adolfo Orive. He had plenty going for him before 1968. Born in 1940 the son of a distinguished and wealthy Mexican engineer and politician, raised in Mexico's highest political company (including the Cárdenas family), Orive had graduated in civil engineering from the National University, studied economics with Charles Bettelheim at the École des Hautes Études from 1961 to 1965, been taken by his family then to see Eastern Europe, the Soviet Union, India, and China, returned to study with Bettelheim (in his most Cultural Revolutionary days) till 1967, and read with Joan Robinson at Cambridge in 1967–68. But once back in Mexico in the summer of 1968 (after the student movement had begun), having organized Economics into the "Coalición Emiliano Zapata," he had put his privileges to dazzlingly effective use for "the people."

In 1977, before Orive went to Chiapas, his Línea published a series of pamphlets to explain in simple terms to militants and masses the crucial importance of the Monterrey issues, what the true Línea was. Excerpts from the third pamphlet follow. Because the language is for clarification inside the movement and occasionally therefore in the movement's jargon, three references cannot be literally translated and convey their real meaning; they remain in Spanish here. For a definition of compañero, see Reading No. 7.

Colonia is literally "colony" (as in Chiapas's canyons), but here really means a neighborhood in the shanty towns that had spread around almost all of Mexico's big cities in the 1960s, and grown in the 1970s. The "social democrats," a literal translation, are concretely the cadres in Monterrey who had not followed Orive's line, and generally the misguided and the misleading in other movements and all parties who act as described in the text. "Brigade," another literal translation, is in this context the tactical unit of the student movement in 1968, by extension the tactical unit of the movement in the colonias and comparable terrain. *Brigadista* is a militant in the movement. An "orientator," yet another literal translation, is a brigadista who orients others, as described here.

P.S. Orive had been Carlos Salinas's most inspiring professor at the University in 1968–69, and the Línea de Masas and the Línea Proletaria remained Salinas's tightest connections on the left while he pursued his political career. Many cadres from both Líneas contributed to Salinas's successes before and during his presidency, and flourished politically from them, to become senator, deputy, governor, assistant minister in the cabinet, or, in the case of Hugo Andrés Araujo, once the main cadre around Torreón, the reformist secretary general of the National Peasant Confederation. But by choice or for lack of their chances Orive did not go into official public service. In 1982, having designed the Union of Union's credit union, he concluded that for the past 11 years, as he later said, "I had been mistaken on the paradigm," and went into private consulting on regional development projects. In 1990 he joined the PRI, but did not run for any office or receive any appointment in the government, until Ernesto Zedillo became president. Then he became technical secretary in the Ministry of Social Development, to design the ministry's projects. In January 1998, soon after the latest massacre in Chiapas, Orive was promoted to "coordinator of advisers" in the Ministry of Interior. In an interview then he said the president's instructions to him were that "the new strategy that the Executive Office if going to present for the solution of all of Chiapas's problems must be inclusive, participatory, and take into account the points of view of all sides involved."

¿QUÉ ES LA LÍNEA PROLETARIA?*

Many compañeros from social-democratic colonias ask us what the proletarian line consists in. After two months of daily struggle with them, it is worth summarizing the main points of our line.

*Línea Proletaria, No. 3 (June 20, 1977), p. 1–12.

1. The Masses Are the Motive Power of History

Through all of human history exploiters and leaders have used the people for their personal benefit. They say that the masses are ignorant, incompetent, and lazy. They say that leaders have to command them and put them to work . . .

The proletarian line puts things totally to the contrary. The masses are those who work, who are in contact with practical problems, who confront the exploiters, and it is therefore they who know most, are most competent.

The working masses in their struggle are those who make history [emphasis in the original, here and below], not leaders or employers or government officials.

Those who do not have full confidence in the masses, who do things in their place, are not proletarian.

2. Political Organization

For the masses truly to make history, and our first point not be just wishful thinking out loud, they have to have in their hands the power of decision . . .

In our colonias we have all agreed that the General Assembly holds the maximum power of decision, not leaders. But so that the General Assembly represents us all, we have to participate in it, give our opinions, and discuss them. There is no point in a General Assembly with little participation, where the leaders and one or another speechifying compañero give their opinions and we simply raise our hands to vote as they say . . .

The Bourgeoisie has for a long time prevented us from learning how to discuss things, how to do politics. It is hard for many of us to speak in public, or we are afraid of making a mistake. Therefore, before the General Assemblies, we must do Block Assemblies. Here we all know each other, and we are fewer. It is easier for us to speak and to learn how to discuss things and make decisions. Then the proposals agreed in each block go to the General Assembly . . .

Once the General Assemblies take accords, an executive body has to put them into practice. We have to elect block commissioners to carry out, with our support, all the accords taken . . .

In other words, the ideas come *from the masses* in their Block or Sector Assemblies; they are systematized in discussions of the block proposals *by the masses* themselves in the General Assembly; and they are brought back *to the masses* by the executive body's commissioners to be realized in practice . . .

3. Ideological Organization

. . . The social-democratic orientation consists in giving ideas and opinions from the top down, as if ideas came from someone who knows more than us and acts as if he were our father. It may be that an idea is good, but this kind of orientation does not teach us how to get ideas.

It is as if someone gave us a fish to satisfy our hunger, but would not teach us how to fish. We are going to have to depend on him forever, and that is what social-democratic leaders want, for us to depend on them forever . . .

The proletarian orientation consists in asking questions so that we ourselves get ideas and accurate opinions. This way, instead of being given a fish, we learn how to fish . . .

There are always some compañeros who at any moment have more proletarian ideas and attitudes than others do. They are the ones who at that moment serve as our orientators. But these same compañeros may not always be the ones who have the best ideas and attitudes. So they do not always have to be the orientators. As we change commissioners, we also can and must change orientators when they no longer serve us in a proletarian way . . .

The orientators of each block meet in the colonia's brigade. The brigade is therefore the colonia's leading ideological organization. It is ideological because its task is to orient, but not to take decisions for the colonia. It is leading in the sense that a school is an ideological organization, but not one deciding the ideas it teaches . . .

Then the brigades from the different colonias meet in the region's leading ideological organization, and so on.

The task of the leading ideological organization is to orient in a proletarian way (on the basis of questions and not orders) the Block, the General Assemblies, the commissioners' executive bodies, etc. . . .

For social democracy, the brigade is *not* subject to the control of the masses. The brigadistas are named by the leaders. They meet behind the back of the masses. And they serve forever as orientators, whatever their ideas and attitudes. It is they who in fact make the decisions, and bring them to the Assemblies only for us to vote them. Social democracy says that the masses do not have the capacity for knowing much and it is not necessary to tell them everything . . .

For the proletarian line, the brigadistas have to be named and recognized by the masses in Block Assemblies and the General Assembly. This way, the brigade is an organization of the masses, inside their movement, and not something that comes to them for above and outside. Only this way can the masses, through their political bodies, control their leading ideological body, which is the brigade. They can make or remove orientators according to whether these are proletarian or not.

But the brigade, as it orients the political bodies such as the Block Assemblies and the General Assembly, is showing them the direction to take. This is why we say it is a leading ideological organization.

The brigade directs and the General Assembly decides and controls. In the diagram of our organization we therefore put the brigade not above or below but alongside the ranked political bodies, because it does not command them, it orients them. And it orients them from inside, not outside, because in each assembly there are brigadista compañeros who from within the assembly, on the basis of questions, show the best direction to take. But if the masses are not in accord with the brigade's orientation, it is the masses who command, who decide, who have the last word, and the brigadistas have to fold into the accord, as the members they are of the masses . . .

4. Forms of Struggle

. . . We know that as ordinary people we cannot resolve our problems except collectively. The bourgeoisie and its government want to keep us asleep, but every day more of us are disposed to struggle for our rights. Because this is a struggle against those who exploit and oppress it, it is a true class struggle . . .

The class struggle happens in all walks of our life.

We fight *economic struggles* to resolve our need for food, housing, work, education, social security.

We fight *political struggles* against the corrupt bosses who prevent us from having our own representatives in the unions, against the police and the army when they repress us, and against the government itself when we demand that it fulfill its obligations to the people or when it tramples on our rights.

We fight *ideological struggles* against ideas and attitudes that the bourgeoisie puts in our head and that divert us from the proletarian path . . .

Not all forms of struggle are proletarian. Although thousands take part in a demonstration, this is not necessarily a proletarian mobilization. The PRI . . . makes demonstrations with millions of workers and peasants, but these are not proletarian.

For a struggle . . . to be proletarian, it has to put proletarian politics in command and proletarian ideology as its objective.

What does it mean to put proletarian politics in command?

It means that a struggle to get water in the colonia or to build a school has to be discussed by the Blocks, decided by the colonia's General Assembly, coordinated according to a program by the executive body's commissioners, and carried out mainly by our own efforts, that is, by the work of the masses . . . At the end of the struggle our organization is going to matter more to us than the water we get. Why does the organization matter more to us than the water? Because with the organization we can continue to resolve all our needs, even transform society and defeat the bourgeoisie and its government, and without the organization we cannot resolve anything by ourselves; we continue to depend on leaders and the government.

What does it mean to put proletarian ideology as the objective?

It means that the struggle to get water or build a school must not have as its main objective our own benefit, but the benefit of all. We must accustom ourselves to struggle to serve others, to serve all the people, more than to serve ourselves regardless of them . . .

5. Theoretical Formation

Social democracy also separates theory from organization and struggle. To start, they do not study theory, and when they do, the study circles are only for the brigadistas. Sometimes they will give theory to the masses, but it is the same old script, and they never try to systematize their own experiences . . .

Theory is the systematization of the just ideas of the people's struggle all over the world. This theory we must all know so that we can all take part in discussions. Otherwise only a few use the experience of the class struggle elsewhere.

Also, theory must be made and learned during the course of struggle, so that it may help us to direct this struggle better.

Only if the people themselves make theory through their organizations and learn it in the course of struggle can it be said that their theoretical formation is proletarian.

6. Forms of Growth

. . . To grow we must follow the masses' tracks . . .

But to follow their tracks is not enough if there is no work of systematic organization, every day. Who must be the orientators of this organization? . . . Our experience in past struggles, our participation in proletarian organizations, lets us be ourselves the orientators of compañeros more backward than we are. So that the orientation is more on target, so that there are more opinions, it is best that the orientator not be a cadre, but a commission of compañeros . . . This way, the orientation is better because it is collective. The orienting commission itself becomes more proletarian because it learns more when it has to teach. Most important is that it is establishing tight connections among different mass organizations. That is, *we are uniting all the people* . . .

7. Relations Between Organizations

Bourgeois ideology penetrates every organization in a different way and to a greater or lesser degree. Therefore the only real way to win the people from the enemy, even within its organizations or in general among the masses with which they work, is by ideological struggle. But this struggle has to be fought not with a lot of words, in discussions that last hours and hours and in which only a few leaders take part, but in work, in the resolution of every colonia's and every work center's concrete problems, in dealing with the masses, in the organization of their own apparatus, in their theoretical formation, to show in fact, in practice, the difference between proletarian and bourgeois forms of organization and struggle. The ideological struggle between organizations would thus show in political practice the accuracy of the proletarian line . . .

CHAPTER THIRTEEN

Agrarian Struggles in the Central Valley: Peasant Mobilization and the OCEZ, 1980–82

San Bartolomé de Los Llanos, Saint Bartholomew of the Plains, did not appear in the Spanish historical record until 1595. A hardy little Tzotzil village, down the cold, rocky highlands toward the hot, fertile, open country along the Grijalva River, on a "bad road" from San Cristóbal, it then impressed a Dominican inspector as a big, "well disposed and hard working," but still idolatrous village. Although eventually the royal highway between San Cristóbal and Guatemala City passed through the village, no one not from there paid the place much mind for another 170 years or so, not royal officials, not Dominicans, not even ladinos looking for Indians to work fertile land. In 1767 San Bartolomé appeared in the record for the first time on its own initiative, clearly guarding by then substantial interests, to petition the Crown to grant it the abandoned lands of an extinct village just north on the river, some 55,000 acres. The Crown granted the petitioners nearly 12,000 acres; the next year they bought the remainder for 200 ounces of gold. All told, the village then owned more than 170,000 acres.

A century later, thanks to Mexican Independence, the Republic, and merchant capital, Liberal land officers and ladino entrepreneurs found the place (as their likes found other such places), settled there, and began their primitive accumulation. San Bartolomé became ever less a Tzotzil village, ever more a mere community of peasants continually losing their land to ladino landlords slowly building a town among them. By 1910 the community had lost vast tracts of land. Thanks to the Revolution, which left ladino counter-revolutionaries in charge in 1920, it lost most of the remainder. In 1924, under the new constitution, the new agrarian code, and a new reformist governor, it applied for restitution of its lost lands, in vain. In 1929 its first agrarian leader was murdered. In 1934 it lost its name too: the then anticlerical state government required all cities, towns, and villages named for saints to take patriotic names; the little town of San Bartolomé and its municipality got the name of the first president under the Revolutionary Constitution, Venustiano Carranza (assassinated in 1920). Five years later under a Cardenista governor the community received a grant for an ejido, but a very small fraction of the lost lands. In disbelief it formed a committee to try to confirm its original titles for another claim for restitution. But when the Cardenista governor left office, the committee suddenly faced menacing obstacles. Despite Carranza's isolation—no road any more there from anywhere or to anywhere, only a motorboat to cross the river—the town's old and new ladino landlords, merchants, and Revolutionary officials had prospered, in particular three allied families that dominated local business and politics, and they forcefully conveyed their determination, in contempt of the community and its committee, to expand their prosperity and power. They promptly co-opted local ejido authorities into their deals.

For 40 years the community of Carranza struggled on its own, in constant danger, continual frustration, and ominously increasing exposure to wealthy and powerful predators. In 1945 it filed yet again for restitution, now figured as 173,000 acres. Years passed. The rich families and political bosses in town flourished. Presidents came and went. In 1962 the first new road, unpaved, opened north to the old San Cristóbal-Tuxtla road. In 1965, incredibly, the community received a presidential resolution for almost 125,000 acres. But most of the land was away toward the highlands, much of it rocky, and all still unsurveyed; the community could not take possession. Local leaders who dutifully pressed its case risked death. In seven years three were murdered. The government expropriated the municipality's biggest industry, the bane of another ejido, the Pujiltic sugar mill, but the landlord kept the land. A new paved road north to the new Tuxtla highway and another east to the San Cristóbal-Comitán (Pan-American) highway promoted local agribusiness, but ruined subsistence farmers. In 1974 the conclusive survey of the presidentially approved restitution allowed the community to recover only 70,000 mostly rocky acres. Carranza ignored the Indian Congress in San Cristóbal that year. Construction of the great Angostura dam on the river gave it some temporary jobs, but the projected lake took most of its remaining good land and compelled divisive relocations; the indemnities due were only half paid. The old bosses lost power, but to federal agencies and the Tuxtla PRI, just as dangerous and harder to avoid or resist. In mounting desperation the community adopted a new strategy—public protests, demonstrations, sit-ins, confrontations, land invasions. Another leader was murdered.

In 1976 the violence reached a new scale. The community rallied in town, stoned the houses of the rich, took up arms, one old boss fled, another was murdered, the army came (in UNICEF pickups), and in a shootout two mutineers and seven soldiers were killed. Thirteen from the community went to jail. The army stayed to occupy the town. In 1978 the community seized the municipal offices, demanding their members' release. The prisoners went free, but advised negotiation in the future, no more confrontation. The community split, most of the elders for negotiation, most of the youngsters for more confrontation.

Embroiled in their own conflicts, both factions ignored the struggle over land and labor at nearby Puijiltic, which resulted in a CIOAC union. The PRI's CNC pretended to mediate in the community, and co-opted the youngsters. Federal and state agencies offered new programs of subsidized credit for fertilizer and seed, and loans to buy disputed land. The community split into several feuding factions.

In 1980 for the first time in the history of the community one faction finally sought strength in an expanded field of struggle. It formed the Chiapas Provisional Coordinating Office, and joined the CNPA, the Coordinadora Nacional "Plan de Ayala." This was a "national front of peasant organizations," founded in 1979 to preserve its affiliates' independence from the government and political parties and provide mutual support in struggle. Significantly, the CNPA was only one of several such "coordinating fronts" then, the most important—and the closest to the CNPA—being the CNTE, the "national coordinator" for "educational workers," leftist schoolteachers.

The new coordinating office used its new allies well, gained affiliations locally and elsewhere in the state, from the Tzotzil north down to the once socialist Pacific Coast, and continued its dangerous confrontations. In 1982 it consolidated and renamed itself the Organización Campesina Emiliano Zapata, OCEZ. It also hosted in Carranza the CNPA's fifth national "encounter" of its affiliates, the most rousing so far, where delegates not only voted support for the armed resistance in Guatemala and the revolution in El Salvador, but talked privately of such action in Mexico. By then the OCEZ was the most extensive, aggressive, and combative popular organization in the Chiapas countryside (not the kind of help Bishop Ruiz wanted for the Unión Qu'iptik). Through the decade, despite a split in 1988 over whether ever to negotiate for land, it remained the most defiant and agitating agrarian movement in the state. As it gained strength in Tzotzil and Tzeltal country, it began to press outright Indian demands. By the early 1990s, from migration of its members down to the jungle and from its organization of migrants there, it had considerable bases in the canyons.

Textual is a periodical review for research and analysis of rural Mexico published since 1979 at the Universidad Autónoma de Chapingo (originally the National School of Agriculture). In the 1980s its editorial committee invited contributions particularly from "militants in the peasant movement."

The following is part of the OCEZ's presentation at the CNPA "encounter" in Carranza in late July 1982.

MOVIMIENTO CAMPESINO: DOCUMENTOS DE LA OCEZ*

We are a mass peasant organization, independent of the rich and their government. We seek to break the isolation in which we peasant groups who are struggling to resolve our problems find ourselves. Therefore our various communities have united, to coordinate better and act together. We do not belong to any political party.

What Does the OCEZ Struggle For?

Chiapas is a state that produces much oil, coffee, corn, cotton, and cattle, but everything belongs to exploiters. On the natural wealth of Chiapas the Mexican and foreign bourgeoisie are getting even richer. The government, which is at the service of the rich, is exploiting the oil in the north of the state and is going to open three more wells in the Lacandón, and all this oil is so that businessmen may increase their profits.

At present the three great hydroelectric dams on the Grijalva River supply electric power to the Federal District, and the Iztantún dam is in construction, and after that the dam on the Usumacinta.

The lumber companies that are stealing Chiapas's best timber are making great profits.

Agricultural production is also important, for there are places where the land is very fertile, and there are very good harvests of corn and beans. This is very important, above all now that there is a serious shortage of corn and beans to feed the Mexican people. Besides, there is much production of coffee and cattle. All this wealth the people produce with their labor, but we are paid very low wages, and when we sell our harvest we are paid very low prices and in exchange have to buy products we need at very high prices.

Nevertheless, the problems and the great backwardness of our state do not give the bourgeoisie the security it wants for exploiting the people of Chiapas even more.

There is much discontent among the peasants over lack of land and delay in agrarian administrative processes. While 44 families hold some 2,500,000 acres, thousands of us peasants do not have anywhere to work.

---

*Textual, September 1982, pp. 141–146.

The people are tired of municipal presidents being imposed on them, and there are ever more municipalities that object to the results of their elections, among them Tapachula, Villa Las Rosas, Motozintla, Chiapa de Corzo, Villa Corzo [all west and south, none in Los Altos], and many others.

Besides, Chiapas is a very backward state, because for lack of land, money, and technical means, each peasant produces very little, hardly enough to eat.

Many of our communities do not have electric light, water, or paved roads, medical service, schools.

Chiapas is a state with much natural wealth, which the rich are beginning to exploit more and more, and where the big bourgeoisie wants to control all production, in order to improve agriculture, so that the countryside will produce more and so that thousands of us poor peasants get well into the capitalist market, selling cheap and buying dear.

To achieve this, they need the Chiapan people under control; they need to make the majority of the population believe that the government is its friend and at the same time not to allow any popular movement.

It is ever more clear what the policy is that the rich and their government want to put into practice against the people. In December 1980 Congress approved in Mexico City the Law on Farm and Ranch Production and Development, and on February 20, 1981, barely two months later, we had the signing in Chiapas of the Agrarian Confidence Agreement, between the state government, the Ministry of Agrarian Reform, the Ministry of Agriculture and Water Resources, and the CNC. Since then the governor says there is no more land to distribute, and therefore they will no longer accept applications for it, or give responses in favor of peasants.

To resolve the land problem without injury to the rich, without using public force, and to control us, the government has been obliging us, principally the most combative ejidos, to buy lands.

With the landlords the policy is different. The cattlemen's associations, private farmers, coffee growers, to them the governor is giving his support, giving them credit to buy machinery, cutting their taxes, building them irrigation works, giving them money like a present to build their offices, and above all protecting them against land seizures.

That is why the army is prepared to evict land invaders, to kidnap and torture combative peasants, as happened at Wololchán [Golonchán] in Sitalá municipality [northeast, in Los Altos, where on June 15, 1980, the army had killed at least 12 and wounded at least 40], at San Caralampio in Venustiano Carranza municipality, and at the ejido 15 de Septiembre in Suchiate municipality [south, on the coast].

They need to control all political discontent, allowing other political parties to participate [in elections], but always making sure that the PRI keeps winning.

This situation makes us live every day in worse misery and see ourselves obliged to defend ourselves from the exploiters. That is why throughout the whole state dozens of our communities are fighting for land, for the enforcement of presidential resolutions [granting communities land], for better wages, for communal and ejido authorities who will represent our interests, for the government to indemnify us for lands affected by the dams, for water, electric light, and paved roads.

Our peasant groups fighting [for these goals] realized that by each group pulling for itself none of us had any strength, and that to advance in the struggle it was necessary to look for unity with other poor peasant compañeros who also suffer exploitation by the rich.

On the other hand, because political parties and other political organizations are not the correct alternative for the solution of our problems, we thought that we had to build our own organization. And so it was that on August 1 and 2, 1980, we held a political event and a General Peasant Assembly in the community of Venustiano Carranza, and agreed among other things to form a regional organization, which for two years we called the Coordinadora Provisional. On July 18, 1982, we decided that our organization would be called Organización Campesina Emiliano Zapata, OCEZ, the Emiliano Zapata Peasant Organization.

We took the name "Emiliano Zapata" because he fought for the land to belong to the peasants, because he fought for the liberty of the peasants subjected to the yoke of the landlords, for the land to be given back to the communities despoiled of it, because he said that it was necessary to defend the land with arms, and because he fought against all foreign and national capitalists' injustices.

The OCEZ therefore takes up the Zapatista ideals and proposes to struggle for the satisfaction of the peasants' demands.

Principles of the OCEZ

The OCEZ struggles principally by means of mobilizations (land seizures, marches, public meetings), combining them with legal action, because we think that legal action alone does not help us resolve our problems. That is why we say it is necessary to combine correctly legal action with the organized mobilization of the masses.

The OCEZ is against organizations that oblige peasants to buy land, because this is a program of the government to control peasants.

We are an organization that attends to the needs of the people, where decisions are taken by the masses at each place [involved in the struggle], and not just by the ejido commissioner.

To guarantee the participation, organization, and development of the consciousness of the communities, we pursue legal action in broad commissions. This form of struggle serves to control the commissioners, so that they do not sell out, or are jailed or murdered, and to avoid tricks and deals behind the people's back.

When we tire of so much legal procedure without any response, we urge the mobilization of the masses so that the problems are resolved. We do not agree with organizations that mobilize peasants for political campaigns.

The OCEZ makes no alliance with nor supports the programs of the government, because we are against two-faced politics.

Demands of the OCEZ

The OCEZ struggles for the fulfillment of presidential resolutions [granting communities land], the expansion of ejidos, indemnification for lands flooded by the dams, and new ejido population centers.

Struggle for better wages and for the recognition of communal and ejido authorities who represent the interests of the peasants.

Struggle for the freedom of political prisoners.

Struggle for the provision of services to the communities, like water, paved roads, light, and credit.

Actions of the OCEZ

The OCEZ's most important mobilizations have been:

Participation in the National Hunger Strike, which was organized by the CNPA and won the freedom of 15 compañeros from Chiapas—seven from Salto de Agua, two from Tenejapa, four from San Caralampio, and two from Venustiano Carranza.

The march of April 20, 1981, to stop the persecution and repression that at that moment the Tzotzil community Venustiano Carranza was suffering.

Participation in other small mobilizations, by which we have also won the freedom of other peasant political prisoners, the indemnification of the community of Tzajalchén and Katzam for more than 2 million pesos, the freedom of Leandro García López from the ejido Plan de Ayala in Ostuacán municipality, etc.

We have won a stop to repression in the community of Venustiano Carranza and kept the rich from imposing their commissioner of communal properties.

On the other hand, experience teaches us that in isolation from other peasants in the country we will not be able to conquer our enemies, and we have therefore decided to join the CNPA on the following conditions:

1. We will be members of the CNPA while it maintains its independence from the government of the rich and from all political parties.

2. So long as the CNPA struggles for the interests of the people.

3. While the CNPA respects the decisions and the autonomy of each [affiliated] organization.

4. So long as legal procedures are combined with mobilizations.

5. So long as there is mutual support among the CNPA's member organizations.

CHAPTER FOURTEEN

Revolutionaries from Monterrey to Chiapas: The FLN, 1980

The great-grandfather of the EZLN of 1994, the Zapatista Army of National Liberation that actually revolted, was the EIM, the Ejército Insurgente Mexicano, or Mexican Insurgent Army, a minute guerrilla force that a prominent Mexican journalist secretly organized in the 1960s, threw into negligible and unreported action in Chiapas in 1968–69, and then disbanded.

Nine veterans of this episode organized the EIM's clandestine heir, the FLN, the Fuerzas de Liberación Nacional, or Forces of National Liberation, in Monterrey, the big city and state capital of the far northeastern state of Nuevo León, in August 1969. They were all male, in their 20s, passionately anti-Soviet (therefore as well hostile to the Mexican Communist Party), passionately pro-Cuban and Che-Guevarist, most of them from locally respected families, and graduates of the State University of Nuevo León. Their first-ranked officer, César Germán Yáñez, then 26, had taught law at the university, and been director of the local Mexican-Cuban Cultural Institute. The FLN had guns, noms de guerre, Yáñez being "Pedro," and a safe house, but it evidently refrained from violent operations. Deeply suspicious of the urban guerrillas then robbing banks and such, it refused connections with them and evidently did no more than organize clandestine cells in other cities around the country. In late 1971 the state police raided the group anyway. Some of those who escaped, including Pedro, went in early 1972 back to Chiapas, down into the Lacandón jungle, quietly rented a farm, and began secretly training themselves as the Emiliano Zapata Guerrilla Nucleus. In February 1974 the police raided another FLN safe house in Monterrey, captured two cadres, and tortured them to confess. At once federal police captured the FLN headquarters outside Mexico City, killing the organization's second-ranked officer and four others. A few days later federal police and the army captured the training camp in Chiapas, killing Pedro and four others.

Three survivors came together in Mexico City to rebuild the FLN, in effect make it anew. "Alfredo," whose responsibility before had been to manage communication among the various cells, took charge. The others were "Juan," formerly the cell officer for Veracruz, and Pedro's younger brother Fernando Yáñez, "Leo," then 30, an architecture student at the University of Nuevo León in the 1960s, graduate of guerrilla training in the north in 1971– 72, most recently the cell officer for Tabasco, often visiting his brother in Chiapas. In 1976 the couple who under torture two years before had betrayed the organization were murdered (by the police?, by the FLN?). The old cells returned to life. Then Alfredo died from injuries in an accident. Consensus among the cells made Leo the FLN's new first officer; Juan, the second. By 1979, when the Sandinistas won their revolution in Nicaragua and revolutionaries in El Salvador went into action, the FLN had live cells in the Federal District and six states, Nuevo León, Veracruz, Puebla, Tabasco, México, and Chiapas (three of them each twice the size of El Salvador), recruiting and training cadres for its immediate and ultimate struggles for revolutionary socialism in Mexico. This was the context in which the FLN high command in 1980 wrote and published its statutes (42 pages of them), to regulate its new clandestine forces and organize them into the already then named Zapatista Army of National Liberation.

Under these statutes (more or less) Leo and Juan commanded the FLN for the next 13 years. Whatever they won on other "Combat Fronts" and "Clandestine Zones," it was Chiapas that produced most results. In statutory terms the FLN's main cadre there in 1980 was an "urban militant." An alumnus of the San Cristóbal seminary, a one-time theology student at the Gregorian University, after that with the Mexican bishops' Commission on Indian Missions, and an aide in 1973–74 at the Indian Congress, "Jacobo" was then 37 years old, married, and a social worker with the diocesan missionaries in Ocosingo. Using old relations in another direction, in Sabanilla, he carefully recruited a Tzotzil leader of land invasions in the north, who in turn carefully recruited other militants there with kinfolk in the canyons. (Two of these, also Tzotzils, cousins, would on January 1, 1994, both as EZLN majors, command two of the Zapatistas' five offensive regiments.) By 1982, from underground, the FLN was running several successful social programs in San Andrés Larráinzar, maybe the poorest and probably the most rebellious of the Tzotzil municipalities, from which many angry young Indians went to the canyons.

By 1983 Jacobo, then separated from his wife, had become regional director of DESMI. That November the entire FLN high command and several cadres, all changing names for the new mission, Leo to "Germán" (for his brother), Juan to "Rodrigo," the brilliant young Captain "Zacarías" to "Marcos," and so on, went secretly down into the canyon country to see how to develop the Zapatista Army there. Jacobo's cover and support through DESMI was a public health program in the district, which his new girl friend, Comandante "Elisa," publicly managed. When the high command returned to Mexico City in early 1984, Comandante Elisa remained in charge of the new "Southeast Combat Front." Over the next four years, during which she and Jacobo split the blanket but continued their clandestine "political-economic" cooperation, she was primarily responsible for the FLN's robust success in the canyons. In 1988 Commander in Chief Germán relieved her of command—married by then to another cadre, she was pregnant—and appointed her outstanding subordinate, Subcomandante (since 1986) Marcos, to succeed her. So under the Statutes of 1980 the structure of authority remained until January 1993, when the high command (minus Rodrigo) transformed the FLN into the Partido de las Fuerzas de Liberación Nacional, the PFLN, with "Germán" as secretary general, interior secretary, and (still) commander in chief of the EZLN, and (on the new Military Secretary Marcos's motion) created the Clandestine Revolutionary Indian Committee, the CCRI, to validate (or not) a PFLN declaration of war.

Nine months later, in September 1993, it was on this new basis of authority in the CCRI, in the fourth generation of revolutionary projects, that Subcomandante Marcos overthrew Supreme Commander Germán and took sole command of the EZLN to lead it in rebellion on January 1, 1994.

The selection that follows is an indication of the FLN's secret plans and organization when its cadres and militants began serious work in Chiapas. Although for some years Bishop Ruiz and other clerics in his diocese often cooperated with FLN officers and militants in struggles to defend the Indian poor there, they have credibly denied—and their worst enemies have so far presented no evidence to show—that they then knew of this clandestine organization's violently revolutionary purposes, or, if they had known, would have approved of them.

ESTATUTOS DE LAS FUERZAS DE LIBERACIÓN NACIONAL*

Chapter II. General Principles

The FLN is a political-military organization whose goal is that the workers in the fields and the cities of the Mexican Republic take political power in order to install a people's republic with a socialist system.

The enemies who oppress and exploit the Mexican people are: imperialism, above all U.S. imperialism, its partners in Mexico, the Mexican bourgeoisie

---

*(Mexico City, 1980), pp. 2–28.

and its puppets who form the bourgeois Mexican state and its armed agents, the police, the army, and the various paramilitary corps . . . To defeat these enemies, *the FLN combines different forms of struggle, principally the political-economic, the political-military, and the ideological* [emphasis in original, here and below].

Political-economic struggle. Despoiled of the means of production, the people own only their labor power, which they have to sell to be able to subsist. But the worker receives in exchange less than what he himself produces with his work: the capitalist appropriates the difference [between what the worker receives] and the wealth that the worker creates with his own hands, which is always greater than his wages. Perpetuating this exploitation is the true purpose of capitalism's laws, its state. . . . And working people, manacled by the laws that their exploiters elaborate, lacking a political-military vanguard, and violently suppressed by repressive forces (police and army), find as their only alternative the struggle for economic and political conquests limited to the bourgeois legal framework. But the FLN considers as reformist and economist the leaders, organizations, and publications that do not carry out action tending to achieve a basic social change to end the exploitation of workers in the city and the field.

The FLN supports and promotes the creation of mass organizations that sustain in fact their independence from the bourgeois state and its apparatus, and those whose demands go beyond the framework of economic struggles and are linked to a political struggle that leads to the people taking power in their own hands.

The FLN promotes among the masses superior forms of organization and struggle, without pretending to take the place of the masses' natural leaders, but incorporating the masses into the popular movement. It works to accumulate and unify the forces that will produce the vanguard of the revolution.

Political-military struggle. Facing the failure of democratic means and the barbarism of bourgeois repression in the cities and the countryside, facing the murder, imprisonment, torture, and disappearance of those who tried to make a definitive change in the country's situation, our organization was born and has consolidated underground, and in a war to the death it confronts imperialism and its puppets, because the state only allows legally the activities of political organizations that do not seriously propose—in theory or in practice—to end capitalist exploitation, but support it, directly and indirectly, justifying the repression of true revolutionaries. The FLN is the answer to the Mexican people's historic need to organize and unleash revolutionary violence to throw off oppression. It is the synthesis of a long process of struggle by our people, a struggle that now combines considerations of a political order with those of a military order. Its fundamental strategy is to move the Mexican people to sustain a long revolutionary struggle to throw off capitalist domination, considering as we do that armed struggle is an extension and higher expression of mass political struggle and proposing as we do to start this struggle in those places where the unredeemed masses are disposed to take up arms, using geographic and strategic conditions duly evaluated by our military authorities, and to develop simultaneously in the rest of the national territory mass political work and armed harassment against purely military objectives.

The alliance of the workers, the peasants, and the progressive levels of the petty bourgeoisie will be the fruit of the struggle itself. That is, the political linkage of proletarian struggles with the battles in the countryside and the direct participation of workers and students from the city in these battles constitutes the objective union of the revolutionary forces that will defeat the common enemy: capitalism represented by the big landlord and the boss, the banker and the usurer, etc., all supported by their repressive forces.

Ideological struggle. With the purpose of perpetuating its unjust system of exploitation, imperialism spreads ideas, thoughts, artistic expressions, and fashions that contribute to the subjugation of the people. The FLN struggles against imperialist ideology, opposing to it the science of history and society: Marxism-Leninism, which has demonstrated its validity in all the victorious revolutions of this century. Therefore, besides struggling against the ideological dominion of capital, we struggle also against those who, infiltrated into the labor movement, the peasant movement, and the bosom of the left, deny the revolutionary essence of Marxism and preach reformism and class collaboration, instead of the struggle to the death by the exploited against their exploiters.

. . . Chapter IV. On Goals

Article 5. *The immediate goals of the FLN are:*

a) To struggle together with the workers in the countryside and the city, guiding them so that they take political, economic, and military power into their hands.

b) To integrate the struggles of the urban proletariat with the struggles of peasants and Indians in the most exploited zones of our country, and form the Zapatista Army of National Liberation.

c) To develop the class consciousness of the proletariat, showing it the historic role that it is called to fulfill as the vanguard of the socialist revolution, and spreading the true history of our people's class struggle.

d) To strengthen the anti-imperialist consciousness of our people, recovering its long history of struggle for definitive independence.

e) To create and strengthen political connections with all progressive and revolutionary forces in Mexico.

f) To establish links with the revolutionary forces and governments of brother countries.

g) To provide combative solidarity to other nations that struggle for their liberation.

Article 6. *The long-range goals of the FLN are:*

a) To defeat the bourgeoisie politically and militarily, in order to liberate definitively our country from imperialist dominion.

b) To install a socialist system that, through social ownership of the means of production, will suppress the exploitation of the workers and distribute among the population the wealth that it creates, according to the principle, "from each according to his ability, to each according to his work," transferring land to the peasants and factories to the workers.

c) To integrate a popular government with representatives of the revolutionary organizations that have participated in an outstanding and intransigent way on the various fronts of struggle (military, political, ideological) against the governing oppressor, in order *to exercise the dictatorship of the proletariat,* so establishing a workers' state, which will attend to the interests of the majority of the population, and in which work will be obligatory.

d) To form a single political party based on the principles of Marxism-Leninism.

e) To organize the workers' state on the following bases:

I. Expropriation of big factories and industrial installations, to put them in the people's hands, respecting the private property of small artisan and family shops, which do not exploit others' labor.

II. Expropriation of big agricultural, ranching, and timber estates, as well as idle lands, to give them to peasants to work.

III. Expropriation of commerce.

IV. Nationalization of credit institutions and establishment of control over foreign exchange.

V. Expropriation of the means of communication and public transportation.

VI. Expropriation of private schools, to use them for the people's education.

VII. Expropriation of private laboratories, clinics, and hospitals, to provide medical services to workers and their families.

VIII. Expropriation of private sport and recreational facilities, to put them at the service of workers and the people in general.

IX. Expropriation of big landlords' land, buildings, residences, and housing projects, to provide workers and their families respectable and decent living quarters.

X. Dissolution of the oppressing army and the formation of a People's Army, starting on the basis of the EZLN.

XI. The end of obligatory military service.

XII. Expropriation of the bourgeoisie's goods for the full benefit of the people.

XIII. To stop the plunder of our wealth in energy resources—above all oil and uranium—and recover these resources, now exploited and used by imperialism and its partners in Mexico, to use them rationally for the good of the country.

. . . Chapter V. On Members

Article 8. Only militants are recognized as members of the FLN. Every militant will carry a means of internal identification expedited by the organisms of command. For present necessities of revolutionary work, we consider as *professional* the militant who has made the socialist revolution his reason for living, dedicating himself full time to the tasks that the organization assigns him, going underground when he is told, and abandoning his position, family, goods, and every link with bourgeois society.

The *urban* is the militant who keeps his family, work, position, etc., because this suits the purposes of the organization, and who is disposed to carry out commissions entrusted to him, putting fulfillment of these duties before his personal, family, and job interests.

The step from urban to professional militant constitutes a recognition of the militant's degree of development and of the needs of the organization .

Article 9. Militants of the FLN are those persons who, having been proposed by a militant who guarantees their discretion and honesty, accept the invitation to struggle in our ranks, follow our political-military lines, respect the discipline that rules us, and are disposed to struggle resolutely against imperialism and the governing oppressor, without concern for the privations and sacrifice this implies.

. . . Chapter IX. On Our Organic Structure

Article 26. The Forces of National Liberation are structured as a complex of organisms and not as an aggregate of members. Because of the necessities imposed by armed struggle, the FLN has military leadership, hierarchy, and discipline; nevertheless, it democratically channels the political activity of its militants through specific organisms.

Article 27. The organisms that form the FLN are:

a) The National Leadership: organism of political-military leadership at the national level.

b) Zapatista Army of National Liberation, in rural zones.

c) EYOL [acronym for Estudiantes y Obreros en Lucha]: clandestine organization of networks and cells of "Students and Workers in Struggle," in urban zones . . .

Article 30. The *Zapatista Army of National Liberation* is so called because Emiliano Zapata is the hero who best symbolizes the traditions of revolutionary struggle of the Mexican people. Its structure is the following:

a) Organism of command formed by professional militants designated by the National Leadership, which will determine the military hierarchy and succession of commands.

b) Combat troops called "insurgents," which will be made up of professional militants from the FLN and those Mexican or foreign combatants who, although not FLN militants, are disposed to subject themselves to military discipline and to respect the succession of commands set by the National Leadership.

c) Commissions for political work designated by the National Leadership, to act under the orders of the commanding officer of each combat unit. Their function will be to raise the political level of all combatants in their unit and to present revolutionary demands and positions to the inhabitants of the zone where their unit operates. They will be called "political officers" of the combat unit.

d) Both military and political responsibilities may fall to the one and the same compañero . . .

Article 31. Functions of the Zapatista Army of National Liberation are:

a) To link the FLN with the working masses in the countryside.

b) To combat head-on the repressive forces of the bourgeois Mexican state and even foreign mercenaries and invaders, until it gains victory over them.

c) To liberate the territory where it operates in order to install in these zones people's revolutionary authorities.

d) To dictate measures and local rules for the benefit of the population that inhabits the zone, above all the workers.

e) To extend its zone of influence till it unites with another combat front or with urban zones, where it will take under its command action by the EYOL . . .

CHAPTER FIFTEEN

The Diocese's Most Radical Declaration: The Plan, San Cristóbal, 1986

The idea that San Cristóbal should have a "diocesan plan" did not come from Bishop Ruiz or his cathedral chapter. It came from Vatican II's calls for applied research to focus and coordinate programs of pastoral action (*Gaudium et spes* 62; *Christus Dominus* 17; *Ad gentes* 26, 29, 34, 41). That the plan appeared so long after Vatican II is not odd. Most bishops everywhere took several years to begin organizing studies for the determination of proper diocesan policies and campaigns. In the United States by 1976 only 32 dioceses had established research or planning efforts. In Mexico in 1986 San Cristóbal was among the first to have a plan.

It was also in accord with Vatican II that a "diocesan general assembly" decided on the plan (*Christus Dominus* 27). Pope Paul VI himself had recommended such "pastoral councils" of clergy, religious, and laity, especially in missionary dioceses (*Ecclesiae sanctae*, August 6, 1966).

The most important contexts of the plan were the Central American wars, Mexican politics, and Liberation Theology, 1979–86. The wars turned bloodiest in these years (thanks primarily to President Ronald Reagan). In 1979 in Nicaragua the Sandinista revolutionary forces had overthrown the Somoza dictatorship and taken power with massive popular support. Since 1981, while they tried to carry out their reforms, they had had to fight CIA subversion and the U.S.-funded and directed "contras." In 1980 in El Salvador, after the assassination of Archbishop Oscar Romero, civilian opposition to the country's murderous armed forces had formed the Democratic Revolutionary Front, gone underground, and endorsed the revolutionary "liberation front" fighting to overthrow the U.S.-backed government. Since 1981, by hook or crook, the United States had funded and advised the armed forces in their campaigns to crush the revolutionaries. By 1986 Washington's surrogates had killed more than 30,000 peasants in massacres and death-squad operations. In 1982 in Guatemala the four main guerrilla armies had unified and opened an offensive all across the country. With U.S., Argentinian, Chilean, and Israeli military advisers, the Guatemalan armed forces had launched a terrific counter-offensive. By 1986 they had destroyed some 400 towns and villages, forced at least 20,000 peasants into strategic hamlets, killed maybe 150,000 people, drafted 800,000 into a paramilitary police, and displaced more than one million, not including 250,000 refugees in Mexico (largely in Chiapas). It makes good sense that the first sentence in the San Cristóbal plan's "referential framework," explicitly geopolitical, locates the diocese in regard to Central America, and the second goes to Guatemala.

On the same reasoning already in 1982 Mexican politics had delivered a military man to govern Chiapas, to close the border to Central Americanization. But he then made the state more like Guatemala. Among all the many oligarchs who have governed Chiapas, General Absalón Castellanos had proved by 1986 that he was one of the greediest, most corrupt, most rigid, and most violent. Coming from a clan in Comitán notorious as "the bosses of the Selva," his kin owning vast politically protected fincas there, himself one of the state's richest cattlemen, the general had spent his entire adult life in the army, in 1980–81 as commander of the Mexican armed forces in Chiapas, at which post he had provided finqueros the full protection of the law and more. (See Reading No. 13.) At 59, he had taken office determined to stamp out "inciters of anarchism, pokers of the fire, fishers in troubled waters, who are not far from the trash the current carries," that is, the CIOAC, the OCEZ, and the Union of Unions. On the federal funding of U.S. $100 million for his Program of Agrarian Rehabilitation he paid landlords in full for land claimed by landless communities, eventually 200,000 acres granted to 159 communities enrolled (in all but a few cases) in the CNC, that is, the PRI. By 1986 he had also given landlords hundreds upon hundreds of exemptions from landless communities' claims, eventually almost 3,000 exemptions covering nearly three million acres. His brother, head of the State Forestry Commission, was stripping large tracts of the rain forest for private profit. The OCEZ had lost more than 20 members killed. In 1985 the CIOAC's state secretary-general and its main lawyer, a Socialist deputy in the federal chamber, had both been murdered, the latter, according to Amnesty International, by hitmen for the governor's brother. (Between 1982 and 1988, when the general's term expired, the number of political assassinations would run to 153, making his governorship one of the most gruesome in Mexico's modern history.)

In part of the "referential framework" not excerpted here, on Chiapas's "political structure," the plan analyzes federal and state political forces and offices in fine detail. The only considerable force it does not mention outright is the FLN, which in September 1985 had moved its Chiapas headquarters from deep down in the jungle up to the deacon of deacon's community, begun carrying diocesan social programs across the canyons, and evidently with pastoral blessing started extensive recruiting for "self-defense." It bears emphasis, however, that the FLN had not yet realized the EZLN. There were in 1986 no actual guerrillas in Chiapas for anyone to approve or disapprove.

Liberation Theology was the grandest context. From Gustavo Gutiérrez's call in Petrópolis, Brazil, in March 1964 for "critical reflection on Christian praxis in light of the Word of God," to San Cristóbal and thousands of other places around the world in July 1986, it had grown into modern Catholicism's most dynamic and complicated "method and movement." It shaped and suffused the diocesan plan. Following religiously Gutiérrez's three basic points (derived consciously or not from Catholic Action), the plan took "the viewpoint of the poor" in "the social analysis of reality [seeing]," did "the theological work" to "interpret this reality in the light of Christian revelation [judging]," and proclaimed "the kingdom of life" in "liberation in Christ [acting]." Quite according to the movement's manuals, it specified "objective, goals, criteria, actions." And directly from the movement's discourse it drew its distinctive adjectives and nouns, some of them Vatican II or Medellín jargon, others apparently ordinary words, but invisibly loaded with theological, philosophical, or Marxist references: ecclesial, salvific, praxis, integrality, change, pastoral, evangelization, prophetic, structural, process, participation, Word of God, the poor, commitment, the oppressed, project, utopia, analysis—and above all the famous neologism *conscientización* (which the great pedagogue Paulo Freire, who coined it, would stop using in 1987), teaching poor souls conscience and critical consciousness.

As Bishop Ruiz indicated in his introduction, the planning had taken "several years." It most likely began between 1980 and 1983, when the Línea Proletaria swung the Union in its own direction. The diocese would then have recognized that it had no coherent program for "sociopolitical" action, and begun preparations to develop one, "the diocesan line." If so, the bishop had initiated the process before the FLN arrived in Chiapas (for the second time). Anyway, the planners made the plan during the years of the Union of Union's crisis, Roots' organization, and unwitting pastoral acceptance of the FLN.

The plan's twice-declared goal of making connections in "Latin America" warrants a comment. Whatever non–Latin Americans may imagine, most Mexicans did not usually have "Latin America" much in mind then. If they thought internationally and culturally, they usually thought, as their language led them to think, of other particular Spanish American countries, for example, Chile. The San Cristóbal planners' interest in "Latin America" is a sign that they wanted connections not only with the impressive Liberationist movements in Chile, Peru, Ecuador, and Colombia, but also with the great

Portuguese-speaking movement in Brazil, then the world's Liberationist powerhouse.

Finally, a few words (among many due) on the plan's "immanentism" and "eschatological" tendencies, that is, how Marxist and how pro-revolutionary it was: Its "referential" six-page sketch of "social classes," not excerpted here (although informing my essay), is good, creative Marxist analysis. Most Liberation theologians and pastors then, although often accused of Marxism and claiming to use Marxism, typically ignored modes and relations of production, never specified any ruling class, and wrote simply of "the oppressed . . . in their totality as a class: the poor, the subjected, the discriminated against," which is mumbo jumbo in Marxism. In contrast, the analysis here is a historically materialist critique of Chiapas's basic social division, concretely "who produces" and "who owns production and controls it." But a fair, contextualized reading of the two "frameworks" and the plan as such would not lead to the conclusion that the diocese was up to any more "immanence" or Marxism than the Vatican's Congregation for the Doctrine of the Faith then allowed; the plan's "general objective" was clearly "transcendent."

As for revolution: Among the Colombian guerrillas then, a few revolutionary priests, like their exemplar Camilo Torres, actually bore arms in combat. For the Salvadoran guerrillas then, many prorevolutionary priests worked in nonviolent but close support. In Chiapas then, there being no guerrillas (as yet), the diocesan planners (in a section on "ideology" not excerpted here) are for the militant but then unarmed, nationalist, Liberationist, and Marxist movements there were. But they foresee *"a new explosion and social change"* (their emphasis), that "independent popular organizations" may "put to themselves the need for a total change." They acknowledge "those [in Chiapas] who affirm that the only path is armed movements and that the rest is reformism." Moreover, they recognize "the tendency toward the upsurge of armed movements in the state [Chiapas]," which implicitly they lament but do not fault. Presumably, as in El Salvador, their aspiration to "a synthesis between faith and politics" (see section on "Evangelization") would not bar nonviolent service to the revolution they indicate might well start soon. A fair, chronologically sensitive reading of the plan would find no promotion of revolution in Chiapas, but no stand against it either.

It is significant that under this plan the diocese did not publicly or privately disapprove of the FLN when it began to realize the EZLN, but did break with the EZLN in 1988, five years before its actual revolt.

PLAN DIOCESANO*

Introduction and Approbation

After several years of joint efforts, in our Diocesan General Assembly of January 1986, we were able to define through common accords a series of elements that will orient pastoral action in our Diocese . . .

The composition of this plan of pastoral work follows the same steps as taken at its genesis: Reflection on reality, hearkening to the salvific will of God, and pastoral accords. They are the three parts that are now introduced as the integrants of our Diocesan Plan.

We all know that it is necessary to look critically at the world to which the call of the Lord is directed and in which our action develops. Only thus will we be able to discover the riches that the Father gave his children even before our humble proclamation of the Good News, and to grasp the negative elements that, being of humankind, limit the development of God's Kingdom. Proper knowledge of our world will help us also to understand many brothers whose efforts also go toward constructing the Kingdom, whether from the perspective of a legitimate autonomy of seculars' action in the Church, or from the action of those who, perhaps without clearly perceiving God's salvific plan, in some way intuit it and commit themselves to the poor, the Gospel's privileged addressee.

It is not possible to put into a few pages God's whole ineffable revelation to his children. The "Doctrinal Framework" tries to gather only some of our most elementary motivations of faith to work for God's Kingdom in the concrete situation of our Diocese of San Cristóbal, without abandoning His explicit will, in communion with the Church Universal and its legitimate pastors, and maintaining an objective vision of the truth, about man and about the Church. This framework cannot, therefore, replace study and meditation on the Holy Scripture, the Holy Fathers, pontifical and episcopal documents, or the reflection of theologians and every reality that feeds, illuminates, and fortifies our faith.

Our diocesan life has already been ruling itself by the objective, goals, and criteria now jointly expressed in the Diocesan Plan. Not all the elements and accords that we have been following in our practice and that guide us are included here. Nor does this Plan pretend to replace the norms of Canon Law, the directives of the Roman Pontiff, or the orientations of our Bishops Conference, but only complements them and makes clearer the spirit with which they must be applied in our reality. . . .

So this Diocesan Plan stands approved, proclaimed, and established. May our Father give us His strength, the Holy Ghost love, and Christ Jesus allow

---

*Diócesis de San Cristóbal (San Cristóbal de Las Casas, 1986), pp. i–46.

us to go on in his service. We pray to the Blessed Virgin Mary to intercede for us and accompany us in our life and work in the vineyard of the Lord.

Given in our see of San Cristóbal de Las Casas, Chiapas, July 17, 1986, the 420th anniversary of the death of Brother Bartolomé de Las Casas, first bishop of Chiapas.

Referential Framework

Chiapas, part of Central American geographically, belongs to Mexico politically. This has made its strategic importance notable, not only because of its location, being the natural passage toward Guatemala, but above all because of the crossroad of interests and systems that intertwine in our state.

It is also necessary to take into account the diversity of geographic regions, the abundant and varied natural wealth, the ethnic pluralism, and the complexity of a social formation resulting from a history of conquests, colonialisms, pillages, dependency, and popular struggles in search of liberation . . .

. . . a first and perhaps fundamental node of the Chiapan problematic is the continuous *production of laborers* [emphasis here and throughout in original]. For some, this has been a constant in Chiapas's social formation for the last five centuries. These are the laborers who if they got a piece of land were exploited by commerce and manipulated by the National Peasant Confederation, and if they did not get land, had to go pick coffee on the fincas of Soconusco [along the Pacific Coast], or who now migrate in search of work to Reforma [the Gulf oil fields], Pujiltic [the big sugar complex], or Villahermosa [Tabasco's once booming capital], or who pile up looking for some opportunity around Tuxtla, Comitán, San Cristóbal, or Ocosingo, or else, driven to the brink by poverty and taking a wrong exit, plant marijuana in several mountainous parts of the state. These are the laborers who, after making interminable efforts to resolve their problems and suffering continual mockeries, have squatted on fincas as the only alternative that landlords, cattlemen, and Agrarian Reform officials leave them. These are the laborers who have made protest marches to the state capital and to Mexico City, who do sit-ins and road blocks on the highways . . ., who struggle against the companies in the jungle, against the bosses in Chamula, against the cantina operators in Oxchuc, against the Mill [Pujiltic], PEMEX, and the Federal Electric Commission, tired as they are of so many abuses and lies, so much exploitation and corruption.

Thus the peasants, finca peons, farm workers, and Indians have remained at the center of the class struggle in Chiapas, and it is this accumulation of laborers, impoverished and taking hard beatings, that points *toward a new explosion and social change.*

After 15 years of struggles, calamities, and advances, independent popular organizations are seeing with greater clarity what is the proper direction and the right road. Not only that, but when they confront power, they do not do so only as groups of Chiapan peasants, but articulated at the national level with other peasants, workers, and students in different regions of the Republic, which gives a different dimension to their struggle, for it allows them to transcend their local objectives and propose broader objectives, even to put to themselves the need for a total change . . .

The proximity to Central American processes, the strategic wealth of Chiapas, the interest of the United States in the zone, and the very confliction of the Chiapan social formation explain the reason for the militarization here and, contrarily, the tendency toward the upsurge of armed movements in the state.

Taking into account all the above, it no longer causes us such surprise that for all Chiapas's wealth we see so much poverty. One wonders how we Chiapans can agree to a system in which so much wealth is carried away and so much misery remains, where the little that is left is so unjustly distributed, a system that, besides despoiling us of our most fundamental political rights, daily sets us one against the other, a system that covers its lies with "modernity, freedom, and progress."

Doctrinal Framework

1. God and His project for men.

> WE BELIEVE IN GOD
> OUR FATHER WHO WILLS THE LIVES OF HIS
>   CHILDREN
> AND A LIFE OF ABUNDANCE

God wants to renew life, where death imposes its laws: "I have seen the oppression of My people and I have heard their cries" (Ex. 3:7).

He shows Himself in our history of conflicts, to reestablish His Plan: to distribute justly the goods of creation (Cf. the Magnificat [the Virgin Mary's song, Lk. 1:46–55]).

God reveals Himself when He accompanies the liberating process of the people and establishes an alliance with them: "I will be Your God, and you will be My people" (Lev. 26:12), so that to be against the people is to be against God.

The Re-creation of man is the work and gift of God, who asks for the collaboration of men themselves. God shows Himself and saves us through men . . .

General Objective

That our Diocesan Church, in union with the Latin American Church, proclaims the practice of Jesus and lives it in fraternal and participative community, committing itself to the people and serving the people, inserting itself as Jesus did into the process of the liberation of the oppressed, in which they are the agents of their history, and together we build the new society in anticipation of the Kingdom.

I.EVANGELIZATION, PASTORAL WORK, AND POPULAR RELIGIOSITY

Goals

To promote and fortify ecclesial communities in rural and urban areas in which property, power, and knowledge will be shared, articulating their practice, experience, and process with other communities in Mexico and Latin America.

To create and fortify liturgical expressions in which the people will celebrate their struggles, achievements, and failures, where Jesus will be discovered incarnate, and hope and liberation made possible.

To provide a spirituality on the basis of the people's struggles against Latin American reality, and search for mechanisms to live and share our experience in the pursuit of Jesus.

Criteria

That the praxis of Jesus be the basis of our liberating action.

That we learn from the people and let ourselves by evangelized by them.

That we confront our reality with the Word of God in such a way that we achieve a synthesis between faith and politics.

That liturgical actions and popular religiosity be realized in such a form that they lead to change.

That urban and rural pastoral work have a common inclination.

That theological reflection always accompany our pastoral practice.

That we take into account those who have remained marginalized from our pastoral work.

Actions

Call to conversion in the face of the needs and abuses that the people suffer.

Revision of the coherence that exists between discourse and practice.

Reflection and celebration of the Word of God expressed in the Bible and in events.

Support for popular religiosity in its liberating aspects.

Provision of ministries to respond to the needs of the people.

Interchange of experiences of faith.

Communitarian and personal prayer.

Systematization with the people of their experience of faith.

Theological workshops.

Courses.

Visits to the communities.

Company for adolescents, the young, and children.

2. CONSCIENTIZATION AND CAPACITATION

Goals

To render ourselves able in reading the Bible to illuminate and make fruitful the historical process of the people.

As a people and pastoral agents, to take consciousness of the oppressive system and its mechanisms.

To train ourselves in the management of structural and conjunctural analyses, so that we give proper answers to concrete situations.

Criteria

That our actions be based on analysis and study.

That the analysis be done in a spirit of faith and from the perspective of the poor.

Actions

Structural and conjunctural analyses of Chiapas, Mexico, and the world.

Workshops of analysis (for pastoral and the people's agents).

Systematic study, reflection, and capacitation.

Courses.

3. ACCOMPANYING THE PEOPLE IN THEIR PROCESS OF LIBERATION

Goals

To accompany and fortify the struggles of the people, assuming the risks that this brings with it.

To create platforms that facilitate knowledge and support of popular movements struggling for justice and that provide their mutual relation.

Criteria

In our support of popular movements, to take into account the riches and the limitations that our vocation in the Church implies.

That we critically respect the process of the people, the subject of change.

That in taking decisions women participate in full equality.

That we favor self-direction, avoiding actions that create dependence.

Actions

Contact with independent popular organizations, dialogue with them, promotion and support of them.

Relation with persons, groups consciously in the struggle, and organizations, favoring always their mutual relation.

Promotion of women.

Promotion of the people's expression of themselves.

Denunciation of the abuses that the people suffer.

Formation of a Committee of Legal Advisory Services.

Search for economic alternatives that will favor conscientization and organization.

4. CRITICAL REEVALUATION OF CULTURES

Goals

To insert ourselves into the culture of our people, to take on ourselves the social utopia hidden there, and to accompany them on their historic path.

Criteria

That we reevaluate the liberating content of cultures.

Actions

To learn the language.

To know the history of the ethnic groups.

To promote cultural expressions.

5. RELATION AND COMMUNICATION

Goals

To increase the mechanisms of communication and to articulate solidarity inside and outside the diocese, especially in Latin America.

To relate areas of work at the base level between zones, inside and outside the diocese.

Criteria

That objective and opportune information be the right of those who do not have it.

That through proper channels the diocese be made aware of actions that implicate it.

Actions

Training of personnel for communications.

Quick communication of news.

Workshops for a people's communications.

6. ARTICULATION AND COORDINATION OF PASTORAL AGENTS

Goals

To share ecclesial responsibility with the laity, creating mechanisms for making decisions jointly.

To promote mechanisms to facilitate fraternal criticism and self-criticism at all levels ecclesial and extra-ecclesial.

Diocesan plan for economic leveling.

Criteria

That every action be planned, organized, coordinated, and subject to periodic evaluation.

That we not make the people come to our present structures, but forge together with them structures in which we can all take part . . .

That the integration of new pastoral agents be pedagogical, so that they will take on themselves the diocesan process.

Disposition to follow the diocesan line.

Actions

To promote personal and group relations . . .

Commitment to coordinated work . . .

Operationalization of Diocesan Assemblies' conclusions.

Interchange of experiences between pastoral bases and agents.

CHAPTER SIXTEEN

Salinas's Form of Social Organization: Solidarity, 1988–94

Of all President Carlos Salinas's programs, he cared most about Solidarity. To him it meant much more than public works, welfare, targeted anti-poverty action. From his father, his university training in political economy, his enduring connections with the Línea de Masas/Línea Proletaria, his experience in government since the early 1970s, and his particular interest, already evident in his Harvard doctoral dissertation, in the applied sociology of organization, he had come through the 1980s to see the deep articulation of the global and the local in his country. If Mexico was necessarily going to open its economy more to foreign (above all American) trade and investment, it could not long maintain much independence unless its government had more legitimacy among its people, fundamentally among the poor, whose real support for the government would increase not as it acted (cleanly or corruptly) for them, but mainly as it enabled them to act more for themselves. National security therefore required social programs by which the poor would organize their own strengths for their own good. Budgetary limits required that the program be productive and eventually self-sufficient. And political reform to protect the program from its most powerful enemies, the PRI establishment in Mexico City, required that it be a cause for which the poor would voluntarily defy the party's traditional bosses and elect its new reformers. Salinas's first official act as president, December 2, 1988, was to create Solidarity. Through the six years of his term it grew into a prodigious complex of struggles to mobilize the poor against their material and institutional poverty.

The program's importance to Salinas is clearest in its increasing share of the federal budget. Social spending altogether expanded from 32 percent of the budget (after debt service) in 1988, to 36 percent in 1989 (Salinas's first full year in office), 38 percent in 1990, 45 percent in 1991, 49 percent in 1992, 52 percent in 1993, and 55 percent in 1994. Solidarity's own line in the budget, in effect Salinas's personal line for "social liberalism," social policy, and social politics, grew faster, from 1.86 percent in 1989, to 2.79 percent in 1990, 3.48 percent in 1991, 3.92 percent in 1992, 3.98 percent in 1993, the year before the EZLN revolt, when the program received and disbursed pesos worth more than $2.5 billion US, a pittance in the United States, but substantial means in Mexico. Although the proportion shrank to 3.72 percent in 1994, the absolute sum grew to $3 billion US.

To keep the program's major enemies from capturing it at birth, Salinas for three years had its funds distributed directly out of the executive office as grants to state and municipal governments, designated federal field offices, and local organizations of the poor for specific projects. Through his term, all told, Solidarity sent about 62 percent of its funds as grants-in-aid to state and municipal governments for "social welfare," for example, water and sewage systems, hospitals and clinics, nutrition, housing, schools, scholarships, electrification, etc.; 20 percent to local offices and organizations of the poor for "support of production," in particular ruined peasants; 16 percent likewise for "regional development," urban and rural community development, including farm roads; and 2 percent similarly for "special cases," migrant workers, poor women, et al. Every year the program operated in every state. By 1994 its grants had reached more than 95 percent of the country's then 2,378 municipalities, including all (170-odd) where an opposition party held town hall.

The material results were impressive. From 1989 to 1994 Solidarity projects numbered nationally almost 525,000, providing, for a few examples, potable water to 13,500,000 people who did not have it before, electricity to more than 20 million, credit "on word of honor" to 2 million peasants (keeping them in production without usurious loans), 12,000 miles of roads in impoverished rural districts, and local improvements in agriculture, livestock, small industry, and transport to nearly 6,400 Indian communities, more than 2 million Indian people.

Still more impressive were the institutional results. Because the program ordinarily required local voluntary associations of the poor to propose projects and do the work on them, "Solidarity Committees" every year organized by the tens of thousands. By 1994 some 250,000 had formed. Nothing like that number survived; maybe three-quarters of the committees lasted no longer than they needed to agree on a proposal, win a grant, and finish their project. But the others were consolidating, able to account for their operations and move their communities in new struggles, some 60,000 enduring organizations of the poor, more or less by the poor and for the poor.

But from the start Solidarity suffered a serious internal difficulty. Since to escape its major enemies it had to go mostly through state governors and municipal presidents, it had continually to negotiate with these officials, over 90 percent of them PRIistas, of whom 80 to 90 percent, in the traditional mode, worked continually to use the new funds to strengthen the PRI the old way and so promote themselves. This was in part why Salinas had one of his political intimates, Luis Donaldo Colosio (not from Línea Proletaria but close to its principal cadres), managing the PRI nationally from 1988 to 1992, to help Solidarity negotiate and to back state and municipal candidates more respectful of the program. But the conflict was continual. Not until 1992 had enough state elections occurred for most governors to owe their positions (ultimately) to Salinas, but even then (to keep some peace in the PRI) most of them were not from his reformist faction. That year he established the new Ministry of Social Development, included both Solidarity and INI in it, and appointed Colosio to head it, for federal protection of Solidarity against provincial bosses. But Colosio still had to negotiate with them, and because his promotion made him a pre-candidate for the presidency in 1994, he could not antagonize many of them at a time.

Besides, governors had their own resources. All of them took federal revenues regularly shared with the states and plowed them into Solidarity projects that their agencies and favorite municipal presidents ran—for paved streets, clinics, shantytown property titles—in return for the favored poor's partisan docility. State-directed Solidarity funds altogether amounted to about a third as much as federal Solidarity funding, a quarter of the program's total commitment, and in all but a few cases their results, including considerable corruption, added to the program's difficulties.

From 1989 to 1994 more federal funding for Solidarity went to Chiapas, Mexico's poorest state, than to any other. It is more interesting that the sum was not remarkable per capita, by which standard Chiapas ranked eighth nationally. The distribution of the funds indicates why this rank was so low, and reveals some of the struggle within Solidarity there. A lower proportion of funds in Chiapas than in any other state but one went as grants to the state government and municipalities for "social welfare," (the worst result being a big new convention hall in the state capital). The proportion going to federal field offices in Chiapas for "support of production," largely to INI's 11 (eventually 15) Coordinating Centers there to support otherwise ruined Indian coffee growers, was only about 60 percent of the national average for production (maybe because not many Indians in the canyons grew coffee). But the amount that went to federal field offices, municipalities, and organizations of the poor for "regional development" was the largest amount so assigned among all the states, larger than the entire federal funding for Solidarity in most states, by far the largest per capita, proportionally more than twice the national average for such matters. Under this rubric INI's centers between 1990 and 1994 gave grants totalling some $20 million US to 20 new Solidarity Regional Funds managed by Indian-elected Indian councils for some 600 Indian organizations representing more than 2,000 Indian communities, which on their grants started and finished some 900 projects of local development (pitifully little but a lot to them). Of INI's Solidarity-funded national budget for such grants, 15 percent went to Chiapas, more than to any other state but Oaxaca. In short, within national political constraints, Solidarity was minimizing contributions to Chiapas's PRI, maximizing contributions where federal offices and local organizations could help the poor do most for themselves.

Even Solidarity's most suspicious critics in Chiapas recognized the change for the better. As a former PRD deputy in congress, a Tojolabal and cofounder of the national Independent Front of Indian Peoples, said in 1992, "The situation in Chiapas is exceptional. . . . This has been achieved because of the maturity of the Chiapas indigenous movement, and a certain division between INI's political clientele and the governor's clientele. . . . As a result, independent indigenous organizations have an important presence in the Regional Funds. . . . When indigenous organizations are able to effectively take the Regional Funds into their own hands, the funds can really become an important space for participation and decision-making . . ."

As federal funding mounted for Solidarity in Chiapas, Governor Patrocinio González (on whom see Reading No. 18) every year put increasingly heavy state resources into the program. (When toward the end he left Chiapas to join the cabinet, his personally chosen substitute did the same, 31 percent of the program's total budget in the state in 1993.) Through 1993 Chiapas ranked fifth nationally, higher than several considerably richer states, in gross contributions to the program's funding in its territory. But from the start this was to do as much of Solidarity as possible the governor's way, for "social welfare" and "support of production," where he controlled the projects strictly for his purposes (ergo, the Tuxtla convention hall). Of the 8,824 Solidarity committees organized in Chiapas by 1993, more than in any other state, probably 75 percent were state PRI creatures. González worked absolutely against "regional development," the cover for INI's struggles for the Indian communities. Of the state's contributions to Solidarity in 1989, only .59 percent went for "regional development"; in 1990, only .16 percent; in 1991, only .89 percent. Then in March 1992, at a critical moment for INI, when its national director had just left to join Salinas's cabinet and a new director had just taken office, the governor struck to capture its administration in Chiapas. He had its state coordinator and two principal officers in Ocosingo arrested on charges of corruption.

Private and public protests (see the following article from *La Jornada*) soon won the INI officers' freedom. But González pushed his men into their offices and took charge of INI's projects in the state. In 1992 he and his successor went into the red on their "regional development," bleeding funds from federal projects to favor their PRIista communities. And as his successor stifled independent projects in 1993, federal funding for "regional development" fell (from 37 percent of total funding in 1989, 43 percent in 1990, 49 percent in 1991, 40 percent in 1992) to 29 percent in the year before the Zapatista revolt.

Of total funding in 1993, state contributions for such projects then were -6.42 percent. This was why Indians in Los Altos raised extraordinarily bitter complaints about the INI in 1993, and one reason why some canyon communities then gave their Solidarity grants to the EZLN.

It was also one reason why Salinas and Colosio visited Chiapas in 1993 (Colosio twice), and why they then committed U.S. $50 million in federal Solidarity to the state, particularly the canyon communities, to regain ground from the state PRI and the EZLN. If not for the prospect of restored and revived Solidarity Regional Funds in the canyons, the EZLN might not have revolted on January 1, 1994. But if this prospect/threat moved the EZLN into action, it also made the revolt less extensive than it would otherwise probably have been.

Two of the figures in the article from *La Jornada* below are noteworthy here, since they make significant (but very different) appearances elsewhere. On Hugo Andrés Araujo, see Reading No. 12. On Eduardo Robledo, see Reading No. 25 on the Chiapas elections of 1994.

La Jornada is an essential Mexico City daily, founded in 1985, usually very critical of the government, and devoutly Cardenista since 1988. It has reported and editorialized so favorably and so amply on the Zapatistas since 1994 that it serves practically as the EZLN-CCRI's newspaper of record; for a while (until the joke got old) some of its critics called it "The Ocosingo News."

Reforma is another essential Mexico City daily. Founded in 1993 by the publisher of the then 55-year-old Monterrey daily *El Norte*, it quickly gained a wide readership and a reputation for professionally impartial journalism.

INDÍGENAS DE CHIAPAS PIDEN SE LIBERE A 3 FUNCIONARIOS DEL INI*

Seven Chiapan Indians, members of a commission from various organizations in Chiapas, met yesterday with the PRI's national leader, Luis Donaldo Colosio, the National Peasant Confederation's leader, Hugo Andrés Araujo, and Assistant Attorney General José Dávalos. They told them, they said, that "in Chiapas we are living a lamentable crisis because of violation of human rights," and requested that three officers from the National Indian Institute (INI), accused of fraud, be released from prison and returned to the posts they held before their arrest.

The INI officers in prison are the institute's state coordinator, Ricardo Paniagua Guzmán; the director of its Ocosingo coordinating center, Argimiro Cortés Esteban; and its chief veterinarian in Ocosingo, Carlos H. Albores.

---

*Rosa Rojas, *La Jornada*, March 21, 1992, p. 13.

After the talks, the commissioners declared that on Monday, March 23, 10,000 Indians will march from Chiapa de Corzo to Tuxtla Gutiérrez, where they will conduct a two-day sit-in in hopes of an answer to their demands. If the answer is not positive, they said, they will march to Mexico City.

The Indians, accompanied by INI Director General Guillermo Espinosa and the institute's national director of development projects, Jesús Rubiel, as well as Chiapas Senator Eduardo Robledo, asked Araujo to arrange meetings with Colosio, officials of the Federal Comptroller's Office and the National Commission on Human Rights, and President Carlos Salinas, in order to secure the release of the INI officers, who have been in the state's Cerro Hueco penitentiary since February 29.

The members of the commission are Mariano Vázquez López, from the executive council of Peasant-Teacher Solidarity (SOCAMA) of Los Altos; Francisco Pérez Sánchez, from the executive council of the Mu'kulum [Solidarity] Cooperative; Vicente Calvo Hernández, from the executive council of the Tojolabal [Solidarity] Region in Las Margaritas; Álvaro Cruz Pérez, from the executive council of the [Solidarity] Regional Funds of Las Margaritas; Mariano Guzmán Pérez, from the executive council of [the Solidarity Regional Funds of] Ocosingo; José Núñez Hernández, from the [Solidarity] Regional Funds of Bochil; and Antonio González Sánchez, from the Mam people in Chiapas's Sierra Madre.

The Indians told Araujo that the detention of the INI officers is an attempt to sabotage the work that their organizations are doing, since "their only crime is working with all kinds of people, whether they sympathize with the government or not. We Indians are offended by their detention. It's clear that there's no fraud or graft. We demand respect. Now that we're learning how to do things, our work gets sabotaged."

They added that the INI officers "are in prison only because we were doing a project a little different. We've brought statements to this effect from several communities, only one missing, because the community's been threatened." They also said that they had brought a message for President Salinas, to ask respect for Indians. "This is a political problem," they declared. "Everything that goes wrong in Chiapas, the authorities there blame on INI. We want to make clear that it's not INI, but our assemblies that make our decisions."

They complained that they had sent the Human Rights Commission several cases of abuse like that of the INI officers, held without warrant, one of them with his two daughters, who were kept several hours in the Cerro Hueco penitentiary. "We got no response," they said.

Araujo offered, they said, "to look for a way out and fast," strictly by the law, "to get our compañeros out of prison and resolve the political problem."

Araujo, the commissioners, and several officials then met with PRI National Secretary Colosio. The Indian representatives repeated to him what they had told Araujo. "Colosio told us that he's very worried about what's happening in Chiapas," they said, and promised that all the reports they gave him would reach the president personally.

Colosio also arranged for them to meet at once with Assistant Attorney General Dávalos. The Indian commissioners said that Dávalos "looked completely amazed at the information that we gave him, and said he was going to do an analysis of the case's documentation," which is now a federal question.

The Indians emphasized that they will continue to struggle not only for the release and restoration of the INI officers, Paniagua, Cortés, and Albores, but also "for the self-determination of Indian organizations and respect for their decisions, as well as the continuation of pluralism in INI's work."

LO MÁS DELGADO DEL HILO: PRONASOL EN CHIAPAS*

"Much remains to do to advance on the road to justice in our fatherland, and if we have already come far, we are not yet at the end," said President Carlos Salinas on September 6 last year at the start of the Fourth National Solidarity Week.

Listening to him were the Indians of Mitontic, a township in Chiapas's Los Altos. Present for the occasion, among other officials, were Luis Donaldo Colosio, then minister of Social Development [by the date of this article the PRI's presidential candidate], and Elmar Setzer, interim governor of Chiapas. Also in the audience and among those who spoke with the president were Indians from San Juan Cancuc and Las Margaritas.

In Guadalupe Tepeyac the president inaugurated the Social Security-Solidarity Rural Hospital, which cost more than 16 million new pesos [then over U.S. $5 million]. That same day he received from the hands of Carlos Rojas [since 1988 Solidarity's national director] a broad diagnosis of the situation "of injustice and poverty" in which Mexican Indians live. Colosio himself had previously been in the state, and announced a grant of 40 million new pesos for special support. Chiapas was worrisome.

Something was up in Los Altos and in the jungle too: 126 days after the visit by President Salinas and Governor Setzer, many of the Indians of that zone, probably some of those who saw them in September, beneficiaries of the highest investment that the National Solidarity Program (PRONASOL) has made, took up arms in rebellion.

From the paradigm of the battle against poverty by producers meeting their payments for "Credit on Word of Honor," Chiapas in violence turned into Solidarity's thinnest thread . . .

---

* Arturo Cano, *Reforma*, January 23, 1994, p. 6.

[PRONASOL's] resources are in reality modest. In 1993 they represented barely 10 percent [sic] of the federal government's social expenditures . . . But . . . these resources have been sufficient, according to official figures, to mobilize no less than 20 million Mexicans in 150,000 Solidarity committees [nationwide]. There have passed through its ranks, in other words, three million more than all those considered "extremely poor" . . .

There is only one group that meets every week, on Mondays, with the president of the Republic: the leaders who attend the courses of the National Institute of Solidarity.

PRONASOL is without doubt the president's program. Under Solidarity's flag President Salinas slept in modest dwellings in Chalco [a big Mexico City shantytown, which Solidarity made one of its major projects], and returned in triumph to La Laguna [in the north, around Torreón, a stronghold of Política Popular since the early 1970s], the same place where he suffered a severe setback in his presidential campaign in 1988.

Under Solidarity's flag he won the early cooperation of a force that had promoted Cuauhtémoc Cárdenas's presidential candidacy in 1988, Durango's Committee of Popular Defense, and this while the controversy over the election was still hot, in February 1989. For Solidarity, President Salinas went to Juchitán, Oaxaca, and signed accords with the Worker-Peasant-Student Coalition (COCEI), one of the sharpest enemies of his party. Under the program's flag he approached opposition municipal presidents and leaders who not long before had questioned the legitimacy of his election. Under this flag he traveled again and again around the country, repeating performances like that of September 10, 1992, closing the Third National Solidarity Week.

There, alone in the middle of the National Auditorium's great stage, he challenged his critics, "Let them grab a shovel like our compañeros and help dig the ditch! Let them carry streetlight poles the way our compañeras do! Let them criticize, but let them work, let them work in Solidarity!"

For several yards around him the space was empty. The lights lit only him. The president drew frequent ovations. "Social involvement, social work, social results, and a people organized are together synonymous with justice and democracy: working together for society, that is justice; people organized, that is democracy."

The lights went on, and the applause rang out and continued.

"PRONASOL is Salinas," a Solidarity leader proudly said, witnessing a scene repeated hundreds of times over the last five years . . .

The Indian rebellion reminded the country that Chiapas holds first place in poverty. Little has been said, however, about the other championship that the state boasts: first place nationally in repayment of Solidarity's Credit on Word of Honor [crop loans without collateral or interest].

Chiapan peasants, the poorest in the country, pay their debts most faithfully. In 1992 they repaid 88 percent of the loans they took from PRONASOL.

In 1993 the figure was over 70 percent. This information comes from "Solidarity in Chiapas for Production, 26 pages of slick paper, in full color, published by the state government of the recently [although not literally] defenestrated Elmar Setzer. "It has been possible to maintain the social impact of the program through 1993 by benefiting more than 133,000 producers (of a total of 241,000), an important figure if we take into account that the state only has credit to give if it is repaid."

This was one of the twists that Setzer's predecessor, Patrocinio González Garrido, gave PRONASOL in Chiapas. . . . the loans "on Word of Honor" (which González Garrido called "Credit to Solidarity," in his eagerness to put his stamp on PRONASOL in the state) were furnished not on the crop but to the producer. Regardless of the harvest, the state government pressured the peasant to repay all his loan.

According to *Solidarity in Chiapas*, credit of almost 94 billion [sic, presumably for 94 million] new pesos was furnished in 1993 to peasants from 3,107 communities. "The region with most [beneficiary] localities," it emphasizes, "is Los Altos, which has 523, inhabited by a largely Indian population characterized by a high rate of repayment of its loans."

It does not explain why, although "faithfully paying its debts," the Indian population of Los Altos suffered a reduction in the resources it received. In 1990 this region, now the scene of armed conflict, received 23 percent of the program's total credit; in 1993 the proportion fell to 16 percent.

Something similar . . . happened in the jungle. In 1990 credit there was 17 percent of the total; in 1991, 13 percent; in 1992, 11 percent; and in 1993 it plummeted to 6 percent . . .

In other states, loan repayments go into a fund that reinvests them in works of direct benefit to the repaying community. In Chiapas the [state] government decided that was not best. It put repayments instead into a state fund that it managed, so that those repaying loans did not necessarily benefit from having kept their word.

Loans under Credit to Solidarity, principally for the production of corn and beans, were channeled through municipal presidencies, not peasant organizations. As late as September 1993, 12 of the state's 19 [sic] representatives of Solidarity Regional Funds met in San Cristóbal and requested the direct transfer of resources [to borrowing communities], since, they complained, municipal councils and local CNC bosses managed them as they pleased.

Some federal officials who worked with independent peasant organizations soon felt the governor's hand. In March 1992, the state government brought an accusation of fraud in a livestock project against three officers of the National Indian Institute, including its state director; all three went to jail.

After January 1 with the outbreak of violence in Chiapas, the new minister of Social Development, Carlos Rojas, gave a detailed account of PRONASOL's investment in Chiapas, and went personally to San Cristóbal to set up a grants board, to cut red tape for peasant organizations' projects, even those proposed by organizations with which Solidarity had had no previous relation.

In September of last year, while he was still minister of Social Development, Luis Donaldo Colosio said, "Whoever the nation's new chief executive may be, Solidarity would have to go on, because more than a program, it's a form of social organization, which is precisely why the people would no longer allow decisions to return to government desks, to bureaucracies, or to the old established powers over them."

PRONASOL's official publication, *Gaceta de Solidaridad*, opted in December 1993 to put the program's plans in black and white: "For opposition political parties, [Solidarity] is only a government sophistry to win votes. For the party in office, it is a demonstration that its government responds to popular expectations." Therefore, *Gaceta* deduces, "In 1994 Solidarity will continue as government action, with more resources, like every year before, in every state and municipality. But besides, now, it will move fully onto electoral terrain."

Gaceta concludes with a prediction: "Among the important considerations in . . . the elections next August . . . will no doubt be the Solidarity Program. From having been essentially an exercise in participatory democracy, it will now have to pass the test of representative democracy."

The critics of PRONASOL are betting that before the elections the program will have to pass a test called Chiapas.

Carlos Rojas's response . . . last January 14 was, "In the face of violence, PRONASOL does not break down. Violence asks of us, demands of us, more and more solidarity."

CHAPTER SEVENTEEN

In Patihuitz Canyon, in the Breach, in Revolt: La Sultana, 1960–94

President Luis Echeverría (1970–1976) took about a year to start *El Con-flicto por La Brecha*, the feud between the federal government and Indian settlers in the Selva Lacandona that became the most important conflict in the canyons in the 1970s and 80s. President Carlos Salinas (1988–94) took 34 days to end it.

Twisted into the standard legalese of the 26 presidential resolutions he signed on January 3, 1989, in his first "agrarian act," are 26 different histories of legal struggle for land inside the "Lacandón Community," none for less than five years, half of them going back 15 years or more, one dating from 1957. There too is Salinas's commitment since before he took office to bring them all to a prompt and just close. Published on El Día de los Reyes (the Twelfth Day of Christmas), Friday, January 6, 1989, in the federal government's official journal of record, the resolutions that day became law. One of them appears in full here. The twenty-second of the 26, it grants the community, which had been petitioning for the land since 1973, an expansion of its ejido of 1,589 acres by 2,074 acres for 75 rightful claimants.

But these communities and many more in the canyons had other grievances that Salinas could not resolve. For example, La Sultana, the Tzeltal community behind the case that follows, had radical grievances in 1989 that turned into revolutionary action in 1994. These grievances were not mainly economic, social, or cultural. They were not so primarily because like many other canyon communities, despite poverty, La Sultana had been from its origins organized, tenacious, resourceful, resilient, adaptable, inventive, and hopeful. Its founding families had formed a community even before they had the ground for one. Among some 30 peon families on El Porvenir (The Future), a small finca in a valley ten hours by horse down from the town of

Ocosingo, they had been the 20-odd who decided in the late 1950s to move together deep down into the Selva. The founding fathers, Lorenzo Gómez, Domingo López, and Pedro Ramírez, had then scouted down Patihuitz Canyon, along the Jataté River, and found, just where the Tzaconejá River joins it, on the Jataté's left bank, the right place. It already had the name La Sultana, so called by legend for a hunting dog, Sultán, that one day long ago mahogany loggers had lost there. In 1960 the founding families had settled their community in the place, kept its infidel, queenly name, and petitioned for legal recognition and an ejido. For sustenance and the market they had raised corn and beans, soon pigs too, and once they got their grant in 1965 sold off the pigs and went into cattle. By 1970, from ever more babies living and youngsters staying, the population had more than doubled; beyond the ejido its landless young men had opened extralegal corn patches. Ocosingo's new-model missionaries and catechists had received a hearty welcome in 1972. The only community in Patihuitz Canyon to fall inside the newly patronized Lacandón zone that year, La Sultana had legally argued in 1973 that its growth entitled it to more land. Its claim practically ignored then by the agrarian agencies, it had been among the 18 founding communities of the Qu'iptik Union of Ejidos in 1975, resisted La Brecha, defied the federal orders to relocate in 1979, and celebrated the Union of Unions in 1980. By then it had negotiated a road from Ocosingo all the way down to its confines, and a little air strip not far east. Although it lost its claim for an expanded ejido in 1983, it had continued as it grew to take adjacent land anyway, eventually a tract bigger than its grant, especially for extra-legal pasture. It had also gained a reputation as *muy fiestero* (always ready to party). And the younger generation had turned out strong. By 1985 one of Lorenzo Gómez's sons, Jesús, was the community's deacon; another, Francisco, was secretary of the Union of Unions. In 1989 the community had won its greatest vindication in the government's acceptance of its expansion.

La Sultana still suffered many grievous wants. Significantly, the 1990 federal census showed 325 "occupants" (less than half the actual population) living there in only 53 dwellings of typically only two or three rooms. And the community would suffer new and sorely painful turns. Because its members had but 20 to 25 acres in coffee groves, the collapse of coffee prices did not hurt much. Salinas's reform of the agrarian law in 1992, however, practically abolished the community's prospects for yet another ejido expansion and its landless members' right to an ejido elsewhere, casting a dark cloud over their future. The almost simultaneous and double-barreled cattle crisis was general and immediate. Nearly every family had invested in a steer. Altogether La Sultana's pastures then were feeding more than 400 head. Many men old and young had borrowed to build their herds, and faced ruin.

But the community also had new support for its work. Through Solidarity it built a drinking-water system, a clinic, a store, and a basketball court for its youngsters' recreation, for seasonally drying the little coffee harvest, and most of all for a year-round paved central plaza. Through Solidarity too it got two trucks for public transport, of people, produce, and livestock, and received special credits for its members to meet payments on overdue loans. For all its troubles, poor as it remained, it was therefore working hard and doing better. (Neither was this the reason for the community's revolutionary action in 1994.)

The radical grievances in La Sultana in 1989 were political. Most likely they arose from the government's having taken ten years to decide on the community's expansion, then, in 1983, refusing approval, then in 1984 "rehabilitating" communities that enrolled in the PRI's CNC. They were so sharp that when the EZLN appeared (clandestinely) in Patihuitz Canyon in 1986, La Sultana was one of the first communities there to adopt it—and this on the lead of Union Secretary Francisco Gómez, soon the cadre "Hugo."

Born in 1958 back in El Porvenir, raised in La Sultana, Francisco Gómez in 1974 had turned 16 there, the age of maturity in the canyons, promptly married a girl from another founding family, and started making babies and taking cargos. At 17 he had worked to organize the first union, La Qu'iptik, learned there from Javier Vargas (among other powers) to read, write, and figure in Spanish, then studied with the Marists in San Cristóbal, and become one of his community's first Tzeltal catechists. If not for his dedication instead to the union, then to the Union of Unions, probably he and not his brother Jesús would have become the community's deacon. In 1985, at 27, known throughout Los Altos for his "very serious" militance in the Union, he had been elected its secretary. There he learned of the EZLN. On his word the next year his brother Jesús and all three of La Sultana's other catechists welcomed the revolutionaries, and practically the entire community became the EZLN's. In 1988, when the Union reformed into an ARIC, Francisco left it and La Sultana for FLN business elsewhere (including a visit to Cuba). Home again in 1991, he publicly tended to his local interests, not only a corn patch, pigs, and chickens, but also a coffee grove (on which he was losing money), stands of cane and palm, and 20 acres of pasture and several cattle, and became the new ANCIEZ representative in Ocosingo, where he organized the big protests in 1992. In secret, by then Captain Hugo, he was at the meeting on January 23, 1993, when the FLN decided to go to war within the year. In June Marcos visited La Sultana and spoke to the community, in castilla. Hugo translated for him.

By then the community was no longer united. Salinas's resolution in 1989 and Solidarity's programs had caused defections from the EZLN. The ejido commissioner wanted to rejoin the Union-ARIC. Others old and young argued that overthrowing the government was not so easy as the EZLN said. But Hugo had never wavered, and the deacon and the catechists remained fervently loyal. So did the founding father who had grown into the community's richest man, old Pedro Ramírez, whose six sons were all in the EZLN militia. He it was who sovereignly sold his 35 steers and the ejido's cattle too to buy arms for the revolution. On Hugo's directions the loyalists contributed their Solidarity credits to the EZLN. Under his command the community's soldiers trained at a camp in the jungle east. In late 1993 La Sultana, the most Zapatista community in the canyons, finally divided: 67 for war, 21 not. The majority made the "counter-revolutionary" minority leave, and burned down some of the empty cabins and shacks.

Before dawn on January 1, 1994, the EZLN's Third Regiment, a force of maybe 600, captured Ocosingo. Its Seventh Regiment drove through the town a little later on its way to San Cristóbal. In this motorized force, along with Sb.-Cte. Marcos, came Capt. Hugo and his company, three infantry platoons, including La Sultana's contingent. Marcos went on to glory. Hugo and his company stayed in Ocosingo, to help secure it. Trying to escape the army's counter-attack there the next day, six from La Sultana were killed in action. One was Hugo. Three others were Eduardo Hernández, Floriberto López (No. 9 below), and Pedro López (one of the catechists, No. 3 below).

RESOLUCIÓN SOBRE PRIMERA AMPLIACIÓN
DE EJIDO, SOLICTADA POR VECINOS DEL
POBLADO DENOMINADO LA SULTANA,
UBICADO EN EL MUNICIPIO DE OCOSINGO,
CHIS. (REG.-22)*

WHEREAS to resolve definitively the process relative to the first enlarge-ment of ejido requested by residents of the settlement called LA SULTANA in the municipality of Ocosingo in the state of Chiapas, and

WHEREAS IN FACT, FIRST.—By writ dated November 12, 1973, a group of peasants established in the settlement in question requested from the governor of the state a first enlargement of ejido, since the lands they then possessed were insufficient to satisfy their agrarian necessities; and once the petition was turned over to the Joint Agrarian Commission, this body initi-ated the respective process, and the petition was published in the *Periódico Oficial* [the official journal of record] of the State Government, dated June 5, 1974, which provided the effects of public notice and thus produced compli-ance with Article 275 of the Federal Law of Agrarian Reform; and the formal census of the settlement was carried out according to the dictates of the law, and showed a total of 75 persons qualified in agrarian matters; there ensued the execution of the due technical and investigative studies.

---

*Secretaría de la Reforma Agraria, *Diario Oficial de la Federación*, January 6, 1989, pp. 52–54.

WHEREAS SECOND.—On the bases of the above elements, the Joint Agrarian Commission issued its opinion, which was approved in the session of September 28, 1982, and submitted it to the consideration of the governor of the state, who on February 18, 1983, issued his order denying the settlement in question the proposed action for lack of actionable land within the radius legally affected, leaving the 75 qualified persons with their rights inviolate.

Said order was published November 30, 1983.

WHEREAS THIRD.—Once the antecedents were reviewed and the records of the respective proceeding analyzed, cognizance of the following was taken: By Presidential Resolution dated March 4, 1965, published in the *Diario Oficial de la Federación*, April 30, 1965, there was conceded to the settlement before us as a grant of lands an area totalling 643 ha. [hectares, 1,589 acres] benefiting 26 qualified persons, the Presidential Resolution having been executed in all its terms; the area conceded as the indicated grant is found to be completely and properly in use, as is affirmed in the official record dated June 20, 1984; from the technical and investigative and complementary studies that were done to duly substantiate the present proceeding, it is deduced that the petitioners in the present agrarian action stand in possession of an area the topographical survey of which shows a total of 839.4258 ha. of unirrigated land and woods that are not included in the area assigned to the Lacandón Community, since this area was excluded from the 614.321 ha. that by Presidential Resolution dated November 26, 1971, published in the *Diario Oficial de la Federación*, March 6, 1972, were recognized and registered as the Lacandóns'; these hectares in the petitioners' possession are national lands, according to the Resolution dated August 16, 1967, published in the *Diario Oficial de la Federación*, August 18, 1967; therefore the possession of said area may be regularized for the settlement in question by the first enlargement of ejido.

On the bases of the above elements the Agrarian Consultative Corps approved its opinion in session on August 10, 1988.

WHEREAS IN CONCLUSION, FIRST.—That the right of the petitioning settlement to the first enlargement of ejido has been demonstrated in the proof that in that same settlement are established 75 qualified persons who lack the lands necessary to satisfy their agrarian needs; that the lands conceded to them as a grant are completely in use; and that the applicants are legally qualified to benefit from the action of first enlargement of ejido, requested in conformity with the provision of Articles 197 and 200 of the Federal Law of Agrarian Reform, giving as a result, in accord with the above, 75 peasants subjects of Agrarian Law, their names being the following: 1. Cornelio López García, 2. Agustín López García, 3. Pedro López García, 4. Vicente López García, 5. María Pérez Hernández, 6. Hermenegildo López Pérez, 7. Alicia López Pérez, 8. Juan López Pérez, 9. Floriberto López Pérez, 10. Martha Velázquez Pérez, 11. Carlos Hernández García, 12. Diego Hernández García, 13. Artemio Gómez López, 14. Mariano Toledo Velázquez, 15. Ma. [María]

Cristina Toledo V., 16. Alejandra de Jesús Jiménez, 17. Antonio de Jesús Jiménez, 18. Tomás González Morales, 19. Francisca Gómez Morales, 20. Domingo Gómez Morales, 21. Virginia Gómez Morales, 22. Antonio Toledo Morales, 23. Vicente López Jiménez, 24. Juan López Jiménez, 25. Rogelio López Hernández, 26. Alejandro López Hernández, 27. Magdalena Hernández G., 28. Javier López Hernández, 29. Marcelo López Hernández, 30. Francisco Morales Hernández, 31. Sergio Morales Hernández, 32. Marcos Jiménez Hernández, 33. Félix Morales Hernández, 34. Alfonso Cortés Toledo, 35. Manuel Cortés Toledo, 36. Pedro Jiménez Pérez, 37. Martín Jiménez Pérez, 38. María Jiménez Pérez, 39. Aurelio Gómez Hernández, 40. Álvaro Morales Gómez, 41. Gerónimo Jiménez Ruiz, 42. Javier Hernández García, 43. Pedro Jiménez Hernández, 44. Vicente de Jesús Pérez, 45. Domingo López Ruiz, 46. Domingo López Morales, 47. Alejandro López Morales, 48. Francisco López Morales, 49. Domingo Gómez Hernández, 50. Pedro Gómez Jiménez.

51. Margarita Gómez Jiménez, 52. Alberto Gómez López, 53. Domingo Gómez López, 54. Nicolás Hernández, 55. Pedro Hernández Jiménez, 56. Román Hernández García, 57. Marcelo Hernández López, 58. Amado Velázquez de Jesús, 59. Marcelo Velázquez Pérez, 60. Enrique Velázquez García, 61. Nicolás Velázquez Pérez, 62. Emilia López García, 63. Antonio Pérez Hernández, 64. Manuel Ruiz Cortés, 65. Julio García López, 66. Rogelio Jiménez Hernández, 67. Marcelo Hernández García, 68. Gilberto Morales Hernández, 69. Marcelo de Jesús Pérez, 70. Mario Jiménez Pérez, 71. Oscar Pérez Hernández, 72. Adán de Jesús Jiménez, 73. Domingo López Hernández, 74. Lorenzo Gómez Velázquez, 75. Antonio Jiménez Ruiz.

WHEREAS SECOND.—That by Presidential Resolution dated November 26, 1971, published in the *Diario Oficial de la Federación*, March 6, 1972, there was recognized and registered to the community called ZONA LACANDONA, located in the municipality of Ocosingo in the state of Chiapas, a total area of 614,321 ha., such Resolution of declarative character recognizes the possession of lands that that community has been using in usufruct, but does not imply the transfer of an area greater than the community possesses, and consequently there was excluded when the survey was done for the Resolution's execution the area of 113,214.8729 ha., which is part of the 160,211 ha. declared national lands, according to the Resolution of August 16, 1967, published in the *Diario Oficial de la Federación* the 18th of the same month and year and on the basis of which diverse agrarian nuclei, among others the one before us, exercise acts of possession.

WHEREAS THIRD.—That by reason of the statement in the previous Whereas, there must be regularized by means of the first enlargement of ejido the possession by the settlement called LA SULTANA in the municipality of Ocosingo in the state of Chiapas of the lands that it holds and which comprise an area of 839.4258 ha. of unirrigated land and woods that, being the property of the Nation, are actionable in accord with the provision of Article 204 of the Federal Law of Agrarian Reform, in relation with Article 3, fraction ii, and Article 5 of the Law of Untitled, National, and Excess Lands. Of the area of reference, a tract will be reserved necessary for the constitution of the agricultural-industrial unit for women, and the rest will be used in a collective form by the 75 qualified persons, as Articles 104 and 130 of the Agrarian Reform Law provide.

WHEREAS FOURTH.—That the regularization of the possession held by the members of the settlement in question has as its object to put a brake on irregular human settlements, to determine precisely to whom correspond the usufruct and utilization of natural resources, to favor rational ranching and forestry, and thereby to cover the agrarian necessities of the members of this petitioning nucleus and at the same time to avoid by regularization and organization the anarchical exploitation of the resources that the nucleus possesses and induce by proper productive processes the profitability and generation of benefits that will incorporate the petitioners into conditions at the cultural and economic level of the country, in accord with the specific projects that are developed in the zone.

For all the indicated conclusive whereases, it is in order to revoke the negative order by the governor of the state.

Therefore and in accord with the imperative imposed on the Executive Office in my charge by fraction x of Article 27 of the Constitution and with bases in Article 8, fraction ii, and Articles 69, 104, 130, 197, 200, 204, 241, 304, 305, and other pertinent articles of the Federal Law of Agrarian Reform, and Article 3, fraction ii, and Article 5 of the Law of Untitled, National, and Excess Lands, it is resolved:

FIRST.—The negative order by the governor of the state, dated February 18, 1983, is revoked.

SECOND.—The action of first enlargement of ejido requested by the peasants of the settlement called LA SULTANA, located in the municipality of Ocosingo in the state of Chiapas, is in order.

THIRD.—There is conceded to the settlement of reference, as first enlargement of ejido, a total area of 839.4258 ha. (EIGHT HUNDRED AND THIRTY NINE HECTARES, FORTY-TWO ARES, AND 58 CENTIARES) of unirrigated land and woods that is the property of the Nation, which will be distributed in the form indicated in the Third Whereas in Fact of this Resolution, must be localized in accord with the map approved by the Ministry of Agrarian Reform, and will pass into the power of the beneficiary settlement with all its accessions, uses, customs, and easements.

FOURTH.—Let there be issued to the 75 qualified persons benefited by this Resolution, and to the agricultural-industrial unit for women, the corresponding certificates of agrarian rights.

FIFTH.—As for the exploitation and utilization of the lands conceded, they will be as provided by Article 138 of the Federal Law of Agrarian Reform and regulations on the matter, and the ejidatarios will be fully instructed on their obligations and rights in this respect.

SIXTH.—Let there be published in the *Diario Oficial de la Federación* and in the *Periódico Oficial* of the State Government of Chiapas, and inscribed in the National Agrarian Registry and the corresponding Public Registry of Property, this Resolution conceding definitively first enlargement of ejido to the petitioning members of the settlement called LA SULTANA, located in the municipality of Ocosingo in the declared state of the federation, for the effects of Law. Let it be announced and executed. Given in the Palace of the Executive Power of the Union, in Mexico City, Federal District, on January 3, 1989.—The Constitutional President of the United Mexican States, Carlos Salinas de Gortari, his signature. Let it be fulfilled: The Minister of Agrarian Reform, Víctor Cervera Pacheco, his signature.

Chapter Eighteen

Governor González's Penal Code: Tuxtla Gutiérrez, 1990

Governor Absalón Castellanos (see Reading No. 13) had Chiapas's penal code reformed in 1984 (and then variously amended) to broaden liability for "crimes against . . . internal security." It must remain for future historians to explain why already in 1988 the state needed or newly inaugurated Governor Patrocinio González wanted a new code. But one reason surely was the new governor's urge to stamp his mark generally on the state, show his stuff in as many capacities as possible, and shoot for the presidency.

Descended from major intellectual (law, history) and political clans in Chiapas and Tabasco, he had much going for him. One uncle had been a federal Supreme Court justice, another a PRI deputy in Congress, another the nationally powerful boss of Tabasco in the 1930's (when Graham Greene wrote about it), and his father, most impressively, a distinguished professor of labor law at the National University, chief administrative officer of the Labor Ministry 1947–52, under-secretary of Labor 1952–58, Labor minister 1958–70, a strong inside competitor for the PRI's presidential candidacy in 1964, and a PRI senator for Chiapas 1976–78.

Beyond his backing, González had his own personal, intellectual, administrative, and political talents. Born in 1934, a student leader at the National University's Law School, where he took his degree in 1956, he had served as chancellor of the Mexican Embassy in London in 1957–59, taken an M.A. in Law and Economics at Cambridge in 1961, directed the Mexican Presidency's Office of Public Investments from 1961 to 1964, married the daughter of the 1958–70 Finance minister (himself another strong competitor for the PRI's presidential candidacy in 1964 and again in 1970), been a PRI deputy for Chiapas in Congress from 1967 to 1970, held high-ranking offices in the Federal District administration between 1970 and 1982, almost won the PRI's gubernatorial candidacy for Chiapas in 1982, and just completed six PRIista years in the Senate for Chiapas. If the new governor could repair his predecessor's mismanagement, regain political control of the state, give some of it a "modern" look, and somehow get into Salinas's cabinet, none of which seemed to him beyond his abilities, then swing his weight and pray hard, he might have a good shot at the presidency in 1994, almost all that any Mexican politician could hope to achieve.

The penal reform, among Governor González's many concerns then a minor operation, took the state legislature two years to accomplish. Essentially a rationalization of the existing code, it refined some definitions (e.g., criminal "responsibility"), reordered Book II's titles, and added a title on "crimes committed in electoral matters." Its most controversial element was the expansion of the already established grounds for legal abortion by a super-modern decriminalization of the act "for reasons of family planning . . . or when it is proved that the abortion was caused by the imprudence of the pregnant woman." After the code had gone into effect in 1990, the diocese of San Cristóbal raised holy hell. Two weeks later the state legislature suspended the chapter in question and restored the previous code's articles on the matter.

The reform's major significance, however, was its impact on leftist social and political movements. In this regard the governor and the legislature generally limited criminal liability but hardened the penalties on the two most agitated issues then, *despojo*, ("despoilment," typically squatters' invasions and occupation of privately owned land), and "crimes against . . . internal security." For "despoilment" the 1984 code had imposed six months to two years in prison and a fine of ten to twenty days' wages; for "rebellion," two to ten years, 100 to 200 days' wages, and suspension of political rights for up to five years; for "conspiracy," two to five years and up to 50 days' wages; for "sedition," two to four years; for "civil disorder or rioting," the same and up to 50 days' wages. Except for "sedition," the penalty for which remained the same, the new code's punishments (see the following excerpts) were all harsher, and the impact heavy on all movements involving public protest.

Consider the risks run by the officers of a militant organization (e.g., the CIOAC or the OCEZ). If by plan they led a mass march through a town's streets to a boisterous demonstration in the park in the main square in front of town hall, then, pushing through a police line, led an occupation of part of the building for a sit-in, in the course of which a demonstrator brandishing a pistol pushed a defiant municipal employee out of his office, they would be liable under Article 215 for "provocation of a crime," under Article 216.iii and 216.iv for "rebellion," under Article 218.i for "invitation to rebellion," under Article 221 for "conspiracy," under Article 222 for "sedition," under Article 223 as "intellectual authors" of sedition, and under Article 225 (almost exactly the same as 1984's Article 135) for "civil disorder or riot," and "responsible" (under Article 11) for same. If charged on all counts and convicted, they could each receive prison terms totaling 60 years and fines amounting to 252.5 days' wages. (The maximum term for first-degree homicide was 20 years.) No social or political militant received so crushing a sentence, but for squatting on a rancher's land, or blocking the streets on a march, or demonstrating in a park, many did go to prison for longer than they would have for armed robbery (six months to three years).

The impact, however, was to aggravate the state's insecurity. Because the new code, for all its rationality, did not abate conflict over land or between the government and its leftist opponents, but only kept the convicted in prison longer, it quickly crowded the prisons—and gave new cause for protest.

On March 3, 1994, two months after the EZLN's revolt and President Salinas's dismissal of Interior Minister González, the state legislature repealed Articles 215, 222, 223, and 224, and amended Article 225 by repealing its second and third paragraphs.

CÓDIGO PENAL PARA EL
ESTADO DE CHIAPAS*

BOOK I

TITLE I
GENERAL RULES ON CRIMES
AND RESPONSIBILITY . . .

CHAPTER II

PERSONS RESPONSIBLE FOR CRIMES . . .

Article 11. Responsibility for crimes falls on all who take part by directing, promoting, or leading, individually or en masse, in the conception, preparation, or execution of same, or lend aid or cooperation of any kind, by concert before or after the commission of same, or induce any person or persons to commit same.

The conduct of the participants will be punishable only if the perpetrator's act has reached at least the degree of an attempt.

Personal considerations for exclusion from punishment will only favor the participant whom they attend . . .

---

*Gobierno Constitucional del Estado Libre y Soberano de Chiapas, *Periódico Oficial*, October 11, 1990, pp. 11, 87–90.

BOOK II

. . . TITLE VII

CRIMES AGAINST PERSONS IN THEIR PROPERTY

. . . CHAPTER VI

DESPOILMENT

Article 202. Imprisonment of two to six years and a fine of 30 to 180 days' wages will be applied to he [or she] who, without the consent of the person who has the right to grant it, by means deceitful or furtive:

I. Occupies real property not his [or her] own, or makes use of such property or of a real right that does not belong to him [or her]. . . .

If the despoilment is done by two or more persons or by violence, imprisonment of six to nine years and a fine of 50 to 180 days of wages will be imposed.

On the intellectual authors of the crime, besides the penalty provided in this article, a penalty of up to one-fourth more than the sanction corresponding to said crime will be imposed.

Article 203. The sanctions provided will be imposed although the right to possession of the property is contested, but if before the sentence is given, in any case, the active subject restores possession and its accessories and pays for the damages and impairments that he [or she] may have caused, then the sanction that would correspond to the crime will be reduced by half . . .

TITLE VIII

CRIMES AGAINST PUBLIC MORALITY . . .

CHAPTER VI

PROVOCATION OF A CRIME AND DEFENSE
OF SAME OR OF ANY VICE

Article 215. Imprisonment of two to six years and a fine of ten to forty days' wages will be applied to he [or she] who publicly calls for the commission of a crime or makes a defense of same or of any vice.

TITLE IX

CRIMES AGAINST THE STATE'S INTERNAL SECURITY

CHAPTER I

REBELLION

Article 216. Imprisonment of two to twenty years will be applied to those who, not being military personnel on active duty [thereby subject to military justice], attempt by violence and use of arms to:

I. Abolish or reform the State Constitution or the institutions that emanate from it.

II. Prevent the election, inauguration, convention, or operation of any of the branches of State Government or any municipal government.

III. Remove any state or municipal public servant from his [or her] office, or prevent the performance of said office's duty.

IV. Withdraw obedience to the State Government by all or a part of any town or any public security force.

Article 217. The penalty prescribed in the previous article will be applied to he [or she] who, resident in territory occupied by the State Government and without resorting to violence, provides arms, munitions, money, food, or means of transport or communication to rebels, or prevents the Government's public-security forces from receiving such support. If he [or she] resides in territory occupied by rebels, the imprisonment will be from six months to five years.

A public servant who by reason of his [or her] office holds documents or reports of strategic interest and provides them to rebels will be penalized by five to 30 years in prison.

Article 218. Imprisonment of four to 10 years will be applied to he [or she] who:

I. In any form or by any means invites rebellion.

II. Resident in territory occupied by the Government, hides or helps rebel spies or scouts, in the knowledge that they are such, or maintains relations with rebels in order to provide them news concerning the operations of the State's security forces, or other news that may be useful to them; and

III. Voluntarily serves in an employment or in an office or on a commission in the place occupied by the rebels, unless he [or she] acts under threat of violence or for humanitarian reasons.

Article 219. Public servants and rebels who after combat cause directly or by their orders the death of prisoners will suffer imprisonment for 15 to 30 years.

Article 220. Rebels will not be responsible for homicides or injuries resulting from combat, but for such as they cause outside same, he [or she] who orders them, as well as he [or she] who, able to prevent them, allows them, and those who actually commit them, will be responsible.

No penalty will be applied to those who lay down their arms before being taken prisoner, if they have not committed any of the crimes mentioned in the previous article.

CHAPTER II

CONSPIRACY, SEDITION,

AND OTHER PUBLIC DISORDERS

Article 221. There is conspiracy whenever two or more persons resolve in concert to commit any of the crimes specified in this Title and agree on the means to carry their decision into effect. The applicable sanction will be from two to seven years imprisonment, or confinement for the same time, and a fine of up to 50 days' wages.

When it is agreed that the means to carry out the rebellion are homicide, theft, kidnapping, despoilment, or pillage, the conspirators will suffer imprisonment of four to eight years and a fine of 100 to 200 days of wages.

Article 222. They incur in sedition those who, united tumultuously, but without arms, resist public authorities or attack them, in order to prevent the authorities' free discharge of their duty, with any of the objectives to which Article 218 of this Code refers.

Article 223. Sedition will be sanctioned with a penalty of two to four years in prison; intellectual authors of sedition will suffer double such penalty and a fine of 50 to 100 days' wages. Insofar as they are applicable to sedition, Articles 219 and 220 will be observed.

Article 224. For all legal effects, only the crimes specified in this Title will be considered as of a political character [considerable for amnesty], except for those specified in Articles 218, 220, and 221 of this Code.

Article 225. They incur in civil disorder or riot those who, on the pretext of exercising a right, unite tumultuously and disturb public order by the use of violence against persons and things, or threaten public authority, its agents, and its servants, or pose grave resistance to them in the discharge of their duties, or on the occasion of such discharge intimidate them or compel them to make any determination. For this crime there will be imposed a penalty of two to four years in prison and a fine of 20 to 50 days' wages.

Without detraction from the crimes in which they may incur in each case, the penalty to which the previous paragraph refers will be increased by up to one-fourth for those who, on the pretext of exercising a right, unite tumultuously to take by assault buildings or public parks or obstruct means of communication by land, sea, or air.

Those responsible under Article 11, besides the penalty provided in this article, will suffer twice the imprisonment and twice the fine.

CHAPTER NINETEEN

A Silent Cry of Sorrowful Warning: Bishop Ruiz's Pastoral Letter, cc. Pope John Paul II, August 6, 1993

Not only "500 years of history," the 33 years of his own work in San Cristóbal, and the last five years of clandestine contention with the FLN weighed on Bishop Ruiz's mind as he drafted a pastoral letter in July 1993. Looming close in the background was a great range of national questions of enormous consequence for Chiapas and his diocese: What would the reform of the agrarian Article 27 do to landed communities and to the landless? How far could "neoliberalism" go? If the U.S. Congress passed NAFTA, how could poor peasants survive? Was it better or worse for Chiapas that Patrocinio González had left the governorship to become Interior minister? Would it make any difference whom the PRI presented as its presidential candidate next year, or who the PRI candidate for governor would be? Could the PRD and Cuauhtémoc Cárdenas come back and win? Which was worse, an authoritarian and corrupt Solidarity, which divided the Union of Unions and allowed the EZLN to regain ground from the diocese's missionary workers, or a popular and honest Solidarity, which made the Union more effective, but also set aside the missionaries? Could the Church alone ever make the Union effective? Could the Union alone ever be effective?

But immediately and awfully before him was a cumulative series of developments that altogether seemed about to lead Chiapas into a war like that in Guatemala. Since January rumors had flown up from the canyons that the EZLN was finally preparing for action. Since then the army had been patrolling up and down the canyons, terrifying all the faithful there. It had found catechists teaching texts (chosen the year before) from the Gospel of Mark ("Marcos") on "the way of life," defined as "our customs, equality, and sharing, the defense of our rights . . . ," versus "the way of death," defined as "the government and other authorities, the [new] Article 27, the State Penal Code . . . ," both of which "ways" the army found seditious. In March the Union of Unions had decided to reconvene the Las Casas Indian Congress (on the pretext of the 20th anniversary of its preparatory Indian assemblies), which, when it met in late May, promised to reassert resistance to the EZLN. But also in March, in the highlands near San Cristóbal, two army officers had been murdered, their bodies quartered and burned. The army had arrested 13 local Indian suspects, whom the diocesan human rights office tried to defend, which the army took as a stain on its honor. In April the CNC in Altamirano had deposed and jailed the municipal president, whom the ANCIEZ locals, hundreds of Indians, defended in angry demonstrations. Then a statewide coalition of "social organizations," including more than 1,500 Indians, had staged a protest march in Tuxtla to demand an end to the army's patrols. Acting Governor Elmar Setzer, who would not meet them, had declared, "They want to test the government of Chiapas, but the government of Chiapas will answer with the Law." On May 22, four days before the Indian Congress was to meet, an army patrol had discovered the big EZLN training camp and, after an exchange of fire in which an EZLN officer and an army officer were killed, took the place, with abundant publicity. The Indian Congress met anyway, more than 1,500 delegates at an ejido in the canyons, representing a substantial reduction in the EZLN's strength. Once the deacon of deacons had then broken with "the armed way," the bishop had personally led his priests and missionaries down into the canyons, to deliver explicit instructions against war. But at the same time Marcos had been managing the receipt and distribution of loads of arms and ammunition among the communities and colonies for war.

With all this on his mind, any reasonable person would have expected that war would soon start between the army and the EZLN, and a war by both against the nonviolent—Chiapas finally made Guatemalan.

The bishop's letter, some 15,000 words long, conveyed several of its messages forthrightly. But the most important message it carried hidden in apparently ordinary language: ". . . we know that God speaks to us urgently . . . we have to know how to read 'the signs of the times' . . . It is precisely at this time that a word of encouragement is most needed. . . . At this moment when contradictions are sharpened. . . . Why not start a different path without waiting . . . ? What prevents us . . . from entering into dialogue . . . ?" In other words, a real war is about to explode. Of all people, considering his position, all who depended on him, all the suspicions of him, the bishop could not give outright his urgent alarm. If he had, he would have most likely provoked the army and the EZLN to act even sooner than he expected they would. He was calling for help to prevent a terrible emergency, but trying in tone and turn of words to keep his call from making the emergency happen.

The date of the letter is telling too. Traditionally, bishops sent pastoral letters to their priests at the start of Lent (February-March) or the start of Advent (around November 30). Bishop Ruiz sent his letter on August 6 (a First Friday, a day of special grace), which is the Feast of the Transfiguration, Jesus's crisis on the mountain, the beginning of "the last days."

Marcos celebrated that day too, the twenty-fourth anniversary of the founding of the FLN, by reviewing 5,000 EZLN troops at one of the FLN's main bases in the canyons.

A copy of the bishop's letter reached Pope John Paul II during his visit to Izamal, Yucatán, on August 11–12. In the pope's "Address to Indigenous Peoples" on August 11, he professed the Church's "emphatic support of your right to have room for your cultural, social, and ethnic identity as individuals and groups." Otherwise, he said, "I also know the difficulties of your present situation, and I want to assure you that the Church, like a concerned mother, is with you and supports your legitimate aspirations and just claims." He insisted that "nothing should slow down the noble struggle for justice, as long as at all times it is inspired by the Gospel principles of cooperation and dialogue, excluding every form of violence and hatred. . . ." As for "the priests, religious, catechists, and pastoral workers . . . in the communities of indigenous brothers and sisters," he warned them: "interests that are foreign to the Gospel cannot be allowed to sully the purity of the mission that the Church has entrusted to them."

It would be a prejudice to conclude that neither the bishop's letter nor the pope's address mattered in the struggles for loyalty in the canyons then. Perhaps in some small part because of these declarations Salinas's minister of Social Development arrived on August 20 in Las Margaritas with a promise of U.S. $50 million mainly for the canyons, visited Ocosingo, met with the deacon of deacons, discussed guerrillas, returned to the region in early September with President Salinas to inaugurate a Solidarity Week and a new local hospital, and in November became Salinas's and the PRI's presidential candidate. And it is at least reasonable to figure that between the revival of the Union of Unions and the newly expanded social programs in the region the EZLN lost support that would have made its rebellion on January 1, 1994, considerably more powerful and extensive than it was.

Bishop Ruiz's letter certainly made a difference to Interior Minister González and Papal Nuncio Girolamo Prigione, as further evidence to justify his removal. In October Prigione privately read the bishop a letter from the Holy Office rebuking him for "pastoral and theological deviations," viz., "particularization" (neglect of the faithful who were not poor) and employment of "elements of Marxism." In November the bishop in charge of the Doctrine of the Faith in Mexico publicly reprimanded Bishop Ruiz for his deviations, "something profoundly deep." If not for the war Ruiz had predicted, to end which he quickly became indispensable, he might very well have had to retire in disgrace.

The following selections from his letter give some of its urgent messages.

Origins is a weekly publication of the Catholic News Service in Washington, D.C.

IN THIS HOUR OF GRACE*

In this hour of grace for the church of Latin America in which the Good News summons us once again in a sign of unity, and on this occasion when the Holy Father returns to this deeply prophetic mission land of Mexico, what better time could there be to express, together with the hopes, longings, and sufferings of our indigenous peoples, our unity with the universal church. The Holy Father, John Paul II, wishes to fulfill his promise and make his voice heard with words of comfort and enlightenment to the representatives of the indigenous peoples of the whole continent in the context of the International Year of the Indigenous People. Our Diocese of San Cristóbal de Las Casas, as a highly indigenous diocese, wants to make its voice heard as well.

. . . If we know that God speaks to us urgently in the cries and even the sorrowful silence of those who still do not have a voice and who sometimes live in desperation, we have to know how to read the "signs of the times," attending carefully to the cries of the poor and the oppressed, of those who live on the margins or are tortured, and of all those who are persecuted because of race or religion or because they have denounced injustice.

. . . Heir of the prophetic vocation of the Dominican friar Bartolomé de Las Casas, the diocese walks among and with the poor, aware of the suffering of the majority of the population: high levels of poverty, disease, and illiteracy; the lack of means of communications; profound marginalization; and racial discrimination.

. . . The present situation of the poverty of our people and their deplorable living conditions, which are even more serious in the indigenous areas of our diocese, are explained by the working of the structures which have been formed over the length and breadth of 500 years of history.

. . . For the Indian peoples the conquest meant that the colonizers brought subjugation and exploitation as well as varying degrees of brutality and violation of the dignity of the indigenous.

*Bishop Samuel Ruiz García, in *Origins*, February 10, 1994, pp. 587–602.

. . . The founders of the national independence movement and, later, of the first modernization program with the Porfirian reforms [by President Porfirio Díaz, 1876–1911] and industrialization, produced the growth and development of the Mexican hacienda with its pattern of forced labor. . . .

. . . The winning faction in the armed conflict of the Mexican Revolution sought to change the structures of land ownership through their proposed agrarian reform, in order to quiet the cry for land and the peasant revolts . . . In Chiapas . . . this process got out of step and slowed down with respect to the rest of the country. We ourselves have been witness to the reality of systems of peonage in the indigenous areas, and in Chiapas generally, until the decade of the [19]80s . . .

The crisis of the industrialized countries and the decrease in the price of oil in the first half . . . of the '80s, together with the burden of the external debt, became intolerable for the economic system. After that, the government undertook the first structural adjustment measures in a neoliberal framework, with high costs for the more vulnerable classes. The government of President Salinas continued and deepened these modernizing measures of structural reform of the national economy, keeping control over concessions that are more strictly political and seeking a new relation between the Mexican economy and the world economy, counting on the North American Free Trade Agreement with the United States and Canada to be its cornerstone . . .

From this perspective, we are now experiencing what we could call "the second modernization of rural Chiapas." This is also happening in the context of the chronic drop of coffee prices at the international level at the same time that the intensity and extension of the agrarian conflicts began to increase. . . . The spearhead of this modernizing agrarian movement is the reform of Article 27 of the Constitution and the new agrarian law [to end the mandate to expropriate and redistribute land, and to allow ejidatarios to take title to their grants as their private property] . . .

Within this broad panorama of inequities, it is not surprising that the recent decades of our diocese have been permeated by a high level of conflict. Because the Indians are among the most vulnerable peoples in the social structure, those in the indigenous areas have been creating their own organizations and methods of struggling to claim their rights to the land and to better living conditions. This road has not been easy; it has been marked by violent responses on the part of those who benefit from the status quo. However, these same difficulties have obliged the Indian people to mobilize in the face of hunger, exploitation, and repression, with different ways of making their presence known, such as marches, sit-ins, demonstrations, hunger strikes, and the like.

. . . Facing the challenges of modernization and the severity of the neoliberalism that we have already confirmed, we lift our voice together with the prophets . . . to say as they did, and together with them, that the poverty that this situation of a lack of material goods generates is evil and totally opposed to the will of God.

The church, through unique individuals and works at various times, has known how to fulfill its prophetic mission. Yet neither can it be denied that at other times it has become worldly, whether by giving ideological legitimacy to the colonial government or to the independent state or by enjoying privileges when it used the forms of systems in fashion for accumulating goods and power.

This particular local church, deeply stamped with the Gospel faithfulness of . . . Las Casas, has opted in these last decades to take its place at the margins of society and with the poorest.

. . . the insertion of the diocese's pastoral workers (priests, [members of] religious [orders], and committed laity) in a conflictive reality has taken us down a long road that has also been a long process of conversion. The world of the indigenous people, who are a majority in percentage of population but even more so in their marginal status, demands of us (if we would be faithful to the Gospel) a response of urgent presence. Therefore our diocese is stamped with inherent characteristics of pastoral care for the indigenous, understanding that this is not only a concern for the Indian but an incarnation of our presence in his world, which is full of needs and at the same time of tremendous values; it is an experience that guides our faith reflection, our pastoral activity, and our ecclesial goal of advancing toward the emergence of a native church that is aware of its own salvation history, that expresses itself through its culture, that is enriched with its own values, that accepts its sufferings, struggles, and aspirations, and that with the strength of the Gospel transforms and liberates its culture.

. . . This option has brought harassment and attacks by the authorities as well as by various groups or sectors of the economically, socially, and culturally privileged. Thus it has had to endure calumny and lies propagated by the mass media, both official and privately owned, and to endure the imprisonment of its pastoral workers, the killing of catechists, the intimidation and even accusations within the church, manipulating and deceiving simple people.

. . . As interpreters and confidants of the people, we sense how hard it is to open doors to hope when we see that the situation in which the majority live is so distressing and the dominating structures so persistent that the very people who dedicate their lives to change see that all of creation is turned upside down by the wickedness of the perverse. The same people who seek the paths of justice are themselves, at times, so upset and frustrated that they do not know what to do or even what to ask for.

It is precisely at this time that a word of encouragement is most needed, a word that at the same time is concrete and that explains why Christians hope.

Today we want to place all that we have done and said on its true and unique foundation: the resurrection. The process of this diocesan church, taking into account these last 33 years, has the Lord's resurrection as its source; because if Christ is not risen, our pastoral work is in vain and your faith futile. This message of the resurrection can be taken as the center that, throughout the various stages, has given us hope because it is the central mystery of our faith, and all that we have done has been inspired by our faith.

. . . We know that the church is not an end in itself nor is it instituted to serve itself, rather it is sent into the world as a servant and a humble but necessary leaven for the building of God's kingdom, the reign of justice, love, and peace. We also know that the kingdom is begun here on earth, although its consummation is not of this world. Today this impels us to the Gospel task of learning to dialogue with all who are of good will and to reflect on the present times in the light of the Gospel, journeying also with our evangelical brothers and sisters.

. . . In Chiapas we experience great sadness and worry because of the increased attempts against life, violating the most elemental human rights and repressing the people's efforts. As the diocesan church, we strive to be faithful to our vocation of building the kingdom of God, offering the values of the Gospel for the humanization of the world and serving preferentially the poorest. We cannot keep ourselves at the margin of what is happening around us. The events make us proclaim: "I have witnessed the affliction of my people in Egypt and have heard their cry of complaint against their slave drivers, so I know well what they are suffering" (Ex. 3:7).

Knowing the grave reality of our brothers and sisters, who are the poorest among the poor, we propose to accompany them, as did the good Samaritan, in their effective search for a new society built on justice and fraternity.

. . . We will only be able to understand the Beatitudes of Christ if we do not set our hearts on wealth and if we are prepared to share as brothers and sisters our social, economic, and cultural goods with those who lack them (Lk. 6:20-26). Blessed are those who, brought by the Spirit of God, are joined in solidarity with the poor (Mt. 5:11–19).

At first our pastoral plans were focused mainly on the neediest. But as we lived with the "poor of Yahweh" and discovered their great suffering, we found ourselves obliged by the circumstances to denounce the plunderings; it was necessary to make a clearer option for the poor in light of a Gospel reflection. We're not talking about any document or a theological exposition, but rather a simple reading of our intentions and where our pastoral activity was heading in light of this painful reality. It was an urgent evangelical decision. We also knew that by making this decision we entered into the conflict of love: to announce from the perspective of the poor a message of conversion to the oppressor and to announce to the oppressed, with whom Christ is identified, a Gospel of hope. . . .

It is difficult to inventory the [Church's local] achievements because several of them are also a result of the work of other institutions, groups, or individuals that are joined with the life of the communities. What we might call an achievement of the diocese's work are the steps that the indigenous and peasant communities have taken from being the object of the decisions of others to beginning to be those who decide their own history. It is worth mentioning that the awareness of their dignity on the part of the Indians and peasants is nourished by Gospel values. They have appropriated the space that belongs to them in the church and thus also in history. They gradually feel and live their own responsibility in the church to which they belong and which belongs to them.

The communities have acquired a critical conscience, a sign of maturity in the faith. They have discovered that united they have the capacity to solve the problems that affect them . . .

At the base of all our pastoral guidance is a Gospel criterion: to announce the Gospel and live a faith that leads to life, life in abundance (Jn. 10:10); in other words, to shed light on the connection between faith and life. It is necessary, therefore, to discern at each step whether or not an action favors the realization of the kingdom of God in justice, truth, love, and peace.

Thus, all pastoral action will achieve legitimacy when it is liberating, when it respects the legitimate decisions of the people of God, when it accompanies the people on their journey, when it favors the weaker, and when their culture, their religiosity, and their needs are taken into account.

Pastoral workers' task of accompaniment must take into account the times that require their presence and those that do not, so as not to supplant the people in that which corresponds to them. It involves helping them mature so that they themselves will be the ones who decide, who question each other, and who evaluate, and in the end, they will be the ones to decide their own history. Frequently the people themselves indicate to us, with wisdom, where our place is and is not. Manipulation, paternalism, and the displacement of others are in the final analysis not Gospel attitudes.

It is important to recognize and to respect the people's place in making civic and political decisions. Even though Christians make their decisions in the light of faith, as pastoral workers we should not head their organizations or plot their course. It is proper to our role to offer informed or enlightening accompaniment and to support their just actions . . .

We have committed many mistakes on our pastoral pilgrimage.

Our first actions, years before Vatican II, were destructive of the culture. We had only our own criterion with which to judge the traditional customs, shaping our judgment with ethnocentrism and moralism, attitudes that regrettably were very common at that time. Our attitudes of compassion and love for the indigenous people and our having lived among them helped make up for our deficiencies.

We were late to see that behind the kindness of the indigenous and their many forms of popular religiosity was the domination the mestizo exercized over them in the economic, political, and even religious realms in order to defraud them. Without having understood, much less analyzed this situation, we were on the side of the oppressors, thinking that through them and their presumed goodwill we could bring about some changes.

We have not yet been able to find a pedagogical method, if indeed there is one, to reach the heart of those who, while geographically near the indigenous and the peasants, are far from them in their hearts. Many methods and activities have been tried in different parts of the diocese that have had transitory effects. However, the conversion of the so-called caxlán or mestizo will, in some cases, require restitution, which will mean leaving land and houses that have been appropriated in specious ways. We are aware that many mestizos are opening their hearts; but we are also aware that many others are hardening theirs. The presence of the poor, their deep sensitivity to God's mysteries, which are revealed to them rather than to the wise (Lk. 10:21), have caused jealousy in the nonindigenous and the feeling that they are on the fringes of the church, the same church with which they had identified and in which they had lived as a place of worship without any commitment to follow Jesus and without any thought for their brothers and sisters (Lk. 16:19–31).

We have not sufficiently taken advantage of the popular religiosity in order to capture its hidden and deep sense of liberation.

Frequent changes of personnel within the religious congregations have affected the follow-up of the evangelizing processes and participation in teamwork.

Events sometimes happen so fast that we feel unable to answer for the consequences that the people will pay. The recent agrarian law reforms, made to accommodate the so-called North American Free Trade Agreement, affect the peasant communities very negatively; but we have not been able to search out alternatives that could be of use to them.

. . . God wants to establish life where death imposes its laws . . . In our history so full of conflict, God has revealed himself to re-establish his plan: to distribute justly the goods of creation (Lk. 1:47–55). God is revealed when he accompanies the liberating process of the people and establishes a covenant with them: "I will be your God, and you will be my people" (Lv. 26:12). God is present with his people in such a way that to be against the people and their legitimate aspirations is to be against God. Jesus made himself poor among the poor, and from that vantage point, proclaims and realizes the Father's plan in the midst of a history full of conflict and death. From there he summons us to choose the road of life, anchored in truth and the hope of resurrection.

. . . The plan of salvation is lived out in a world full of choices that energize our lives and history itself. They define the Christian option whose truth is shown forth in the dead and risen Christ. We can choose between eternal life or death, between God or the idols of power and money, between freedom or oppression, between living and building community or submerging ourselves in individualism. We can choose between discovering, loving, and defending Christ in the poor or oppressing and stripping him, between living in and building a just world or destroying ourselves with injustice. In a word, we can proclaim and build the living kingdom of God or we can build a kingdom of death. Each of the options for life, which are also an expression of following Jesus, increase life in us and clarify our pilgrimage, which is a commitment that cannot be reversed.

. . . God, creator of the universe, makes his creation a gift to all men and women. However, human beings, in their desire to always have more, kill their brother in order to be the sole owner of what God, in his love, gave to all of us; that is the structure of social sin.

God is a God of life who accompanies his people, who are revealed in Christ, poor, suffering, and risen, who opts for the poor. God wants life for all his children, especially for those who have the least and are depised by our society; he desires the well-being of his people.

God is revealed to us in history; his salvific action is brought about in the world with our participation.

God makes a convenant with his people. In that covenant he calls us to be faithful, to free ourselves from situations of injustice and death, to form community and to work together to build the kingdom.

. . . The different responses that the rich and the poor give to the presentation of the Gospel generate division and contradiction within the human household (Lk. 12:51) and provoke serious conflicts against those who preach love and justice. We can only lament the fact that the reproaches of Jesus to the scribes and pharisees (Lk. 11:37–12:1) continue unfortunately to be fully applicable in our diocese. The poor demanding their rights through legal means are repressed, businesspersons engage in speculation with the products of the field, the jails are full of innocent people, hunger and malnutrition are a permanent condition for many of the indigenous.

In the face of this situation, so common in Latin America, our diocese has felt compelled to emphasize its prophetic ministry, reading the "signs of the times" in the light of the Spirit, and calling for such a conversion that gathers all together for the building of a just society. This interpretation of history is part of the service that the church offers the world, joined to its prophetic ministry of proclaiming the justice of God.

. . . At this moment when contradictions are sharpened in our country and many are profiting from the changes, the responsibility of Christians to search for the truth is ever greater. By trying to know in our hearts the suffering and anguish of the other, we will have greater capacity to understand and know each other, to listen and to change. Neither selfishness nor our own convenience can be a platform for dialogue at a time when the other needs us.

The Lord helps us understand that acting from selfishness and convenience dehumanizes and shatters. Creation itself protests against the way of plunder and concentration of wealth that our social system generates, signaling the urgency of a change of course for humanity, lest our planetary survival itself be jeopardized.

Why not start a different path without waiting until the social structures change because of the desperation of those who have been crushed since antiquity? What prevents us, for example, from entering into dialogue for fresh initiatives by the *ejidos* unions instead of forming new farming structures that will bring about a new form of land concentration?

Dialogue, which is a condition for fraternal relationships, supposes a prior willingness to listen and has as its platform the acceptance of the other, without presuming him to be of excessively bad faith. To designate those who have good words, a good heart, and high moral standards will largely assure a successful dialogue.

Persons, groups, or communities that may have clashed should seek bridges of communication that connect one with the other, so as to experience the transforming dimension of Christian forgiveness.

The poor, the broken ones of society, know how to give witness to the love that Jesus made the sign of his church. They know that the Lord has showered them with his love, which no one merits, that he calls them to share their values to transform society, a society in which they strive to benefit everyone. It is not a transformation in which I will exclude my enemy but rather include him, because his enmity is based on the type of fratricidal society that we seek to change so as to establish the kingdom of God.

. . . The Holy Trinity is our reason for being . . . In the bosom of the Trinity, no person is inferior to another nor do they compete with one another or possess something that another lacks. Striving for a social system whose behavior and structures tend toward eliminating plunder and which has the sharing of goods as a goal, so that the poorest will no longer be so, will bring about irreversible gains in history . . .

CHAPTER TWENTY

ENOUGH!:
The Zapatista Declaration
of War, January 1, 1994.

The EZLN officers who read the Declaration from the Selva in the towns their forces had taken on the first morning of 1994 were not masked whites leading Indians, but masked Indians themselves, mostly born in Los Altos, infuriated in the Selva, returned in command on native ground. It was fitting that they should read the declaration, because on textual evidence it was they who had determined its substance and form.

To its credit the declaration had no intellectual finesse. Marcos would later (almost apologetically) describe it as "a confluence of various ideas, . . . a cocktail, . . . a general synthesis, a mixture of patriotic values, of the historic heritage of the clandestine Mexican left of the '70's, of elements of Indian culture, elements from Mexico's military history, of lessons from the Central American and South American guerrillas, from movements for national liberation, . . . the text of minimal agreement. . . ." (Sous-Commandant Marcos and Yvon Le Bot, *Le rêve zapatiste* [Paris: Seuil, 1997], pp. 164–67.) But this first declaration from the jungle shows more conscious logic than that, as Marcos also noted. It was a wrathful, entangled, but nevertheless deliberate statement of radical national popular sovereignty.

First, it thrashed through an introduction without any likely ideological reference for justification, not a word from or about Marx, Lenin, Mao, or Che. Second, shifting from Mexican history and patriotism for justification, it at once claimed constitutional protection under Article 39, the people's sovereign right to change the form of the country's government. Third, it was a declaration of war, but not against the entire government, only against the army acting in defense of the then chief (illegitimately so, in its judgment) of the executive branch, Carlos Salinas; it appealed to the other, unchallenged legislative and judicial branches of government to exercise their constitutional authority to remove Salinas and "restore" the rule of law, so that the country could have (somehow, not indicated) "a free and democratic government." Fourth, it did not even mention Indians. According to Marcos, this omission followed the lead of the most Indian Indians on the drafting committee, who insisted that the struggle was not particularly Indian but national. Fifth, the "General Command" explicitly claimed belligerent status for the EZLN, which (if neutral powers elsewhere recognized it) would not only, as the General Command indicated, oblige the Mexican army and the EZLN to abide by international laws on war, but also assume a government de facto responsible for the EZLN. Sixth, the declaration nowhere purports simply to call national attention to ignored outrages (which is all some Zapatistas and their supporters later said was its intent). Instead, it states the most ambitious marching orders for the EZLN: to defeat the Mexican army and capture the national capital for the Mexican people.

The historical references, familiar to Mexican schoolchildren, may stump many American readers. Here is a guide for the puzzled:

"500 years of struggle": Since Columbus in 1492 discovered a world new except to natives and Norsemen, suggesting a native struggle, but allowing that "we" may include anyone of any ethnicity in the struggle.

"slavery": Spanish imperial rule from 1521 to 1821, and probably peonage too.

"the War of Independence": in Mexico, from 1810 to 1821.

"American imperialism": the war the United States made on Mexico, 1846–48, as a result of which the United States acquired over half of Mexico's territory.

"our constitution": the Mexican Liberal Republican Constitution of 1857.

"the French Empire": French imperial military occupation of much of Mexico, 1862–66.

"Porfirista dictatorship": Porfirio Díaz's presidencies, 1876–80, 1884–1911.

"Reform Laws": Liberal decrees abolishing Catholic clerical legal immunities (1855) and compelling the Catholic Church to sell its real estate and forgo future acquisitions (1856), the latter of which eventually allowed many villages to lose their land.

"Hidalgo": Father Miguel Hidalgo (1753–1811), the Mexican priest who started the war for independence.

"Morelos": Father José María Morelos (1765–1815), the Mexican priest who continued the war for independence.

"Vicente Guerrero": a leading commander (1783?–1831) in the war for independence, a hero especially popular after independence for his hostility to Spanish landlords and merchants still in Mexico, president in 1829, overthrown, retired, arrested, and executed. (He is supposed to be a particular hero of Marcos: The watchword of his forces, "To Live for the Fatherland or Die for Liberty" became the EZLN's.)

"foreign invader": the United States, 1846–48.

"European prince": Maximilian (1831–67), the Austrian Hapsburg archduke installed by the French as emperor of Mexico in 1864, captured by the victorious Republicans in 1867 and executed.

"Porfirista 'scientists'": educated politicians in Díaz's government who (in a faint echo of their theoretical hero Auguste Comte) claimed that their administration of public affairs was scientific.

"Oil Expropriation": President Lázaro Cárdenas's nationalization of foreign oil companies in Mexico, 1938.

"railroad workers": members of the PRI–controlled national industrial union of railroad workers who went on a wildcat strike in 1958, won their demands, won control of the union, struck again in 1959, and lost, thousands of them going to jail.

"the students": the university and secondary-school students and their hundreds of thousands of supporters who in Mexico City in the summer and early fall of 1968 mounted massive demonstrations against a particularly right-wing government; the army and federal police crushed this movement in the massacre of October 2, 1968.

"the tri-color flag": the Mexican national flag—red, white, and green.

"the colors red and black": the old anarchist colors, which the Mexican labor movement since the 1910s has used for its own.

DECLARACIÓN DE LA SELVA LACANDONA*

Today We Say Enough!

To the people of Mexico:
Mexican Brothers:

We are a product of 500 years of struggle: first against slavery, during the War of Independence against Spain led by the insurgents; afterward to avoid being absorbed by American imperialism; then to promulgate our constitution and expel the French Empire from our soil; and later the Porfirista dictatorship denied us just application of the Reform laws, and the people rebelled, forming their own leaders; Villa and Zapata emerged, poor men like us, who have been denied the most elemental preparation so as to be able to use us as cannon fodder and pillage the wealth of our country, without it mattering to them that we have nothing, absolutely nothing, not even a decent roof

---

* January 1, 1994, www.ezln.org

over our heads, no land, no work, no health care, no food, or education; without the right to freely and democratically elect our authorities; without independence from foreigners, without peace or justice for ourselves and our children.

But TODAY WE SAY, ENOUGH! We are the heirs of those who truly forged our nationality. We the dispossessed are millions, and we call on our brothers to join in this call as the only path in order not to die of hunger in the face of the insatiable ambition of a dictatorship for more than 70 years led by a clique of traitors who represent the most conservative and sell-out groups in the country. They are the same as those who opposed Hidalgo and Morelos, who betrayed Vicente Guerrero, the same as those who sold over half our territory to the foreign invader, the same as those who brought a European prince to rule us, the same as those who formed the dictatorship of the Porfirista "scientists," the same as those who opposed the Oil Expropriation, the same as those who massacred the railroad workers in 1958 and the students in 1968, the same as those who today take everything from us, absolutely everything.

To prevent this, and as our last hope, after having tried everything to put into practice the legality based on our Magna Carta, we resort to it, to our Constitution, to apply Constitutional Article 39, which says:

"National sovereignty resides essentially and originally in the people. All public power emanates from the people and is instituted for the people's benefit. The people have, at all times, the unalienable right to alter or modify the form of their government."

Therefore, according to our Constitution, we issue this statement to the Mexican federal army, the basic pillar of the Mexican dictatorship that we suffer, monopolized as it is by the party in power and led by the federal executive that is presently held by its highest and illegitimate chief, Carlos Salinas de Gortari.

In conformity with this Declaration of War, we ask the other branches of the Nation's government to meet to restore the legality and the stability of the Nation by deposing the dictator.

We also ask that international organizations and the International Red Cross keep watch over and regulate the battles that our forces fight, in order to protect the civilian population, for we declare now and forever that we are subject to the stipulations of the Geneva Convention's Laws on War, the EZLN forming a belligerent force in our struggle for liberation. We have the Mexican people on our side, we have a Fatherland, and the tri-color Flag is loved and respected by the INSURGENT fighters. We use the colors red and black on our uniforms, symbols of the working people in their struggles on strike. Our flag bears the letters, "EZLN," ZAPATISTA ARMY OF NATIONAL LIBERATION, and under our flag we will always go into battle.

We reject in advance any attempt to diminish the just cause of our struggle by accusing us of narco-traffic, narco-guerrilla war, banditry, or any other term our enemies may use. Our struggle sticks to constitutional law, and justice and equality are its banners.

Therefore, and in conformity with this Declaration of War, we give our military forces of the Zapatista Army of National Liberation the following orders:

First: Advance to the capital of the country, conquering the Mexican federal army, and in the course of your liberating advance protecting the civilian population and permitting liberated peoples to elect their own administrative authorities freely and democratically.

Second: Respect the lives of prisoners and turn over the wounded to the International Red Cross for their medical attention.

Third: Initiate summary judgments against soldiers of the Mexican federal army and political police who have taken courses or have been advised, trained, or paid by foreigners, either in our country or outside it, under accusation of treason to the Fatherland, and against all those who repress and mistreat the civilian population and rob or transgress against the people's goods.

Fourth: Form new ranks with all those Mexicans who declare their enlistment in our just struggle, including those who, being enemy soldiers, surrender without fighting our forces and swear to follow the orders of this General Command of the Zapatista Army of National Liberation.

Fifth: Request the unconditional surrender of enemy garrisons before engaging in combat.

Sixth: Suspend the plunder of our natural resources in the places controlled by the EZLN.

PEOPLE OF MEXICO: We, upright and free men and women, are conscious that the war we declare is a last resort, but it is just. The dictators have been applying an undeclared genocidal war against our people for many years. Therefore we ask for your decided participation in support of this plan of the Mexican people in their struggle for work, land, housing, food, health care, education, independence, liberty, democracy, justice, and peace. We declare that we will not cease fighting until we achieve the fulfillment of these basic demands of our people by forming a free and democratic government in our country.

JOIN THE INSURGENT FORCES OF THE ZAPATISTA ARMY OF NATIONAL LIBERATION.

General Command of the EZLN, 1993

CHAPTER TWENTY-ONE

Revolutionary Legislation: The EZLN's New Laws, January 1994

Another indication that on January 1, 1994, the General Command of the EZLN was not simply calling for national attention to ignored outrages, but had deliberate, radical plans for taking national power, is the batch of ten "Revolutionary Laws" it then distributed. These are laws for EZLN-liberated territory (ultimately the entire country), for all Mexicans there, with no reference to Indians or Chiapas in particular. And they go beyond the declaration of war, in that they tacitly disavow the entire Mexican government, including Congress and the courts, and assume a national revolutionary authority enacting and enforcing the Mexican people's will. Distributed with the laws was a code of military conduct, "Instructions for EZLN Commanders and Officers," Article 9 of which referred to a "Law of Revolutionary Government," which, however, did not appear. Another law (translated here) also refers to "the revolutionary government."

This does not mean that the same sort of Indians who framed the declaration of war did not take a substantial part in framing the laws too. It would seem that they did, from the laws' inexpert (as opposed to expert) combinations of clarity, convolution, detailed specifications, oversights, congruities, and contradictions. The laws are not lawyerly statutes, but guidelines and principles and positive mandates. It seems most likely that the General Command and the CCRI wrote them, more or less according to earlier FLN drafts, between September and November 1993, after Marcos's eviction of the PFLN, but before preparations for the mobilization.

The subjects of the laws, in the order of publication, were war taxes, the rights and duties of "peoples in the struggle," the rights and duties of the "Revolutionary Armed Forces," the agrarian question, women, "urban reform," labor, industry and commerce, social security, and legal justice. The fourth, fifth, and sixth are here below.

The "Revolutionary Agrarian Law" begins in a respectful recollection of the original Zapatista struggle. But the language slips then into a slight but significant confusion. It is a nearly universal and incorrigible belief in Mexico, in all political circles, that the original Zapatista agrarian program of 1911–16 was the program that the Constitution of 1917 adopted and mandated in its Article 27, and that Salinas's reform of the article in 1992 abolished. Anyone who examines the original Zapatista program and Zapatista practice from 1911 to 1916 and Article 27, consequent federal agrarian codes, and federal policies and practice from 1917 to 1992, not to mention the reform of 1992, will see some basic differences. If this were only a common, harmless historical error, it would not be worth notice. But there is more to it than that. Whereas a major distinction of the original Zapatista agrarian reform was its recognition of various forms of tenure, arrangements of work, and modes of production as valid, the EZLN law is notably prescriptive.

Some of its provisions are immediately interesting. The new limit on private farms in Article 3, 50 hectares (nearly 125 acres) of good land, 100 ha. of poor land, would be one of the strictest in Latin American history. The original Zapatista Agrarian Law of October 26, 1915, allowed 100 ha. of prime irrigated land in hot country, as much as 1,500 ha. of untilled range land in northern ranching states. Under the Mexican Constitution since 1917 the limits have been from 100 ha. of good land to 200 ha. of poor land. In Guatemala from 1952 to 1954 they were 90-200; in Bolivia from 1952 to 1970, 24-50,000; in Cuba from 1959 to 1963, 400, and from 1963 to date, 67; in Chile from 1967 to 1973, from 80 "standard basic irrigated hectares" to "the equivalent" elsewhere; in Peru from 1969 to 1976, 35-1,500; in El Salvador in 1980, projected but never fulfilled, 150-500; in Nicaragua from 1981 to 1985, 510 on the Pacific coast, 850 on the Caribbean.

According to Article 4, existing communities and cooperatives may hold unlimited tracts of land. Do they have to use it all? Do they have to farm or ranch it themselves? May they rent or sell it?

Under Article 5, unlike grantees under the existing agrarian code, who legally hold grants of the national domain on conditional tenure, beneficiaries of the new law will own their land as "collective property." And under Articles 5, 8, and 10, unlike the great majority of grantees in the existing system, beneficiaries of this reform "must" work their property collectively. By the exceptional Article 11, big agribusinesses will be nationalized for their presently employed workers to "administer" collectively. It is clear from Articles 5, 6, 7, and 16, as in the Cuban, Chilean, Peruvian, Salvadoran (projected), and Nicaraguan reforms, that cooperatives are a preferred form of organization, but collectives are the most preferred.

According to Articles 8 and 10, beneficiaries "must" produce to support local and national self-sufficiency in food; only regions that do not produce certain products and other regions that do produce them may engage in domestic commerce in them, and only "excess production" may be exported.

In Article 15 the accords of the Indian Congress of 1974 resound again, ordering the creation of "fair" markets, health and recreation centers, schools, housing, roads, clean water, etc.

Following Article 17, all debts due by the rural poor and landless to anyone not among the rural poor and landless, or not a Mexican self-employed or hired worker, are abolished.

The "Women's Revolutionary Law," for women's rights, actually guarantees (on paper) no more than existing law does (on paper), with one important exception. Implicit in Article 1, explicit in Article 9, this is the right to hold rank in "the revolutionary armed forces." It applied not only to clerical staff and the medical corps, but to combat forces as well. The FLN's first Southeast Combat Front commander and organizer of the EZLN in Chiapas from 1984 to 1988 had been a woman, "Elisa." There were female captains in command of EZLN assault units in January 1994, for example, another "Elisa," "Laura," and "Irma." The highest ranking woman then was Major "Yolanda" (reportedly Marcos's wife), who led the EZLN's Seventh Regiment in the capture of San Cristóbal and the attack on the nearby army base.

The law on "urban reform," to provide housing for "dispossessed families," is more generous than the Cuban Urban Reform of 1960. For example, whereas the Cuban law required tenants to continue to pay their previous rents (no longer to landlords but to the government) and gave them ownership of the premises in five to 20 years, this law requires rent of only ten percent of the household head's income, and no rent after continuous residence of 15 years (although the law says nothing about eventual ownership).

All ten laws deserve much closer analysis for an indication of the CCRI-EZLN high command's plans for national economic and social reorganization.

They were evidently first published in the first number of the EZLN's new underground newspaper in Mexico City, *El Despertador Mexicano* ("The Mexican Alarm Clock"), in December 1993, for distribution in the city and wherever else possible in early January.

EL DESPERTADOR MEXICANO,
ORGANO INFORMATIVO DEL EZLN, MÉXICO,
NO. 1, DICIEMBRE 1993*

Revolutionary Agrarian Law

The struggle of poor peasants in Mexico continues to claim the land for those who work it. After Emiliano Zapata and against the [most recent] reforms of

---

*La palabra de los armados de verdad y fuego: Entrevistas, cartas y comunicados del EZLN, 3 vols. (Mexico City: Editorial Fuenteovejuna, 1994–95), vol. I, pp. 14–18.

Article 27 of the Mexican Constitution [ending the mandate to redistribute land and allowing existing ejidatarios to take title to their grants in new forms of tenure], the EZLN takes up the just struggle of rural Mexico for land and liberty. With the purpose of establishing a general rule for the new agrarian redistribution of land that the revolution brings to the Mexican countryside, the following REVOLUTIONARY AGRARIAN LAW is issued.

First. This law is valid over the entire territory of Mexico, and is for the benefit of all poor peasants and farm workers in Mexico, regardless of their political affiliation, religious creed, sex, race, or color.

Second. This law affects all agricultural properties and national or foreign farm and ranching businesses within the territory of Mexico.

Third. All tracts of land that are more than 100 hectares [nearly 250 acres] of poor quality and more than 50 hectares of good quality will be subject to revolutionary agrarian action. From landowners whose properties exceed the aforementioned limits, from them the excess land will be taken away, and they will remain with the minimum allowed, so that they can stay as small landowners or join the peasant movement of cooperatives, peasant societies, or landed communal associations.

Fourth. [Existing] communal lands, ejido lands, and popular cooperatives' lands, although they exceed the limits mentioned in this law's third article, will not be subject to agrarian action.

Fifth. The lands affected by this agrarian law will be redistributed to landless peasants and farm workers who apply for it as COLLECTIVE PROPERTY for the formation of cooperatives, peasant societies, or farm and ranching production collectives. The land affected must be worked collectively.

Sixth. PRIMARY RIGHT of application [for expropriated land] belongs to the collectives of poor landless peasants and farm workers, men, women, and children, who duly verify not having land or land of bad quality.

Seventh. For the exploitation of land to benefit poor peasants and farm workers, action [under this reform] on big landed estates and farm and ranching monopolies will include means of production such as machinery, fertilizer, storage, financial resources, chemical products, and technical consulting.

All these means [of production] must pass into the hands of poor peasants and farm workers, with special attention to groups organized as cooperatives, collectives, and societies.

Eighth. Groups benefited by this Agrarian Law must dedicate themselves preferentially to the collective production of foods necessary for the Mexican people: corn, beans, rice, vegetables, and fruit, as well as animal husbandry for cattle, pigs, and horses and bee-keeping, and [to the production] of derivative products (milk, meat, eggs, etc.).

Ninth. In time of war, a part of the production of the lands affected by this law will be allotted for the support of orphans and widows of revolutionary soldiers and the support of the revolutionary forces.

Tenth. The purpose of collective production is to satisfy primarily the needs of the people, to form among the beneficiaries a collective consciousness of work and benefits, and to create units of production, defense, and mutual aid in rural Mexico. When in one region some good is not produced, [some other good that is produced there] will be exchanged [in trade for the needed good] with another region where it is produced, [this trade to occur] in conditions of justice and equality. Excess production can be exported to other countries if there is no national demand for the product.

Eleventh. Big agricultural companies will be expropriated and pass into the hands of the Mexican people, and be administered collectively by the same [companies'] workers. Farm machinery, tools, seed, etc. that sit idle in factories and businesses and other places will be distributed among rural collectives, in order to make more extensive the land in production and begin to eradicate the people's hunger.

Twelfth. Individual monopolization of land and means of production will not be permitted.

Thirteenth. Virgin jungle zones and forests will be preserved, and there will be reforestation campaigns in the principal zones.

Fourteenth. Headwaters, rivers, lakes, and seas are the collective property of the Mexican people, and will be protected by avoiding pollution and punishing misuse.

Fifteenth. In benefit of poor peasants, the landless, and farm workers, besides the agrarian redistribution [of land to them] that this law establishes, commercial centers will be created that will buy the peasant's products at a fair price and sell to the peasant at fair prices the merchandise that he needs for a life worth living. Community health centers will be created with all the latest modern medicine, with trained and conscientious doctors and nurses, and with medicine free for the people. Entertainment centers will be created so that peasants and their families may have decent [places to] relax instead of cantinas and brothels. Education centers and free schools will be created where peasants and their families may get an education without regard to their age, sex, race, or political affiliation, and may learn the technical skills necessary for their development. Centers will be created for housing and highway construction, with engineers, architects, and necessary materials, so that peasants can have decent housing and good roads for transport. Service centers will be created to guarantee that peasants and their families have electric light, piped and drinkable water, drainage, radio and television, besides everything necessary to facilitate housework, stoves, refrigerators, washing machines, mills, etc.

Sixteenth. There will be no taxes for peasants who work collectively, or for ejidatarios, cooperatives, or landed communal associations. FROM THE

MOMENT THIS REVOLUTIONARY AGRARIAN LAW IS ISSUED, ALL DEBTS ARE ABOLISHED THAT POOR PEASANTS AND FARM WORKERS OWE FOR CREDIT, TAXES, OR LOANS TO THE OPPRESSING GOVERNMENT, FOREIGNERS, AND CAPITALISTS.

Women's Revolutionary Law

In its just struggle for the liberation of our people, the EZLN incorporates women into the revolutionary struggle without regard to their race, creed, color, or political affiliation, the only requirement being that they make their own the demands of the exploited and that they promise to fulfill and execute the laws and regulations of the revolution. Besides, taking into account the situation of working women in Mexico, their just demands for equality and justice are incorporated in the following WOMEN'S REVOLUTIONARY LAW:

First. Women, without regard to their race, creed, color, or political affiliation, have the right to take part in the revolutionary struggle in the place and to the degree that their will and capacity determine.

Second. Women have the right to work and to receive a fair wage.

Third. Women have the right to decide the number of children they can have and care for.

Fourth. Women have the right to take part in community affairs and to hold community office if they are elected freely and democratically.

Fifth. Women and their children have the right to PRIMARY CONSIDERATION in [provisions for] health and food.

Sixth. Women have the right to education.

Seventh. Women have the right to choose their mate and not to be obligated by force to contract marriage.

Eighth. No woman may be beaten or mistreated physically, either by members of her family or by others. The crimes of rape and attempted rape will be severely punished.

Ninth. Women may occupy positions of leadership in the [revolutionary] organization and hold military rank in the revolutionary armed forces.

Tenth. Women will have all the rights and duties that the [other] revolutionary laws and regulations indicate.

Law of Urban Reform

In urban zones controlled by the Zapatista Army of National Liberation the following laws go into [immediate] effect in order to provide decent housing for dispossessed families:

First. Residents who own their own home or apartment will pay no more real estate taxes.

Second. Tenants who pay rent and have been living more than 15 years in a residence will pay no more rent to the landlord until the revolutionary government triumphs and legislates on the matter.

Third. Tenants who have been living less than 15 years in a residence and paying rent for it will pay only ten percent of the wage that the head of the family earns, and will stop paying rent once they have been 15 years in the same place.

Fourth. Urban lots that already have public services may be occupied immediately, with notice to civil authorities freely and democratically elected, in order to build housing on these lots, provisional or not.

Fifth. Vacant public buildings and grand mansions may be occupied provisionally by several families who divide the interior among themselves. To this end, civil authorities will name neighborhood committees that will decide on the applications that are presented and grant rights to housing according to need and available resources.

CHAPTER TWENTY-TWO

Thanks to the Zapatistas: Chamula and Its Exiles, January-February 1994

The EZLN's drive up into the highlands on January 1, 1994, triggered several local Zapatista uprisings there, mainly in the northern municipalities of Huixtán (65 percent Tzotzil, 30 percent Tzeltal), Simojovel (60 percent Tzotzil, 15 percent Tzeltal), and Larráinzar (97 percent Tzotzil). Some EZLN officers and many troopers in the offensive, born and raised in these places, were close kin to the highland rebels.

No such action, however, took place in San Cristóbal (25 percent Tzotzil, 6 percent Tzeltal), or in the adjacent townships of Zinacantán or Chamula (both 99 percent Tzotzil). It would have been suicide to revolt in Chamula. In 1990 a jurisdiction of 330 square miles, 52,000 souls, one small town, two villages, and over 100 hamlets, this had long been the major bastion of Indian bossdom in Los Altos. Since the 1950s its ladino-connected "traditional" chiefs had developed an oligarchical dictatorship in control not only of the municipal government but also of land, credit, markets, transportation, federal offices, the PRI, and the Catholic Church, and eliminated cohort after cohort of opposition. The dead told no tales (although their ghosts and survivors did). The emigrants had gone for pioneers to the Selva. The expelled, the banished, the displaced, the exiled, the wretched, including the opposition that had become Protestant, had accumulated in other highland townships, Chenalhó, San Cristóbal, Teopisca.

Even so (or therefore), the EZLN capture of San Cristóbal struck dread in Chamula. The ceasefire barely relieved the panic. No one in the township in January-February 1994, guilty as they nearly all were, could be sure that the Zapatistas would not surge forth again, worse than before, and the wretched themselves rebel in powerful revenge.

Among the uprooted Chamulas and others like them around San Cristóbal, 90 percent of them landless and poor, the EZLN's sudden appearance was at first terrifying (caught in a war away from home!), then exhilarating. First, there was the Zapatista evasion and then siege of Rancho Nuevo, the army base just south of San Cristóbal. It was wonderfully sweet to learn of the army's humiliation, the arrogant officers, who had long strutted their professional, practically omniscient, technically invulnerable capacity to snuff rebellion in the bud, and their briskly alert, highly lethal soldiers, who had seemed absolutely invincible, all made fools and scared, if only for a day or two. Then there was the prospect of Zapatista justice, which undid bosses not only in Chamula but in San Cristóbal as well. Justice actually done would be better, but the mere idea of local lords and masters in hiding gave some satisfaction, and fueled many jokes. And before long the disappearance of direct official controls sucked away poor people's fear of officials and the routines of official contempt, and inspired among the poor a miraculous feeling, the possibility of defiance.

In every town in Mexico there is a market, a real place, always near the center of town, and for every market there is an administrator, the municipal official who manages the assignment of stalls in the market and the collection of due fees, sales taxes, and bribes. An occupational requirement for this position in a city such as San Cristóbal is the *licenciatura* (literally the license, a college degree), that is, that the occupant of the office be a *licenciado*, a college boy. As the army officer is a master of the killing trade, the college boy running a city market, in sunglasses, clean white shirt, and shiny shoes, is a master of the bribing, vilifying, and intimidating trade. The best installed in the market, who have paid dearly for their privilege, despise him. The poor, who cannot afford even the fees to get into the market, obey and loathe him, and sell on the street. (See Reading No. 10, on Indian complaints about markets in 1974, which had not changed by 1994.) When the EZLN took San Cristóbal, however socialist its principles, the defiant poor opened a free market.

The author of the following is a Tzotzil from Chamula, a migrant worker in his childhood, since the early 1980s relocated to a Protestant squatters' settlement on the edge of San Cristóbal, and a master of truthful, ironic, playful, and strong stories about his people.

Already introduced (in Reading No. 4) is the scholar who collected and translated these stories, Jan Rus.

THE FIRST TWO MONTHS OF THE
ZAPATISTAS: A TZOTZIL CHRONICLE*

Early January: Preparations and Visits

Before the invasion of San Cristóbal, everyone always talked about how the soldiers at the army base overlooking the southern approach to the city had spread booby traps all around their land, how they had fixed it so no one would ever dare attack them. If the poor Indians ever came to make trouble, everyone said, the soldiers would finish them off right there, before they even got out of the forest. The army officers are maestros of killing, they said, and all they have to do every day, their only chore, is to teach the young soldiers how to kill. And as if all of that weren't enough to scare away a bunch of raggedy peasants, all the people said, the soldiers also have mounds of bombs stored behind their fort. Nothing but special bombs for killing Indians!

K'elavil, look here: According to what people said, the soldiers had strung a special wire around their barracks that was connected to a bomb every few steps. If the damn Indians ever did come around, they said, all the soldiers would have to do was lean out of their beds and touch the wire with a piece of metal—like, say, a beer can—and the bombs would all blow up. And if the Indians tried to cut the wire, it would also blow up. But of course, the soldiers are famous for never sleeping, so the Indians would never even get close to the bombs in the first place. No one, the soldiers figured, would ever get past them.

But after all those preparations, what happened? On January 1, the soldiers were asleep when the Zapatistas arrived in San Cristóbal! But snoring! They didn't see the Zapatistas go by their checkpoints with the other passengers on the second-class buses! They didn't notice the Zapatistas get out of their buses at the station and walk into the center of town! They didn't see anything! And when the soldiers woke up, the Zapatistas had already seized the *Palacio de Gobierno* [the municipal building] and set up their own guards around the city! After all, it was the army that was left outside of town, safely holed up in its barracks! The Zapatistas won by just ignoring them! Not until the next day, when they had finished their business in town, did the Zapatistas finally go to pay a visit on the soldiers!

The Zapatistas are only Indians, but what the army officers forgot is that Indians too are men. And since they are men, they also could be armed and trained, just like the army. All they needed was the idea. And as it turned out, their thinking was better than the army's! They fooled the officers, who are

---

*Marián Peres Tsu, in *Indigenous Revolts in Chiapas and the Andean Highlands*, Kevin Gosner and Arij Ouweneel, eds., (Amsterdam: CEDLA, 1996), pp. 122–130. (Translation from the original Tzotzil into Spanish and English by Jan Rus.)

maestros of killing! Since that day, all of us, even those who are not enemies of the government, feel like smiling down our shirts.

If there is a sad part to all of this, it is that even though the Zapatistas are men, they will have to live in hiding from now on. They won't be able to sleep in their own beds in their own houses, but will have to stay hidden in caves in the jungle. If they want to make babies like everyone else, they'll even have to screw in the caves, like armadillos!

Early January: Uncertainty in Chamula

When word first came that the Zapatistas had occupied San Cristóbal, all the Chamulas said that they weren't afraid. But that was a lie; they were. Just to keep up appearances, though, everyone said that the only one who really had anything to be scared of, the single person responsible for all the bad things that have happened in Chamula, was the municipal president. In truth, of course, all of them knew that they too had participated in the round-ups and expulsions of their Protestant neighbors, and they were all afraid the Zapatistas were going to come and exact justice. They had heard that the Zapatistas were well armed and figured they wouldn't waste a lot of time listening to excuses, that they would just kill all the Chamulas who had beaten the Protestants and burned their property. And what could the Chamulas do about it? They didn't have any good weapons, just some .22 rifles, a few pistols, and one or another old shotgun—enough to scare their unarmed neighbors, maybe, but against real soldiers they wouldn't have a chance. Instead of fighting, they all said, everyone in the whole town would be better off if they just stayed in bed and screwed one last time.

As you can imagine, however, if everyone else was worried, the municipal president himself was terrified. He was so scared about what the Zapatistas and Protestant exiles would do to him if they ever caught him that he walked around for a week with a hard-on. But stiff! He better than anyone knew all of the terrible things that had been done. But he wasn't alone. To tell the truth, the whole town was afraid.

Finally, since there was no other defense, the *presidente* announced that the whole town should offer candles and incense at the sacred caves and mountain tops and ask for the protection of God and the saints. Since Chamula's *j-iloletik* (shamans) are famed for their power, this seemed like such a good idea that the officials of the *municipios* of Zinacantán, Amatenango, Mitontic, and Huistán decided to join in as well. Together, they thought, maybe their prayers would be powerful enough to keep the Zapatistas away.

On the appointed day, scores of officials and dozens of chanting shamans, all dressed in their ceremonial clothes and many carrying candles and *yavak'aletik* of burning incense, assembled at the church in Zinacantán. From the church and sacred mountain of Zinacantán, they proceeded together to the sacred cave at the border of the *municipio* of San Andrés, and then to the mountain of Chaklajun on the road between the *cabecera* [the municipal seat] of Chamula and San Cristóbal. They prayed for more than an hour at each site. *Kajval!* [Lord]: There was so much incense it was like a fragrant fog, and the whole entourage seemed to hum like bees as each man murmured somberly in his own prayers:

> Have mercy, *Kajval,*
> Have mercy, Jesús,
> Make yourself present among us, *Kajval,*
> Make yourself present in our incense, Jesús,
> With us, your daughters,
> With us, your sons.
>
> We have brought you food, *Kajval,*
> We have brought you drink, Jesús,
> To awaken your conscience,
> To awaken your heart,
> That you might lend us your feet,
> That you might lend us your hands,
> That you might discharge your rifle,
> That you might discharge your cannon.
>
> What sin have we, *Kajval?*
> What guilt have we, Jesús?
> Don't you see that we are here, sacred lightning?
> Don't you see that we are here, sacred thunder?
> We beg that you close the roads to your sons who are coming,
>
> We beg that you close the roads to your daughters who are coming,
> That you bind their feet,
> That you bind their hands,
> That you silence their rifles,
> That you stifle their cannons,
> If only for an hour,
> If only for two hours, *Kajval,*
> Although they come at night,
> Although they come in the day,
> Although they come at sundown,
> Although they come at sunrise.
>
> Holy guardian of the earth,
> Holy guardian of the sky,
> Because we come on our knees,
> Because we come bent over,

Accept this bouquet of flowers,
Accept this offering of leaves, *Kajval*.
Accept this handful of incense,
Accept this offering of smoke,
That we come to offer at your feet,
That we come to offer to your hands,
Holy Father of sacred Chaklajun,
Holy Mother of sacred Chaklajun.

As the days passed and the Zapatistas never came, it seemed that the prayers had worked . . .

Early January: The Evangelicals' Prayer

The traditional officials and *j-iloletik* were not the only ones who were afraid during the siege of San Cristóbal, however. The Chamula evangelicals—the *expulsados* [the Protestants who had been expelled]—were also scared. Since they live in colonies on the outskirts of the city, it might even be true that at the beginning they were even more frightened than the traditionalists. But even later, when they saw that the Zapatistas meant them no harm, they continued praying because now they were afraid the national army was going to kill them. Their prayers sound just the same as the traditionals, but if you listen to the words they say different things. Here's the prayer of the pastor of the colony *Paraíso* [Paradise]:

Our Lord Jesus Christ,
God, who art in heaven,
Lord, we are your daughters,
We are your sons,
Look, Lord, at the thoughts of those who are invading,
Look at how they don't want the good you bring,
How they are coming with arms,
How they are coming with machetes,
But listen to our words, Eternal Father,
You alone decide what will be,
You alone prepare what will be.
We, Lord, without you can do nothing,
We, without you, are not complete.
Listen, Lord Jesus Christ,
You who accompany us on your path,
You who accompany us on our walk,
There is nothing we can do without you,
There is nothing we can start without you, Lord.
Look at us,
See us,

On your path,
On your trip, Lord.
We only ask your favor, Lord,
That they not come to hit us,
That they not come to fight us,
In our houses,
In our homes.

You, Father,
You, Lord,
Accept our thanks,
That what you say will be done,
That your children will do only what you have thought.
Look, Lord, pardon us,
That we do not know how to communicate with you more respectfully,
That we are not worthy to address you, Lord.
This is the only way we know,
Only like this,
In our own language,
With our heads bowed, Lord,
Hallclujah,
Hallelujah,
Hallelujah.

Late January: Toward a Free Market

For the first two weeks or so after the seizure of San Cristóbal, not a single *kaxlan* [same as caxlan] official showed his face in public—not a policeman, not a parking officer, not a collector of market fees. Not one. They disappeared! They were so terrified of the Zapatistas that they hid. But the moment they were sure the Zapatista Army was gone and wasn't coming back, Ha!, immediately the parking officers were back unscrewing license plates [for parking violations and bribes], the municipal police beating up drunks, and the market collectors chasing away poor women trying to sell tomatoes and lemons on street corners. With the Zapatistas gone, suddenly they were fearless again. But when the Zapatistas were here, they stayed in their bedrooms with the shades closed, quaking with fear. They couldn't even get it up with their wives they were so scared.

You see what that means? They were afraid of *Indians*, because that's what the Zapatistas were, Indians. When we other Indians realized that, we felt strong as well. Strong like the Zapatistas. The *kaxlanetik* of San Cristóbal have always pushed us around just because we don't speak Spanish correctly. But now everything has begun to change.

One example of this is that in mid-January, when the *kaxlan* officials were all still hidden, the Indian charcoal sellers got together and formed the "*Or-*

ganización Zapatista of Charcoal Sellers." Then, without asking anybody's permission, they moved from the vacant field where they had always been forced to sell in the past to the street right next to the main market. The thing is, *ak'al* [charcoal] is really dirty—everything around it gets covered with black dust—so the market officials had always kept it far away from the part of the market frequented by "decent people" and tourists. With no one to stop them, however, the charcoal sellers came to be near everyone else.

But there are a lot of other Indians who have always been relegated to the edges of the market, too. When these people saw that the charcoal sellers had changed their location without asking anyone's permission, they started coming around and asking if they could change as well. *Híjole* [Son of a gun]! Suddenly there were a couple of hundred people sitting in orderly rows selling vegetables and fruit and charcoal in what used to be the parking lot where rich people left their cars! The first day they gathered there, the leader of the charcoal sellers gave a speech. *"Brothers and sisters!"* he cried, *"Don't be afraid! There are too many of us selling here in this street now! Let all of those who have been forced to sell out of the backs of trucks, all of those who have been driven to the edges of the market, come sell right here in the center with us! Let them come and take a place here in these rows we have made, and then we'll see if the* caxlan *officials dare say anything! Only one thing to all of those who join us: I don't want to hear anyone talking about being afraid! If we remain united and firm, we have nothing to fear!"* All the Indian peddlers jumped to their feet. *"We're with you!"* they responded joyfully.

So every morning early all of these people came and formed themselves into neat rows and spread their goods out on the ground. But then the day finally came when the Market Adminstrator returned. Since he's the boss of the market and all the surrounding streets, he stomped up to the first charcoal seller he saw and demanded, *"Who gave you permission to sell here?"* *"No one had to give us permission because we belong to an organization."* *"What fucking organization? Pick up all this shit and get the hell out of here before I lose my temper,"* the Administrator screamed. *"I don't want to hear another word from any of you assholes! Are you going to fucking obey or not?"* Mother of God! He seemed pretty mad. *"No, we're not going to move. We're poor and hungry and we have to sell to eat,"* the Indian said stubbornly. Then the leader of the charcoal sellers spoke. *"You sound pretty brave now,"* he said evenly to the Administrator, *"but when the Zapatistas were here you didn't say anything because you were hiding behind your wife's skirts. Not until now have you had the balls to talk. So who's the asshole? Maybe it would be better for you if you kept quiet, because if you run us off we're going to make sure the sub-comandante of the Zapatistas gets your name, and then we'll find out how much of a man you are. You might win today, but maybe you ought to think about what it's going to cost you in the long run."*

Hijo! [Boy!] The Administrator had never been talked to like that by an Indian before! He started to tremble, who knows whether from fear or rage, and then he turned and fled without saying another word, taking all of his fee collectors with him.

And that's where things remain at the beginning of March. Thanks to the Zapatistas, the Indians are learning to stand up for themselves.

Early February: The Governed Do Not Consent

Then there's what happened in Teopisca [the next town south of San Cristóbal, mainly ladino]. In February, some Indian squatters from outside the town seized the *kaxlan* municipal president. They said he hadn't kept his campaign promises, and just grabbed him. He tried to make excuses for himself. *"I already spent my entire budget on you,"* he begged. *"I paved your streets, I brought electricity to your houses, I brought you water faucets, I made new roads for your trucks . . . What more do you want?"* But according to all of the people, none of what he said was true. The streets aren't paved, there's no electricity, no faucets, no roads; nothing. In truth, the president and his friends just stole all the money.

Well, the squatters almost lost their heads and killed the president. Some wanted to hang him and they say someone even took a shot at him. But eventually others calmed the crowd down, and in the end all they did was truss him up like a pig, throw him in a pick-up truck, and send him back to the state government in Tuxtla.

The thing is, those squatters were Indians, Chamulas! There was a handful of poor ladinos among them too, but most were Chamulas! And they managed to capture and depose the president of a *kaxlan* town! Of course it was the president's own fault; no one forced him to steal the municipality's money. But now all the politicians have to be careful. We "poor dumb Indians" aren't afraid the way we used to be. Now we've all learned from the Zapatistas how to meet our collective problems: with unity. Obviously, the squatters didn't have machine guns and grenades like the Zapatistas—just .22s and shotguns. No; it was their unity that gave them strength!

Mid-February: The Festival of Games

Since everyone in Chamula was still afraid at the beginning of February that the Zapatistas were coming, *K'in Tajimol* (the Mayan New Year, celebrated at Carnival [Mardi Gras]) didn't go well this year. Instead of coming and staying two or three days as in the past, visiting with their friends and sleeping on the ground, everyone came down from their hamlets to watch for just a few minutes before scurrying back to their houses and closing the doors. Nobody wanted to be part of a crowd in the town center.

As if that weren't enough, the army had forbidden fireworks [traditional at all festivals in Los Altos]. No one could have skyrockets . . ., firecrackers, or pinwheels. Nothing. The head religious officials were able to have just a few *cohetes* [rockets] for the celebration itself, but only by getting a special permit from the army. The municipal president had to go ask in person, and only won out after explaining that the religious officials had been saving for 20 years each to put on the fiesta, and that it—and their lives—would be ruined without rockets.

In San Cristóbal, on the other hand, fireworks are absolutely prohibited. No exceptions. But *cohetes* are just as much a part of their traditions as ours, so all their fiestas are very sad. Of course, there are still marimba bands, games, and always a little bit of liquor. Nevertheless, the fiestas are sad and fearful. The soldiers don't even want anyone to drink; if they catch a drunk, they beat him up. They don't want anyone to be noisy or out of order.

After all, though, neither the army nor the Zapatistas came to Chamula's *K'in Tajimol*. Not many other people came either, for that matter. The fiesta didn't go well.

Mid-February: Mayan Justice

When the negotiations with the government began in mid-February, the Zapatistas, as a sign of good faith, freed the former governor, Absalón Castellanos Domínguez [see Readings No. 13 and 15], whom they had captured at his ranch at the beginning of the revolt. They say he got sick at the end, that he wouldn't eat anything. Maybe it was because his hands were tied behind his back for six weeks, who knows . . . Personally, I think he got sick because he couldn't stand the Zapatistas' cooking! It was nothing but Indian food: corn and a little beans. No meat. There is no one in the Zapatistas' camp in the jungle but Indians, and Indians aren't used to eating meat. We can never afford to buy it, and even if an animal dies we have to sell it. Poor old *don* Absalón: since he's rich, he's not accustomed to going without meat every day . . .

Still, when they freed him, outside of his hands, which were a little swollen, he seems to have been okay. That's more than you can say for Indians who are arrested by the authorities, rebellion or no rebellion. When Absalón was Governor, they were always beaten, whether they were guilty or not, even before they were questioned, "so they would learn to have respect." All the Zapatistas did to Absalón, on the other hand, was take his ranch away from him and divide it among peasants who have no land. Who knows whether they will get to keep it . . .

CHAPTER TWENTY-THREE

The Zapatistas Are Indians, the Government Is Responsive: San Cristóbal, Mexico City, February 21–March 2, 1994

It surprised the EZLN's high command that the Mexican government offered "dialogue" (January 10) and ordered its armed forces in Chiapas to cease fire (January 12). ". . . we thought it was a trap," recalled Marcos in 1997. Reflecting on their disastrous military situation, the CCRI-EZLN too ordered a cease-fire and prepared conditions for the proposed talks that they assumed the government would reject but that might gain time for missing units to escape back into the canyons. As the fighting died down and they remade contact with cadres in Mexico City, it dumbfounded them to discover the national response to their rebellion. "The people" nationwide had not joined them, but had not ignored them either, did not want them to fight, but did not want the army to fight them either, and by the hundreds of thousands were demonstrating for them and for peace. If, as the CCRI-EZLN reasoned, "the people" had obliged the government to offer negotiations, they were also urging the CCRI-EZLN to accept negotiations. "Civil society has intervened . . . ," as Marcos later put it, and after some sharp internal debate the CCRI-EZLN cautiously agreed, if Bishop Ruiz would mediate, to "dialogue." They did not expect the talks to resolve any important question, but hoped to use them to learn who "the people" demonstrating for them and for peace were, to present their cause attractively (and disarmingly) to them, and so continue the struggle politically. (See Reading No. 28.)

The grievances the CCRI-EZLN sent to San Cristóbal in the cold rain on

February 21 were therefore a mixture of old positions (some of them going back 20 years to the Indian Congress of 1974) and new propositions. Not surprisingly among those most on their mind were some already evident in the Declaration of January 1 and the Revolutionary Laws (Readings Nos. 20 and 21), for example, over the PRI's monopolization of the country's politics and office. By far the most numerous and finely detailed, however (not surprisingly either), were over injustices inflicted specifically on Indians in Chiapas.

The welcome the CCRI-EZLN negotiators received on their arrival in San Cristóbal amazed them. Despite the weather and the federal police, tens of thousands people cheering and applauding made a "peace cordon" for them to the cathedral. The media loved not only Marcos, but also the Indians. In a week of "dialogue" the Zapatista delegates formulated their grievances in a statement of 34 "demands," explained them, listened to the government's objections, explanations, and concessions, and learned much about the new terms of struggle. The first selection here is from their statement released at the "dialogue"'s close on March 1, addressed (significantly) not only to "the people of Mexico," but to "the peoples and governments of the world" and "the national and international press" as well, telling again why "the indigenous peoples of the State of Chiapas" had rebelled, and spelling out the demands they asked "the whole people of Mexico" to resolve. It is worth notice that unlike the Declaration of January 1, which made no reference to Indians or Chiapas, this statement was heavy on both such counts: 15 of its 34 demands were explicitly for Indians, six explicitly for Chiapas. (Four of them, Nos. 4, 14, 16, and 17, all on Indian autonomy, would later comprise the CCRI-EZLN's primary demand, on which see Readings Nos. 27 and 32.)

Once Salinas offered to negotiate, he had gone to work on two agenda. He had to continue to promote the just started presidential campaign of his carefully prepared successor, the former minister of Social Development and primary protector of Solidarity, Luis Donaldo Colosio. And given the barely contained rage among his enemies on the right and the massive displays of sympathy for the rebels and support for peace among "the people," he had to promote the negotiations—find among his political intimates a famous negotiator (to show how seriously he took the talks) and have him so engage the EZLN as to give every indication of a search for honorable compromise to ensure peaceful elections. He had put much into both promotions, but one could not succeed for the other. While Colosio tried through January and February to refocus national attention on his campaign, the negotiator, Manuel Camacho, the charismatic former mayor of the Federal District (once as close to Salinas as Colosio was), who had quit in public anger when Salinas had not chosen him to be his successor, then agreed to serve as minister of Foreign Relations, then resigned to represent the government in Chiapas, attracted ever more attention. Colosio's campaign did not gain momentum. Camacho flourished in San Cristóbal.

The second selection here (after Salinas's introduction) is Camacho's negotiated response to the CCRI-EZLN's demands, also on March 1. Inevitably Salinas hailed it. Colosio's campaign faltered. Except to Colosio and his campaigners (and the right), Camacho was a national hero.

These were the commitments that the CCRI-EZLN took back to their communities in early March for consideration and a vote.

Before their deliberations had concluded, Colosio was assassinated on March 23. Politically Camacho was suddenly dead too. The communities rejected the commitments. (See Reading No. 28 for Marcos's explanation three years post factum.)

COMUNICADO DEL CCRI-CG, PLIEGO DE DEMANDAS, 1 DE MARZO*

To the People of Mexico
To the peoples and governments of the world
To the national and international press

Brothers:

The Clandestine Revolutionary Indian Committee-General Command of the EZLN respectfully and with honor addresses you all to let you know the statement of demands presented at the negotiating table during the Sessions for Peace and Reconciliation in Chiapas:

"We do not ask for charity or gifts, we ask for the right to live with dignity as human beings, with equality and justice like our ancient fathers and grandfathers."

To the People of Mexico:

The indigenous peoples of the State of Chiapas, risen in arms in the Zapatista Army of National Liberation against poverty and bad government, present the reasons for their struggle and their principal demands:

The reasons and causes for our armed movement are that the government has never given any real solution to the following problems:

1. The hunger, poverty, and marginalization that we have been suffering from the beginning.
2. The total lack of land where [we could] work to survive.

---

*La palabra de los armados de verdad y fuego: Entrevistas, cartas y comunicados del EZLN, 3 vols. (Mexico City: Editorial Fuenteovejuna, 1994–95), vol. I, pp. 263–269.

3. Repression, eviction, imprisonment, torture, and assassination as the government's response to the just demands of our peoples.

4. The intolerable injustices and violations of our human rights as indigenous peoples and impoverished peasants.

5. The brutal exploitation that we suffer in the sale of our products, in our working day, and in the purchase of basic necessities.

6. The lack of every indispensable service for the great majority of the indigenous population.

7. The lies, tricks, promises, and impositions of governments for more than 60 years. The lack of freedom and democracy to decide our destiny.

8. The constitutional laws have not been fulfilled by those who govern the country; on the other hand, they make us indigenous and peasants pay for the littlest mistake and throw on us the whole weight of a law we did not make and that those who did make it are the first to break.

The EZLN came to dialogue really and truly pledging its word. The EZLN came to say its word about the conditions that gave rise to its just war, and to ask the whole people of Mexico to resolve the political, economic, and social conditions that drove us to the point of taking up arms in defense of our very existence and our rights.

Therefore we demand . . .

First. We demand that a really free and democratic election be held, with equality of rights and duties for [all] the political organizations that struggle for power, with true freedom to choose one or another proposal, and with respect for the will of the majority. Democracy is the fundamental right of all peoples indigenous and not indigenous. Without democracy there can be no freedom or justice or dignity. And without dignity there is nothing.

Second. For there to be really free and democratic elections, it is necessary that the titular head of the Federal Executive resign, as well as the titular heads of state executives who came to power by means of electoral fraud. Their legitimacy does not come from respect for the will of the majority but from its usurpation. In consequence, it is necessary that a government of transition be formed so that there will be equality and respect for all political currents. The [existing] federal and state legislative branches, elected freely and democratically [sic!], must assume their true function of making laws that are just for all and must be vigilant in assuring their enforcement.

Another way to guarantee the realization of really free and democratic elections is for the great laws of the nation and local laws to make effectively legitimate the existence and the work of citizens and groups of citizens who, without partisan commitment, would oversee the entire electoral process, sanction its legality and results, and, as the real maximum authority, guarantee the legitimacy of the entire electoral process.

Third. Recognition of the Zapatista Army of National Liberation as a belligerent force and its troops as authentic soldiers, and the application of all international treaties to regulate military conflicts.

Fourth. A new pact among the states of the federal republic that will end centralism and allow regions, indigenous communities, and municipalities to govern themselves with political, economic, and cultural autonomy.

Fifth. General elections for the entire state of Chiapas and legal recognition of all political forces in the state.

Sixth. Producing electricity and oil, the state of Chiapas pays tribute to the federal government without receiving anything in return. Our communities do not have electrical power, [and] the economic overflow resulting from oil exports and domestic sales produces no benefit for the Chiapan people. Therefore it is of primordial importance that all Chiapan communities receive the benefit of electrical power and that a percentage of the income from the sale of Chiapan oil be applied to construction of industrial, agricultural, commercial, and social infrastructure for the benefit of all Chiapans.

Seventh. Revision of the Free Trade Agreement signed with Canada and the United States, since in its present form it does not consider indigenous populations and sentences them to death for not having any labor skills.

Eighth. Article 27 of the Magna Carta [the federal Constitution] must respect the original spirit of Emiliano Zapata: the land is for the indigenous and the peasants who work it, not for big landlords. We want the big tracts of land that are in the hands of finqueros and national and foreign landlords and others who occupy much land but are not peasants, to pass into the hands of our peoples who totally lack land, as is established in our revolutionary agrarian law. The grant of land must also include farm machinery, fertilizer, insecticide, credit, technical advisers, improved seed, cattle, fair prices for rural products like coffee, corn, and beans. The land that is redistributed must be of good quality and must have highways, transport, and irrigation. The peasants who already have land also have the right to all the support above-mentioned to facilitate work in the field and to improve production. Let new ejidos and communities be formed. The Salinas reform of Article 27 must be annulled and the right to land must be returned to our Constitution.

Ninth. We want hospitals to be built in the municipal seats, with specialized doctors and sufficient medicine to treat patients, and field clinics in the ejidos, communities, and hamlets, as well as training and a fair wage for the health agents. And where there already are hospitals, have them rehabilitated as soon as possible, and equip them for a full range of surgery. In big communities, have clinics built, and let them also have doctors and medicine to give the people closer attention.

Tenth. Guarantee the right of the indigenous to accurate information about what happens at local, regional, state, national, and international levels with an indigenous radio station, independent of the government, directed by the indigenous and managed by the indigenous.

Eleventh. We want housing to be built in all the rural communities in Mexico, and that they have necessary services: light, potable water, roads, drainage, telephone, transportation, etc. And also let them have the advantages of the city, such as television, stoves, refrigerators, washing machines, etc. The communities must have recreational centers for the healthy amusement of their people: sports and culture that dignify the human condition of the indigenous.

Twelfth. We want an end to illiteracy among indigenous peoples. To this end we need better primary and secondary schools in our communities, that they have free teaching materials and supplies, and teachers with university training who are at the service of the people, not to defend the interests of the rich. In the municipal seats let there be free primary, secondary, and college-preparatory schooling, and let the government give the students uniforms, shoes, meals, and study supplies for free. In big communities located far from municipal seats there must be secondary boarding schools. Education must be totally free, from preschool to the university, and must be offered to all Mexicans without regard to race, creed, age, sex, or political affiliation.

Thirteenth. That the languages of all the ethnic groups [in Mexico] be official and that their teaching be mandatory in primary, secondary, and preparatory schools and at the university.

Fourteenth. That our rights and dignity as indigenous people be respected, and our culture and tradition taken into account.

Fifteenth. We do not want to continue to be the object of the discrimination and disregard that we the indigenous have been suffering from the beginning.

Sixteenth. As the indigenous people we are, let us organize and govern ourselves with our own autonomy, because we no longer want to be submitted to the will of the national and international mighty.

Seventeenth. That justice be administered by the indigenous peoples themselves, according to their customs and traditions, without the intervention of illegitimate and corrupt governments.

Eighteenth. We want to have an always decent job with a fair wage for all workers in the fields and in the cities of the Mexican Republic, so that our brothers do not have to work at evil things, like drug trafficking, crime, and prostitution, to be able to survive. Have the federal labor law apply to rural and urban workers with bonuses, benefits, vacations, and a real right to strike.

Nineteenth. We want a fair price for our farm produce. To this end we need to be free to look for a market or have one where we can sell and buy and not be subject to *coyote* [tricky, cheating] exploiters.

Twentieth. Let there be an end to the sacking of our Mexico's wealth, and above all that of Chiapas, one of the richest states of the republic, but which is where hunger and poverty every day abound more.

Twenty-first. We want the cancellation of all debts with high interest for credit, loans, and taxes, because they cannot be paid anymore, because of the great poverty of the Mexican people.

Twenty-second. We want an end to hunger and malnutrition, because they have only caused the death of thousands of our brothers in the countryside and in the city. In each rural community there must be cooperatives, supported economically by the federal, state, or municipal government, and let prices be fair. Also there must be trucks belonging to the cooperatives, for the transport of merchandise. Also the government must send free food for all children under 14 years of age.

Twenty-third. We ask for the immediate and unconditional freedom of all political prisoners and the poor unjustly imprisoned in all the jails of Chiapas and Mexico.

Twenty-fourth. We ask that the Federal Army and the public-security and judicial police no longer go into rural areas, because they go only to intimidate, evict, rob, repress, and bomb peasants who organize to defend their rights. Our peoples are tired of the presence of soldiers and public-security and judicial police, because they are so abusive and repressive. Have the federal government return to the Swiss government the *Pilatus* airplanes used to bomb our people, and let the money coming in return be applied to programs to improve the lives of rural and urban workers. We also ask that the government of the United States of America withdraw its helicopters, because they are used to repress the people of Mexico.

Twenty-fifth. The indigenous peasant people rose up in arms, and the fact is that of their own they do not have anything but their humble huts, but when the Federal Army bombs the civilian populations, it destroys these humble houses and all the few poor belongings in them. We therefore ask and demand that the federal government indemnify the families that have suffered material damages caused by the bombings and the action of the federal troops. And we also ask indemnification for the widows and orphans of the war, civilians as well as Zapatistas.

Twenty-sixth. We, as indigenous peasants, want to live in peace and tranquility, and be left to live according to our rights to liberty and a decent life, a life worth living.

Twenty-seventh. Get rid of Chiapas's Penal Code, because it does not let us organize except in arms, because all legal and nonviolent struggle is punished and repressed.

Twenty-eighth. We ask and demand the cessation of expulsions of indigenous people from their communities by *caciques* supported by the government. We demand guarantees for the free and voluntary return of all the expelled to their lands of origin and indemnification for their lost goods.

Twenty-ninth. Petition by Indigenous Women

We, peasant indigenous women, ask for the immediate solution of our urgent needs, to which the government has never given a solution.

a) Birth clinics with gynecologists so that peasant women receive necessary medical attention.

b) That child-care centers be built in the communities.

c) We ask the government to send sufficient food for the children in all rural communities, such as milk, corn meal, rice, corn, soy, cooking oil, beans, cheese, eggs, sugar, soup, oatmeal, etc.

d) That kitchens and dining halls be built for the children in the communities, that have all the necessary services.

e) That corn mills and tortilla-pressing machines be put in the communities, depending on the number of families that the communities have.

f) That they give us farm projects for chickens, rabbits, lambs, pigs, etc., that have technical advisers and veterinarians.

g) We ask for bakery projects that have ovens and supplies.

h) We want artisan shops to be built that have machinery and raw materials.

i) For artisanry, that there be a market where it can be sold at a fair price.

j) That schools be built where women can receive technical training.

k) That there be preschools and infant care in the rural communities, where children can enjoy themselves and grow up morally and physically healthy.

l) That as women we have transportation sufficient to travel from place to place and transport our products from the different projects that we will have.

Thirtieth. We demand a political trial of Patrocinio González Garrido, Absalón Castellanos Domínguez, and Elmar Setzer M. [See Readings Nos. 13, 15, 16, and 18.]

Thirty-first. We demand respect for the lives of all members of the EZLN and that it be guaranteed that there not be any criminal trial or repressive action against any of the members of the EZLN, soldiers, sympathizers, or collaborators.

Thirty-second. That all groups and commissions in defense of human rights be independent, that is, nongovernmental, because those that are from the government only hide the government's arbitrary actions.

Thirty-third. That there be formed a National Commission of Peace with Justice and Dignity composed in its majority of people who do not belong to the government or any political party. And that this National Commission of Peace with Justice and Dignity be the [commission] that oversees compliance with the accords that the EZLN and the federal government may reach.

Thirty-fourth. That humanitarian aid for the victims of the conflict be channeled through authentic representatives of the indigenous communities.

As long as these just demands of our peoples have no solution, we are disposed and determined to continue our struggle until we reach our objective.

For us, the smallest of these lands, faceless and without history, but armed with truth and fire, we who come from the night and the mountain, true men and women, the dead of yesterday, today, and always . . . for us, nothing. For everyone, everything.

Liberty! Justice! Democracy!

Respectfully,
From the Mexican Southeast
CCRI-CG del EZLN

EL PRESIDENTE DE LA REPÚBLICA, LIC. CARLOS SALINAS DE GORTARI, EMITIÓ LA SIGUIENTE DECLARACIÓN . . . ,*

The president . . . issued the following declaration regarding the conclusion of the Sessions for Peace and Reconciliation in Chiapas:

"It is truly encouraging news that the dialogue in the Sessions for Peace and Reconciliation in Chiapas has already had notably positive results.

"The statement of petitions has been answered in a spirit of true attention and heed to the claims of justice, well being, and dignity for Indians.

"The government has taken its commitments seriously. In the following days the decisions necessary to guarantee their execution will be made. We hope for backing from society as a whole for the points agreed. In support of these results we will waiting to take care of all the details necessary to reach the final signature of the peace accords . . ."

Commitments for a Worthy Peace in Chiapas

Declarative

1. Declarative: To attend to [this petition] is a path that would make a political solution impossible.

2. Declarative: During this month an extraordinary session of Congress will be convened to discuss reform that will guarantee the involvement of independent citizens in conducting the electoral process with no advantage to any political force.

Resolutory

3. Full guarantees to the EZLN and treatment worthy and respectful of those who form it. The Zapatista Army will decide the type and the nature of its participation in society and politics in the future.

El Financiero, March 3, 1994.

4. Promulgation of a General Law of Rights of Indian Communities (which considers the petitions of the communities that comprise Indian municipalities to govern themselves in political, economic, and cultural autonomy).

5. General elections in Chiapas with legal recognition of all political forces in the state, which requires the preparation of a new electoral law to guarantee the impartiality of the process.

6. Expansion of programs of electrification in rural communities to double the annual rate of growth of this service.

7. Careful evaluation by the Ministry of Trade and Industrial Development of NAFTA's impact on Indian communities and on pertinent lines of production in Chiapas.

8. To generate a solution to the many agrarian conflicts in the country. The process for achieving this goal would be connected to the discussion, passage, and promulgation of the General Law of Rights of Indian Communities.

9. Health. The rehabilitation of hospitals and new funding for them in order to strengthen the network of care at the primary and secondary levels.

10. The Ministry of Transport and Communication will issue the concession required for an independent Indian radio station, directed and managed by Indians.

11. Housing. To support the construction and improvement of housing in rural and Indian communities, as well as the introduction of the basic services of electricity, potable water, roads, and installations to control and improve the use of the environment.

12. Education. Establishment of programs to raise the quality of public education in the zone.

13. To include bilingual education in Indian communities

14. Respect for the culture and tradition, rights and dignity of indigenous peoples, which includes their concrete expression in terms of government, administration of justice, and culture.

15. Modification of the values of children and young people to direct them away from discrimination against indigenous peoples and lack of respect for them.

16. Creation of new municipalities in the present territories of Ocosingo and Las Margaritas.

17. Reforms of the State Constitution of Chiapas, the Organic Law of the Judiciary in the state, the Organic Law of police forces there, and other ordinances.

18. Decent jobs and fair wages for workers, which requires an improvement in their skills and education, in investments to increase their productivity, and in legislation to strengthen workers' rights to defend themselves.

19. On prices for farm produce, decisions will be adopted to compensate

partially for the effects on Indian communities of the abrupt changes in international prices.

20. Protection of the region's natural resources. Commitment of the federal government, international institutions, foundations, ecological organizations, and Indian communities to coordinate their operations in support of technology transfer and finance for the conservation of natural resources.

21. Establishment of a commission in the Ministry of Finance and Public Credit to assess the magnitude of the problem (the state's financial and fiscal problem), which commission will take into account the conflict's economic consequences [in the state] and make a budgetary proposal.

22. Realization of a program to provide medical care for children from birth to six years who suffer from extreme malnutrition.

23. On the day after the peace accord is signed, the Law on Amnesty, federal and state, will go into effect, to favor persons against whom criminal charges may have been filed, federal or state, based on acts committed in the conflict in Chiapas.

24. To reconcile the objectives of compliance with the law and full respect for the rights of Indian communities.

25. Monetary support for the victims, widows, and orphans of the conflict.

26. The combination of the decisions contained in this political commitment to a worthy peace in Chiapas and those contained in the state peace accord sustain this petition.

27. Repeal of Chiapas's current State Penal Code and the promulgation of a new code designed to respect individual freedoms and political rights.

28. To include in the new penal code the crime of expulsion of Indians from their communities.

29. To improve the condition of peasant and Indian women. To offer support for [such] women to find new spaces of well being and freedom.

30. Establishment of accords to confront the tensions that have generated rancor [in Chiapas], which accords will include all Chiapans on questions that are political.

31. Respect for the life of all members of the EZLN, and the guarantee there will be no criminal charges or repressive action against them, as soldiers, sympathizers, or collaborators.

32. More involvement of civil society in the National Commission on Human Rights or in new organizations for the protection of human rights.

33. The government will support the creation of a National Commission for Peace with Justice and Dignity to oversee compliance with the accords contained in this political commitment for a worthy peace in Chiapas.

34. To channel through Indian communities the humanitarian aid from NGOs and government agencies for the victims of the conflict, under terms on which all the concerned agree.

CHAPTER TWENTY-FOUR

The Sovereignty of Civil Society: The Second Declaration, June 10, 1994

After the assassination of Colosio on March 23, 1994, and the CCRI-EZLN's consequent decision to refuse the government's commitments to reform (Reading No. 23), the Zapatista leadership was without a strategy. As Marcos later admitted, ". . . we found ourselves in a completely unforeseen situation, and we didn't know what to do" (Reading No. 28). Taking stock through April, they saw three major facts: 1) they could not make their rebellion important nationally unless they allied with other clandestine revolutionary organizations, none of which they trusted; 2) the most important and only national uprising so far had been nonviolent, that of "the people," who since January had been demonstrating massive sympathy for Zapatista demands but deep opposition to war; 3) national elections would happen on August 21, with the PRI's new presidential candidate, Ernesto Zedillo, not a masterful or masterly politician, against a brilliant debater but determined loser, Diego Fernández, candidate of the Partido de Acción Nacional, the PAN, the old official right, and "the people"'s hope and hero, but a pitiful politician, Cuauhtémoc Cárdenas, candidate for the Partido de la Revolución Democrática, the PRD, the new independent left. From near and far the EZLN high command received much unsolicited advice about the course to pursue. PRD counselors especially urged Marcos to declare Zapatista support for Cárdenas (whose campaign in 1988 had had fateful results for the EZLN then).

But on its own, "improvising," the CCRI-EZLN decided on a new, explicitly supra-political strategy. It would rally Mexican "civil society" to organize and demand "democratic" elections, and then when the PRI won and "civil society" took to the streets in massive national protests, forcing a political crisis that the government could not resolve, it would join "civil society" in constituting a transitional government for "liberty and democracy." On May 15, on a well publicized trip into rebel territory, Cárdenas met Marcos, hoping at least for a friendly welcome. He did not get it. Marcos said nothing for his campaign, and pronounced the PRD no better than the PRI. On June 10 the CCRI-EZLN high command released its Second Declaration from the Lacandón, dismissing the government's offers of reform and calling on "civil society" to form a National Democratic Convention to create the transitional government and the body to write a new constitution.

Whatever part the Indians of the CCRI may have had in defining this declaration's content, whoever actually wrote the thing, it is, unlike the first declaration, certainly in Marcos's intellectual style. The thought, the argument, and the language are clear, consecutive, articulate, cutting, powerful, aggressive, grand, vivid, commanding, mystical, arresting, heroic, and theoretically right in the swing of Mexico City's cosmopolitan discourse.

The newly central concept is "civil society." Drawn from Gramscian arguments for Euro-Communism, it had entered debates on the Mexican left in the 1970s about the nature of "hegemony" in Mexico. It meant then pretty much what Gramsci had meant: as opposed to "political society," essentially "the State," or the government in all its various branches, levels, and forms, including of course the army and the police, "civil society" was essentially the total combination of private or autonomous institutions and voluntary associations of all classes, for example the Church, universities, social and political movements, political parties. The main difficulty for Mexican Gramscians was the PRI, not a party in any European (or American) sense, practically the government's electoral agency, but also heir to much of the country's nationalist populism, both dominant, through coercion and corruption, and "hegemonic," through consent. For years the debate remained very intellectual. The concept gained sudden plausibility and public currency in 1985, however, when a tremendous earthquake wrecked much of Mexico City, and while for days the government and the PRI sat stunned, hundreds if not thousands of private institutions and voluntary associations emerged to rescue and organize surviving victims to help themselves and demand official services. Thereafter "civil society" was nearly as common as "crisis" in political discussions in the capital and the provinces, right, left, and center.

But in this CCRI-EZLN declaration the concept bears a new meaning and power. "Civil society" now is "all honest Mexicans of good faith." It appears to exclude only corrupt and homicidal politicians. It is "the people" at large. And although "civil society" does not appear in the Constitution, it is now sovereign. Its delegates in a national convention would therefore represent the will of the Mexican people.

Two other points want emphasis. Despite the many demands for Indians and Chiapas in the dialogue in San Cristóbal, this declaration (like the first) does not once refer to Indians, and there is only one reference to Chiapas—that its conflict is an integral part of the great national struggle for "democracy."

For all the public fascination with Marcos and the Indian rebels, "civil society" at first only speculated on the call for the National Democratic Convention. A month passed. On July 9, with the elections the convention was to protest only seven weeks off, the CCRI-EZLN embraced a newly formed Chiapan State Democratic Convention and summoned the national convention to meet in San Cristóbal on August 6.

"Civil society" certainly did respond then. A few named by "committees of the convention" (as the Second Declaration had suggested), most of them envoys or volunteers from one or another of the myriad leftist associations, movements, parties, leagues, fronts, and such around the country, some 15,000 enthusiasts applied for credentials to attend. Excitement mounted when the event became exclusive: the Zapatistas could accommodate only 6,000, including 600 from the media and 300 guests and observers. Marcos heightened the drama. If the convention did not "jell," he declared, "the immediate consequence for the country will be civil war." The 5,000-plus accredited delegates, presumably then representing the sovereign will of Mexico, convened in San Cristóbal on Saturday, August 6, divided into five working groups (on "Transition to Democracy," "Inviability of the State-party," "Non-violent Ways to Democracy," "Elections, Civil Resistance, and Defense of the Will of the People," and "Formulation of a National Project . . ."), argued all day, and reached preliminary conclusions. Probably most important was the refusal to endorse Cárdenas. Among the media, guests, and observers following the debates was most of the cream of Mexico's leftist (and very pro–Cárdenas) intelligentsia.

The convention then turned into real fun. At 5 a.m. on August 7 the 6,000 on the list left in a long caravan of buses for Zapatista country, east of Las Margaritas, down the canyons to the end of the road, Guadalupe Tepeyac, where the last arrived at 3 a.m. on August 8, and from where they all had to hike another couple of hours along a Zapatista trail into the jungle, to reach the place Zapatista soldiers in the last month had built for them and the high command had named Aguascalientes. This was a piece of historical drama. Eighty years before, in October 1914, delegates from Villa's, Zapata's, and Carranza's triumphant revolutionary armies had met as the "Sovereign Revolutionary Convention" in the northern Mexican city of Aguascalientes to frame a program of reforms and oversee the election of a government to realize them. That day at Aguascalientes II passed, as an astute and amply experienced cultural critic there wrote, "variously as Woodstock, Avándaro [the Mexican Woodstock], a mining camp, *Mad Max IV*." In the evening there was

music, Marcos welcomed the delegates, introduced the proud Zapatista organizers and help, spoke brilliantly, professing the EZLN's subordination to
"civil and nonviolent mobilizations . . . even to the point of disappearing as
an alternative," there were more greetings and speeches, then a crowd-
scattering, gully-washing, flag-ripping, toad-strangling rainstorm. Already
exhausted delegates, media persons, guests, and observers passed that night in
a cold, wet, "vast and comfortable solidarity." August 9 had been scheduled
for final debate and resolutions. Instead, because it looked like another storm,
the organizers announced that they would be returning the conventioneers to
San Cristóbal; the resolutions would remain pending. Marcos gave the media
an interview, performed brilliantly, and left them in the sun, laughing, happy,
hopeful.

The elections on August 21 impressed the country at large as the cleanest in
living memory. Officially Zedillo took 49 percent of the vote, Fernández 26
percent, Cárdenas 17 percent. Cárdenas denounced the elections as fraudu-
lent, but the PRD made no call for popular action. There were no protests in
the streets (except over the state election in Chiapas, on which see Reading No.
25). The National Democratic Convention languished, surviving as only one
more of Mexico's many agitating societies. The EZLN got a page on the
World Wide Web.

SEGUNDA DECLARACIÓN
DE LA SELVA LACANDONA*

Mexican Brothers:

In December of 1993 we said ENOUGH! On January 1, 1994, we called on
the legislative and judicial branches of government to assume their constitutional responsibility to block the genocidal policy that the Federal Executive
imposes on our people. . . .

[They] ignored our just demand and allowed the massacre . . . Civil Society assumed the duty of preserving our fatherland. . . . We all understood
[then] that the days of the eternal party in power . . . cannot
continue. . . . This all honest Mexicans of good faith, Civil Society, have
understood. The only ones who are opposed are those who have based their
success on theft from the public treasury, those who, prostituting justice, protect the drug traffickers and assassins, who resort to political assassination and
electoral fraud to impose themselves [on the country].

Today we do not call on these bankrupt powers . . . that did not know

---

*June 10, 1994, www.ezln.org

how to fulfill their constitutional duty. . . . It is in CIVIL SOCIETY that our sovereignty resides; it is the people that can at any time alter or modify our form of government. . . .

First. We have without any violation carried out acts of war within the internationally established conventions on war: this has granted us the tacit recognition of Mexicans and foreigners as a belligerent force...

Second. We order our regular and irregular forces in the entire national territory and abroad TO UNILATERALLY EXTEND THE OFFENSIVE CEASE-FIRE. We will maintain respect for the cease-fire in order to permit civil society to organize in the forms it considers pertinent for achieving the transition to democracy in our country . . .

Third. We condemn the threat that hangs over Civil Society as [the government] militarizes the country . . . on the eve of . . . federal elections . . .

Fourth. We propose to all independent political parties . . . that they pronounce themselves ready to assume a government of transition . . . toward democracy.

Fifth. We reject manipulation and the attempt to disconnect our just demands from the Mexican people . . .

Sixth. We repeat our disposition in favor of a political solution in the transition to democracy in Mexico.

We call on Civil Society to recover the protagonistic role that it took to stop the military phase of the war and to organize itself to lead the nonviolent effort toward democracy, liberty, and justice. Democratic change is the only alternative to war.

Seventh. We call the honest elements of civil society to a National Dialogue for Democracy, Liberty, and Justice for all Mexicans.

. . . The fulfillment of the commitments [that the government made as a result of the dialogue in the San Cristóbal cathedral and that the CCRI-EZLN communities had rejected] implies necessarily the death of the State-party system. By suicide or by the firing squad, the death of the present Mexican political system is a necessary condition, although not sufficient, for the transition to democracy in our country. Chiapas will have no real solution if Mexico is not solved . . .

The problem of power will not be who nominally holds it, but who exercises it. If the majority exercises power, the political parties will be obliged to confront this majority and not each other.

To reframe the problem of power in this framework of democracy, liberty, and justice will necessitate a new political culture within the parties. A new class of politicians will have to be born, and no doubt political parties of a new type will be born.

We are not proposing a new world, but only something very prior to that: the waiting room of the new Mexico. In this sense this revolution will not end in a new class, or class fraction, or group in power, but in a free and democratic "space" of political struggle. This free and democratic "space" will be born on the stinking cadaver of the State-party system and presidentialism. A new political relationship will be born. A new politics whose basis will not be a confrontation between political organizations, but the confrontation of their political proposals with the different social classes, for on the real support of these classes will depend the title to political power, not its exercise . . .

Current Mexican law is too narrow for these new political relations between governors and the governed. A National Democratic Convention is necessary, from which a Provisional or Transition Government will issue, either by the resignation of the federal executive or by the electoral path.

The National Democratic Convention and the Transition Government must issue in a new Magna Carta in whose framework new elections will be held . . .

The EZLN has a conception of a system and a path for the country. The EZLN's political maturity, its maturity as representative of the sense of a part of the Nation, is in the fact that it does not want to impose this conception on the country. The EZLN claims what is evident to itself: Mexico's maturity and its right to decide, freely and democratically, the path it is to take. From this historic waiting room not only will a better and more just Mexico emerge, but also a new Mexican. On this we stake our lives, to bequeath to Mexicans of the day after tomorrow a country in which it is not a shame to live . . .

. . . thieves of hope suppose that behind our arms are ambition and heroics, that this will guide our behavior in the future. They are mistaken. Behind our firearms are other weapons, those of reason. And hope animates both. We will not let them steal hope from us.

Hope with a trigger had its place at the beginning of the year. Now it is necessary for that hope to wait. It is necessary that the hope that goes in the great mobilizations return to the protagonistic place that corresponds to it by right and reason. The flag is now in the hands of those who have names and faces, good and honest people who walk roads that are not ours, but whose goal is the same that our steps long for. Our greetings to them, and our hope that they carry this flag to where it ought to be. We will be waiting, upright and with dignity. If this flag falls, we will know how to raise it again . . .

Let hope organize, walk now in the valleys and the cities as it did yesterday in the mountains. Let them fight with their own weapons; do not worry about us. We will know how to resist to the end. We will know how to hope . . . and we will know how to return if again all the doors close, so that dignity may walk.

Therefore we address ourselves to our brothers in nongovernmental organizations, in peasant and Indian organizations, workers in the field and in the city, teachers and students, housewives and squatters, artists and intellectuals, in the independent parties . . .

We call you to a national dialogue on the theme of Democracy, Freedom, and Justice. Therefore we release this:

Convocation for the National Democratic Convention

We, the Zapatista Army of National Liberation, struggling to achieve the democracy, liberty, and justice our country deserves, and considering:

First. That the supreme government has also usurped the legality that the heroes of the Mexican Revolution bequeathed to us.

Second. That the Magna Carta that rules us is nothing more than the popular will of Mexicans.

Third. That the departure of the usurper of the federal executive is not enough, and that a new law is necessary for our new fatherland, which is to be born from the struggle of all honest Mexicans.

Fourth. That all forms of struggle are necessary to achieve the transition to democracy in Mexico.

We call for the realization of a Democratic Convention, national, sovereign, and revolutionary, from which would result proposals for a transition government and a new national law, a new Constitution that will guarantee the legal fulfillment of the popular will.

The fundamental objective of the National Democratic Convention is to organize civic expression and the defense of the popular will.

The sovereign revolutionary convention will be national in its composition and representation, bound to include all the states of the Federation, pluralist in the sense that all patriotic forces will be represented, and democratic in decision-making, making use of national consultation.

The convention will be freely and voluntarily presided over by civilians, public personalities of recognized prestige, without regard to their political affiliation, race, religious creed, sex, or age.

The convention will be formed through local, regional, and state civic committees, in ejidos, urban and rural settlements, schools, and factories. These convention committees will take charge of gathering popular proposals for the new constitutional law and the demands to be fulfilled by the new government emanating from this constitution.

The convention must demand free and democratic elections and struggle without rest for respect for the popular will.

The Zapatista Army of National Liberation will recognize the National Democratic Convention as the authentic repesentative of the interests of the Mexican people in its transition to democracy . . .

Mexican Brothers:

Our struggle continues. The Zapatista flag still waves in the mountains of the Mexican Southeast, and today we say: We will not surrender!

With our face to the mountain we spoke with our dead so that in their word might come the good path for our muffled face to go.

The drums sounded, and in the voice of the land our pain spoke, and our history spoke our pain and our history spoke.

"For everyone, everything," our dead say. So long as this is not so, there will be nothing for us.

Speak the word of other Mexicans; find the ear of the heart of those for whom we struggle. Invite them to walk in the worthy steps of those who have no face. Call on everyone to prevent anyone from taking anything from those who order by commanding. Make of "Don't Sell Yourself" a common flag for the others. Ask that not only a word of encouragement come for our pain. Ask others to share the pain, ask that they resist with you, that they reject all the charity that comes from the mighty. May all the good people in these lands today organize the dignity that resists and does not sell itself. Let this dignity tomorrow organize to demand that the word that goes in the heart of the majority hold truth and greeting from those who govern. Let the good path be imposed, that he who commands, commands in obedience.

Do not surrender! Resist! Do not dishonor the true word. Resist with dignity in the land of true men and true women, and let the mountains cover the pain of the men of corn. Do not surrender! Resist! Do not sell yourselves! Resist!

Thus spoke the word from the heart of our ever dead. We saw that the word of our dead is good. We saw that there is truth and dignity in their advice. Therefore we call on all our Mexican Indian brothers to resist with us. We call on all peasants to resist with us, workers, employees, squatters, housewives, students, teachers, those who make thought and words their life. On all those who have any dignity or sense of shame, we call on you all to resist with us, for this bad government wants no democracy in our land. Nothing will we accept that comes from the rotten heart of this bad government, not a single coin, not medicine, not a rock, not a grain of food, not a crumb of the charity they offer in exchange for our path in dignity . . .

Brothers: Do not sell yourselves! Resist with us. Do not surrender. Resist with us. Repeat with us, brothers, the word of "We will not surrender! We resist!" Let it be heard not only in the mountains of the Mexican Southeast. Let it be heard in the north and in the peninsulas. On both coasts let it be heard. Let it be heard in the center of the country. In the valleys and the mountains let it become a cry. Let it resound in the city and in the countryside. Unite your voice, brothers, give a cry with us, join your voice with ours:

"We will not surrender! We resist!"

Let dignity break the siege with which the dirty hands of the bad government strangle us. We are all besieged, for they will not let democracy, liberty, and justice enter Mexican lands. Brothers: we are all besieged. We will not surrender! Let us resist! Let us be upright and trustworthy! Let us not sell ourselves!

Of what use to the powerful is all their wealth, if it does not buy what is most valuable in this land? If the dignity of all us Mexicans has no price, what is the power of the powerful for?

Dignity does not surrender!

Dignity resists!

Democracy!

Liberty!

Justice!

From the mountains of the Mexican Southeast.

Clandestine Revolutionary Indian Committee-General Command of the Zapatista Army of National Liberation

Mexico, June 1994

Chapter Twenty-Five

The Movement for National Liberation: The Third Declaration, January 1, 1995

When the federal elections resulted in a PRI victory but no massive pro-tests, the CCRI-EZLN high command had come another cropper. As Marcos later admitted, "we [had] fooled ourselves yet again . . . There was nothing else to do," he said, "but wait for Salinas to leave, and see what the new president proposed" (Reading No. 28). But there was actually more to do, and still along the lines of the Second Declaration, the EZLN did it.

Besides the presidential and congressional elections, four states had regular gubernatorial elections that summer. One was Chiapas, on the same day as the federal elections, August 21. The PRI's candidate for governor was a strong reassurance to the state's businessmen and landlords, a professional PRIista who had run the state PRI under Governor González, at least once crossed him (see Reading No. 6), but done much for him to corrupt, pervert, and prostitute Solidarity, Eduardo Robledo. Likewise the PRD had fielded a strong candidate for its constituency, the CEOIC's hero and hope, one of the few popular ex-mayors of San Cristóbal, a rousing, populist newspaper pub-lisher, Amado Avendaño. On July 2–3, while "civil society" nationally, de-spite the Second Declaration, failed to generate a National Democratic Convention, the PRD in Chiapas, the CEOIC, other local associations and movements sympathetic to the Zapatistas, and now nonviolent Zapatistas themselves in Los Altos had formed the State Democratic Assembly of the Chiapan People, a coalition of altogether 180 organizations, to promote Av-endaño and serve as his "civil society." On July 14 Avendaño had gone to

Guadalupe Tepeyac, addressed the Zapatistas as "compañeros," and practically adopted the Second Declaration as his platform, promising if elected to form a "transitional government" for Chiapas and convoke a constitutional convention of Chiapas's "civil society" to write a new state constitution.

The Chiapas elections on August 21 showed officially 50 percent of the vote for Robledo, 35 percent for Avendaño. Unlike the opposition nationally, the State Democratic Assembly at once denounced "electoral fraud" and proclaimed its candidate triumphant. On August 28 the state electoral commission validated Robledo's victory. The State Democratic Assembly at once called for *resistencia civil*, "civil disobedience." A week later its campaign began, blocking highways, seizing radio stations, occupying farms and ranches from the Pacific Coast to the highlands, demanding recognition of Avendaño as governor-elect to take office on the prescribed date, three months down the road, December 8.

In the absence of such movement nationally, the EZLN high command tried to shame (if not blackmail) "civil society" into it. In mid-September it praised Cárdenas for his personal campaign "to prevent Zedillo's usurpation," denounced the PRD for compromising, accused "civil society" of forgetting its duty, warned that the Zapatistas would go back into war if nonviolence failed, and boosted again the National Democratic Convention, "the hope for a new national revolutionary movement." There remained two and a half months for the strategy of the Second Declaration to work before the presidential inauguration on December 1.

The assassination of the PRI's new national secretary general in Mexico City on September 28 hit the Salinas government almost as hard as Colosio's murder six months before. It eliminated Salinas's last powerful political ally, his main operator then against the PRI's traditional bosses, and his choice for chief of the Chamber of Deputies in the next congress (carrying much more clout than "speaker of the House"). The obvious conspiracy for the crime suggested that "the State-party system" might well fall apart on its own before December 1, all the more reason to press "civil society" for a national "transitional government." On October 6 the CCRI-EZLN high command issued its "proposals" (guidelines) for the National Democratic Convention's second meeting: stop squabbling, get organized, keep the leadership clear of all partisans (i.e., from the PRD) "who have not made explicit their subordination" to the convention, and publish a specific program of struggle (recommendations for which followed).

Chiapas would show the way. On October 8, commemorating the death of the *Comandante de América*, Che Guevara, the CCRI-EZLN announced it would no longer negotiate with the government, had mined roads into its territory, and installed anti-aircraft "units." On October 12, anti-Columbus Day, the State Democratic Assembly marched 25,000 strong into San Cristóbal, disavowed the federal and state governments, announced a "civil insurgency" for Avendaño, and declared the establishment of "transitional governments" in nine henceforth "autonomous multi-ethnic" districts, which federal and state officials could not enter and where residents would not pay taxes, utility bills, or debts on federal, state, or municipal loans until Avendaño took office. (Cf. Reading No. 4, on Tzajalhemel's secesion in 1867–70.) Bishop Ruiz urged new negotiations. Ignoring him, Marcos declared, "If Robledo is imposed as governor, there is going to be war here. And here means Mexico, not just Chiapas." On October 14 Marcos gave the National Democratic Convention a stern lecture on how to run its affairs, particularly its next meeting, by then set for Chiapas in three weeks. On November 2 the CCRI-EZLN high command "proposed" the meeting's agenda. On November 4–6 the State Democratic Assembly hosted the meeting (4,000 delegates) in Tuxtla, to plan a national campaign of civil disobedience. On November 6 Avendaño told a PRD rally there that to prevent Robledo's inauguration "the people" should occupy the state capitol on December 8. Three days later Cárdenas and Marcos met again in rebel territory. Among other things Cárdenas allowed, "There has to be generated a national movement with more strength." The CCRI-EZLN high command agreed, and declared Cárdenas "a valid political interlocutor for the EZLN." This was the first conscious connection that would culminate in the Third Declaration.

The State Democratic Assembly's campaign continued to build. On November 17, recalling the eleventh anniversary of the EZLN in Chiapas, Marcos made a show for the media of receiving the CCRI's "staff of command," in final preparation for the war he threatened if "civil insurgency" failed. On November 20, recalling the Revolution of 1910, the CEOIC announced that Indian marches were beginning from most of the state's 111 municipalities to concentrate in the state capital on December 8 in a massive force for Avendaño.

But the National Democratic Convention continued to flounder. Without national popular or partisan protest, Zedillo took office smoothly on December 1. More ominously for the CCRI-EZLN, his Interior minister in talks with Avendaño at once defused the preparations for December 8, confirming Robledo's official claim to the state capitol, but allowing Avendaño a ritual inauguration and offices in San Cristóbal to run a "parallel government" for the "autonomous multi-ethnic" districts. (Cf. Readings Nos. 4 and 23.) That way led away from crisis. The convention's weakness was no longer only a national embarrassment to the EZLN high command. It was also exposing the "civil insurgency" in Chiapas to isolation. Civil negligence in Mexico City endangered even armed insurgents in the canyons. On December 4 Marcos called on the convention and Cárdenas to head together "a great broad opposition front" to force Zedillo's resignation, form a "transitional government," etc. On December 6, to resharpen the crisis, the Zapatista high command denounced Robledo's coming inauguration as a federal breach of the cease-fire, recognized Avendaño as the state's constitutional governor, and declared the "autonomous" districts rebel territory.

On December 8 Robledo took office in Tuxtla, Avendaño took office in San Cristóbal, and the CCRI-EZLN high command published orders for its troops to advance on "military missions." At Robledo's request the army expanded its patrols. On December 11 the Zapatista high command announced the creation of nine "new rebel municipalities" in the canyons. On December 13 Cárdenas met again with Marcos. Four tense days later the high command refused Zedillo's offer of a congressional commission to negotiate, accepted Bishop Ruiz's CONAI as a mediator, and called again on the National Democratic Convention and Cárdenas to show "Mexican society" how to reach "peace with justice and dignity." Then early on December 19, without firing a shot, EZLN troops "broke the siege," emerging from under cover to establish military positions in 38 municipalities, all east of the Grijalva, but most of the country there, all of Los Altos, the north, and the Lacandón, all declared rebel territory under the Zapatista "revolutionary laws of 1993." To President Zedillo, Marcos wrote, "It is my duty to inform you that you have an Indian rebellion in the Nation's southeast." Bishop Ruiz started his fast for peace. National and international pleas for peace followed. On December 20 (for entirely different reasons) the government quite ineptly devalued the peso, which threw the country into a national economic crisis. Ten days later the Zapatista high command announced a truce from January 1 to January 6, to allow "a new dialogue." On the first day of the truce it issued its Third Declaration from the Lacandón jungle.

Three observations may be useful. (1) In this declaration "civil society" has disappeared. "Civic effort," "civic struggle," "civilian population," yes, but of "civil society," nothing. (2) There is a significant emphasis on "the indigenous." The national revolution the EZLN proposed on January 1, 1994, is "the Chiapan Indian rebellion" on January 1, 1995. (3) In the early 1960s ex-President Lázaro Cárdenas briefly led a leftist *Movimiento de Liberación Nacional*, a Movement of National Liberation. Here the CCRI-EZLN calls for a *Movimiento para la Liberación Nacional*, (a Movement for National Liberation). If the prepositions mean anything important, it may be a new Zapatista gradualism.

Even so, the CCRI-EZLN high command could not yet make the National Democratic Convention into the force it wanted. In February the Movement for National Liberation proved a political disaster for the Zapatistas.

TERCERA DECLARACIÓN
DE LA SELVA LACANDONA*

To the people of Mexico:
To the peoples and governments of the world:
Brothers:

. . . The pre-electoral process in August 1994 brought hope to many sectors of the country that the transition to democracy was possible by the electoral road. Knowing that elections are not, in the current conditions, the path to democratic change, the EZLN gave orders in obedience to the popular will that it would stand aside in order to give legal political opposition forces the opportunity to struggle. The EZLN pledged its word and its effort, then, to the search for a nonviolent transition to democracy. Through the National Democratic Convention the EZLN called for a civic and peaceful effort that, without opposing the electoral struggle, would not be consumed by it, would seek new forms of struggle including other democratic sectors in Mexico, and would connect with democratic movements in other parts of the world. [The federal elections on] August 21 ended the illusions of an immediate change by nonviolent means . . . Reports from the National Democratic Convention, the Civic Alliance, and the Commission for Truth brought to light what the great mass media were hiding, with shameful complicity: a gigantic fraud. Multitudinous irregularities, inequity, corruption, blackmail, intimidation, robbery, and falsification were the framework in which took place the dirtiest elections in Mexico's history. . . . not satisfied with this, the State-party system repeated the fraud [at the local level,] . . . imposing governors, municipal presidents, and state legislatures . . . The electoral process of August 1994 is a crime of state . . .

Meanwhile the federal government was preparing a military solution for the Chiapan Indian rebellion, and the Nation sank into despair and disgust. Deceptively indicating a will to dialogue that only hid its desire to liquidate the Zapatista movement through asphyxiation, the bad government let time pass and death happen in indigenous communities throughout the country . . .

Seeing that the government and the country were again laying oblivion and uninterest over the original inhabitants of these lands, seeing that cynicism and negligence were again taking possession of the sentiments of the Nation and that, besides being denied their rights to the minimal conditions of life with dignity, Indian peoples were being denied the right to govern . . . according to their own reason and will, seeing that the deaths of our dead were becoming useless, the EZLN took the risk of breaking the military siege that

---

*January 1, 1995, www.ezln.org

was containing it, and marched in aid of other indigenous brothers who, non-violent means having been exhausted, were sinking into desperation and misery . . . With the offensive of December 1994, the EZLN sought to show, to Mexico and to the world, its proud indigenous essence and the impossibility of resolving the local social situation unless there are profound changes in political, economic, and social relations throughout the country.

The indigenous question will not have a solution if there is not a RADICAL transformation of the national pact. The only form of incorporating, with justice and dignity, the indigenous into the Nation is by recognizing their specific characteristics in social, political, and cultural organization. Autonomy is not separation; it is the integration of the most humiliated and forgotten minorities in contemporary Mexico . . .

Today we repeat: OUR STRUGGLE IS NATIONAL . . .

Today we reaffirm: FOR EVERYONE, EVERYTHING; NOTHING FOR US! . . .

Today, after having called the people of Mexico first to arms and later to a civic and nonviolent struggle, we call them to struggle BY ALL MEANS, AT ALL LEVELS, AND IN ALL PARTS OF THE COUNTRY, for democracy, liberty, and justice, by means of this

Third Declaration of the Lacandon Jungle

in which we call on all social and political forces of the country, all honest Mexicans, all those who struggle for the democratization of national life, to form a MOVEMENT FOR NATIONAL LIBERATION, including the National Democratic Convention and ALL forces, without distinction by religious creed, race, or political ideology, that are against the State-party system. This *Movement for National Liberation* will struggle in common accord, by all means and at all levels, for the installation of a transitional government, a new constitutional congress, a new Magna Carta, and the destruction of the State-party system. We call on the National Democratic Convention and Cuauhtémoc Cárdenas Solórzano to head this Movement for National Liberation, as a broad opposition front.

WE CALL ON THE WORKERS OF THE REPUBLIC, THE LABORERS IN THE COUNTRYSIDE AND THE CITIES, THE PEOPLE IN SQUATTERS SETTLEMENTS, THE TEACHERS AND THE STUDENTS OF MEXICO, THE WOMEN OF MEXICO, THE YOUNG PEOPLE OF THE WHOLE COUNTRY, THE HONEST ARTISTS AND INTELLECTUALS, THE COMMITTED CHURCHMEN, THE GRASSROOTS MILITANTS OF DIFFERENT POLITICAL ORGANIZATIONS, acting in their own situation and by the forms of struggle that they consider possible and necessary, to struggle for the end of the State-party system, joining the NATIONAL DEMOCRATIC CON-

VENTION if they do not belong to a party, and the Movement for National Liberation if they are active in any of the opposition political forces.

Therefore, in keeping with the spirit of this THIRD DECLARATION FROM THE LACANDÓN JUNGLE, we declare that

First. Custody of the Fatherland is removed from the federal government.

The Mexican flag, the Nation's constitution, the Mexican Hymn, and the Great National Seal will now be under the care of the forces of the resistance until legality, legitimacy, and sovereignty are restored in all the national territory.

Second. The original Political Constitution of the United Mexican States, issued on February 5, 1917, is declared valid, incorporating into it the Revolutionary Laws of 1993 and the Statutes of Inclusive Autonomy for the indigenous regions, and adherence to it is decreed until the new constitutional congress is installed and a new Magna Carta is issued.

Third. The call is given to struggle for the recognition, as "a government of transition to democracy," of the government that the various communities, social organizations, and political organizations may give themselves, keeping the federal pact agreed in the 1917 Constitution, and that are included, without regard for religious creed, social class, political ideology, race, or sex, in the *Movement for National Liberation*.

The EZLN will support the civilian population in the task of restoring national legality, order, legitimacy, and sovereignty, and in the struggle for the formation and installation of a national government of transition to democracy with the following characteristics:

1. That it liquidate the State-party system and actually separate the government from the PRI.
2. That it reform the electoral law in terms that guarantee: clean elections, credibility, equity, nonpartisan and nongovernmental civic participation, recognition of all national, regional, and local political forces, and that it hold new general federal elections.
3. That it convoke a constitutional congress for the creation of a new constitution.
4. That it recognize the particularities of indigenous groups, and recognize their right to inclusive autonomy and their citizenship.
5. That it again give direction to the national economic program, putting aside deceit and lies and favoring the country's most dispossessed sectors, the workers and peasants, who are the principal producers of the wealth that others appropriate.

Brothers:

Peace will come from the hand of democracy, liberty, and justice for all Mexicans. We cannot find the just peace to which our dead lay claim if it is at the cost of our Mexican dignity. The earth has no rest; it walks in our hearts. The mockery of our dead demands struggle to wash away their grief. We will resist. Infamy and arrogance will be defeated.

As with Benito Juárez in the face of the French Intervention, the Fatherland marches today at the side of the patriotic forces, against the anti-democratic and authoritarian forces. Today we say:

The Fatherland lives! And it is ours!

Democracy!

Liberty!

Justice!

From the mountains of the Mexican Southeast

CCRI-CG of the EZLN

Mexico, January 1995

Civil Society and the Zapatista Front: The Fourth Declaration from the Jungle, January 1, 1996

Salinas's worst enemies had been the PRI's traditional bosses, who opposed his economic policies, political reforms, and negotiations with the CCRI-EZLN, which they wanted the army to crush. He had maneuvered and scared them into subordination or desperation. Zedillo's worst enemies were the same. But unlike Salinas, Zedillo could not maneuver or scare them. By February 1995, having thrown the economy into a crash, his government was fighting to survive from day to day. To regain an image of competence, it began resorting to displays of force in the name of law. Its first target was the EZLN. On February 9 the president announced the identities of some leading Zapatistas (including Marcos), the issue of federal warrants for their arrest, and a military offensive to recover control of rebel country.

Militarily this action was successful: a force of 25,000 in a few days capturing all EZLN strongholds in the canyons, the people there fleeing into the depths of the remaining jungle. But politically it was another Zedillo disaster. It erased public memory of the recent Zapatista fiasco in the Movement for National Liberation. It revived the PRD, which on February 11 led a march of 100,000 protesters into the capital's central plaza. And it provoked notable pro–Zapatista demonstrations in the United States and across Western Europe (two in Paris), making Marcos an international pop idol and the Indians of Chiapas globally famous and fantastically attractive. On February 14 Zedillo called a truce, and Governor Robledo resigned (for another PRIista). Promising an amnesty on one hand, demanding on the other that the EZLN pursue its goals legally and politically, the president was virtually pleading to renew negotiations.

Its public credit so restored, and considering the chance then apparently strong that the Zedillo government would soon fall, the CCRI-EZLN high command returned to the courtship of "civil society." If the government needed "dialogue" again to show its peaceful intentions, the Zapatista high command needed "dialogue" to consolidate its public support (always independent of the PRD) and try again to organize a popular movement to act when the "State-party system" collapsed; otherwise its own militants might return to arms. On March 28 it therefore published a sophisticated proposal of "basic principles" and "rules of procedure" for direct talks—to take place in Mexico City, after the army's withdrawal to its positions of February 8—on "the political, economic, social, and cultural causes of the war." "Not viable," said the Interior minister; the talks had to be in Chiapas (to localize their significance), and the army would not move. Accordingly, under the new amnesty, with the help of the new COCOPA and through the good offices of Bishop Ruiz's CONAI, government and EZLN delegates met on April 9 in an abandoned Zapatista canyon community, surrounded by the army, and painfully agreed on the "principles" under which the talks could start.

The first session took place on April 20–21 in San Andrés Larráinzar. A little Tzotzil town (97 percent) some 20 miles north of San Cristóbal, a hotbed of Zapatismo, which the EZLN there the previous December had de-ladinoized to San Andrés Sakamch'én (White Cave) de los Pobres, which the army had retaken and now surrounded, it was not a place for the slow or the timid. At the EZLN's request, because the Mexican army continued to run heavy patrols everywhere in eastern Chiapas, some 5,000 Indians had crowded into the town's square as security for the Zapatista team. The government's team complained that it lacked security. Not until late on the second day, after the Indians had left, would it talk with its counterparts—and then only to insist that the EZLN concentrate at three designated points in eastern Chiapas, accept federal security and supplies there, and change into "a legal organization," that is, disarm.

The second session opened on May 12 in San Andrés. It passed entirely in arguments about security. The Zapatista team reported the CCRI-EZLN's rejection of the government's plan to concentrate, control, and disarm them, complained of continuing military patrols and provocations, and asked again that the army withdraw to its positions of February 8. The government team proposed that while the army retained its militarized roads into the canyons, it regroup in only 11 of the 21 communities currently occupied, leaving the EZLN to concentrate where it chose. Late on May 15 the arguments ended in agreement only on a date for resumption.

On June 7 the third session at San Andrés began. The Zapatista team rejected the government's proposal and presented an EZLN plan to relocate the occupying army units, which the government team rejected. By June 9 the delegates had again agreed only on the date of the next meeting.

Far more important, however, was Marcos's surprising call on June 7 for the National Democratic Convention to intervene in the "dialogue." So that the government and the CCRI-EZLN would know what "civil society" thought, the convention on its anniversary in August should conduct "a grand national poll" on six points: (1) if the original Zapatista demands for land, housing, etc. were "the principal demands of the Mexican people"; (2) if "democratizing forces" should unite in a "broad civic, social, and political front"; (3) if there should be "a deep political reform to guarantee democracy"; (4) if the EZLN should turn into "a new and independent political force"; or (5) if it should unite with other organizations to form "a new political force"; and (6) if women should be guaranteed "equitable presence and participation" in all representative offices in civil organizations and the government.

In economic misery and political crisis the government continued to flounder. On June 22 Cárdenas demanded Zedillo's resignation, congressional appointment of an interim executive, and a new presidential election. Despite the army, more villagers in Chiapas seized town halls and organized "autonomous" councils. (See Reading Nos. 4, 23, and 25.) And bedeviling the PRI and the PRD there, "rebel" Governor Avendaño announced that his Democratic Assembly would abstain from state legislative and municipal elections in October.

At the fourth session in San Andrés, July 4–6, deliberately in light of publicity for "the grand national poll," the Zapatista team proposed a substantive agenda of national proportions, nothing less than Democracy and Justice, Indian Rights, Political Liberties, and Women's Rights. The government team objected that it could not discuss national questions, only Chiapas. The fifth session, July 24–26, was useless, except for the government and the CCRI-EZLN to blame each other for the impasse.

Finally "the grand national poll" happened, not by the convention (which could not manage it), but by the Alianza Cívica, the national organization of election observers. From August 23 to August 27, in every state, at more than 8,000 polling tables, some 40,000 volunteers collected 1,200,000 electronic ballots: 97.7 percent for the Zapatista demands for land, housing, etc., 92.2 percent for a "broad opposition front," 95 percent for "reform to guarantee democracy," 57 percent for the EZLN's transformation into an "independent political force," 43 percent for its union with other organizations, and 90 percent for equity for women. Electronically as well the poll went international; in 28 countries some 55,000 cosmopolitans expressed themselves in about the same proportions. It was a triumph impressive to Zapatistas civil and still armed.

Suddenly the talks at San Andrés turned positive. At the sixth session, September 5–10, the delegates agreed on an agenda (practically what the Zapatistas had earlier proposed), which question to treat first (Indians, on which see Reading No. 27), and a procedure (as the Zapatistas had initially proposed), first "dialogue," then "negotiation," then "accord," finally "commitment." The reason for this new tractability was not that either side now expected the talks to lead to any real agreement. It was simply a congruence of new calculations in the struggle for public support. In anticipation of the EZLN's metamorphosis into a mere left-wing political organization, Zedillo and his ministers would use "dialogue" and official powers to prove their sensitive, responsible, effective commitment to reform, and make nonviolent Zapatismo irrelevant. In anticipation of the regime's collapse, the CCRI-EZLN high command would use "dialogue" to demonstrate the government's and the PRD's incapacity for reform, captivate "civil society," and build the new popular force to replace its armed force on the imminent day of redemption. On October 1 the delegates opened their "dialogue" on "Indigenous Rights and Culture." Despite continual feuding—PRD fury at Zapatista abstention (and the consequent PRI triumph) in Chiapas's elections on October 15, Marcos's declarations of scorn for the PRD, mysterious maneuvers through the federal police to sabotage the "dialogue," displays of mutual disgust at San Andrés, and provocations by the army—the two teams cooperated sufficiently through October, November, and December, directly and through COCOPA and CONAI, to negotiate debatable drafts for an accord.

By mid-December it was public knowledge that the EZLN was meanwhile constructing four new "Aguascalientes" in the canyons, for "cultural encounters" with "civil society" and to celebrate the rebellion's anniversary on January 1. The army intensified its patrols. Marcos warned these were "the shadow of war." On December 25 villagers in Los Altos started seizing town halls to prevent PRI mayors-elect from taking office on January 1. On December 28 Zapatistas and guests from "civil society" inaugurated the new "Aguascalientes" with parties, music, and a show.

Hopefully then, on New Year's Day 1996, the Zapatista high command issued its Fourth Declaration from the jungle, announcing the birth of the Frente Zapatista de Liberación Nacional, the FZLN, the Zapatista Front of National Liberation.

This was the most artful declaration so far, fully in Marcos's style. In deliberate consideration of the current negotiations on "Indigenous Rights and Culture," it was also the most Indian, in its turn of words and traditionalist incantation and imagery, its explicit authorial projection, and its historical and rhetorical allusions (including the reference to 63 indigenous peoples in Mexico). It was traditionally Indian too in its offer of authority, "political force that does not aspire to take [official] power." But in line with the Second Declaration it rendered (mostly in historical parts omitted here) much homage to "civil society, national and international." The excerpts here are the most figurative and expository.

Predictably, PRI, PAN, and PRD leaders criticized the notion of political solutions without political parties. More troublesome for the CCRI-EZLN was that the government continued to survive, and "civil society" did next to nothing for the newborn FZLN.

CUARTA DECLARACIÓN
DE LA SELVA LECANDONA *

Today we say:
We are here!
We are rebel dignity, the forgotten heart of the fatherland! . . .

To the people of Mexico:
To the peoples and governments of the world:

Brothers:

The flower of the word will not die. The masked face of he who names the flower may die today, but the word that came from the depth of history and the earth can no longer be pulled up by the arrogance of power . . .

Our struggle is to make ourselves heard, and the bad government shouts arrogance and closes its ears with cannon.

Our struggle is because of hunger, and the bad government gives us lead and paper for our children's stomachs.

Our struggle is for a decent roof over our heads, and the bad government destroys our houses and our history.

Our struggle is for knowledge, and the bad government spreads ignorance and contempt.

Our struggle is for land, and the bad government offers us cemeteries.

Our struggle is for a fair and dignified job, and the bad government buys and sells bodies and shame.

Our struggle is for life, and the bad government offers death as the future.

Our struggle is for respect for our right to govern and to govern ourselves, and the bad government imposes the laws of the minority on the majority.

Our struggle is for freedom of thought and the road, and the bad government lays out jails and graves.

Our struggle is for justice, and the bad government is full of criminals and assassins.

Our struggle is for history, and the bad government proposes oblivion.

Our struggle is for the Fatherland, and the bad government dreams of a foreign flag and language.

---

* January 1, 1996, www.ezln.org

Our struggle is for peace, and the bad government announces war and destruction.

Housing, land, work, bread, health, education, independence, democracy, liberty, justice, and peace. These were our banners at the dawn of 1994. These were our requests during the long night of 500 years. These are, today, our demands.

Our blood and our word lit a small fire in the mountain, and we walked it along the path that goes to the house of might and money. Brothers and sisters of other races and languages, of another color, but of the same heart, protected our light and drank in it their own fires.

The mighty one came to put us out with his violent puffing, but our light grew into other lights. The rich man dreams of putting out the first light. It is useless; there are now too many lights, and they are all the first.

The arrogant want to put out a rebellion that their ignorance locates in the dawn of 1994. But the rebellion that today has a dark face and a true language was not born today. It spoke before in other languages and in other lands. In many mountains and many histories rebellion has taken its path against injustice. It has already spoken in Nahuatl, Paipai, Kiliwa, Cúcapa, Cochimi, Kumiai, Yuma, Seri, Chontal, Chinanteco, Pame, Chichimeca, Otomí, Mazahua, Matlatzinca, Ocuilteco, Zapoteco, Solteco, Chatino, Papabuco, Mixteco, Cuicateco, Triqui, Amuzgo, Mazateco, Chocho, Ixcateco, Huave, Tlapaneco, Totonaca, Tepehua, Popoluca, Mixe, Zoque, Huasteco, Lacandón, Maya, Chol, Tzeltal, Tzotzil, Tojolabal, Mame, Teco, Ixil, Aguacateco, Motocintleco, Chicomucelteco, Kanjobal, Jacalteco, Quiché, Cakchiquel, Ketchi, Pima, Tepehuán, Tarahumara, Mayo, Yaqui, Cahíta, Ópata, Cora, Huichol, Purépecha, and Kikapú. It spoke and speaks Spanish. Rebellion is not a matter of language, but a matter of dignity and being human.

They kill us for working, they kill us for living. There is no place for us in the world of power. They will kill us for struggling. But this is how we will make a world where we all fit and all live without death in the word. They want to take the land away from us so that there is no ground under our feet. They want to take history away from us so that in oblivion our word will die. They do not want us Indians. They want us dead.

For the mighty one our silence was his desire. Being silent, we were dying. Without the word we did not exist. We struggle to speak against oblivion, against death, for memory and for life. We struggle for fear of dying the death of oblivion.

Speaking its Indian heart, the Fatherland goes on in dignity and remembering . . .

Today, with the heart of Emiliano Zapata and having heard the voice of all our brothers, we call on the people of Mexico to participate in a new stage of the struggle for national liberation and the construction of a new fatherland, through this . . .

Fourth Declaration from the Lacandón Jungle

in which we call all honest men and women to participate in the new national political force that is born today: the

Zapatista Front of National Liberation

a civil and nonviolent organization, independent and democratic, Mexican and national, which struggles for democracy, liberty, and justice in Mexico. The Zapatista Front of National Liberation is born today, and to participate in it we invite the workers of the Republic, the laborers of the countryside and of the cities, the indigenous peoples, the shantytown squatters, the teachers and students, Mexican women, the young people all across the country, honest artists and intellectuals, responsible priests and nuns, all Mexican citizens who do not want power, but democracy, liberty, and justice for ourselves and our children.

We invite national civil society, those without a party, the civic and social movement, all Mexicans, to construct a new political force, a new political force that will be national, a new political force based on the EZLN.

A new political force that forms part of a broad opposition movement, the Movement for National Liberation, as a place of civic political action where other political forces of the independent opposition may flow together, a space for wills to meet, and a coordinator of actions in unity.

A political force whose members do not hold or aspire to hold elected positions or government office at any level. A political force that does not aspire to take power. A force that is not a political party.

A political force that can organize citizens' demands and proposals so that he who commands, commands in obedience to the popular will. A political force that can organize a solution to collective problems even without the intervention of political parties and the government. We do not need to ask permission to be free. The function of government is the prerogative of society, and it is society's right to exert that function.

A political force that struggles against the concentration of wealth in a few hands and against the centralization of power. A political force whose members have no other privilege than the satisfaction of their duty done.

A political force with local, state, and regional organization that grows from the base, from its social sustenance. A political force born of civic committees of dialogue.

A political force that calls itself a Front because it tries to incorporate nonpartisan organizational efforts, and has many levels of participation and many forms of struggle.

A political force that calls itself Zapatista because it is born with the indigenous hope and heart that, together with the EZLN, again descended from the Mexican mountains.

A political force that calls itself Of National Liberation because its struggle is for the freeom of all Mexicans all across the country.

A political force with a program of struggle with 13 points, those of the *First Declaration from the Lancandón Jungle* enriched through two years of insurgency. A political force that struggles against the State-party system. A political force that struggles for democracy in everything, not only in elections. A political force that struggles for a new constitutional convention and a new Constitution. A political force that struggles so that there will be justice, liberty, and democracy everywhere. A political force that does not struggle to take political power but for the democracy where those who command, command by obeying.

We call on all the men and women of Mexico, the indigenous and those who are not, on all the races who form the nation; on those who agree with struggling for housing, land, work, bread, health, education, information, culture, independence, democracy, justice, liberty, and peace; on those who understand that the State-party system is the principal obstacle to the transition to democracy in Mexico; on those who know that democracy does not mean alternation in power but government of the people, for the people, and by the people; on those who agree with making a new Magna Carta that will incorporate the principal demands of the Mexican people and the guarantees that Article 39 be fulfilled through plebiscites and referendums; on those who do not aspire or try to exercise public office or elected positions; on those who have their heart, will, and thought on the left side of their breast; on those who want to stop being spectators and are disposed to have no pay or privilege at all other than their participation in national reconstruction; on those who want to construct something new and good, [we call on them all] to form the Zapatista Front of National Liberation.

Those citizens without a party, those social and political organizations, those civic committees of dialogue, movements, and groups, all those who do not aspire to take power and who subscribe to this *Fourth Declaration from the Lacandón Jungle,* commit themselves to participate in the dialogue to resolve by common consent the organic structure, plan of action, and declaration of principles of the Zapatista Front of National Liberation.

With the organized unity of civic Zapatistas and combatant Zapatistas in the Zapatista Front of National Liberation, the struggle initiated on January 1, 1994, will enter a new stage. The EZLN does not disappear, but its most important effort will go to the political struggle. In its time and under the right conditions, the EZLN will participate directly in the formation of the Zapatista Front of National Liberation.

Today, January 1, 1996, the Zapatista Army of National Liberation signs this *Fourth Declaration from the Lacandón Jungle.* We invite the people of Mexico to subscribe to it.

Brothers:

Many words walk in the world. Many worlds are made. Many worlds make us. There are words and worlds that are lies and injustices. There are words and worlds that are truths and truthful. We make true worlds. We have been made by true words.

In the world of the mighty one only the great and their servants fit. In the world we want we all fit.

The world we want is one where many worlds fit. The Fatherland that we construct is one where all the peoples and their languages fit, where all steps may walk, where all may have laughter, where all may live the dawn.

We speak unity even when we are silent. Softly and gently like rain we speak the words that find the unity that embraces us into history, to refuse the oblivion that confronts and destroys us.

Our word, our song, and our cry is that the dead not die more deeply dead. So that they may live, we struggle. So that they may live, we sing.

Long live the word! Long live the cry, Enough! Long live the night that becomes morning! Long live our worthy journey along with all those who weep! To destroy the mighty one's clock of death we struggle. For a new time in life we struggle.

The flower of the word does not die, although our steps walk in silence. In silence the word is sown. So that it may flower shouting, it goes quiet. The word becomes a soldier in order not to die in oblivion. To live the word dies, sown forever in the womb of the world. Being born and living, we die. We will always live. Only those who surrender their history will return to oblivion.

Here we are. We do not surrender. Zapata lives, and in spite of everything the struggle continues.

From the mountains of the Mexican Southeast
Clandestine Revolutionary Indian Committee-General Command of the Zapatista Army of National Liberation
Mexico, January of 1996

CHAPTER TWENTY-SEVEN

The First Accords:
Indian Rights and Culture,
San Andrés, February 1996

O f the several great questions that the CCRI-EZLN high command put on the agenda for negotiation in March 1995, why was the first to be negotiated "the political, social, economic, and cultural rights of the indigenous in Mexico"?

Without archives and memoirs no one not privy to both sides' calculations then can confidently tell. Among various hypotheses the likeliest now is that not until after the Zapatistas' "grand national poll" (which asked nothing about Indians) did either side decide on a substantive agenda, and that both sides then decided to give "the Indian question" priority for different but overlapping reasons. The government would take this question first, because for all its symbolic importance it seemed at once the least important materially, involving only about eight percent of the country's population, and the most provincial, the easiest to confine to Chiapas. The Zapatista high command would take it first, because it seemed the most promising to then badly beleaguered and bitterly suspicious Zapatista forces and their families.

Whatever the reasons for the choice, the question of Indian rights was an issue of enormous complications. Historically, not counting ancient Indian peoples' rights in regard to each other, it dated from the Spanish Conquest. The paramount legal and moral problem of Spanish rule for three centuries, it had after Independence so exasperated Liberals and Conservatives in their rival struggles for nationhood that ultimately they could only try together to will it away, admitting no status in the nation but that of citizen, trusting repression, education, and the superiority of "the white race" gradually to expunge "barbarism" and yield "civilization" (their final solution, on which see Reading No. 4). In the same vein nothing about the indigenous or Indians appeared in the Revolutionary Constitution of 1917. Since the 1930s, by law since 1948, INI, the National Indigenous Institute, had been "at the service of . . . indigenous communities," but working deliberately into the 1980s still to de-indigenize them, "integrate" them into the "true nation." Even so every decade more Indians had figured absolutely in the national census. By 1990, speaking one or another of 70-odd indigenous languages, there were some seven million, half in four far southern and southeastern states, half in 28 other very different states. INI then was "at the service" of some 3,000 indigenous organizations, and failing by any standard. Since the 1960s national economic booms and busts, migration, urbanization, social programs, Protestant and Catholic missionary campaigns, guerrilla movements, leftist politics, and anthropological criticism inside and outside INI had complicated beyond all historical criteria the conditions and meaning of being indigenous in Mexico. Indians no longer stuck to their native language, village, or corn patch. In Mexico City, speaking good Spanish, there were quite real Indian street venders, midwives, truck drivers, welders, politicians.

Lately, despite the objections of national states everywhere, the question of aboriginal rights had resurfaced internationally. Since 1982 a UN Working Group on Indigenous Populations had been meeting every year, debating drafts of a "universal declaration on the rights of indigenous peoples." The World Council of Churches, the Latin American Bishops Conference, OXFAM, Cultural Survival, the Inter-American Foundation, the Human Rights Commission of the Organization of American States, the World Bank, the Inter-American Development Bank, and most ominously the U.S. Agency for International Development were all pressing for recognition of specifically indigenous rights in Latin America.

Anti-INI anthropologists in Mexico had taken a special interest in these developments. They studied most closely the case of Nicaragua. In the early 1980s the Sandinista government, extending its reforms and rule from Managua, had run into deep indigenous resistance on the country's Caribbean coast. Challenged not so much on their reforms as on their claim to centralized rule, and under heavy foreign pressure, friendly and hostile, to respect the resistance, the Sandinistas sponsored hot debates (including sympathetic Mexican anthropologists) on Nicaragua's "national-ethnic question," in 1984 created a National Commission for Autonomy to negotiate with the indigenous, in 1985 surveyed indigenous opinion in the contested region, in 1986 hosted an international symposium on "the State, Autonomy, and Indigenous Rights," wrote such rights and a mandate for indigenous "autonomous governments" into Nicaragua's new Constitution, and in 1987 passed an indigenous bill for these governments into national law.

Mexican anthropologists and politicians had also carefully pondered the International Labor Office's adoption in 1988–89 of a new "Convention on

Indigenous and Tribal Peoples in Independent Countries." Its old Convention No. 107 (from 1957) had been for "integration." The new Convention No. 169 held that "all peoples have the right to self-determination" (although it stipulated that "peoples" here did not necessarily mean "peoples" in international law).

President Salinas had at once committed Mexico to the new convention. And at his direction the Mexican Congress in 1990 had amended the constitution to define "the Mexican Nation" for the first time in its history as "multicultural" and mandate the first federal law "to protect and promote" indigenous "languages, cultures, practices, customs, resources, and specific forms of social organization. . . ." The PRI's traditionalists and the army had accepted the change grudgingly, for in their classic Liberal nationalism they read it as a threat to national unity and sovereignty. A political struggle had followed, Salinas's movement in the PRI trying to unite all major Indian organizations for a consensus on the new law's provisions, the PRD trying to draft its own bill, especially to establish Indian "autonomous regions"; the result, a stalemate. Dissension deepened in the controversies leading up to the Quincentennial Columbus Day in 1992. After the EZLN revolted, Salinas in line with the commitments of San Cristóbal and despite objections from the PRI's traditional bosses and the army had directed another effort to write an Indian law, which also failed.

By then the CCRI-EZLN had its own plan for constitutional reform and "multi-ethnic autonomous regions." Declared on October 12, 1994 (see Reading No. 25), these authorities had quickly taken form in eastern Chiapas, and still functioned in April 1995, when the talks at San Andrés began. Through the summer of 1995 a new and expertly advised National Multi-Indigenous Assembly delivered to the government, CONAI, the PRD, and the EZLN its detailed plan for several constitutional reforms and a law on indigenous rights, above all for "autonomous Indian regions." This plan the PRD and the EZLN promptly adopted.

On September 1, 1995, in his first Annual Report to the Nation, President Zedillo had called on Congress to enact an Indian law. INI began "a broad consultation." In turn the PRD urged Congress to act on the National Multi-Indigenous Assembly's proposal.

These in brief were the complications bearing on the government's and the CCRI-EZLN's delegates when they met in San Andrés on September 5 and agreed on an agenda the first item of which was "Indigenous Rights and Culture." Under so heavy and thorny a charge both teams would need help, not only in contending with each other, but also for their rival ulterior purposes of gaining public sympathy and respect. They therefore agreed too that each team could bring technical advisers to the ensuing talks.

When the teams opened their first substantive "dialogue" in San Andrés on

October 1, they both had advisers. The government's were mainly INI's in-house critics, who knew the history and law of "indigenous rights and cultures" nationally and internationally, opposed "integration," and championed Indian communities in the preservation and promotion of their "languages, practices, customs . . ." and in their struggles for economic development. The CCRI-EZLN's advisers were a different sort. They numbered over 100. Their chief was a sophisticated, scholarly, shrewd 59-year-old Jesuit who for the last 31 years had lived and worked with the Tarahumara people in the mountains of Chihuahua. He came with some of Mexico's most distinguished social scientists. And he brought experts who knew the comparative history and law of nationality, ethnicity, and autonomy backward and forward, could identify not only "ethnocide," but "ethnopaghy," "ethnopopulism," and "ethnicism" as well, and stood absolutely for "self-determination," the correct form of which in Mexico, they held, was autonomy. As the "dialogue" proceeded, the government's advisers tended to agree with the Zapatistas'. By the time "dialogue" ended on October 22, the government delegates were talking of autonomy as "a solution."

When the second phase of the talks, formally "negotiation," began in San Andrés on November 13, the government team had almost no advisers. It formally accepted autonomy as "the indigenous peoples' contribution to the necessary transition to democracy," then insisted on classic Liberal stumpers: national sovereignty, equality, civil rights . . . The Zapatista team had brought its full company of advisers, and the experts among them, scoffing at the government delegates for their ignorance of ethnic studies, gave them lectures and required reading for the next session. By December 13 both teams had drafts for coherent debate.

They agreed then to suspend talks for the Zapatista high command to make sure independent Indian organizations around the country would approve its positions. There followed the Fourth Declaration, on January 1, 1996, for the FZLN, and a National Indigenous Forum in San Cristóbal, January 3–8, where eventually some 350 delegates from 27 indigenous peoples in 17 states ratified the CCRI-EZLN's stands.

"Negotiation" resumed in San Andrés on January 10. Under pressure from Zedillo, who hoped (in vain) to make a state visit to Europe soon without having to face nasty demonstrations there, the government's team now pushed to bring the talks quickly to a praiseworthy end. For traditional nationalists, it vehemently defended national sovereignty (which the Zapatistas had not questioned) and saved the federal Constitution from any mention of autonomy (which the Zapatistas most wanted). It also contrived to de-link Indian rights and culture from such questions as agrarian reform, which would have to wait for later. But it conceded many other positions, for example, constitutional "rights of jurisdiction" and federal legislation to recognize Indian communities as "entities of public law." On the other side, under contradictory pressures from the PRD, independent Indian organizations, and its own bases, the Zapatista high command could not find public support for its team to win more. On January 18 "negotiation" ended in several tentative "accords."

The government's team reported its success to its superiors. The Zapatistas' advisers argued among themselves. Without clear Zapatista victories on autonomy, rights to land, etc., were the accords acceptable unconditionally? The CCRI consulted its local committees. It received approval of the accords as "minimal," but also a vote of 96 percent protesting the failure to solve other demands and ordering the EZLN to continue (by means unspecified) to struggle for them.

On February 13 the delegates met again in San Andrés. On February 16 they finally signed the accords, making them "commitments." The Zapatista team attached an addendum to detail the missing points for which the CCRI-EZLN would continue to struggle.

So complicated in their background and negotiation, the Accords of San Andrés were of neverthless obvious importance as the government's and the CCRI-EZLN's first formal compact. The title of the agreement is itself suggestive: San Andrés is just San Andrés, neither Larráinzar nor Sakamch'én de los Pobres. But it remains impossible to tell what was honest and mutually understood agreement, what was honestly agreed but actually misunderstood and still in dispute, what was deliberately phrased by one or another side to feign agreement, or what mattered most to either side for publicly avowed or ulterior purposes.

The excerpts below are the substantive parts. Two comments may be pertinent. First, whoever proposed it, whoever consented to it, whatever its purpose, whatever its consequences, the shift in discourse from "self-determination" to "free determination" was ingenious (for good or ill). It allowed claims and commitments to Indian rights without regard to sovereignty. Second, Mexico being constitutionally a federal republic (unlike Nicaragua, a unitary republic), whichever side framed the agreement as "a new federalism" undermined the Zapatista side. Federalism allowed federal support for autonomous Indian communities and associations among them, but explicit recognition of autonomy only in state constitutions (e.g., Chiapas's), for state legislatures to determine its extent, that is, its limits.

In the wake of the massacre at Acteal in December 1997, badly needing some good press, President Zedillo on March 15, 1998, sent a diluted version of the agreement to Congress as a bill on "Indigenous Rights and Culture." Nothing on the question has yet become law (August 22, 1998).

ACUERDOS DE SAN ANDRÉS*

Joint Announcement That the Federal Government and the EZLN Will Send to the Courts of National Debate and Decision . . .

III. COMMITMENTS BY THE FEDERAL GOVERNMENT TO INDIGENOUS PEOPLES . . .

1. To recognize indigenous peoples in the federal Constitution. The government must promote the recognition, as a constitutional guarantee, of the right to free determination of the indigenous peoples that have descended from populations that inhabited the country at the time of the conquest or colonization and establishment of the present borders and that, whatever their juridical situation may be, conserve their own social, economic, cultural, and political institutions, or part of them. Consciousness of their indigenous identity must be considered a fundamental criterion to determine the groups to which the dispositions on indigenous peoples apply. (Definition of "indigenous peoples" according to Convention 169 of the International Labor Organization, Article 1, paragraphs h and e, accepted by the Mexican government.) The right to free determination will be exercised in a constitutional framework of autonomy, assuring national unity. Indigenous peoples will consequently be able to decide their own form of internal government and their own ways of organizing themselves, politically, socially, economically, and culturally. The constitutional framework of autonomy will permit the effective achievement of social, economic, cultural, and political rights with respect to their identity.

2. To broaden political participation and representation. The government must press for juridical and legislative changes that broaden the local and national participation and representation of indigenous peoples, respecting their diverse situations and traditions and strengthening a new federalism in the Mexican republic. The claim that indigenous voices and demands be heard and heeded must carry over to the recognition of indignous peoples' political, economic, social, and cultural rights, within the framework of the Mexican nation, and to a decisive reform of the government on the matter of institutional practices. The federal government will promote the constitutional and legal reforms that correspond to the accords and consensus achieved.

3. To guarantee full access to justice. The government must guarantee [indigenous] peoples' full access to Mexican courts, with recognition and respect for cultural specificities and their internal normative systems, guaranteeing

---

*February 16, 1996, pp. 11–19.

full respect for human rights. It will promote a reform so that Mexican positive law recognizes the authorities, norms, and procedures for resolving conflicts internal to indigenous peoples and communities, in order to apply justice on the basis of their internal normative systems and so that by simple procedures their judgments and decisions are validated by the government's juridical authorities.

4. To promote the cultural manifestation of indigenous peoples. The government must press for national and local cultural policies of recognition and amplification of the spaces of indigenous peoples for the production, recreation, and diffusion of their cultures; the promotion and coordination of activities and institutions dedicated to the development of indigenous cultures, with the active participation of indigenous people; and the incorporation of the knowledge of diverse cultural practices into the plans and programs of study of public and private educational institutions. The knowledge of indigenous cultures is an enrichment of the nation and a necessary step to eliminate lack of understanding and discrimination against the indigenous.

5. To assure education and training. The government must assure the indigenous an education that respects and uses their knowledge, traditions, and forms of organization. With processes of integral education in the communities that broaden their access to culture, science, and technology; professional education that improves their prospects for development; training and technical assistance that improve productive processes and the quality of their goods; and training for organization that raises the negotiatory and managerial capacity of the communities. The government must respect the educational work of the indigenous peoples within their own cultural space. The education that the government gives must be intercultural. It will press for the integration of regional educational networks that offer communities the possibility of acceding to different levels of education.

6. To guarantee the satisfaction of basic necessities. The government must guarantee indigenous peoples conditions that allow them food, health, and housing in a satisfactory form and at least an acceptable standard of living. Social policy will press for prioritized programs so that the levels of health care and nutrition among the indigenous peoples' infant population improve, and will support the activity and training of indigenous women.

7. To press for production and employment. The government must build up the indigenous peoples' economic base with specific strategies of development, agreed on with them, that use their human potentialities in industrial and agro-industrial activities that cover their necessities and produce surpluses for markets; that help generate employment through productive processes that increase the added value of their resources; and that improve the endowment of basic services in the communities and their regional environs. Programs of rural development for the indigenous communities will be sus-

tained in planning processes in which the role of their representatives will be central from the design of the program to its execution.

8. To protect indigenous migrants. The government will press for specific social policies to protect indigenous migrants, within the country and beyond its borders, with inter-institutional action in support of jobs and education for women and health and education for children and young people, which in rural regions will be coordinated in the zones of supply and of demand for agricultural day laborers.

IV. PRINCIPLES OF THE NEW RELATION . . .

1. Pluralism. Mutual treatment among the peoples and cultures that form Mexican society is to be based on respect for their differences, on the premise of their fundamental equality. As a consequence, it is to be the policy of the government to conduct itself accordingly and to promote in society a pluralist orientation, which actively combats every form of discrimination and corrects economic and social inequalities. Also it will be necessary to take measures toward the formation of a juridical order nourished by plurality, which reflects intercultural dialogue, with norms common for all Mexicans and respect for the internal normative systems of indigenous peoples. The recognition and promotion of the pluricultural nature of the nation means that, with the purpose of strengthening the culture of diversity and tolerance in a framework of national unity, the action of the government and its institutions must be realized without making distinctions between indigenous and non-indigenous or before any collective socio-cultural option. The development of the nation must be based on plurality, understood as peacefully, productively, respectfully, and equitably living together in diversity.

2. Sustainability. It is indispensable and urgent to assure the survival of nature and culture in the territories occupied and used in any way by indigenous peoples, as Article 13.2 of the ILO's [the International Labor Organization's] Convention 169 defines them. Respecting the cultural diversity of indigenous peoples, governmental action at all levels must consider the criteria of sustainability. The traditional modalities that indigenous peoples and communities put into practice in using natural resources form part of their strategies of cultural survival and their living standard. Recognition will be promoted, in legislation, of the right of indigenous peoples and communities to receive indemnization when the exploitation of natural resources by the government causes damage in their habitat that does harm to their cultural reproduction. For cases in which the damage has already been done, and the [indigenous] peoples demonstrate that the compensation given does not permit their cultural reproduction, mechanisms of review will be established to permit the government and those affected to analyze jointly concrete cases. In

both cases, compensatory mechanisms will seek to assure the sustainable development of indigenous peoples and communities . . .

3. Integrality. The government must urge integral and concurrent action by its institutions and lower levels that bear on the life of indigenous peoples, avoiding partial practices that fracture public policies. It must likewise propitiate the honest and transparent management of public resources destined for the development of indigenous peoples, by greater indigenous participation in decision making and in social control of public expenses.

4. Participation. The government must favor institutional action in support of participation by indigenous peoples and communities, and respect their forms of internal organization, in order to attain the purpose of fortifying their capacity to be decisive actors in their own development . . . And it must assure adequate coreponsibility of the government and indigenous peoples in the conception, planning, execution, and evaluation of actions that affect the indigenous. Because policies in indigenous areas must not only be conceived with the [indigenous] peoples themselves, but implemented with them, the present institutions for indigenous affairs and social development that operate in these areas must be transformed so that the indigenous peoples themselves conceive projects and operate jointly and in concert with the government.

5. Free Determination. The government will respect the exercise of indigenous peoples' free determination in each of the areas and levels in which they use and practice their differentiated autonomy, without impairment of national sovereignty and within the new normative framework for indigenous peoples. This implies respect for their identities, cultures, and forms of social organization. The government will also respect the capacity of indigenous peoples and communities to determine their own development. And so long as the national interest and the public interest are respected, none of the different levels of government will unilaterally intervene in the affairs and decisions of indigenous peoples and communities, in their organizations and forms of representation, or in their prevailing strategies of using natural resources.

V. NEW JURIDICAL FRAMEWORK

. . . The federal government commits itself to promote the following actions:

1. Recognition in the federal Constitution of indigenous demands that must remain consecrated as legitimate rights.

a) Political rights. To strengthen their political representation and participation in state legislatures and government, with respect for their traditions and to guarantee that their own forms of internal government continue to exist.

b) Rights of jurisdiction. So that their own procedures for designating their authorities are accepted, as well as their normative systems for the resolution of internal conflicts, with respect for human rights.

c) Social rights. So as to guarantee their forms of social organization, the satisfaction of their fundamental human needs, and their internal institutions.

d) Economic rights. In order to develop their plans and alternatives for the organization of work and for the improvement of efficiency in production.

e) Cultural rights. In order to develop their creativity and cultural diversity and the permanence of their identities.

2. Recognition in national legislation of [indigenous] communities as entities of public law, the right to free association in municipalities with indigenous majorities, as well as the right of various municipalities to associate [among themselves] in order to coordinate their action as indigenous peoples. The competent authorities will carry out the orderly and gradual transfer of resources, so that they [the indigenous] themselves may administer the public funds assigned to them, and so as to strengthen [them] in their different areas and levels. It will be for state legislatures to determine in each case the functions and faculties that can be transferred to them.

3. Recognition that in state legislation there must be established the characteristics of free determination and autonomy that better express the diverse and legitimate situations and aspirations of native peoples . . .

4. Several articles of the federal Constitution must be amended. The federal government promises to promote the following amendments.

a) Article 4. So that the demands indicated above (points 1 and 2) are consecrated as legitimate rights.

b) Article 115. So that the federal pact is strengthened and the participation of indigenous communities is guaranteed in the integration of town councils and municipalities of indigenous majority. . . .

c) Other articles derived as a consequence of the above amendments, and to state expressly in the Magna Carta the content of the government's new relationship with native peoples.

5. In the corresponding regulatory laws and juridical instruments of federal character dispositions must be assured to make them compatible with the constitutional amendments on new indigenous rights. In this respect, the federal government promises, on the basis of the constitutional amendments, to press for federal legislation to provide immediately juridical mechanisms and procedures so that

a) revision and modification of various federal laws may begin;

b) the states may enact legislation.

6. In state legislation relative to the characteristics of free determination and indigenous autonomy, the federal government recognizes that the following elements must be taken into acount:

a) Where diverse indigenous peoples coexist, with different cultures and geographic situations, with different types of settlement and political organization, it will not do to adopt a uniform criterion on the characteristics of indigenous autonomy to be legislated.

b) Concrete modalities of autonomy must be defined with the indigenous themselves.

c) To determine in a flexible way the concrete modalities of free determination and autonomy in which each indigenous people will find best reflected its situation and its aspirations, diverse criteria will have to be considered, such as, among others: the permanence of its internal normative systems and community institutions; the degrees of its intercommunity, intermunicipal, and interstate relations; the presence of the indigenous and the nonindigenous and the relations between them; the pattern of population settlements and geographic situation; and the degrees of indigenous participation in the courts of political representation and levels of government.

The federal government promises, in a framework of full respect for republican principles, to press state governments and legislatures to consider these elements among others as criteria for the legislation that will construct the characteristics of free determination and indigenous autonomy.

CONCLUSION

1. The conflict that began January 1, 1994, in Chiapas produced in Mexican society the feeling that government and society needed a new relationship with the indigenous peoples of the country.

2. The federal government assumes the commitment to build, with the different sectors of society and in a new federalism, a new social pact that reforms at the roots the existing social, political, economic, and cultural relations with indigenous peoples. The pact must eradicate the forms that in common daily practice and in public life generate and reproduce subordination, inequality, and discrimination, and must make effective the rights and guarantees to which indigenous peoples are entitled: the right to their cultural difference; the right to their habitat; the use and enjoyment of a territory, in conformity with Article 13.2 of ILO Convention 169; the right to community self-management in politics; the right to the development of their culture; the right to their traditional systems of production; the right to the management and execution of their own development projects.

3. The new relation between the government and indigenous peoples is based on respect for differences, recognition of indigenous identities as intrinsic components of our nationality, and the acceptance of their particularities as basic consubstantial elements in our juridical order, based on multiculturality.

The new relation between indigenous peoples and the government must guarantee inclusion, permanent dialogue, and consensus for development in all its aspects. Neither unilaterality nor underestimation of indigenous capacities to build their future will define the government's policies. Quite the contrary, it will be the indigenous who, within the constitutional framework and in full exercise of their rights, will decide the means and forms in which they are to conduct their own processes of transformation . . .

CHAPTER TWENTY-EIGHT

Marcos's Reflections: Just Another Organization or Something Truly New? *La Realidad*, August, 1996

On March 10, 1996, again in San Andrés, the government's and the CCRI-EZLN's teams began their "dialogue" on "Democracy and Justice in Mexico." On these questions, the background of which would take several books to describe, no one but a child could have expected agreement. The talks now served only ulterior purposes. The government wanted them to continue as a reason to give hyper-patriots for not going to war again (yet), as a reassurance to the public of its peaceful intentions, and as a forum in which to discredit the EZLN and CONAI (in particular Bishop Ruiz), all the while working otherwise to reduce local, national, and international support for the Zapatistas so that at some point it could plausibly claim or deniably provoke EZLN violation of the ceasefire—and then smash the rebels and send Marcos to his reward. For its part the CCRI-EZLN high command wanted the talks as a reason for the government not to launch another offensive, as a reassurance to national and international "civil society" of its own commitment to "nonviolence," and as a forum in which to discredit "the State-party system" and the PRD, all the while working otherwise to promote the newborn Zapatista Front of National Liberation, the FZLN—which when the government fell would lead the making of the "new Mexico."

Consequently on March 19 in Mexico City Zedillo signed an "agrarian settlement" with 69 of some 250 Chiapan peasant organizations whose members were illegally squatting on more than 200,000 acres of private property. The government would buy the land in dispute and sell it on the cheap to the signatory organizations' members; "to reestablish the rule of law," it would evict all others. In word or in effect most of the signatory organizations had already or then declared themselves to be PRIista, anti-Zapatista. The biggest of them, the CIOAC, remained, however, as independent as ever. The land in dispute was mostly in the state's northern Indian townships, once CIOAC turf, since 1994 strongly Zapatista. On March 20 the government's and the CCRI-EZLN's delegates met again in San Andrés for "dialogue" on democracy and justice. The government's team brought four advisers. The Zapatista team brought 50, including "intellectuals, artists, and writers." The very next day, on six occupied properties, one for which the CIOAC had signed, the others held by squatters whose organizations had refused to sign, state police began violent evictions. In two days of conflict five peasants and three policemen were killed, some 20 peasants wounded, more than 100 arrested. CONAI protested, and suspended the "dialogue."

For its purposes the CCRI-EZLN high command staged another media event. On April 3 it inaugurated in La Realidad, a tiny community far down in the canyons, a Continental Encounter for Humanity and against Neo-Liberalism. The invitees included more than 250 famous U.S. and Latin American human rights and environmental activists, leftish politicians, artists, poets, intellectuals, union leaders, Indian leaders, and movie people, among them (from the United States) Noam Chomsky, Francis Ford Coppola, Oliver Stone, Robert Redford, Kevin Costner, Jane Fonda, and Jodie Foster. Some came, and so therefore did foreign media. For several days hosts, delegates, and guests discussed humanity and neoliberalism, particularly how to stage an intercontinental encounter on the same concerns later in the summer. The event received newly controversial treatments from the foreign media, some as if from war correspondents actually on the front line of humanity's really reviving resistance to inhumanity, others as if from critics at a ridiculous performance of a show about to close. However, as the Zapatistas had hoped, the stars and the media there usefully provided another run of foreign coverage, both publicity and insurance.

On April 9 "dialogue" on democracy and justice in Mexico resumed in San Andrés. As it proceeded, the CCRI-EZLN hosted another National Indigenous Forum at one of its new "Aguascalientes." The state government ordered more evictions in the northern Indian townships and and backed PRIista villagers there in violent disputes with PRDista and Zapatista neighbors. From France, bringing more foreign coverage, Danielle Mitterand appeared at San Andrés, and took a seat among the Zapatista delegates!

National politics in Mexico slipped deeper into disorder that summer. The government and opposition parties wrangled over "reform of the State," how to have fair congressional elections in 1997. Through May speculation in the capital mounted that Zedillo would resign in the next few months. To show resolve and force, his Interior and Justice Ministries and the army intensified pressure in Chiapas, and the state government increased evictions in the northern townships, protecting loyalists in now often deadly conflicts with local unregenerates. In response the CCRI-EZLN high command announced the Intercontinental Encounter on Humanity and Against Neo-Liberalism, to take place in La Realidad in late July. And it refused to send its team to San Andrés for the "dialogue" scheduled on June 5; the talks remained suspended. In a few days in mid-June, in the highly tense northern townships of Sabanilla, Simojovel, and Tila, 12 villagers of various partisan loyalties, PRI, PRD, and others, were killed in ambushes. The state government blamed local PRDistas and Zapatistas. The diocese blamed the landlords' "white guards" and the PRI's "paramilitary groups." On June 20 Marcos conferred with COCOPA, the next day with the media, proposing a dramatic change in the San Andrés talks, each branch of the federal government to send delegates to discuss democracy and justice with the CCRI-EZLN's and "civil society"'s delegates. COCOPA could not agree. On June 28, mysteriously and alarmingly, well-armed guerrillas surfaced in Guerrero and called for a national revolution. Zedillo at once sent the army to contain, catch, and crush them, and gained immediate public support right, left, and center. It seemed to many then, in hope or dread, that he would use the army likewise in Chiapas.

But in a rare stroke of some political skill the government decided to make a distinction (which it did not yet draw in public) between the new "terrorists" and Zapatista "insurgents," and relented on the latter. And the Zapatista high command extended its campaign for support in "civil society." On July 16 its team returned to San Andrés for "dialogue," urging not only (as the government's team was emphasizing) new guarantees for democratic elections, but "direct democracy . . . social and participatory democracy," in which "the people have, maintain, and exercise power" and "those who come to represent the citizenry use their authority in obedience to the citizenry." On July 19–21 the high command staged an exultant meeting in La Realidad with leaders of a new nationally militant organization of debtors (ruined in the crash of 1994–95), and announced with them an alliance against the government's economic policies. On July 23–24 it hosted another National Indigenous Forum. And on July 27 it inaugurated the Intercontinental Encounter, already in jokes "The Intergalactic," welcoming (after registration at U.S. $100 a head) eventually some 3,000 delegates and guests from Mexico and 42 other countries, among them, some daffy, some serious, celebs, old hippies, flakes, old ex-guerrillas, fastidiously coiffured punks, movement people, anarchists, socialists, communists, and scholars, plus (at only $15 a head) some 350 foreign-media people. This was a jubilee for the daffy. It was the chance of a lifetime for the serious, to meet each other in tropical fog, rain, mud, and swarms of bugs, and wonder together, sometimes seriously, how to organize against capitalism's newest, boldest, and most artfully denied rampage. It was a five-ring surrealist circus for the media, which lavished witty and ironic pity on rebels reduced to such—the French, of course, had the word for it—

mediatisation. But many of all kinds there, daffy and serious, knew quite well what they were mainly doing, which was simply, as some *mediatistes* reported, raising an international human shield against the government to protect the Zapatistas for yet another while. In closing on August 3 Marcos joked that the next encounter really would be "intergalactic . . . We're going to invite the Martians!"

"Negotiation" on democracy and justice began in San Andrés on August 6. It yielded only more displays of theoretical interest, and recessed on August 12, to resume on September 4.

Zedillo by mid-August needed the talks to reach some accord soon, to meld it into the "reform of the State" that he hoped to accomplish in the next session of Congress, opening in September. But the Zapatista high command had good reasons to slow the talks down. Considering the government's preoccupation with the new revolutionaries in Guerrero, the success of the Intercontinental Encounter, the predictable dissension in congress over "reform of the State," and the prospect of congressional elections in mid-1997, which, if the PRI won or lost, would agitate "civil society," the sub-comandante and his fellows would do best to play for all the time and media they could get for the FZLN.

This was the multiply reflective context in which one of the serious scholars who had attended the Intercontinental Encounter interviewed Marcos at length in late August. That the CCRI-EZLN high command agreed to the interview, about the Zapatista movement in any dimension, indicates how seriously it wanted an engaging image in Europe, especially in France. For months it had had trouble with *Le Monde*'s correspondent in Mexico, who had reported its defects and whom someone speaking for the EZLN (fingers pointed in various directions) had barred from the "encounter" at La Realidad. It had welcomed Che Guevara's old camp follower become French socialist sage, Régis Debray, for a two-day visit with Marcos and a ruminating essay on the movement in *Le Monde*. But the interviewer it now accepted was a real risk, an objective, sophisticated, mature, deeply learned, and acutely inquisitive French historical sociologist, who knew more than any other European scholar about popular struggles in violence in modern Spanish America.

Yvon Le Bot, member of the Centre d'Analyse et d'Intervention Sociologique de l'École des Hautes Études en Sciences Sociales, director of Latin American research at the Centre National de la Recherche Scientifique, began his studies of Latin America in the field in 1968. Since 1972 he had concentrated on the Guatemalan highlands, which he knew intimately. Since 1974 he had published numerous articles and six books on social, religious, ethnic, and political movements and violence in various Latin American countries. He had often served on UN and Amnesty International missions there. His major scholarly works, drawn from his doctoral dissertation under Alain

Touraine's direction at the École des Hautes Études, were *La guerre en terre maya: Communauté, violence et modernité au Guatemala, 1970–1992* (Paris, 1992) and *Violence de la modernité en Amérique latine: Indianité, société et pouvoir* (Paris, 1994), a comparative study of war on native ground in modern Nicaragua, Colombia, Ecuador, Peru, and Bolivia. He had not come to La Realidad to cheer virtuality, but to learn more about the truly real (and usually awful) problems he had explored all his adult life.

Interviewing Marcos and two other leading Zapatista officers, Le Bot and a colleague pushed them hard. They suffered some old evasions, but won loads of new and important memories, confessions, observations, accusations, analyses, and judgments, some consistent, others contradictory, some self-serving, others revealing, candidly and inadvertently.

Here Marcos tells about Zapatismo from late February 1994 to late August 1996. Most significant may be his worry that the movement will consolidate into only one more address on the Mexican left, and not contribute "something truly new." In an interesting passage not here, he declares his (envious?) admiration for the "impressive moral authority" of the Alianza Cívica.

LE RÊVE ZAPATISTE[*]

. . . 1994: A Chaotic Year

Y [Le Bot]: When was civilian Zapatismo born? In the course of the "talks in the cathedral"?

M [Marcos]: Maybe when they formed that absurd and marvelous "cordon of peace," which took us completely by surprise. Remember, when we'd left San Cristóbal we were going to our death; we were sure we were going to get killed somewhere along the way. Then, see, we came back to San Cristóbal and people were waiting for us, applauding us, jostling each other to see us. They'd even organized themselves to make that cordon in the cold, under the rain. People of no party or organization, who weren't obeying any orders, any line, who got no advantage from their presence there. They were hungry, taking risks, getting photographed there, they could lose their job. All that just because they believed in it.

It was our first contact with them; we didn't expect this encounter. I wouldn't call it Zapatismo yet. It's a movement barely emerging, people of all classes, from high to low, who sympathize with certain ideas of Zapatismo and who come to see, who want to meet us, get to know us.

When we decided to attend the dialogue, the discussion wasn't easy, believe me. Some thought it was a trap, that it was out of the question to accept.

---

[*]Sous-Commandant Marcos and Yvon Le Bot (Editions du Seuil: Paris, 1997), pp. 200–211.

Besides, the government sent us its star negotiator, Camacho Solís, who had succeeded in neutralizing and winning over parties like the PRD. In the Committee [the CCRI], some thought we were going to get had, that Camacho was going to roll us over. Others said we had to use this space to talk, to understand what was happening. They said that we had to go there to talk with people, that the most important thing wasn't the dialogue with the government; it was to talk with people to try to understand what was happening. Finally, we decide to take the risk. The question was knowing if the dialogue would be used by the government or by the Zapatistas. And I think that we're the ones who won.

Y: That is to say?

M: The dialogue allowed the Zapatistas to make themselves known, to enter into contact with a lot of people, especially through the media; at that point we hadn't had direct contacts. Besides, the government wasn't able to buy us or win us over. Finally, all this process of dialogue went to hell March 23, when Colosio was assassinated.

Y: That's the decisive event?

M: Yes, that shows the government is in crisis and can't negotiate. The bullet that killed Colosio killed the possibility of a peace accord with the EZLN. We can't sign any pact with someone who isn't even capable of guaranteeing his heir's life. Why would he guarantee that of his enemy? Also, it reflected a political crisis so deep that we couldn't have reached any result.

Y: It's then that you decide to wait for the elections in August?

M: To wait and prepare the resistance. . . . our problem was that we found ourselves in a completely unforeseen situation, and we didn't know what to do.

Y: There you've gotten into a very obscure question. According to Jorge Castañeda's interpretation [Castañeda is an important Mexican intellectual and political analyst], Marcos had the chance then to enter the political game; he bungled it, and since then he hasn't stopped fading. Did Zapatismo then have the chance to transform its symbolic politico-military force into a political force?

M: Maybe, but we didn't see it. We didn't see it because we were improvising, and our problem was to decide on the next step. The question was knowing what to do with those people who'd stopped the war. Were they ready to do anything, and if so, what? We had to meet them and talk. They were the same ones who sent humanitarian aid; they'd continued to help, even after the dialogue in the cathedral.

We'd never proposed to reach power; that wasn't our objective. It was for others to do that, to get to power and satisfy our demands. Eventually an option on the left or in the center like Cárdenas, or someone in the PRI who could do it, who could resolve these problems . . .

Y: Your bet on the elections in '94, was it that Cardenismo could win, or not?

M: We thought the PRI was going to win, but by a fraud so enormous that people would revolt. I'm not talking about taking up arms, but about a great protest movement. We told ourselves that we had to wait for the elections and that people would realize that the PRI, the State-party system, wasn't going to commit suicide. That was what we demanded of it, sure, that it commit suicide, but that's impossible.

So we had to wait and let the elections unroll as foreseen by the government, so that no one could say that we'd interfered with them. We had people passing us information on what was being hatched in the State apparatus, and we warned Cárdenas that the government's intention was to relegate him to third place. The objective wasn't to beat him, but to deprive him of any possibility of protest. That's what we told him on May 15 [1994]. . . . If he believed that he'd come in second and could fight for the presidency, he was fooling himself. He'd be third. That was the maneuver.

They didn't believe us. Cárdenas said it was impossible, that the PAN had no chance, that the PRI was deliberately inflating its figures. That's normal. In his place I'd have thought the same thing. He was convinced he was going to win. If not, he wouldn't have run. If you don't have confidence, it's not worth the trouble. [Earlier in the interview Marcos said that at the end of 1993, six months earlier, the PRD had no illusions about its chances of victory.]

A lot of people say the Zapatista movement got in Cárdenas's way, but I believe on the contrary it helped him, because it made him look like the chance for a peaceful transition, in contrast with the violent transition represented by us.

Y: Wasn't there a fear vote, by sectors that voted for Zedillo for fear of the destabilization of the regime?

M: That's one possible reading. I'm not so sure of it. The electoral result in '94 was so perfect that it makes you think. For example, look at the percentages: altogether, they give 50 percent to the PRI, 30 percent to the PAN, 15 percent to the PRD, and 2 percent to the PT [Partido del Trabajo]. Everywhere. For the presidential election, you have the same result in Lomas de Chapultepec or Polanco [Mexico City neighborhoods], where people live very well, as in La Lagunilla [another Mexico City neighborhood, but poor], for example, or in Chiapas, or in Guerrero, corners of the country where people are barely surviving. You find the same percentages [in the presidential vote], when they vary for congressional elections, for local elections.

That'd mean you're dealing with extraordinarily politicized people who want the PRI in the presidency but not [necessarily] for deputy or senator, or for mayor. For the presidential elections, the percentages are the same in all quarters, in all sectors, with a stupefying precision.

Apart from that, there was an obvious, proven financial inequality. Zedillo spent much more than the others. He himself recognized it. He also had much better media coverage. But I'm convinced that on top of that there was fraud. We didn't feel fear among the people, especially not fear of Zapatismo. No one ever demonstrated in support of the government when it wanted to liquidate us. On the contrary, people demonstrated to stop it from that. I'm not talking about militants, workers. I'm talking about the middle class, well-off sectors, artists, intellectuals.

Y: Maybe not Zapatismo, but didn't the assassination of Colosio make people afraid?

M: That certainly counted, but people thought if the regime was capable of that, it was capable of anything.

In any case, the elections showed several things. It's the first time the PRI doesn't have the majority. Most people voted against the PRI, even if they divided among abstention, PT, PAN, PRD, and even Zapatistas. There were not a few votes, annulled, that were for the EZLN. It's a vote against the PRI, but diluted between abstentionism and the different opposition forces.

Y: The massive protest you were expecting, however, didn't take place?

M: There we fooled ourselves yet again. Like in January '94. And the same question came up again: now what? There was no massive protest, and the National Convention, which was our bridge to the outside, enters a period of internal crisis after the electoral setback. There was nothing else to do but wait for Salinas to leave and see what the new president proposed. That's what the Committee decides. The dialogue remains at an impasse. When Ruiz Massieu [secretary–general of the PRI, a staunch ally of Salinas] is assassinated [September 28, 1994], we break the dialogue with Salinas and wait to see what Zedillo is going to do. Zedillo makes contact with us by letter and promises to resolve the problem as soon as he takes office. We tell him that for the moment we can't have dealings with him, but are disposed to engage in dialogue when he's president.

Once he's president, the first thing he does is support Robledo Rincón [elected by the PRI as governor of Chiapas in August 1994, over general opposition protest, on which see Reading No. 25.]. Fraud was impossible to prove in the case of the presidential election, but for Robledo's election . . . really, it jumped right out before your eyes. There were proofs; a tribunal of many observers met and was able to prove the fraud. Despite everything, Zedillo's first decision when he got into office was to go attend Robledo's inauguration. For us, it was clear. We had to do something to remind them we were still here. We decided then to break the army's encirclement, in December '94.

The objective was to tell Zedillo, as we'd told Salinas, "Remember, you've got guerrillas in the southeast, and you're going to be obliged to find a solution, military or political." So we do this action of breaking the siege, and the government decides then to launch an economic crisis that, as we found out later, was already brewing, to make us bear the responsibility for it. The peso went to hell, the stock market collapsed, capital flight and all the rest . . .

Y: Maybe your action really served as a detonator of the crisis, no? . . . The financial crisis, national and maybe international. The governor of the Bank of France was able to say that the international financial system is so fragile that a handful of Indians in Chiapas, in the far depths of Mexico, can dangerously disturb it.

M: Poets, a handful of poets, as the EPR [the guerrillas lately appearing in Guerrero] would say!

In any case, that means that the crisis was already brewing. I believe our action poked a hole in a boiler under pressure, and it all exploded. In a shot the misery of the Indians was all of a sudden generalized to millions of Mexicans. That changes everything. The government, facing a real source of agitation, decides to liquidate it. It chooses betrayal. You understand, this wasn't anymore a struggle of Indians that they can keep at a distance. A lot of people who found themselves in a shot in the same situation of misery were now maybe going to see us as eventual compañeros in the struggle. That's why the coup in February '95.

There Are Several Zapatismos in Zapatismo

N [another interviewer, with Le Bot, Maurice Najman]: Are you developing at that point the conception of organized civil society, new political forms?

M: Not yet. We were still thinking about Zapatismo, about the Zapatismo of the EZLN, nothing more. We hadn't yet realized that Zapatismo was beginning to change through the relation between armed Zapatismo and civilian Zapatismo. People who see the National Democratic Convention as a setback don't understand that. Why a setback? Because Cárdenas didn't win? Because the CND didn't become a political force? Really it's with the Convention that you can begin to talk of a civilian Zapatismo alongside armed Zapatismo. The EZLN even begins to modify its discourse and its initiatives to reinforce this relationship. It's then that there begins to ripen what'll become the dialogue of San Andrés, where the guerrillas invite everybody to take part. It's the beginning of what'll issue later in the Consultation, the Fourth Declaration, and later the Forums and the Encounters. After the CND, we begin to talk of a Zapatismo that no longer amounts to the EZLN.

Y: Well, then, that's the question: what is Zapatismo? Neo-Zapatismo? My hypothesis is that there are three components, a military component, which inherits everything you talked about before January 1, a component that we could call social, and a political component. I don't know if you agree?

M: In my opinion, there's a series of intersections. There's the Zapatismo of the EZLN, with the communities and the combatants. I distinguish the two because the communities establish relations with the outside through their army, the EZLN, which is a military structure. This is important. Zapatista discourse and practice are still marked by a certain military authoritarianism, a certain impatience, let's say.

Y: War economy, society at war . . .

M: Yes, but also the habit of seeing initiatives executed immediately and the exasperation when that's a little slow: we took such and such a decision, why don't they react right away, we're at war!

So there's the EZLN as such, the Indian communities. That's original Zapatismo, let's say. Then civilian Zapatismo, which appears in the dialogue of San Cristóbal, then in the National Democratic Convention, and looks for how to organize. I mean, it begins as a kind of diffuse committee of solidarity, focused on what's happening here, and that evolves into a political organization.

Y: The Zapatista Front?

M: We hope so. We'll see . . . You could say an organized civilian Zapatismo is beginning to develop. The EZLN envisions one day joining this organization, if conditions allow it to continue to evolve in this sense. Then there's the third Zapatismo, bigger, more dispersed, people who have sympathy for the EZLN and are ready to support it, but who have no intention of organizing or who already belong to other political or social organizations.

These are the three great components of Zapatismo at the national level: armed Zapatismo, civilian Zapatismo, and a social Zapatismo . . .

Beyond that, since February '95 and since the Encounters, an international Zapatismo is beginning to appear. In '94, we didn't interest the great world outside, not like now. Some time had to pass for Zapatismo to make itself known on the outside, be digested, assimilated. It's after the betrayal of '95 that people remember us. Then the movement took off and took form with the preparation of the Intercontinental Encounter . . .

You can't truly call this Zapatismo. Zapatismo is the common point, or the pretext for converging. Each one has his own logic, but recognizes himself in certain very general propositions of Zapatismo. I see no resemblance at all among the Basque, Catalán, Greek, Kurdish, Swedish, Japanese Zapatistas, except that they all come here and each has its idea of Zapatismo or of what it should be. In any case it's a phenomenon that exists, and beyond the solidarity with the Indian movement, it aims more and more to retrieve a series of universal values that can serve as well for Australians, Japanese, Greeks, Kurds, Cataláns, Chicanos, Indians from Ecuador, for example, or the Mapuche [Indians in Chile].

N: More profoundly, maybe after 15 years of crisis on the left, of decomposition, people find here a point of departure for their recomposition. It's not only a projection of dreams or wishes . . .

M: Zapatismo has maybe only helped them remember that it's worthwhile to struggle, that it's necessary. For us, it's important to be very clear on this matter, not to look to create a universal doctrine, to take the direction of a new International or that kind of thing. Especially I believe that the generality, the lack of definition of Zapatismo, is particularly important in this case, that we have to maintain it. For the communities, you have to understand that the contact with this "international Zapatismo" represents especially a protection that allows them to resist. This protection is more effective than the EZLN, the civilian organization, or national Zapatismo, because in the logic of Mexican neoliberalism, the international image is an enormous stake. There's a kind of tacit accord: people from abroad find here this point of support, this recall they need to regain their spirit, and the communities get the support that allows them to survive.

. . . There it is, crudely, that's how I see things. I believe the EZLN is going to have to define its relations with these four courts: with military Zapatismo, that is to say itself and the communities, with the organized Zapatismo of the Front, with social Zapatismo, and with international Zapatismo. The challenge is to know when to look at your finger and when to look at the star, as Old Antonio used to say. [Old Antonio figures in Marcos's stories about the struggle in Chiapas: "When you dream, you have to look at the star all up there high, but when you struggle, you have to look at the hand pointing at the star . . ."] Alain Touraine spoke of not confusing the levels, universal, international, national, Indian. That's in sociological terms what Old Antonio expressed in a poetic way. It's Zapatismo's most serious problem at this point. More than the soldiers, the rupture of the dialogue, the planes, and the tanks. That's what's going to decide its future. As it tries to define itself, Zapatismo takes the risk of becoming just another organization, or on the contrary contributing something truly new . . .

CHAPTER TWENTY-NINE

Organizing the Zapatista Front: Principles, Proposals, and Virtual Force, August 1997

Announced as "born" on January 1, 1996, the Frente Zapatista de Liberación Nacional, the FZLN, the Zapatista Front of National Liberation,
went for months without form or substance. "Civil society" had not taken
much initiative in constructing the National Democratic Convention. It had
done less to constitute the Movement for National Liberation. It did nothing
now to make "the new national political force" real. Neither did the CCRI-
EZLN high command. It had other pressing concerns, the talks at San Andrés, the evictions and violence in the north, preparations for the
Intercontinental Encounter, evidently too much to give serious attention as
well to raising the FZLN. It did not even have an agent on the job. Not until
early June 1996 did anyone appear to assume responsibility for the front.

He was Javier Elorriaga, no Marcos, but an able fellow. Son of a rich Spanish family in Mexico City, he had graduated with honors in history from the
National University in 1987, with a thesis on "Geopolitics and Revolutionary
Change in Central America," and joined the Fuerzas de Liberación Nacional
underground in Chiapas the same year. There he had not only survived training, but had also, as 2nd Lt. Vicente (then 25 years old), married EZLN Comandante Elisa (then 31). Reassigned with her in 1988 to FLN business
elsewhere, he had been promoted in September 1993 to director (succeeding
his wife) of the PFLN's Commission on Ideology and Political Education. In
the showdown then between Germán and Marcos he and Elisa had sided with
Marcos. Working, above ground, for a media production company in Mexico
City, making (among other things) soap operas, and connected to the Internet,

Elorriaga in January 1994 had managed the distribution of Marcos's first rebel communiqués to the capital's press, and shortly coproduced a fine piece of Zapatista propaganda, a video, "Voyage to the Center of the Selva." A year later he had served as Marcos's intermediary in the secret negotiations with the Interior minister to resume "dialogue" between the government and the rebels, which Zedillo destroyed in the offensive of February 9, 1995. He had not been available for any assignment for the next 16 months. Arrested in Chiapas on February 10, 1995, he had gone to the Cerro Hueco penitentiary on charges of conspiracy, rebellion, and terrorism. Despite the government's amnesty of March 11, 1995, Elorriaga had remained in prison, been judged guilty on all counts on May 2, 1996, and received a sentence of 13 years. As soon as another judge made him available, revoking his sentence and releasing him on June 6, 1996, the Zapatista high command secured his services for the FZLN.

This turn relieved the government and its partisan opposition. All but hyper-patriotic politicians looked forward then to the EZLN becoming an FZLN, if only, as "just another organization," to simplify congressional elections in 1997. The FZLN the Zapatista high command wanted, however, would do "something truly new"—comprise all Mexicans committed to a national, multiclass, multiethnic, nonpartisan, nonelectoral, nonviolent struggle for "democracy, liberty, and justice," in 1997, 2000, and beyond. Within two months, by the time of the Intercontinental Encounter, Elorriaga had organized more than 400 basic "civil committees of dialogue" around the country, articulated them through the Internet, and started CD-ROM production of their virtual presence in La Realidad. Questioned by Le Bot (Reading No. 28), Marcos spoke of this work as only a "project." Implicitly he looked forward to imbedding the EZLN, maybe still armed (if only for the symbolism), in an FZLN much bigger, more trusted, more amenable, and more influential even than the Alianza Cívica.

Without deep evidence, which would probably take years of research to find, it is impossible to explain confidently why (as of August 1998) the Frente Zapatista has barely survived. But three hypotheses seem worth adopting. One is that for the last few years the U.S. government, in particular the Defense Department, has wanted "low-intensity" warfare in Mexico. To many Americans this may appear far-fetched, but only if they ignore the history and contemporary dynamics of U.S.-Mexican relations. Since the Louisiana Purchase (1803), which first put the United States on the border of the territory that would become Mexico (1821), it has been necessary to take U.S. interests into account to understand any major Mexican crisis. And every major Mexican crisis has resulted in foreign gains in Mexican affairs, which Mexicans have then had to struggle for years to overcome. Since the Union victory in the U.S. Civil War and the Mexican victory against the French Intervention in Mexico (1863–1867), Mexican crises have always brought Americans the most gains. Since World War I and the Mexican Revolution, only Americans have gained such advantages. During the Cold War, from 1945 to 1989, the U.S. government supported a wonderfully stable Mexican government. As the Cold War ended, it supported a wonderfully reformist Mexican government. Since 1995, however, it has used Mexico's economic and political crises to gain new American advantages. The Zedillo government's weakness particularly impresses the Pentagon, which has prudently fortified its bonds with Mexico's Defense Ministry. War within the limits of "low intensity" (i.e., counter-insurgency in Chiapas, Guerrero, Oaxaca, and elsewhere, policing the Federal District, and pursuing drug traffickers throughout the country), has grossly expanded the budget and the mission of the Mexican armed forces, ever more Pentagon trained. Its continuation will make the Pentagon's partners still stronger, the better, by U.S. logic, to prevent or contain a constitutional crisis.

A second hypothesis is that on the whole Mexicans are politically more conservative than the CCRI-EZLN high command figured. It is important that in the "grand national poll" in 1995, to determine the EZLN's future, more than one million registered intense sympathy with the movement. But it remains nevertheless important that 97.6 percent of the Mexican population 18 and older did not take the trouble to register anything. This failure does not mean that Mexicans are nearly as conservative as, say, Americans. But it does suggest that even on the left wing, among partisan regulars and vicarious progressives, relatively few have been ready to act even as virtual Zapatistas. In most movements anywhere it is hard for militants to imagine how hard it is for the people they champion to organize, come to continual meetings, reach decisions without division, act as agreed, own the movement, carry it on. The CCRI-EZLN and its high command have had a very hard time reading their country's "civil society." They do not seem to have recognized that it includes many institutions and organizations actually hostile or contrary or apathetic to them, or only virtually or putatively for them, not many really for them. Ten years in formation underground and inside, stunningly defeated by the government in battle outside in January 1994, amazingly saved by public compassion in February-March 1994, successively betrayed, amnestied, glorified, and depreciated in 1995, they still trusted in 1996, in the logic of La Realidad, that Mexico's "honest men and women" would flock to their cause. If any of them by then suspected otherwise, or knew better, it was Marcos. His messages from Reality were doing only unreal harm to Mexico's enduring bourgeois hegemony. But if he knew, he did not demoralize the others.

Neither condition—the Pentagon's stake in Mexico or the Mexican public's conservatism—would have obstructed Elorriaga from developing the FZLN into a new and considerable national political force. But either would have made his work more difficult; both, much more difficult.

The third hypothesis is that precisely during the time when the Mexican government most wanted an FZLN, the Zapatista high command put it on hold. For both sides the reason was the same threat. On August 28, 1996, the revolutionaries who had surfaced in June in Guerrero, the Ejército Popular Revolucionario, the EPR, resurfaced in coordinated attacks on military posts and police stations in Guerrero, Oaxaca, Puebla, and Mexico state, killing 13, wounding 22, and staged five roadblocks on main highways in Chiapas, offering support to the EZLN if it quit negotiating with the government. The government needed more legitimacy on the left, pronto, including an avowedly civilian EZLN, viz., an FZLN, for the immediate crisis and for credible elections in 1997. On August 29 the CCRI-EZLN high command suspended the talks in San Andrés. But Marcos at once publicly told the EPR that its action in Chiapas had been at best "useless and stupid," at worst "a provocation," that the EZLN did not need or want its help, but would continue its distinctive struggle, not for "power," but for "democracy, liberty, and justice." On September 1, in his Second Annual Report to the Nation, Zedillo intimated his offer to the EZLN: if it became an FZLN, a law for Indians would follow. The Zapatista high command would not play the "good guerrilla" so soon, so cheap. Not until mid-October, after threatening a march to Mexico City for "national dialogue" on anti-Columbus Day (to show it was no patsy), did it make the government an offer: if first a law on Indigenous Rights and Culture, then peace at San Andrés and the FZLN. Secretly the Interior Ministry, the Zapatista high command, and advisers negotiated through CO-COPA to work the San Andrés accords into law. In November Elorriaga and his wife went to Paris and Strasbourg to advertise the FZLN. At last on November 29 the negotiators had a final draft. The next day Marcos approved it. COCOPA and the Zapatistas expected peace by Christmas, with the FZLN in January starting to define issues for the elections in July.

By then, however, the government had much worse troubles. Among the minor of these was that the EPR (trailed by the Defense Ministry) had extended its raids into other states and the Federal District, killing 17 more along the way, and other revolutionary groups had surfaced. The main trouble came from the PRI. In November its large majority in Congress had ruined the government's electoral reform, flagrantly favoring the PRI over other parties and humiliating the president. If the PRI's rebellion continued, the elections in 1997 would be a national disgrace, with dreadful consequences for the country. To save the elections, Zedillo had to regain leverage in the PRI that he had earlier let go. For this recovery he had to placate the party's traditional bosses. Whether or not he had ever seriously pondered an Indian law acceptable to Zapatistas, he could not afford one now, much less its result—an FZLN in the streets before the elections. In December he proposed revision of the COCOPA agreement. The CCRI-EZLN had to refuse.

From January 1997 into the summer, the local violence in Chiapas's northern Indian townships thickened into civil war, and army patrols went deeper into the canyons. COCOPA kept trying to restart negotiations. But without the already negotiated Indian law the Zapatista high command would not budge. In June, to rally foreign support again, it sent EZLN delegates to Spain to plan a Second Intercontinental Encounter for Humanity and Against Neo-Liberalism in July.

The elections happened on July 6. Praised as "the first fully democratic elections in Mexican history," they were a great and vital victory for Zedillo. For the first time in its history the PRI lost its majority in the Chamber of Deputies (although it still held most seats, 239 of 500). Cárdenas and the PRD were elected to govern the Federal District, with high hopes for the presidency in 2000. (In Chiapas, in protest against the PRI, Zapatistas abstained, and prevented others from voting wherever they could.)

At this historic juncture, as the public indulged a tremendous surge of faith in elections, it correspondingly lost interest in Zapatistas, army or front. All parties advised the CCRI-EZLN to quit its now only virtual rebellion and finally found the FZLN (which, they reckoned, would no longer amount to much and none of them would need anyway). Delegates to the Intercontinental in Spain, July 25–August 2, brought back similar advice. On August 8 Marcos warned the PRD not to back Zedillo's presumed plan to use the new Congress "to annihilate us," but accepted the elections as opening "a space that can be one of democracy, liberty, and justice," and announced that "1,100 Zapatista men, women, and children—100 for each of the indigenous communities that support the EZLN"—would soon march to Mexico City to attend the founding congress of the FZLN on September 13–16 (Mexico's Independence Day).

Elorriaga reminded the media why the country still needed the FZLN. Political parties "are very distanced from the people, and their only objective is electoral." Separately from the EZLN, which would remain armed, the FZLN would struggle nonviolently and beyond elections, "with ideas, organization, and mobilizations," to realize Zapatista goals. Formal construction of the FZLN was going to be "a titanic job, because we have something of everything, anarchists, communists, Christians, socialists, democrats, centrists, mariachis, peasants, miners, schoolteachers, students, punks, homosexuals, lesbians, I mean everything." But once the front existed, it would spare "civil society . . . having to take up arms and go off to the mountains." Even if it were just a bit of Mexico's "much broader Zapatismo," it would help make for "*un pueblo consciente*, a people conscious and conscientious, which will not let parties think that the vote they win gives them a blank check to do to the people whatever they want."

On September 8 the EZLN marchers gathered in San Cristóbal, now 1,111

Indian men, women, and children representing 111 communities. The next day they left, not on a march, but in a caravan of 38 buses. Over the following two days along the way some 3,000 supporters and delegates from Oaxaca, Michoacán, Puebla, Guerrero, and Morelos (the original Zapatista country) joined them. Increased to 158 buses, trucks, vans, and cars, the caravan stopped on September 12 (a Friday) in vastly jammed traffic on the southern edge of the Federal District, for the riders and their hosts in the capital, the Second National Indian Congress and the FZLN committees there, to march leading thousands of others down the avenues (which the original Zapatista army had taken to occupy the old city in November 1914) to the megalopolis's ancient central plaza, where a more or less great crowd welcomed them, maybe (according to Elorriaga's staff) 80,000, maybe (according to the police) 25,000. On September 13 Marcos clarified that the EZLN would not yet join the FZLN. On September 15, with Elorriaga as master of ceremonies, following the FZLN National Organizing Committee's exposition of motives, declaration of principles, and proposal for struggle (included here), some 2,000 FZLN delegates formally founded the Zapatista Front of National Liberation.

This was much too little, much too late, to be anything but a merely virtual force in national politics. It could do nothing real even about local conflicts, (e.g., the feuds then rending Indian communities in northern Chiapas). By mid-1998, thanks primarily to the devotion of Zapatista advisers, it survived at best as a kind of Zapatista think tank, a network of committees of electronic correspondence with some influence in Mexico's southern states on local social legislation and policy.

CUADERNILLO NÚM. I: DOCUMENTOS DE DISCUSIÓN PARA EL CONGRESO DE FUNDACIÓN DEL FRENTE ZAPATISTA DE LIBERACIÓN NACIONAL*

. . . Exposition of Motives and Declaration of Principles

On the soil and under the skies that border the Rio Grande in the north and the Suchiate in the southeast, between two oceans, in the city and in the countryside, recovering the past in order to fight in the present for a better future, speaking with those to whom no one speaks, listening to those to whom no one listens, raising rebellion as a banner, living dignity as a life project, and

---

*Comisión Nacional Organizadora del FZLN, August 1997, pp. 4–9.

CONSIDERING . . .

First. That in Mexico there are two projects for the Nation, which contend with each other to define the future of the country: One, that of Power, is the project of immobility. It implies the destruction of the Mexican Nation, denies our history and roots, sells our sovereignty, makes treason and crime the bases of modern politics, subterfuge and mendacity the stairway to political success, imposes an economic program that only makes profits in the destabilization and insecurity of all citizens, and uses repression and intolerance as the government's arguments.

The other project, that of Mexican men and women of the people, with or without an organization, is the project of movement. It implies the reconstruction of the Mexican Nation in the only form possible, that is, from the bottom up; it recovers the history and roots of our people, defends our sovereignty, struggles for a transition to democracy that does not simulate change but makes itself the country's reconstruction project, struggles for a country that has the truth and for government in obedience to the people as the norm of political work, struggles for democracy, liberty, and justice to be the national patrimony, struggles for dialogue, tolerance, and inclusion to build a new form of doing politics.

Second. That the political life of our country goes beyond what the Mexican State, excluding the immense majority of the people, imposes; and that the struggle to maintain Power or to take it has defined a form of doing politics that leaves great hollows in national political life.

Third. That the Zapatista uprising of 1994 not only revealed the crisis within the State-party system and the oblivion to which it was trying to condemn Mexican Indians, but also showed the need and the possibility of a new form of doing politics, without aspiring to take Power and without vanguardist positions, but recognizing and establishing bridges with an emerging civil and nonviolent movement, nonpartisan and heterogeneous, civil society.

Fourth. That civil society, in organized or spontaneous ways, has been filling the great hollows that political parties leave, and in recent years and in waves ever more important has won the most significant gains in modern Mexico, has become, in the company of some political forces, the principal driving force in the transition to democracy and the essential constructive force of a new society, plural, tolerant, inclusive, democratic, just, and free, which is possible today only in a new Fatherland.

Fifth. That the real transition to democracy is the only hope that all citizens, men and women, will recover their right to make use of Article 39 of our Magna Carta, which specifically says: "Sovereignty resides essentially and originally in the people. All public power flows from the people, and is instituted for the people's benefit. The people have at all times the unalienable right to alter or modify the form of their government"; and that this right is the basis for the construction of a new country.

Sixth. That the construction of the project for a New Fatherland is a process whose leadership does not belong to a hegemonic force or to an individual, but to a broad national movement, popular and democratic. And . . .

Seventh. That a political force is necessary that will not struggle to take Power or by the old methods of doing politics, but will struggle to create, aggregate, promote, and empower civic and popular movements, without trying to absorb them, lead them, or use them; a political force whose struggle is not electoral, but that recognizes that the electoral terrain has become a space of valid and necessary civic action, and that the struggle to broaden and democratize it is indispensable; a political force that adds its struggle to the struggle of other forces to achieve real democratic transformation; a political force that by its practice contributes to the construction of a new form of doing politics; a political force that struggles so that political work will be a civic space, that does not use citizens but is a vehicle and pretext for social and political movement; a political force that does not gaze upward along its way and in its aspirations, but directs itself to those by its side, in its words, attention, and efforts; a political force that always raises the banner of rebel dignity high wherever it finds itself.

THEREFORE . . .

It is necessary to think about new forms of relation between political organization and the whole of society, new forms of relation where ethics and politics are not enemies.

It is necessary that movement and political organization not only not be set against each other, but that one be at the service of the other.

What is necessary is dialogue with and between the spaces of participation and the movements, the capacity to convoke one and the other, to promote actions together, to add to their initiatives, and to join them.

We need a space of participation that, facing the movements and along with them, can organize demands for popular rights and their satisfaction, can organize resistance and the development of social forms of self-management, can recognize the appearance of new social actors and accompany their mobilizations, can organize and promote civic vigilance over the authorities, and can create new spaces of mobilization.

It is necessary that the space of political participation have interior movement, in order not to freeze ideas as unmovable truths, but so that thought be in continual confrontation with reality, and the space of participation generate a thinking critical toward Power and toward itself.

It is necessary that the space of participation have a place for the voice of all who find themselves there.

It is necessary that the space of participation make collective construction its principal interest.

For all this, to try to fill an empty space, not to compete with others, to try to bring something new, not to fight over a monopoly of the old way, to try to add something, not to subtract, to try to build, not to destroy, to try to convince, not to conquer, to try to give company, not to lead, to try to include, not to exclude, as a group of Mexican men and women answering the convocation made by the EZLN in its Fourth Declaration from the Lacandón Jungle, we propose to build the Zapatista Front of National Liberation, according to the following . . .

DECLARATION OF PRINCIPLES

The Zapatista Front of National Liberation adopts the following principles that define its social and political identity:

1. The Zapatista Front of National Liberation is a Mexican political organization, present throughout the entire country, that uses civil and nonviolent forms of struggle to realize in our country a free, just, democratic, and participatory society, open to all currents of thought, plural in its cultural and ethnic composition, inclusive in regard to every type of minority, and just in its economic and social order. For this goal the FZLN is based on the ethnic, cultural, and historical roots that form the Mexican nation, to strengthen our identity as peoples and to enrich our multi-cultural character, and picks up the tradition of struggle that our people have developed over more than 500 years, to liberate themselves from the different types of domination that they have suffered.

2. The Zapatista Front of National Liberation declares itself independent ideologically, politically, and economically from political parties, churches, the Mexican State, and any other State in the world.

3. The Zapatista Front of National Liberation, with the inclusive character it holds high, because it knows that its ojective cannot be the work of a single force, but a collective labor, recognizes that it is necessary to promote and take part in a broad national movement where other independent opposition political forces will flow together and whose task is the transformation of Mexico into a country with democracy, liberty, and justice for all.

4. The Zapatista Front of National Liberation does not aspire to take Power. Its reason for being is the construction of organizational structures in the bosom of the people so that they can take collectively the political decisions that answer to their interests and exercise their sovereignty over economic, political, and social development.

5. The Zapatista Front of National Liberation assumes as a fundamental

principle that government must be in obedience to the governed, which is opposed to the commanded obedience that comes from Power and seeks to infiltrate all of society. The FZLN proposes to the entire nation that it adopt this principle as the basis of all social and political relations in Mexico.

6. The Zapatista Front of National Liberation assumes the principle of "Everything for everyone, nothing for us," for its deep communitarian content and because it reflects the decision of its militants not to seek individual, sectarian, or partisan benefit in the development of the struggle, but to struggle for the collective welfare.

7. The Zapatista Front of National Liberation knows that its struggle is part of the new international movement that opposes neo-liberalism, and in this great battle it proposes to contribute, working from its country, to the victory of all the peoples of the planet in favor of humanity and against neo-liberalism, the construction of a world with room for many worlds.

The FZLN's Proposal for a Program of Struggle . . .

CONSIDERING THAT . . .

[a] the program of the FZLN must reflect the fact that we are a political force that does not seek to take power, that does not pretend to be the vanguard of a specific class, or of society as a whole; [and that]

[b] the program of a political force of the new type must pick up the entirety of demands by diverse social actors and citizens, individual and community rights, not from an academic perspective, but from active and conscious participation in a social movement in struggle, working so that society, beginning with the citizen, appropriates politics.

THEREFORE WE PROPOSE . . .

To group as six programmatic axes the 13 fundamental demands of the EZLN: Work, Housing, Land, Food, Health, Education, Independence, Democracy, Justice, Liberty, Culture, and the Rights to Information and Peace, together with the other three added during the Civic Consultation in August 1995, Security, the Battle against Corruption, and Defense of the Environment, and the entire set of proposals elaborated for the present Congress of the FZLN.

These six axes would be:

DEMOCRACY

JUSTICE

LIBERTY

INDEPENDENCE
NEW CONSTITUTION
CONSTRUCTION OF A POLITICAL FORCE
OF THE NEW KIND

On the axis of DEMOCRACY we place everything that has to do with breaking the command-obedience relationship that the State imposes on society, as well as the necessary construction of new democratic relations in the very bosom of society.

Here we would take up again authentic federalism, the establishment of organs where the people exercise their sovereignty (direct democracy), the struggle for a State of Law, a true political reform—in which the instruments of civic control are guaranteed, such as the referendum, recall, public accounting, authentic citizenization of all electoral organs, demilitarization of the country, the struggle to democratize the means of communication.

On this axis and also of great importance is the struggle for an authentic and profound Reform of the State, understood as a new relation among the Nation's different parts, as a reformulation of the role of diverse social actors in their relationship with the State, beginning with payment of the historic debt that the Fatherland owes the Indian peoples. An authentic Reform of the State has to be consistent with Mexico's multi-ethnic character and to recognize native communities as the origin and essential part of the Nation, accepting their right to autonomy, just as it was formulated in the accords of San Andrés Sakam'chén de los Pobres.

A Reform that puts an end to the State-party system and all that this implies at the social, political, ideological, and cultural level. That makes the Free Municipality a reality. That guarantees the right to information, the broadening of civil rights, especially human rights. That puts an end to discrimination by gender or sexual preference. And that incorporates all that is necessary to achieve the democratic reconstruction of Mexico.

On the axis of JUSTICE we place everything that has to do with the objective of achieving a life worth living:

Here we group: Work, Land, Housing, Food, Health, Education, Justice, Culture, Security, Anti-Corruption, Defense of the Environment. The struggle against official impunity, the struggle against the concentration of wealth, against neoliberalism; for the establishment of new criteria and courts for the administration of justice; for unemployment insurance; for a wage that allows the satisfaction of fundamental necessities; to recover the original spirit of Article 27 of the Constitution [which mandated agrarian reform]; against the AFORES law [to privatize pensions]; for the defense of social security [against privatization]; for democratic participation in the communities in order to apply programs for the use and distribution of drinking water in an equitable form; to promote scientific, democratic, and popular and quality education at all levels, without exclusion or entrance exams; to orient an economic program favoring the country's most dispossessed sectors; and many other struggles that reflect the constant mobilization of our people to change the terrible social deterioration into which they have been submerged.

On the axis of LIBERTY we place the demands that seek to break the bonds that prevent us from living freely:

The struggle against corporatism and bossism; for the freedom of unions to affiliate as they will; freedom of expression and public demonstration; the defense of human rights; freedom for political prisoners and the disappeared; and so many other struggles that day to day are expressed in the streets and villages of our country.

On the axis of INDEPENDENCE we place the initiatives of the majority of us Mexicans who are not resigned to mortgaging our future to the irrationality of "the new world order":

The struggle for the defense of National Sovereignty, which is expressed particularly in the defense of our natural and human resources; the struggle against the presence of police or military corps from other countries in Mexico; against the North American Free Trade Agreement that the Mexican government signed; for the development of our own technology; for self-sufficiency in food; for self-determination of all peoples; for solidarity with peoples struggling for national liberation; and for all those struggles that the Mexican people in their wisdom fight to avoid the destruction of our national fabric.

On the axis of NEW CONSTITUTION, we want to note the importance that it has for many of the previously noted points:

The realization of a new Constitutional Congress that will write a new Constitution; take up again the best of the 1917 Constitution; leave to the side the countless antipopular modifications that have been done to it since the State-party system arose; and take into account the different voices and attitudes that from outside positions of power have been appearing in this regard in recent times. The objective would be to put at the center of the Constitutional Congress's attention the needs of citizens and their organizations.

On the axis of CONSTRUCTION OF A POLITICAL FORCE OF A NEW KIND we place precisely our decision and our commitment to try to build it day to day, in deeds. An organization that must also be built by applying to its internal operations the programmatic axes of DEMOCRACY, JUSTICE, LIBERTY, AND INDEPENDENCE; that struggles not to fall into double-talk and double-dealing morality. That has as its object to act on its internal questions as it proposes to society that it will act. We do not want to develop an inhospitable space of political participation. We struggle for a Democratic, Just, Free, and Independent FZLN.

The idea that we want to express with these definitions of our program of struggle is that the FZLN seeks to take up the most sensitive demands that society has been formulating, and at the same time have a flexible program that will take up those that new social movements will be framing. Therefore it is not a program of government, nor is it made for the FZLN to take power; it has a different objective, possibly smaller: to help unleash all the social energy to build new human relations that will permit society to possess what is really due to it: control of its destiny.

Therefore we understand the program as a bridge from the FZLN to society and social movements, a space of permanent dialogue, a common territory, where every answer generates a new question. It is the instrument by means of which we Zapatista civilians integrated in the FZLN seek to organize the struggle to satisfy civil popular rights, to organize resistance and the development of social forms of self-management, to recognize the appearance of new social actors and join their mobilizations, to organize and promote civic vigilance over those who govern, and help create new spaces of mobilization . . .

CHAPTER THIRTY

The Civil War
in the Highlands:
Acteal, December 22, 1997

Dirctly north of San Cristóbal is the Tzotzil municipality of Chamula. Across Chamula's line north are the Tzotzil municipalities of Bochil, Larráinzar, Chenalhó, and Mitontic. From San Cristóbal it is about 18 miles as the crow flies to Chenalhó's municipal seat, some 25 long miles by the twisting mountain road there, to San Pedro Chenalhó, where Saint Sebastian's statue sweated and Saint Peter's beamed light before the great Indian revolt of 1712, and whence Tzotzil militia hunted and killed Tzotzil fugitives from the ladino reconquest of Chamula in 1869–70. Only a bit more than a quarter the size of Chamula, Chenalhó covers not quite 88 square miles. It is all green mountain rises and slopes, valleys, streams, rain in the summer, fog in the winter, cold at night all year round. In the forests of pine and oak men cut timber to make their rough shacks. In shaded groves they and their households tend coffee trees, in cleared patches corn and beans, on the open slopes sheep, in the valleys sugar cane and cattle. In 1990 the township counted nearly 31,000 souls in 101 localities, San Pedro Chenalhó (pop. 1,564) the biggest, 20 other villages (pop. from 1,227 to 507), and 80 hamlets (from 471 to maybe six). Of these people probably 99 percent were Chenalhó natives. Of those older than five, 98 percent spoke an Indian language, 93 percent Tzotzil (the others Tzeltal); over 40 percent spoke only Tzotzil.

Since the Revolution 60-odd years ago, "when we stopped being crushed," more than 50 of Chenalhó's villages and hamlets (all those eligible) have received ejidos, which comprise about nine-tenths of the township's territory. But the overwhelming majority of the people remained poor, not so miserably poor as in the cañadas, or in Chamula, but still poor. In 1990, of the people who ever made money from their work there, in all some 7,000 (so few because more than 40 percent of the population was under 12), nine-tenths worked in "the primary sector," on their ejido plots or as hired hands, and nine-tenths made less than the minimum wage. Historically, comparatively, mostly, Chenalhó was just another sad highland township.

Its post-Revolutionary history, however, did have some distinctive features. While young bilingual Indian hustlers captured authority in other highland townships in the 1940s, Chenalhó's elders held their ground. They began losing converts to the Presbyterians in the 1950s, but did not shun or banish them. The INI-trained bilingual teachers took charge in the 1960s faster there than elsewhere in the highlands, and made a tougher bossdom. In the name of the PRI, teachers from the Arias family and the Ruiz, the Cruz and the Méndez, the Paciencia, the Gómez, the Pérez, and the Hernández for 25 years dominated Chenalhó's politics, together against outsiders, against each other locally. And since 1965 there had been a tough and savvy parish priest resisting them, Normandy-born and bred, 34 when he moved to Saint Peter's, a veteran of red Ivry-sur-Seine, fresh from a crash course with Ivan Illich, pledged to Bishop Ruiz and Vatican II, Father Michel Chanteau. Within a few years his respect and work for the parish's poor won him much influence among them. Like the missionaries in the canyons, he learned the poor's language, studied the new catechism, and continually recruited catechists. In 1973–74 "Padre Miguel" served as one of the Tzotzil zone's two "promoters" of the Indian Congress, where (as his catechists stirred) Chenalhó's delegates told of the struggle of the villages of Los Chorros and Puebla to protect their ejidos against an invasive landlord, demanded Los Chorros's amplification, told of Puebla's successful struggle to free an unjustly jailed villager, complained about federal agencies' local incompetence and corruption, about extortion in San Pedro Chenalhó's market, forced labor on the roads, exploitation on fincas, illegal liquor sales, useless doctors, useless schools, and accused one teacher by name, a former municipal president's brother, of sexually abusing the older girls in his school.

The teachers retained their PRI franchise and their bossdom. They mourned only in rhetoric the passing of the last elders and the departure of the angriest youngsters for the canyons. They easily divided the remaining "traditionalists" between the patronized and drunk and the screwed and drunk. They nevertheless enjoyed (for being "educated") the support of the township's increasingly numerous (and dry) Presbyterians. Their only serious frustration was the new-fangled Catholics around Padre Miguel.

This regime began to crack in 1988. Not only did the PRI divide nationally, but the Chenalhó teachers lost control over municipal elections: their PRIista for municipal president, backed by the Presbyterians, lost to a fellow backed by a new coalition of "traditionalists" and Padre Miguel's catechists. More cracks opened then. A union of ejidos and coffee growers organized. Solidarity appeared. Out near the township's eastern line, in Los Chorros (pop. in 1990, 1,065), even local Cardenistas formed a committee, and won the federal concession of a local sand-and-gravel pit for their new Solidarity construction cooperative. Suspicious of them, other Cardenistas in the area joined the PRD. Others, disgusted with Solidarity and the PRD's decline in 1991, enlisted in the new Alianza Nacional Campesina Independiente Emiliano Zapata, AN-CIEZ. Thanks to Solidarity and the ANCIEZ's abstention, the teachers' PRI reconquered the "traditionalists" and beat the local PRD for the municipal presidency in 1992. Separating from the parties and their factions, the parish's catechists then induced the organization of Las Abejas, "the Bees," a civil association for the sorts of reforms the ANCIEZ promoted.

Unlike some other northern townships in 1994, Chenalhó did not evidently harbor many (if any) EZLN combatants or militia. One reason may be that more of the poor there were like the Cardenistas in Los Chorros, who kept the Cardenista name, but (if only to guard the little they had of material value) supported the government; another reason, that the Bees really were nonviolent. Anyway the teachers' PRI won the municipal presidency again in 1995, for Jacinto Arias, a Presbyterian. But suddenly in April 1996 (two months after the San Andrés accords, most notably on Indian "autonomy"), the teachers got the most insolent and dangerous shock in their collective history—the proclamation of an "autonomous municipality" in Chenalhó. Based in the township's northeastern corner, in the hamlet of Polhó (pop. in 1990, 450), a coalition of local PRDistas and nonviolent pro-Zapatistas claimed jurisdiction over 11,000 souls in 36 communities in the township's northeastern quarter.

Municipal President Arias could not long ignore the Polhó "Zapatistas" (as he called them). In August 1996 the "autonomous municipality" seized the Chorros cooperative's sand-and-gravel pit, or (as the Polhó "autonomous" council declared) "expropriated it for the benefit of the communities," allowing its use only on Polhó's permission; PRIistas and their new "Cardenista" allies need not apply. Even so, for months while civil war spread elsewhere in the highlands, PRIistas/"Cardenistas" and Polhó loyalists in Chenalhó's northeastern villages and hamlets exchanged at worst angry words, and "neutrals" (whatever their private political inclinations) went on about their work and worship. The union of ejidos remained intact. The Bees reconcentrated on prayers for peace.

In April 1997, however, the Polhó council heard that Arias had received a shipment of 200 high-powered rifles and that the state police were recruiting and training "paramilitaries" at several places in the "autonomous municipality," Santa Martha, Pechiquil, Yaxgemel, Los Chorros, and Puebla. This had probably happened, justified as security against a possible EZLN challenge. It may have happened too that on May 23, across the valley south of Polhó, in Yaxgemel, "Zapatistas" committed "aggressions" on PRIistas (including "shots fired"). On May 24 the first political killing of the season certainly happened, when "paramilitaries" surrounded Yaxgemel, shot to death a Polhó council member, and wounded two local "Zapatistas." Other Polhó loyalists and some neutrals fled. More tried to, but their PRIista neighbors would not let them. On June 10 Arias sent to Tuxtla the first of several requests that Acting Governor Julio César Ruiz meet with a Chenalhó delegation. He wanted to "personally explain the municipality's problems," in the hope of more state support "to solve the security problem." The governor must have already known how matters stood in Chenalhó; his secretary for Indian Affairs was Arias's uncle. Maybe to avoid political blackmail, he avoided the meeting. Two months later he made a Social Development grant worth some U.S. $500,000 to a municipality notorious for its "paramilitaries" (Peace and Justice). Maybe Chenaló needed more notorious "paramilitaries."

The war began during the week of September 14. That Sunday, union of ejidos be damned, Puebla's PRIista ejido commissioner announced a special collection "to buy cartridges and repair weapons." Three days later ejido officers there beat and jailed four villagers who refused to contribute. The same day at an ejido assembly three miles northeast, in Los Chorros, the "Cardenista" commissioner reported rumors that EZLN soldiers were coming to kill people there. Fellow "Cardenista" Antonio López and 30 followers promptly overthrew him, demanded "war on the Zapatistas," distributed rifles, and went out and killed three neighbors, burned down the local Bees' chapel, and looted and burned 15–20 "Zapatistas" houses. Some 60 Bees fled to other villages and hamlets, most of them four or five miles northwest to Acteal (pop. in 1990, 471), a couple of miles north of Polhó. "Paramilitaries" then went shooting, looting, and burning in Naranjitic, Yibeljoj, Pechiquil, and La Esperanza too (all within three miles of Polhó), holding local "Zapatistas" and neutrals hostage if they could. Hundreds of Polhó loyalists and neutrals fled into the forests, wherever possible toward Polhó. Some refugees started shooting back.

It did not take long before "alleged Zapatistas" had killed "alleged PRIistas," and burned their houses, too. On October 1 in San Cristóbal, Arias asked President Zedillo's permission for (his) Chenalhó civilians to carry weapons in "self-defense." The Bees protested. Permission (not granted) was blatantly not necessary. In Chimix on October 28 an army patrol found a cache of 20 rifles, and returned them to the local PRIistas who claimed them. In Los Chorros in October and early November Antonio López collected at least US $10,000 in "war taxes" to buy AK-47s, .22s, an Uzi, and ammunition in San Cristóbal for a major offensive. In other villages and hamlets PRIistas collected "war taxes" in installments, and when households had paid in full (US $75), gave them "immunity" and let them (or made them) paint "PRI" on their shacks. Elsewhere innocents painted "civil society" or "neutral zone" on theirs. Arias went to Tuxtla and asked the governor's lieutenant, Homero Tovilla, for more state police, "to reinforce security." Tovilla said he would send another 160 officers. Some came. Arias complained they were not enough. Tovilla told him, "First, you Indians reach your own agreement, and then come see me." By November, 14 six "alleged PRIistas" had died at the hands of "alleged Zapatistas."

Good Tzotzils always say what they intend to do next. On November 15 in San Pedro Chenalhó Municipal President Arias stopped Father Chanteau on the street and told him that if he did not "control" the "Zapatistas" and the Bees, he (Arias) would kill him and burn down his church with him in it. Coffee-picking time had come. Three days later, some wearing red masks, some in dark uniforms (like the state police), some with state police escorts, "paramilitaries" launched their major offensive, attacking in Nueva Aurora, Pechiquil, Bajoveltic, Canolal, Chimix, Acteal, Yaxgemel, and Tzajalhucum, killing at least eight "Zapatistas" or neutrals, trucking off their newly harvested coffee, ransacking and burning 40 to 50 houses, holding hostages, and making hundreds more refugees. On November 26, as Arias had arranged with the state police colonel responsible for the township's northeastern precincts, a state police captain went with Los Chorros ejidatarios on their pick-up trip to San Cristóbal to buy and bring back more AK-47s and ammo. Like the army commander of the "mixed detachment" (soldiers and state police) at Majomut, a mile up the road east of Acteal, the colonel was by then instructing subordinates who asked for orders regarding armed civilians, "If they're *verdes* ["greens," political slang for PRIista peasants], let them be." Even without instructions police often had little choice. As Los Chorros's new ejido commissioner told the captain after the ammo run to San Cristóbal, police officers' weapons were no good for anything, because the villagers' had better. Boasts and rumors of such firepower scared hundreds more into flight.

On December 1 the Chiapas office of Mexico's National Human Rights Commission received from the San Cristóbal diocese a detailed report on Chenalhó's "paramilitaries." CONAI and COCOPA then pressed for negotiations to stop PRI-patronized violence there. The union of ejidos (its peaceable members desperate to pick what was left of their coffee), the Bees, and Polhó quickly accepted. Arias twice refused. The governor told him to accept. On December 5, in the presence of the National Human Rights commissioner for Los Altos, the state's Human Rights commissioner, secretary for Indian Affairs, deputy attorney-general for Indian Justice, and field agent for Los Altos, and observers from the diocesan Human Rights Center, the union, and the Bees, the Chenalhó town council and the Polhó "autonomous" council met in the hamlet of Las Limas (halfway between San Pedro Chenalhó and Polhó) for "a dialogue for peace." Meeting under the same auspices in Las Limas on December 11, they agreed to a ceasefire and a "Verification Commission." Two representatives each from the national, state, and diocesan human-rights offices, the state Indian Affairs department, and the Bees, three Chenalhó PRIistas, and three Polhó loyalists would make a two-day tour of the embattled villages and hamlets to see if both sides kept the truce. At a third meeting scheduled for December 19 the commission would report, and the two councils would take appropriate action to maintain peace. On December 11, December 13, and December 14 Polhó complained of PRIista rearmament. On December 15, surely not accidentally, the Vatican's apostolic nuncio in Mexico commenced a four-day visit to the northern highlands (though no stop in Chenalhó). The Verification Commission met on December 16, headed east, and before the crossroads to Polhó and Yaxgemel had to halt before a 100-man PRIista roadblock.

The next day near Quextic, less than a mile northeast of Acteal, a man died in an ambush. According to the state police report, five armed and masked men fired on four or five others, killing Agustín Vázquez, a PRIista, and the surviving victims recognized two of the attackers, whose masks fell off when they fired, as PRDistas and pro-Zapatistas from Acteal. According to the Verification Commission, PRIistas fired on other PRIistas for not joining their "paramilitary" campaigns, killing Vázquez and wounding seven. On December 19 Polhó accused PRIistas of expelling 200 people from Quextic in the last 48 hours, and announced that for lack of security on the road to Las Limas it was suspending participation in negotiations indefinitely. More refugees hit backcountry paths for a maybe safer village or hamlet, PRDistas and pro-Zapatistas mainly in Polhó, neutrals mainly in Acteal. The diocese declared that because of the "paramilitaries" a fifth of Chenalhó's population, some 6,000 people, were refugees living in camps. Around Acteal, its population swollen by then to ca. 900, scores of men, women, and crying, coughing children, refugees from Los Chorros, La Esperanza, Chimix, Pechiquil, Quextic, Tzajalhucum, and elsewhere, were living out under the trees, in the cold mist and mud. When the Bees there heard the negotiations were off, they intensified their prayers for peace; many began fasting.

Governor Ruiz announced that "paramilitaries" did not exist in Chiapas, "displaced persons" were returning home, and his government would compensate them for their losses. His lieutenant Tovilla insisted particularly that "armed 'white guards'" were impossible in Chenalhó, "because land in that municipality is in ejidos, and there are no big landlords to pay for 'paramilitaries.'" On Sunday December 21 PRD's lone state rep called the governor three times about rumors "paramilitaries" were going to attack Acteal, and every time got only a secretary's promise that the governor would call her right back.

Since December 17 Agustín Vázquez's PRIista and "Cardenista" relatives and compañeros, above all his 70-year-old father in Los Chorros, Antonio Vázquez, had been aching for revenge. They were certain who had killed Agustín, "Zapatistas" from Acteal. If not actually directed by Municipal President Arias or Los Chorros's ejido commissioner, then abetted by them (materially with weapons, ammunition, and trucks), and protected by their deals with the local army and state police commanders, old Antonio and his son Manuel planned an attack on Acteal. From Chimix, Yaxgemel, Canolal,

Puebla, La Esperanza, Bajoveltic, Yibeljoj, Los Chorros, and Acteal, the leading avengers and late recruits gathered in Quextic, where Manuel Vázquez and another of old Antonio's sons lived. On Sunday evening December 21 maybe 20 of them met at Manuel's house to decide details for the attack in the morning, to kill first "the Zapatistas . . . and then Acteal's civil society." They wanted even men without guns to join them; while the armed did the killing, the unarmed would sack the place and steal its harvested coffee. They sent to Los Chorros to ask for more men to join them. Antonio López promised his men, and proposed the whole attacking force dress in state police blue and wear red masks. Some of the group in Quextic spent the night there, others at a cabin in the forest, to meet at 5 a.m. with the contingent from Los Chorros, give them breakfast, and together hit Acteal early. Three of the recent recruits left to find the makings for breakfast.

Actually these three were PRIista conscripts, and from Acteal. On a trip to Chimix they had fallen foul of the municipal officer there, who had not only fined them, but ordered them to join the PRI, or "we kill you." At once they had joined. Now in the night around Quextic they fled home. In Acteal they found the catechist who led the Bees, and told him of the impending attack. The catechist thanked them, but decided that since "God only knew what might happen," the Bees would stay and continue their prayers for peace. One of the three Quextic runaways took off with a friend for San Cristóbal, to tell the diocese.

December 22, 5 a.m. in Chenalhó: in the dark, all across the township, 6,500 women patting tortillas for their household's breakfast; two hours later, daybreak, still no blood anywhere. Maybe because it was a Monday, maybe because Quextic's avengers did not have breakfast ready for Los Chorros's, maybe because the attacking force could not get its uniforms right, maybe because of waiting for old Antonio, who later complained "they left him behind," the force did not move out from Quextic—some 60 men in three trucks—until after 10:30 a.m. By then most of Acteal's "Zapatista" men had gone to work out in the coffee groves. Others up near the road were building a camp for the refugees. Up at the school basketball court by the road a small detachment of state police guarded the main entry to the hamlet. A couple hundred yards down near the little frame chapel a few men and some women were sorting state-donated clothes for the refugees. Some men and most of the women and children (none armed) were down in front of the chapel, where the catechist was leading the Bees in their prayers. There was a board sign: "Peace, Neutral Zone." About 11:00 the three trucks from Quextic appeared on the road. The dark-uniformed and (mostly) red-masked men piled out, took the heights east and south of the hamlet, and came down after the people they saw below, shooting to kill, taking no fire in return. The catechist and several Bees died where they had been praying. The wounded and the as yet unhurt, the children screaming, fled into the coffee groves or down the hill northwest, to hide along the brush and banks of the creek at the bottom. The state police up at the basketball court fired some shots in the air, then laid low. (State police on the road not far away stopped a state civil-defense employee driving toward Acteal; he could go no further, they said, because of "a shoot-out.") Around noon a diocesan vicar, Father Gonzalo Ituarte, received reports of shooting in Acteal. He at once called Tovilla in Tuxtla and told him. Tovilla called the state police commander in the area, who told him nothing was happening there. The shooting went on all afternoon. It was not sustained fire, as the chief state police adviser (a retired army brigadier general) heard for himself up at the basketball court from 1 p.m. to 4:30, but fire every three to five minutes in bursts and single shots, as the chief recognized, from AK-47s, AR-15s, .22s, shotguns (also at least one .30-.30, a 9 mm pistol, and a .38 special). It was hunting fire, Tzotzil hunters shooting Tzotzil prey down by the creek. The chief did not send any of the eventually 40 state police up by the road during the afternoon down to investigate. Neither did the army commander at Majomut intervene. Around 2:00 the third Quextic runaway reached San Cristóbal, ran to the diocesan Human Rights Center, told his story, ran on the center's directions to the state Indian Affairs office, found it closed for Christmas vacation, and did not know then what to do. As night fell in Acteal, the shooting stopped. The attacking force had killed 45 people: seven men, 20 women (four of them pregnant), and 18 boys and girls (one an infant). It had shot 43 of them to death (23 in the back), beat the other two's heads in, and wounded at least 25 others, including eight or more children. (None of the victims had fired a weapon.) In the dark the force then withdrew. About 6 p.m. a different state police unit arrived, went down and found some dead and wounded around the chapel, hauled the wounded up to the road, and filed a report. Other wounded and scores of fugitives, some of whom had recognized their cousins among the killers, were on their way to Polhó and beyond to San Cristóbal. Around 7:30, informed by Polhó of the attack, Father Ituarte called Tovilla again. Tovilla assured him nothing had happened at Acteal, only four or five shots fired, that he had 15 state police in the area "to deal with the situation," and would give him the latest information tomorrow. At 7:50 the state police commander for Chenalhó requested the use of municipal vehicles to transport wounded from Acteal to the municipal seat. Arias provided three trucks, which brought 14 families to shelter in town. The avengers who returned to Quextic told old Antonio Vázquez they had killed many people, which so pleased him that he gave them "food and drink." By 10 p.m. the first wounded were coming into San Cristóbal's regional hospital, and the diocesan chancellor was hearing their accounts of the day. About 11 p.m. the state police who had earlier entered Acteal found 30-odd bodies down by the creek. About the same time in Tuxtla the governor was meeting privately with his top security officials: on Acteal both Tovilla and the state police chief reported *sin novedad*, "all quiet."

Around 4 a.m. on December 23 the state deputy attorney-general for Indian Justice and a state Red Cross official arrived in Acteal. The state attorney did not secure the site, have it photographed, or gather evidence. He did call the municipality for trucks again. At 5 a.m. an aide awoke the chief police adviser still up by the road "with the news . . . that down below there are many people dead." During the morning three Chenalhó trucks took the 45 bodies to Tuxtla for state police autopsies. Hundreds of refugees were pouring into Polhó. The news spread fast. The CCRI-EZLN high command issued a communiqué blaming "the massacre of Indians in the community Acteal" on Zedillo, his Justice Ministry, Governor Ruiz, Tovilla, his deputy, and the state police (the first reading here). At noon the diocese put its version on the Internet. An hour later Bishop Ruiz delivered his "communication . . . to all of God's people . . . and pastoral workers in the diocese," trying to make Christian sense of the killing, begging the state government to return the bodies for mourning, begging the guilty for contrition, begging the aggrieved for fidelity to the Sermon on the Mount (the second reading). Governor Ruiz's spokeswoman said she had no information about any massacre. The state attorney-general allowed that he had started an investigation, but could not confirm an attack. Interviewed at 2:30, Arias was more expansive. "What happened is an act of revenge. It's not a political problem, and that's why you can't solve it." He laughed at Polhó's accusation that he had provided weapons for the act. "Let them prove it on me. That's just a lot of hot air. God is my witness it's not true." He added that the governor had not yet called him about Acteal. At 4 p.m., on Zedillo's instructions, the federal Justice Ministry assumed jurisdiction in the case. Federal police took custody of the bodies in Tuxtla, and occupied an empty, sacked Acteal. Some 500 troops of Mexico's U.S.-trained Airborne Special Forces Group arrived on the scene. The army surrounded Polhó, to protect it (and prevent reprisals). On December 24 federal police trucked the 45 bodies in coffins there. The mourning could start.

At dawn on Christmas Day, under federal security, men from several villages and hamlets who had taken refuge in Polhó went to Acteal to dig the graves. In a clearing among banana plants, near the road where the refugee camp was going to be, they made two trenches, six feet wide, 50 feet long, not common but "communitarian" graves. When the sun was high and hot, amid crowds of media, federal police, and National Human Rights Commission officials, the funeral procession of Bishop Ruiz, the pallbearers, 15 small coffins in white bunting, 30 of the standard size in blue and black, priests, religious, and hundreds of other mourners left Polhó for Acteal. Along the way, at a curve in the road, a municipal truck and a state police van headed south stopped for them. In the back of the truck were men whom mourners recognized from Monday as killers. (Arias had called them from Quextic and Los Chorros to the municipal seat, so that they could get their stories straight.) Some mourners began yelling "killer" at the men, pulling them out of the truck, beating and kicking them. The state police, improvising, explained that as soon as the procession passed, they were going to arrest the men. This inflamed the gathering crowd. In the furor the bishop quickly consulted with the federal police commander, whose officers arrested everyone in the truck, commandeered the state police van, and brought the men back to San Pedro Chenalhó for a federal interrogation. As the dust settled, the procession proceeded. At Acteal it met an army unit with machine guns guarding the place. Before a little table for an altar out in the open the pallbearers laid the coffins in four rows, the small ones in front. At the foot of each coffin catechists lit tall white candles. Bishop Ruiz said a Christmas Mass with special prayers for the dead, whose names survivors called out. In his homily he could not do much more than repeat his earlier "communication" (the second reading below without redundant passages), again begging the guilty for contrition, the aggrieved for fidelity to Jesus's sayings on the mountain. Then a Presbyterian minister spoke, urging an end to rancor and violence. Afterward survivors and others from Acteal who since Monday had not been able to find their kin opened the coffins to try to identify the bodies in them. The lids off, they had to unzip body bags, peel away sheets stiff with dried blood, and through the suffocating stench of putrefaction and sudden plague of flies look at blasted, perforated, sliced human remains for some trace of familiar, loved features. They identified 29. Their survivors could not dress them for burial, but put blankets, clothes, shawls, favorite shoes in the coffins with them. Catechists closed all the coffins. The pallbearers carried them to the trenches and lowered them into the graves. The gravediggers covered them. The procession returned to Polhó, where the Acteal refugees would try to keep together.

COMUNICADO DEL COMITÉ CLANDESTINO REVOLUCIONARIO INDÍGENA-COMANDANCIA GENERAL DEL EJÉRCITO ZAPATISTA DE LIBERACIÓN NACIONAL*

To the people of Mexico,
To the peoples and governments of the world,
To the national and international press,
Brothers:

In regard to the massacre of Indians in the community Acteal, in the municipality of San Pedro de Chenalhó, Chiapas, committed yesterday, December 22, 1997, the EZLN makes known:

---

*December 23, 1997, www.ezln.org

First. In accord with the information obtained so far, some 60 paramilitaries from the PRI (sponsored by the federal and state governments) were those who attacked with high-powered firearms the displaced Indians taking refuge in Acteal.

Second. As a result of this attack, which lasted up to four hours, at least 45 Indians were murdered, among them nine men, twenty-one women, and fifteen children (one of them less than a year old). Besides the dead, seven males were wounded (four of them children), and ten females (four of them children).

Third. In accord with radio transmissions from the Chiapas state government (intercepted by the EZLN), police from the Chiapas Public Security force on the outskirts of Acteal and at the time the massacre was being committed backed the attack, and during the evening and night collected bodies to hide the massacre's magnitude. Homero Tovilla Cristiani and Uriel Jarquín, Chiapas's state secretary and undersecretary of government, respectively, commissioned the police to back the crime. Governor Julio César Ruiz Ferro was constantly informed as the "operation" developed (at least from noon on December 22, when the massacre had already been going on for an hour). Approved by the federal and state governments, plans for the attack were refined on December 21 in a meeting of paramilitaries that the PRIista municipal president, Jacinto Arias, convened from the communities of Los Chorros, Puebla, La Esperanza, and Quextic, all in Chenalhó township.

Fourth. The direct responsibility for these bloody acts falls on Ernesto Zedillo Ponce de León and the Interior Ministry, who for the last two years have given a green light to the counter-insurgency project proposed by the army. This project is an attempt to turn the Zapatista war into a conflict between Indians, motivated by religious, political, or ethnic differences. To accomplish it, the government has committed itself to pay for the equipment and arms (with funds from the Ministry of Social Development) and to give military training (by army officers) to Indians recruited by the PRI. To allow time for these death squads to get ready, the federal government designed a parallel strategy of feigned dialogue, consisting in a process of negotiation without any intention of fulfilling its agreements and at the same time increasing the military presence in Zapatista zones. The state government was left in charge of guaranteeing the impunity of the paramilitary groups and facilitating their operation in the principal rebel zones, Chiapas's north, the jungle, and the highlands.

Fifth. In this manner the federal and state governments, the PRI, and the army united their forces. Their objective is synthesized in the "war cry" of the paramilitaries called "Red Mask": "We are going to finish off the Zapatista seed," that is, "we are going to finish off the Indian communities."

Sixth. As part of his style of governing and a show of his "peaceful intention," Ernesto Zedillo by various channels made threats to the EZLN's General Command with the following message: "I would rather pass into history as a repressor than keep agreements with the EZLN." He certainly has kept his word in this case. Zedillo has now passed into history as a murderer of Indians and has the blood of Acteal on his hands.

Seventh. The media's opportune attention to Chiapas and the just indignation of national and international public opinion at what has occurred have provoked the brains behind the crime to fall all over themselves washing their hands and promising investigations "to get to the bottom of things." They are not going to punish the responsible parties; impunity is guaranteed, because those who are investigating the crime are the very ones who planned it. For this reason the declarations by Zedillo and his subalterns are nothing more than demagogy.

Eighth. As a result of the Acteal massacre the government and its spokesmen again are calling for dialogue, but without mentioning their determination not to fulfill agreements already made and only for the purpose of carrying their counter-insurgency strategy forward. In this sense, the recent and ridiculous declaration by COCOPA (which decided to go on vacation instead of work for peace) on what was done at Acteal is remarkable. The congressmen forget that the one who is murdering children, women, and men is the government. They forget that the one who is using firearms is the government. They forget that the one who refuses a serious dialogue is the government. It is to the government that they must address themselves when they speak of not resorting to violence and of the need for dialogue.

Ninth. Again, the EZLN calls on national and international civil society and on independent organizations not to let themselves be fooled, and to demand true justice and no subterfuges.

Tenth. The Clandestine Revolutionary Indian Committee-EZLN General Command is at this moment completing its investigation and analyzing what happened in order to take the necessary and pertinent decisions.

Democracy!
Liberty!
Justice!

From the mountains of the Mexican Southeast,
Sub-comandante Marcos . . .

COMUNICACIÓN*

> . . . a voice was heard in Ramah,
> lamentation, and bitter weeping;

---

* Mons. Samuel Ruiz García, San Cristóbal de Las Casas, December 23, 1997, curiasc@laneta.apc.org

Rahel weeping for her children
refused to be comforted for her children,
because they were not.   (Jer. 31:15; Mt. 2:18)

To all of God's people who like pilgrims live this mortal life in our suffering Diocese of San Cristóbal de las Casas,
To all our brother and sister pastoral workers:

If perhaps we had forgotten that the true Christmas happens in a tragic context of oppression and domination (Lk.2:1-2), of insecurity and closed doors (Lk.2:6-7), of persecution and exile (Mt.2:13-15), and even of real genocide (Mt.2:16-18), the events of these days in Chenalhó have come to remind us of it.

The greatest happiness the world has known, the birth of God's Word in our human form, happened in the painful setting of the greatest suffering. The true light shown out in the midst of the thickest fog.

Christmas this year for the Christian people of our diocese, our state, our entire country, is a sorrowful Christmas.

Ignominious is not only the so far proven number of dead (45) and wounded (25), many of them minors in age, but also and above all the climate of growing and unpunished violence, duly and zealously reported to the authorities who could have stopped it before it reached this disgraceful conclusion.

There are so many aggravating circumstances that make this painful event a true crime against humanity:

The fact that the attack was perpetrated by grown men, armed, against a group mostly of women and children, unarmed.

The fact that this group of victims—the Bees—was precisely a group that had made a profession to the four winds and for a long time of its option for civil, peaceful, and nonviolent means for the satisfaction of its demands, although they live and work in the heart of a zone where violence reigns.

The fact that the victims were a group of persons recently harassed to the point of being obliged to leave their homes and hamlets, for they were in Acteal as displaced persons.

The fact that the attack happened precisely at the moment when they were meeting in the hamlet's chapel, praying for Peace, and surely praying for those who were persecuting them. We know that such is the Christian quality of these brothers and sisters. What a horrible paradox that on the very day when the newspapers announce that in the states's northern zone and thanks to the instances and efforts of the apostolic nuncio, it was possible to open some chapels that had been closed and occupied by armed groups of civilians and [state] public security police, on this very day, in a chapel in the zone of Los Altos, all these Christians have been massacred! In the space of the sacred, violence bursts out. And against this people so profoundly religious! The whole Judeo-Christian tradition, for centuries, that temples are "sanctuaries" for the persecuted (Dt.19) has here been trampled on.

The fact that today, at a very early hour, the state authorities have ordered all the bodies collected, perhaps with practical legal or sanitary arguments (they may speak of the need to do autopsies or avoid disease) has turned into one more offense, and not a small one, to the massacre's survivors. They have come to us, pleading: "We want to bury our dead! They won't let us take them!" Whoever knows the Indian soul knows to what degree it is existentially indispensable to them to do their mourning, to weep for their dead. Will it be that even this consolation is going to be torn away from them?

How much work it takes at this moment to say, "Merry Christmas." To our human sensibility it seems that the baby is born dead.

Only by faith and with the help of revelation can we understand that this is how the true Christmas is. This Christmas, not that of consumer society, is what allows us to understand to its depths the mystery of the Incarnation. Here in Chiapas something new is being born, and the labor will not end without these anguishing doses of pain (Jn.16:21-23; Rom.8:18-27).

But it is precisely when we reach these limits of irrationality that the hope that new paths of fraternal life together may open grows forth with force from many hearts that before lived in lethargy. This is why Hope is the theological virtue that illuminates the Christmas season.

Herod wanted—but was not able to!—finish off the baby. Today he will not be able to do it either, although so many innocents have to fertilize this hard and arid ground with their blood.

We ask, we vehemently exhort, we beg in the Name of the God of Peace those who have perpetrated this crime to seek peace with God and with their conscience, laying down, more than only their arms, the gratuitous attitude of hate and violence, be this induced, imposed, or their own.

To our dear Tzotzil brothers and sisters of San Pedro Chenalhó we want to say that we are with you on the saddest Christmas of our life, and that we pray to the Father of Jesus that you remain faithful to the Sermon on the Mount and that your heart does not succumb to the understandable temptation of hate and revenge. Do honor to the convictions that inspired the victims and inspire their survivors!

All the parishes and missions of our Diocese, Don Raúl [Vera, the coadjutor], presently in Rome, and I exhort you to declare this Christmas of '97 the "Day of Mourning in Hope," and find with your communities the proper forms to give this tint to the celebration of the birth of the Lord, both in reference to liturgical expression and in decisions that you may agree on for support and solidarity with the massacre's victims.

To all the men and women of good will who, personally or in groups in solidarity, in Mexico and abroad, have sent their word of support to these communities, or their protest and denunciation to the responsible authorities, we give our most sincere thanks.

May the Lord God of heavens and the earth, who sent his Son so that, taking on our humanity, he be sacrificed for our salvation and bring His peace, bless us all.

CHAPTER THIRTY-ONE

Marcos and the Ark on the Mountain: San Cristóbal, July 15–16, 1998

On July 15, 1998, breaking more than four months of silence, Marcos issued two communiqués. He addressed the first to the Mexican and Guatemalan armies, Interpol in Paris, and Mexican military intelligence. In big letters it read, "Yepa, yepa, yepa! Ándale, ándale! Arriba, arriba! Yepa, yepa! From the mountains of the Mexican Southeast, Subcomandante Insurgente Marcos, alias 'El Sup Speedy González,' or, what amounts to the same thing, 'the rock in the shoe.'" The second, addressed to the Mexican people and the peoples and governments of the world, signed on behalf of the CCRI-EZLN high command, and in big letters read, "¡Nemi Zapata! ¡Nemi Zapata! ¡Nican ca namotata, ayemo miqui! ¡Nemi Zapata!," which in Nahuatl means, "Zapata lives! Zapata lives! Here your father continues, he has not yet died! Zapata lives!"

The next day the subcomandante really let loose. This third communiqué was one of his longest, 24 pages. It was also one of his most Joycean. Selections from all its parts follow. Two of its declared political points deserve special notice: the emphasis on divisions within the Mexican army, between honorable and dishonorable officers, and the insinuation that while the CCRI-EZLN would not negotiate with the government's executive branch, it would with Congress, through COCOPA. It is interesting too that "civil society" has disappeared again, except for one passing mention (not in the following selections). Its elements are here, "laborers, peasants, housewives," et al., but the collective is now only an aggregate, "millions of Mexicans," or "the majority of Mexicans." In Part IV below Marcos suggests why.

The literary and film references are numerous. Most obvious is that to Mariano Azuela's classic novel of the Revolution, *Los de abajo* (1915), translated into English as *The Underdogs* (New York: New American Library, 1963).

"The 300" for whom Marcos signed the communiqué are "the [EZLN] transgressors of the law" he mockingly imagines (in a part not selected below) the army having counted in Chiapas. They include "the masked clown who commands them."

MÉXICO 1998: ARRIBA Y ABAJO — MÁSCARAS Y SILENCIOS*

Of the public man, particularly the politician, it is necessary to ask that he possess the public virtues, all of which may be summed up in one: fidelity to his own mask . . .

Endeavor, . . . those of you who go into politics, to make your mask, as much as possible, your own work. Make it yourselves, to prevent your enemies or your co-religionists from putting it on you, imposing it on you. And do not make it so rigid, so impervious, and so impermeable, that it suffocates your countenance, because sooner or later you have to show your face.

Antonio Machado . . .

I. Mexico, mid-1998 . . .

Resting on my shoulder, the sea sighs on seeing the complicated plans of this new construction, conceptualized in long and silent dawns, pondered from behind the masks we are. Suddenly an unexpected wind rises, moving the trees that are our windows . . .

Mid-1998 in Mexico, and a wind rises to break silences and tear off masks.

After a long and heavy drought, the rains begin to loom on the horizon of this country whose government persists in carrying it to catastrophe. Protected by a whisp of cloud, from the privileged and gilded balcony that the sea offers me for these cases, damp and astonished, I see mid-1998 pass and the last death rattles of a century that refuses to retire without scandals and outrages . . .

I see . . . millions of Mexicans in the role in which the powerful always want to see them, the role of spectators.

Far from here the World Cup concentrates and convokes emotions . . .

On this side of the ocean, the tragi-comedy of national political life also turned into a spectacle . . .

---

*July 16, 1998, www.ezln.org

In the spectacle of "high" Mexican politics, the confusion of masks and parliaments prevents us from knowing with certainty who is the judge and who the criminal, who is the fraud and who the defrauded.

But it is ever more clear that Mexico at the end of the twentieth century has in its State-party system its most criminal face. In this Mexico the growing criminality of the State . . . is only equalled by the impunity given by money, influence, and proximity . . . to the select circle around him whom some still call (not without blushing, it is true) "Mr. President."

This face, the most irrational the Mexican State has had in all its history, hides its horrifying image behind a mask. And the sound of the blood it collects day to day is hushed behind a silence.

It would appear evident that masks hide and silences hush.

But it is also true that masks reveal and silences speak.

To hide and to hush, to reveal and to speak masks and silences. These are the signs that will help understand this end of a century in Mexico.

Yes, this is a country of masks and silences. I tell it to the sea, and she answers me, from behind her ski mask, with a silent but more than eloquent gesture of paradox . . .

But I tell her and I tell myself, there are masks and masks, silences and silences . . .

II. Masks and Silences Above

The Mask of Modernity. Do you find it attractive? Functional? Aerodynamic? Biodegradable? "Cool"? "Light?" It is none of that. But it is sold and consumed with those kinds of arguments. The Modernity of neoliberal governments in Mexico reveals a country empty and dry. Despite publicity and marketing, and notwithstanding the millions invested in cosmetics and makeup, the mask of Mexican Modernity is ever faster crumbling to pieces. And it is ever more difficult not to see what it is hiding: the destruction of the material bases of the Mexican State, that is, the bases of National Sovereignty . . .

With the masks of "industrial reconversion," "adjustment to globalization," "rationalization of public expenditures," "elimination of subsidies preventing free competition and economic development," "the international struggle against narco-trafficking," and "the end of the populist State," Mexican governments since 1982 have worked a veritable campaign of extermination against the fundamental grounds of national sovereignty . . .

The Mask of Macroeconomics. Here you have Zedillo's speeches, a display of contagious optimism, where he explains-scolds-warns that the-economic-recovery-is-irreversible-and-the-strength-of-our-economic-indicators-demonstrates-that-we-can-resist-the-crises-at-minimum-cost-and-how-lucky-you-fellow-citizens-are-to-have-me-as-your-president!-bla-bla-bla-bla-bla-bla-bla . . .

The destruction of Mexico as a Nation must be hidden. So another mask is necessary, that of Chauvinism. Driven by an eagerness for peace and trying to stop the extermination of Indians that the Mexican government has underway in the lands of Chiapas, hundreds of men and women from Mexico and other parts of the world arrived in the Mexican Southeast. Since there was nothing more uncomfortable for the criminals than having witnesses of the extermination laboratory they had set up on Indian soil, from the ineffable Interior minister came the double recipe: for Mexicans, jail; for those from other countries, expulsion (after a xenophobic campaign in the press and on radio and television). Suddenly, with explanations more than stupid, the principal vender of National Sovereignty had an attack of patriotism and, to the cry of "the good foreigner is the dumb and blind foreigner!," devoted himself to persecuting, harassing, and expelling all those born on other soil who add their heart to the struggle for a peace with justice and dignity. Hundreds of foreign observers suffer beatings, rapes, threats, insults. For foreign "investors," servile caravans abound, flattery, adulation.

And, as a grotesque embellishment of this mask, comes the silence of Betrayal. Yes, betrayal of the work pledged in San Andrés. Betrayal of those who believed in the path of dialogue . . . And betrayal, destruction, oblivion need an ideological support . . .

So here comes the Mask of "Intellectual Objectivity." It is worn by various personages of cultural life in Mexico who have a free pass into the halls of political, economic, and religious power . . .

Reason, history, legitimacy, and the Nation all lost, little is left to the Mexican political system. It thinks that now only one mask can save it and bring it alive (though not safe and sound) to the other shore of this century: The Mask of War . . .

III. The Mexican Army: Between Angels and Orchards

[After a mockery of President Zedillo's military "victories" in Chiapas, the first being Acteal, come these portraits of generals in the old, pre-Revolutionary army:]

General Felipe Ángeles [which means Angels]. From the old army at the time of the Mexican Revolution, he joined the rebel ranks and put his genius and training at the service of the oppressed. He fought under the orders of Francisco Villa in the Division of the North. His comrades in arms in the government's army then accused him of betraying the Fatherland. History recalls him as a military patriot.

General Victoriano Huerta [which means orchard]. From the old army at the time of the Mexican Revolution, he put himself under the orders of the

U.S. ambassador and executed President Francisco I. Madero [the first Revolutionary president]. He headed the counter-revolution and organized massacres of Indians and the destruction of villages in his military campaign against a transgressor of the law who called himself "Emiliano Zapata." His comrades in arms in the government's army then exalted and extolled him as a patriot. History recalls him as a traitor to the Fatherland . . .The mask of war, *with it comes the silence of death. And with death come* . . .

IV. Masks and Silences for Those Below, The Underdogs

. . . To maintain itself and grow, the neoliberal model demands the perpetuation of a crime concretized in millions of small and big crimes, and the State is in charge of the actual and effective collection from the victims below.

So that this complicated (and useless) set serving for the political system's death scene can function, it is necessary to distribute great quantities of masks and silences for the underdogs. Anonimity, desperation, rancor, apathy, impotence, resignation, scepticism, individualism, and cynicism are offered wholesale for consumption by millions of the Mexican men and women who eke out their lives in this country . . .

The masks of anonimity and individualism that frenetic globalization tries to impose on men and women all over Mexico hide not the singularity of each being, but the concrete nightmare of the underdogs' misery. The daily injustice that the system does to Mexicans dilutes its impact precisely in the vast multiplication of its little crimes: someone fired here, a rape there, someone unjustly jailed over here, a robbery over there, someone disappeared for his politics on that side, a fraud on this side, hunger and misery within four walls on all sides . . .

And the masks come with other masks, as apathy and cynicism want to multiply among the underdogs. It is a matter of joining "I don't care about anything" with "I'm all that counts and so what." Thus power would fulfill one of its principal objectives: to impose immobility and prevent fraternity.

Then come the silences. The silence of rancor against anyone or no one, concretized against whoever is at hand. The silence of the impotence of feeling too small before an enveloping, ungraspable, and nevertheless omnipresent power. The silence of desperation from seeing and knowing oneself alone, without even a suspicion that things could be better tomorrow. The silence of resignation that assumes the inevitability of injustice and victimization. . . .

New forms of struggle go creating their own masks and forging their silences. Little by little, growing and multiplying, is the mask of resistance—"I don't give up," "I don't surrender," "I keep struggling," "I don't back off," "Go to it!" Behind the very mask of anonimity, Indians, laborers, peasants, housewives, people in the shantytowns, union members, students, teachers, Christians in the communities, the retired, the disabled, taxi drivers, merchants, political and social militants, women, young people, children, and old people . . . refuse to remain like-this-as-if-nothing-bro-sis-and-now-well-we-cannot-give-up-we-have-to-struggle-and-organize-and-turn-it-all-over-and-redo-it-new-and-it-is-not-true-that-we-are-few-and-it-is-not-true-we-are-weak-and-it-is-not-true-we-will-always-lose-and-it-is-not true-that-this-and-it-is-not-true-that-that-and-wait-man-and-now-you-are-going-to-see-and-it-is-not-true-that-it-is-not-true-and-no-and-because-no-and-no-and-because-yes-and-no-and-now-no-NO-NO-MORE . . .

And with resistance walks and arises a terrible silence: the silence that accuses and names.

V. The Seven Victims of the Government's New Strategy for Chiapas

. . . seven are the victims of [the government's war in Chiapas]: peace, dialogue as a way to solve conflicts, Indians, civil society national and international, national sovereignty, the transition to democracy, the Commission of Concord and Pacification, and the National Mediation Commission [which actually amount to eight] . . .

Dialogue as a way to solve the conflicts is one of the most important casualties in the war in the Mexican Southeast. By failing to fulfill the accords he signed [sic], Zedillo knocked confidence in his government to smithereens. Without confidence, it is impossible to reach agreements. And if it is not to reach agreements, what is dialogue for? . . .

Two victims deserve special mention: the first is levelled near death, the other lies irremediably dead.

The first is the Commission of Concord and Pacification . . . COCOPA has been mocked, ridiculed, abused, scorned, humiliated, and forgotten by the government . . .

The EZLN will not do the same . . .

Simultaneously with the sabotage against COCOPA, the Interior Ministry carried on . . . a total war against . . . CONAI, especially against . . . Bishop Samuel Ruiz . . . After suffering an intense and long campaign of attacks and insinuations, [CONAI] was dissolved . . . , but its [members'] search for peace has not ended.

VI. Old Antonio against Morning-After, Dead-Tired Maoism

. . . Old Antonio tells a story that the oldest elders of his community told him. He tells the story that once upon a time there was a very handsome fish that lived in a river. They say a lion saw the fish and wanted to eat him. The lion went to the river, but saw he could not swim in the river and catch the fish. Then the lion asked the possum for technical advice, and the possum said, "It's very simple. The fish can't live without water. All you have to do is drink the river's water, and that way the fish won't be able to move, and then you can catch him and eat him." The lion was very satisfied with the possum's technical advice, and gave him a position in his kingdom.

The lion went down to the river bank and began to drink the water.

He died bursting from the water.

The possum wound up unemployed . . .

VII. The Seventh Mask and the Seventh Silence

. . . 1998. Mexico. While the government heads toward war and tries desperately to gather wind, animal grunts, and sorceries above to push the heavy sails of the ship of death, these Mexican Indians, who added the name of Emiliano Zapata to their history, in silence prepare the justice and dignity that are to come despite their death (or maybe through their death).

In silence these Indians look at the heavens and the earths to foretell the winds below that blow through the fields of Mexico and the world, through the dusty streets of little villages and hamlets, through the disorderly sprawl of metropolitan shantytowns, through the headquarters of honest unions, through the offices of committed political parties, through theaters-moviehouses-auditoriums-coliseums-art galleries, through laboratories and scientific-research centers, through university cubicles, lecture rooms, and hallways, through meetings and assemblies of social and political organizations, through churches of the poor, through international committees of solidarity, through national and foreign non-governmental organizations, down the turnpikes, down the highways, down country roads, down barely blazed trails, sailing on rivers, on lakes, and on the seas of this country today prodigious in humidity, and of this world awakening, late, it is true, but awakening.

In silence these Indians see, and see each other, themselves.

In silence they feel where the winds of the worlds below are blowing.

In silence these Indians know.

In silence they are finishing this new and absurd Noah's ark, and knowing that the wind is blowing for democracy, liberty, and justice, they hoist high the double sail of hope, engine and light for this ship, the boat of those of always, the ship of life.

With art and science they built the ark, and chose thousands of their own for the crew.

The rest will wait in harbor for what may come.

If war and destruction come, they will resist as they have learned to resist in the hard school of centuries, that is, with dignity.

If democracy, liberty, and justice come, they will know to share it as they have known to share through their history.

Mexico, mid-1998

After a long silence these Indians speak a boat and convoke all to board it.

After so much silence these Indians speak a boat, a Noah's ark, a navigating tower of Babel, an absurd and irreverent challenge.

If there were any doubt who mans the ship and is directing, the super-solemn fellow at the prow is sporting—a ski mask! Yes, a ski-mask, the mask that unveils, the silence that speaks. A "For everyone, everything, nothing for us" adorns the flag of the five-pointed red star on a black background waving from the mast. In golden letters, to port, to starboard, and before the wind, the "Votán Zapata" [a mythical Mayan Zapata] names the origin and destination of this ship, so powerfully fragile, so clamorously quiet, so visibly hidden.

"All aboard!" we hear the voice of the captain cry-order-invite. The only ticket necessary is honesty. Several thousand rowers wait. Ready to leave? No, something is missing . . .

With that strange and reiterated tendency they have to complicate their life, these men and women of masks and silences built their ship—in the middle of a mountain!

"And now?" I ask them.

As was to be expected, a silence is the reply. But behind their masks there is a smile when they give me a message and a bottle.

I do what for myself I do in these cases: I put the message in the bottle, plug the bottle tight with some chewing gum and a little chamoy the sea gives me, I plant myself firmly on one ridge of the Ceiba [the great tropical "silk-cotton" tree, the God tree], and with all my strength I throw the bottle with the message into the distance. A whisp of cloud catches it, and navigating, it carries it to let's-see-where-it-carries-it. There goes the bottle. Whoever finds it, if he breaks it, can break the silence and find some answers and many questions. Also he will be able to read the . . .

Fifth Declaration from the Lacandón Jungle?

Well, that's all.

So long. Good luck, and be prepared. Get your umbrellas, raincoats, and life-vests out! Who will deny now that the word can convoke humidities?

From the mountains of the Mexican Southeast
Subcomandante Marcos
In the name of the 300
Mexico, July, 1998

CHAPTER THIRTY-TWO

Recognize Indian Rights and Stop the War: The Fifth Declaration, July 19, 1998

The hope inspiring the Fourth Declaration is here forced and thin (see the following selections). Indians are still the subject; Indian rights are the principal objective; the turn of words, the incantation, imagery, and allusions are in large part still Indian, and 63 indigenous peoples again make their appearance. But in odd inversions Indians here are also often the object, of representation, gratitude, honor, recognition, inclusion, respect, national opinion, the CCRI-EZLN high command's appeals. The EZLN's original and here transparently overdue "Indian debt" weighs heavy. The concentrated Indian point of view is shifting to a pro-Indian point of view, the art of Indian declaration becoming explicit, artificial. "Civil society," whose near extinction Marcos had virtually explained three days before, is back in putative strength. But it is not so coherent or dynamic as the "civil society" in declarations of yore. It is more a disposition of grievance, an array of people with categorically disparate grievances, the categories of which come listed as if from Javier Elorriaga's updated directory of the aggrieved.

In making its "declarations" reflective, interpretive texts, to attract "honest minds" and "worthy hearts" in other walks of life, the CCRI-EZLN high command has created for itself an increasing difficulty in communication. Except in rituals, the same mode and tone too often lose their power to move. Even in advertising, the same message too often loses its meaning. "We resist!" had a power and meaning in the Second Declaration, in June 1994, that "We resist!" does not have here, where, although in bold print, it feels more like (what it may also mean in Spanish) "We endure!," which is impressive, but not rousing. This difficulty is not the authors' fault. Thomas Jefferson could not have written five successive and equally powerful Declarations of Independence. The difficulty is in the discourse.

This declaration also suffers from excessive internal repetitions. These are not the "Indian" chants ("since then . . . , since then . . . ," "we saw . . . , we saw . . ."), which retain rhetorical effect. Rather they are the strained repetitions of watchwords, slogans, alerts, and direct addresses, for example, the repeated roll call of "civil society." Most telling (of Elorriaga's hand?) is the ceremonious repetition of a pseudo-legal formula for the simple act of communication ("For this purpose . . ."). The deterioration of style indicates fatigue.

The one concrete demand here, coming toward the end of the preamble, is actually a strategic surrender, amazingly simple and easy to honor. All the Zapatista high command now declares it wants is an addition to the Mexican Constitution's new Article 4, a sentence specifically assuring Indians "respect and the possibility [which the Constitution already guarantees among the rights of all citizens] of struggling for what belongs to them. . . ." (This is not to predict that if the Constitution were so amended, the CCRI-EZLN would accept a "right" as a "possibility.")

The one concrete proposal is a new "national poll," a sort of popular referendum, on "COCOPA's Indian bill." With help from the Indian peoples themselves, the new Congreso Nacional Indígena (CNI), civil society, "honest" political parties, Congress, and COCOPA (no mention of the FZLN there or elsewhere in the declaration), Zapatista delegates will go to every municipality in Mexico to ask the local public's opinion of the bill and if "the war of extermination" should end. This would be a phenomenal accomplishment; at last count there were 2,504 municipalities in Mexico.

On the practical matter of how actually to do the poll, only the National Indian Congress, the CNI, gave a prompt, definite, and promising response. Now closer than any other serious national organization to the EZLN, the CNI on July 20 welcomed the Zapatista proposal as "the only authentic and visible peace proposal at this point," demanded that the federal government guarantee the freedoms of travel, expression, and association necessary for the poll, and committed its membership to "participation [according to "its own strategies"] in this important initiative." Only a few other major organizations in "civil society" showed even tentative interest. Most positive was the National University workers' union, whose leader offered the union's "availability" for "collaboration" in "the search for peace in Chiapas." Plans for the poll remain in the air.

QUINTA DECLARACIÓN
DE LA SELVA LACANDONA*

Today we say:
Here we are!
We resist! . . .

Brothers and sisters:

We understand that the struggle for the place we deserve and need in the Great Mexican Nation is only a part of the great struggle of all for democracy, liberty, and justice, but it is a fundamental and necessary part. Again and again, from the beginning of our rebellion on January 1, 1994, we have called on all the people of Mexico to struggle together and by all means for the rights the mighty deny us. Again and again, since we saw and spoke with all of you, we have insisted on dialogue and encounter as the path for us to walk. Since more than four years ago never has war come from our side. Since then it has always come in the mouth and the steps of the government. From there have come lies, deaths, miseries.

Following the path you asked us to walk, we dialogued with the mighty and we reached accords that would mean the beginning of peace in our lands, justice for Mexico's Indians, and hope for all honest men and women in the country.

These accords, the San Andrés Accords, were not the result of only our will. To San Andrés came representatives of all the Indian peoples of Mexico, and there was their voice represented and their demands presented. Shining was their struggle, which is lesson and path. Their word spoke, and their heart defined . . .

Like then, today we continue walking together with all Indian peoples in the struggle for the recognition of their rights. Not as vanguard or leadership, only as a part.

We kept our word to seek a peaceful solution.

But the government broke its word and did not fulfill the first fundamental accord we had reached: the recognition of Indian rights.

To the peace we offered, the government opposed the war of its stubborness.

Since then the war against us and all Indian peoples has continued.

Since then the lies have grown.

Since then the country and the entire world have been fooled by imitating peace and making war against all Indians.

---

*July 19, 1998, www.ezln.org

Since then they have tried to forget the government's word has not been kept, and they have wanted to hide the betrayal that governs Mexican lands . . .

Silence, dignity, and resistance were our strengths and our best weapons. With them we fought and defeated an enemy mighty but lacking reason and justice in his cause. From our experience and the long and luminous history of Indian struggle that our ancestors, the first inhabitants of these lands, left to us, we took up these arms and turned our silences into soldiers, our dignity into light, and our resistance into a wall.

Although in the time that our being quiet lasted we did not take direct part in national problems with our position and proposals, . . . great were the steps that forward we walked and saw.

We saw that they could no longer keep our dead quiet. Our dead spoke dead, the dead accused, the dead cried out, the dead lived again. Our dead will never die again. These our dead are always ours and always of all who struggle . . .

We saw the mighty government grow irritated at not finding either a rival or a surrender. We saw it then turn against others and hit those who did not take the same path as we did, but raised the same banners . . .

We saw also that the government is not one, nor is the vocation of death that its chief displays unanimous. We saw that inside the government there are people who want peace, who understand it, who see it as necessary, who regard it as indispensable. Being quiet, we saw that other voices inside the machine of war spoke to say no to its path . . .

We saw, being quiet, that we could better hear voices and winds from below, and not only the rude voice of the war above.

We saw, being quiet ourselves, that the government buried the legitimacy that reason . . . and the will for peace give . . .

We saw, being quiet, that stronger spoke the resistance of our peoples against trickery and violence . . .

We saw that our silence was shield and sword against him who wants war and imposes war . . . We saw that in each new attack he won less and lost more. We saw that by not fighting we were fighting . . .

A national Indian law must respond to the hopes of the Indian peoples of the entire country. In San Andrés the Indians of Mexico were represented, not only the Zapatistas. The accords signed are with all the Indian peoples, not only with the Zapatistas . . .

Although it does not incorporate all the San Andrés Accords . . . , the bill composed by the Commission of Concord and Pacification is a proposal that was born from the negotiation process and . . . is a firm base that can open a peaceful solution of the conflict. . . . Therefore we today ratify that we support the bill . . . and demand that it be taken up to constitutional rank . . .

On dialogue and negotiation we say that they have three great enemies that must be defeated for them to be able to constitute a viable, effective, and credible path. These enemies are the absence of mediation, war, and noncompliance with accords taken . . .

Dialogue and negotiation will be pertinent, viable, and effective when, besides . . . mediation, confidence and credibility are restored. Until then it can only be a farce, in which we are not disposed to take part . . .

The EZLN has managed to survive as an organization one of the most ferocious offensives that have been unleashed against it. It has kept intact its military capacity, expanded its social base, and gained strength politically as the justice of its demands became evident. The EZLN's Indian character has been strengthened. . . . Indians are today national actors, and their destinies and proposals form part of national discussion. . . . What is Indian is no longer tourism or artisanry, but struggle against poverty and for dignity . . .

Despite the war we suffer, despite our dead and our brothers and sisters in jail, we Zapatistas do not forget why we struggle and which is our principal banner in the struggle for democracy, liberty, and justice in Mexico: that of the recognition of the rights of Indian peoples.

For the commitment made since the first day of our rebellion, today we turn to put again in first place . . . the demand that the rights of Indians be recognized by an amendment to the Constitution that assures them all respect and the possibility of struggling for what belongs to them: land, housing, work, food, health care, education, democracy, justice, liberty, national independence, and a worthy peace . . .

Today, with the Indian heart that is the worthy root of the Mexican nation and having heard now the voice of death that comes in the government's war, we call on the Mexican People and on the men and women of the entire planet to unite their steps and their forces with us in this stage of the struggle for liberty, democracy, and justice, in this

Fifth Declaration from the Lacandón Jungle.

In which we call on all honest men and women to struggle for the

RECOGNITION OF THE RIGHTS OF INDIAN PEOPLES AND FOR THE END OF THE WAR OF EXTERMINATION.

There will be no transition to democracy, or reform of the State, or a real solution to the principal problems on the national agenda, without the Indian peoples. With the Indians a better and new country is necessary and possible. Without them there is no future at all as a Nation.

This is the hour of the Indian peoples of all Mexico. We call them so that, together, we may continue struggling for the rights that history, reason, and the truth have given us. We call them so that, together and gathering our heritage of struggle and resistance, we may mobilize through the entire country, and make known to all, by civil and nonviolent means, that we are the root of the Nation, its worthy foundation, its present in struggle, its inclusive future. We call them so that, together, we may struggle for a place of respect at the side of all Mexicans. We call them so that, together, we may show that we want democracy, liberty, and justice for all. We call them to demand to be recognized as a worthy part of our Nation. We call them so that, together, we may stop the war that the mighty are making on us all.

This is the hour of National Civil Society and of independent social and political organizations. It is the hour of peasants, workers, teachers, students, professionals, committed religious men and women, journalists, shantytowners, small merchants, debtors, artists, intellectuals, disabled people, HIV-positives, homosexuals, lesbians, men, women, children, young people, old people, unions, cooperatives, peasant groups, political organizations, social organizations. We call them so that, together with the Indian peoples and us, we may struggle against the war and for the recognition of Indian rights, for the transition to democracy, for an economic model that serves the people and does not use them, for a tolerant and inclusive society, for the respect of differences, for a new country where peace with justice and dignity is for all.

This is the hour of Congress. After a long struggle for democracy, headed by the opposition political parties, there is in the Chamber of Deputies and in the Senate a new correlation of forces that hinders the arbitrariness typical of presidentialism, and points with hope to a true separation and independence of the branches of government. The new political composition of the lower and upper chambers presents the challenge of making legislative work dignified, the expectation of turning Congress into a space at the service of the Nation and not of whoever happens to be president, and the hope of making a reality of the title "Honorable" that goes before the collective name by which deputies and senators are known. We call on the deputies and senators of the Republic, from all registered political parties, and on independents, to legislate for the benefit of all Mexicans. To command in obedience. To fulfill their duty by supporting peace and not war. Making effective the division of powers, to oblige the federal executive to stop the war of extermination it has underway on Mexico's Indian populations. With full respect for the prerogatives that the Constitution confers on them, to hear the voice of the Mexican people, and that this voice be the one that commands them at the moment of legislation. To support firmly and fully the Commission of Concord and Pacification, so that it can effectively and efficiently carry out its work of helping in the peace process. To answer the historic call that demands full recognition of the rights of Indian peoples. To contribute to the creation of an international image worthy of our country. To pass into the nation's history as a Congress that stopped obeying and serving only one person, and fulfilled its obligation to obey and serve us all.

This is the hour of the Commission of Concord and Pacification. It is in the commission's hands and within its abilities to stop the war, to fulfill what the federal executive refuses to fulfill, to open the hope for a just and worthy peace, and to create the conditions for the peaceful coexistence of all Mexicans. It is the hour for true compliance with the law for dialogue and negotiation in Chiapas. It is the hour to respond to the confidence placed in this commission not only by the Indian peoples who came to the table at San Andrés, but all the people who demand that words pledged be kept, a stop to the war, and a necessary peace.

This is the hour of the struggle for the rights of Indian peoples as a step toward democracy, liberty, and justice for all.

As part of this struggle . . . for the recognition of Indian rights and an end to the war, ratifying our motto, "For everyone everything, nothing for us," the ZAPATISTA ARMY OF NATIONAL LIBERATION announces that it will directly and all across Mexico carry out a

NATIONAL POLL ON THE COMMISSION OF CONCORD AND PACIFICATION'S BILL FOR AN INDIAN LAW AND FOR THE END OF THE WAR OF EXTERMINATION.

. . . we propose to take the commission's . . . bill to all the municipalities in the country, so that all Mexican men and women can declare their opinion on this proposal. The EZLN will send a delegation of its own to each one of the municipalities of the entire country to explain the content of COCOPA's bill and to take part in conducting the poll. For this purpose, the EZLN will at an opportune time publicly address itself to national civil society and to political and social organizations to make known to them the express convocation.

We call on:

The Indian peoples of all Mexico, for them, together with the Zapatistas, to mobilize and demonstrate in demand of recognition of their rights in the Constitution.

The brothers and sisters of the National Indian Congress, for them to take part, together with the Zapatistas, in the task of polling all Mexican men and women on COCOPA's bill.

Laborers, peasants, teachers, students, housewives, shantytowners, small farmers, small merchants and businessmen, retired people, disabled people, religious men and women, young people, women, old people, homosexuals and lesbians, boys and girls, for them individually or collectively to take part directly with the Zapatistas in the promotion, support, and conducting of this poll, as one more step toward peace with justice and dignity.

The scientific, artistic, and intellectual community, for it to join the Zapatistas in the tasks of organizing the poll all across the national territory.

Political and social organizations, for them, with the Zapatistas, to work on conducting the poll.

Honest political parties committed to the people's causes, for them to furnish all the support necessary for this national poll. For this purpose, the EZLN will at an opportune time publicly address itself to the national leadership of the political parties in Mexico.

Congress, for it to assume its commitment to legislate for the benefit of the people, to contribute to peace and not war by supporting the work for this poll. For this purpose, the EZLN will at an opportune time publicly address itself to the Congressional leadership of all parties and to independents in the Chamber of Deputies and the Senate.

The Commission of Concord and Pacification, for it, in compliance with its labors of helping in the peace process, to smooth the way for conducting the poll on its bill. For this purpose, the EZLN will at an opportune time publicly address itself to COCOPA's members . . .

Brothers and sisters:

The time has now passed when the war of the mighty spoke. Let us not allow it to speak any more.

Now has come the time for peace to speak, the peace we all deserve and need, peace with justice and dignity.

Today, July 19, 1998, the Zapatista Army of National Liberation signs this Fifth Declaration from the Lacandón Jungle. We invite all to read it, to distribute it to others, and to join in the effort and work that it demands.

DEMOCRACY!
LIBERTY!
JUSTICE!

From the mountains of the Mexican Southeast
Clandestine Revolutionary Indian Committee-General Command of the Zapatista Army of National Liberation
Mexico, July 1998

Permissions

The author is grateful for permission to reprint the following materials:

Cover photo © Emiliano Javier Thibaut Muchnik.

Map of "Diocesan Chiapas, 1986," Diócesis de San Cristóbal de Las Casas.

Map of "Cities, Towns, and the Villages of Chiapas's Central Highlands, ca. 1960" © 1995 Jan Rus.

Historia de la Provincia de San Vicente de Chiapa y Guatemala de la Orden de Predicadores, Libros I y II, Serie "Biblioteca Goathemala" Volumen XXVIII, 1977, pp. 370-373 © Academia de Geografía e Historia de Guatemala.

Thomas Gage's Travels in the New World, edited by J. Eric S. Thompson © 1958 by the University of Oklahoma Press, Publishing Division of the University.

"Las causas de una rebelión india" © 1995 Juan Pedro Viqueira.

"Whose Caste War?" by Jan Rus, reprinted from *Spaniards and Indians in Southeastern Mesoamerica: Essays on the History of Ethnic Relations* edited by Murdo J. MacLeod and Robert Wasserstrom, by permission of the University of Nebraska Press. © 1983 by the University of Nebraska Press.

En la escuela y en la milpa, la plática no es la misma © 1984 Andrés Aubry.

Trozas © 1977 by R.E. Luján. English translation © 1994 by Allison & Busby. Reprinted by permission of Ivan R. Dee, Inc.

Abtel ta Pinka: Trabajo en las fincas, © 1990 Jan Rus, Diane Rus, and José González Hernández, translators and editors.

"Evangelisation in Latin America" © 1970 Consejo Episcopal Latinoamericano, CELAM.

"Estamos buscando la libertad" and "Plan Diocesano," Diócesis de San Cristóbal de Las Casas.